KUBRICK

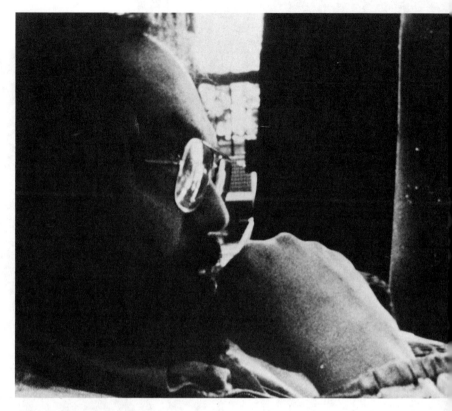

The Palace is not infinite.
The Library is limitless and periodic.

—BORGES

KUBRICK
Inside a Film Artist's Maze

New and Expanded Edition

Thomas Allen Nelson

INDIANA UNIVERSITY PRESS • Bloomington & Indianapolis

This book is a publication of
Indiana University Press
601 North Morton Street
Bloomington, IN   47404-3797 USA

http://www.indiana.edu/~iupress

Telephone orders   800-842-6796
Fax orders   812-855-7931
Orders by e-mail   iuporder@indiana.edu

The paper used in this publication meets the
minimum requirements of American National Standard
for Information Sciences—Permanence of Paper for
Printed Library Materials, ANSI Z39.48-1984.

Manufactured in the United States of America

Library of Congress Cataloging-in-Publication Data

Nelson, Thomas Allen, date
Kubrick, inside a film artist's maze / Thomas Allen Nelson.—
Expanded and rev. ed.
p.   cm.
Includes filmography (p.   ), bibliographical
references (p.   ), and index.
ISBN 978-0-253-33742-9 (cl) —
ISBN 978-0-253-21390-7 (pa)
1. Kubrick, Stanley—Criticism
and interpretation. I. Title.

PN1998.3.K83 N45 2000
791.43'0233'092—dc21
99-087689

4   5   6   7   8   12   11   10   09   08   07

The acknowledgments on page ix
constitute a part of this copyright page.

For Judy
In keeping with the situation

CONTENTS

ACKNOWLEDGMENTS

The author wishes to express appreciation to Mr. Kubrick, who, in the years between 1980 and his untimely death in 1999, kindly responded to a cry for help on more than one occasion, to include his permission to use some of the photographic material found in this book. In addition, I am grateful to Jan Harlan, Julian Senior, Louis C. Blau, and other representatives of Mr. Kubrick for their generous assistance in helping me secure the necessary permissions for the stills found in both the first edition and this new and expanded edition. I also owe a debt of gratitude to Jane Lyle, Joan Catapano, and the staff of Indiana University Press, who provided me with invaluable assistance and encouragement during the preparation of the new and expanded edition.

Below are the sources for the stills used in this book:

Fear and Desire, p. 22: Joseph Burstyn.

Killer's Kiss, pp. 23, 27: United Artists. Courtesy of United Artists.

The Killing, pp. 35, 37: United Artists/Harris-Kubrick. Courtesy of United Artists.

Paths of Glory, pp. 20, 42, 47, 50, 52: United Artists/Harris-Kubrick. Courtesy of United Artists.

Lolita, pp. 56, 68, 70, 71, 72, 77, 78: Metro-Goldwyn-Mayer/Harris-Kubrick. Courtesy of Metro-Goldwyn-Mayer.

Dr. Strangelove, pp. 6, 82, 86, 90, 94, 97, 101: Columbia Pictures/Hawk Films. Courtesy of Columbia Pictures.

2001: A Space Odyssey, pp. 11, 103, 127, 128: Copyright 1968 Turner-Entertainment Co. A Time Warner Company. All Rights Reserved.

A Clockwork Orange, pp. 136, 151, 161: Copyright 1971 Warner Bros. Inc. and Polaris Productions, Inc. All Rights Reserved.

Barry Lyndon, pp. 4, 166, 185, 191: Copyright 1975 Warner Bros. Inc. All Rights Reserved.

The Shining, pp. 195, 218, 224: Copyright 1980 Warner Bros. Inc. All Rights Reserved.

Full Metal Jacket, pp. 228, 242: Copyright 1987 Warner Bros. Inc. All Rights Reserved.

Eyes Wide Shut, pp. 260, 280: Copyright 1999 Warner Bros., a division of Time Warner Entertainment Company, L.P. All Rights Reserved.

The frontispiece and the stills on pp. 1, 140, 170, and 202 are used by permission of Stanley Kubrick/Hawk Films.

The jacket photograph, reproduced on p. 298, and the photograph on p. 231 are used by permission of Jan Harlan.

KUBRICK

1 KUBRICK AND THE AESTHETICS OF CONTINGENCY
The Shaping of a Film Imagination

The remarkable vision of one of the twentieth century's greatest film directors shut down for perhaps the first and only time in the early morning hours of March 7, 1999. Within a matter of days after the completion of *Eyes Wide Shut,* his thirteenth feature film and one of his greatest achievements, death came suddenly and un-expectedly to Stanley Kubrick at the age of seventy. His dark, pen-etrating eyes would no longer look out with fascination into the vari-ous sensory masks worn by a contingent world and its people. They would no longer attempt to penetrate the dynamic, often decora-tive, and always uncertain surfaces of psychological life and probe for those poignantly absurd but revealing moments of repressed fear and desire that had been a dominant obsession in his creative life for more than fifty years. His mind no longer would roam over an eclectic range of ideas and personal speculations, nor struggle to find unique ways of translating thought and sardonic observation into the dramatic, visual, and emotional structures of film narrative. And most regrettable of all, his eye no longer would look through a camera's viewfinder and put his imagination into a frame for us to look at on a movie screen. Hopefully, in his final moments of life, Stanley Kubrick also no longer had to fear the annihilation of death—as so many of his film characters unconsciously had—but instead was confident in the knowledge that his presence in the world would survive in the memories of a loving family and in the distinguished film record he left behind for the twenty-first century and beyond.

Stanley Kubrick's career as a filmmaker probably began in earnest on July 26, 1941, when his father, Jack Kubrick, a New York City doctor, gave him a Graflex camera for his thirteenth birthday. Besides photography, his father also gave his son a love of chess and of the storytelling traditions of literature. Although young Stanley was a poor student academically, and seems to have never seriously considered pursuing a college degree, he developed an almost scholarly passion not only for still photography, literature, and chess, but for physics, music (swing and jazz), baseball, and movie-watching. With his camera around his neck or concealed in a bag, he roamed the New York City streets taking pictures and playing chess, from his Bronx neighborhood, to the bustling center of Manhattan around Times Square, to the bohemian haven of Greenwich Village. He haunted the city's movie theaters and saw practically everything made, whether it was the first-run products of Hollywood shown at Loew's Paradise on East 188th Street, double features at Manhattan's numerous retrospective houses, new foreign films shown at the Guild and World Cinemas near Times Square, or the almost daily program of classic foreign films at the Museum of Modern Art on West 53rd Street. By the time he graduated from William Howard Taft High School in 1945, Kubrick was working as a staff photographer for *Look* magazine; at age seventeen, he was already in advanced training for a career as an image-maker. It would be only a matter of time before this introverted and highly imaginative young photographer would want to create emotion rather than merely record it. By 1951, now married and outwardly living the life of a bohemian artist in Greenwich Village, Kubrick had completed a documentary about a young prizefighter named Walter Cartier (*Day of the Fight*) that grew out of a *Look* magazine assignment. In the next two years, he would make two more documentaries for money (*Flying Padre*, 1951, and *The Seafarers*, 1953) and complete his first feature, *Fear and Desire* (1953). From all accounts, it appears that by the time of his twenty-fifth birthday in 1953, Stanley Kubrick had decided to become a great film director.*

Even in the photographs published in *Look* and in his three documentaries, Kubrick showed an early desire to rework the inherently impersonal nature of photographic surfaces into the dramatic and psychological forms of fictional narrative. His first published photograph—of a newsstand vendor's expression of sadness framed by the *Daily Mirror* headline "F.D.R. DEAD"—was instrumental in his getting the job with *Look*. Kubrick was able to invest the ordinary and mundane with humor and emotion in pictorial stories about a trip to the dentist or an amorous interlude between a male stranger and a woman in the balcony of a movie theater. He showed an early interest in theories of evolution—again humorously rendered—in a four-shot sequence that started with a stock shot of a monkey in a zoo ("How a Monkey Looks to People"), followed by three photographs by Kubrick of onlookers—who now appear to be inside the cage—gazing into the monkey's world ("How People Look to a Monkey"). Significantly, the three separate shots of the people on the other side of the cage's vertical bars form a progression that in a motion picture would be shown in a single panning or tracking shot.

Even though his best photographs are framed and staged in ways that suggest the photographer's interpretive presence, they retain their authenticity as realistically recorded moments in time. They quietly evoke an emotional human drama going on within a more impersonal, documentary-like simulacrum that ambitiously strives to overload each image with both humor and intellectual speculation. Stylistically, the sixteen minutes of *Day of the Fight* (1951) combine a newsreel form of narrative compression and visual authenticity with an expressive imagery that recalls the American *film noir* of the 1940s. In the editing and camera work, you can sense the young Kubrick

---

*See the "Notes & Trivia" section for a listing of sources consulted in the preparation of this book. Throughout, I use the notes to document quoted or paraphrased material and to extend my description and analysis into tangential but relevant areas.

Games of chance and games of love in the candlelit
formality of *Barry Lyndon*

working out a tightly compressed approach to storytelling that invests the dynamic and emotional elements intrinsic to an event such as a boxing match with an interpretive subtext. Walter Cartier's routines on the "day of the fight," for instance, take on an authentic and mechanical quality that brings under control the disorderly emotional undercurrents of anticipation and fear. In the film's climax, Kubrick uses his handheld camera (a 35mm Eyemo) to capture the violent disorders that exist within both the boxing ring and the fragile structures of human routine and emotional stoicism. Surprisingly, *Day of the Fight*, particularly in its technical qualities, shows none of those telltale signs that would expose it as the product of a very talented but still amateurish film novice. At the age of twenty-two, without the resources of a university film curriculum or a studio apprenticeship to tutor him, Stanley Kubrick was already well on his way to becoming a professional filmmaker with an artist's ambition to infuse his work with the narrative power of myth and archetype.

During this busy period in his life, Kubrick continued to be an omnivorous and eclectic viewer of films, which included the silent classics of Chaplin and Eisenstein, contemporary American studio releases by directors such as Huston and Wilder, and the film festi-

val–endorsed works from the other side of the Atlantic of emerg
auteurists such as Bergman and Fellini. And because American {
criticism in the early 1950s was dominated by writers with a literary
orientation, Kubrick had little choice but to seek out books written
by European filmmakers and theorists, who had treated film as a
serious art form since its inception. Thus Kubrick discovered not
only the brilliant, highly subjective theoretical works of Sergei Eisenstein but also the clarity and logic of V. I. Pudovkin's *Film Technique*
(1929). Not only would he recommend Pudovkin's book as an invaluable primer for years to come—"it is the most instructive book
on film aesthetics I came across"—but it probably had the greatest
influence of any single written work on the evolution of his own
private aesthetics. Consequently, in later years critics would contend,
either explicitly or by default, that Kubrick should be treated as a
European auteur who just happened to have a Bronx accent, even if
at times he might go slumming for satiric effect in mainstream Hollywood genres. But as the following chapters will show, Stanley Kubrick eventually would pursue a less pretentious and more ambitious
goal. In charting Kubrick's development as a film artist from *Killer's
Kiss* (1955) to *Eyes Wide Shut* (1999), I will have little difficulty demonstrating how Kubrick's work reveals his belief in film as an art
form for the expression of a complex personal vision. However, I
also will try to show how his collected work reveals an equally important conviction—that film, as a popular commercial form, can touch
the lives of millions of people in profound ways only when it explores the universal (i.e., generic) myths and archetypes of both our
shared cultural experience and our collective unconscious.

For Pudovkin, two essential factors elevated film from a photographic process to a cinematographic art: an artist-director's con-
trolling vision and editing, the "creative force of filmic reality." Pudovkin's most famous principle maintains that a film must be *built*,
not shot, and in this construction process the director must strive to
achieve a "compulsory and deliberate guidance of the thoughts and
associations of the spectator." Kubrick once said that "the writer-director is really the perfect dramatic instrument," and that the combination of these two functions has "produced the most consistently
fine work." And Kubrick's films, particularly after *Fear and Desire* and
Killer's Kiss, stand as testaments to a meticulous architectonics in the
organization of their temporal rhetoric. The intricately layered and

On the set of *Dr. Strangelove* (Stanley Kubrick, Jack
Creley, Peter Sellers, George C. Scott)

at times classic structures of *2001: A Space Odyssey* (1968), *A Clockwork
Orange* (1971), *Barry Lyndon* (1975), *The Shining* (1980), and *Eyes
Wide Shut* serve as later, grandiloquent extensions of a Kubrickian
trademark that can be traced back to the organizational precision of
such earlier films as *The Killing* (1956), *Paths of Glory* (1957), and *Dr.
Strangelove; or How I Learned to Stop Worrying and Love the Bomb* (1964).
They leave no doubt that for Kubrick, the working out of shots into
scenes, scenes into sequences, sequences into acts, and acts into con-

sciously modulated wholes involved an essential creative activity both during the preparation of the script and in the final editing. However, the fact that, even in the early years of *Day of the Fight* and *Fear and Desire*, Kubrick believed in total directorial control does not, in itself, separate his work from that of a number of other directors. What does distinguish Kubrick's films from most others, including Pudovkin's, is the remarkable ability that he had to convert cinematic form into a variety of complex cinematic meanings.

On this issue of the relation between a film's thematic content and its style of presentation, Kubrick once said that good writing starts with a "writer's obsession with his subject, with a theme and concept and a view of life and an understanding of character. Style is what an artist uses to fascinate the beholder in order to convey to him his feelings and emotions and thoughts." In other comments, Kubrick expressed his belief that "a preoccupation with originality of form is more or less a fruitless thing," and that if he had to choose between a filmmaker like Eisenstein ("all style, no content") and one like Chaplin ("all content, no style"), he would take Chaplin. But we must not neglect the importance of Kubrick's final words on the subject: "Obviously, if you can combine style and content, you have the best of all possible films." Similarly, Pudovkin envisioned a film director as an inspired and benevolent despot whose aim it was to guide audiences toward a clear understanding of theme and to produce a prescribed feeling in them. "One must try to express one's concepts in clear and vivid visual images," Pudovkin said, so that the "psychic guidance" of the spectator can be directed toward an understanding of how a given film's "searching glance" reveals a truth that exists beneath the superficially apprehended surfaces of reality. Like Eisenstein, Pudovkin trafficked in the thematic and psychological implications of a simplified Marxist aesthetics—a necessary strategy, he felt, for expression in a medium not far enough advanced in the 1920s to deal with large and complex themes. Thus Kubrick's judgment that Eisenstein's films (and, by inference, Pudovkin's) were more sophisticated stylistically than thematically seems sound enough. Yet Kubrick's own films, to include what we know about the care with which they were conceived and planned, demonstrate working principles very close to those recommended by Pudovkin.

As early as *Day of the Fight*, Kubrick too believed that a director must, first and foremost, formulate a conceptual understanding of his subject, what Pudovkin called "theme." But the lessons of *Killer's*

Kiss, and the difficulties of producing quality work from a poorly prepared script, would teach Kubrick to respect another recommendation by the Russian filmmaker. Following the formulation of theme, Pudovkin believed that the next step should be the full integration of the conceptual elements into the construction of what he called "action" and "treatment." During the time that *Killer's Kiss* was in release, Kubrick formed a partnership with producer James B. Harris that not only would ensure his continued independence but eventually would lead him toward a solution to the many problems that troubled his first two features, *Fear and Desire* and *Killer's Kiss.* Harris found a crime novel by Lionel White that excited Kubrick and would eventually become *The Killing,* the first of several exceptional films that bear the unmistakable imprimatur of Stanley Kubrick. Thus began Kubrick's practice of adapting novels to the interests of his own unique film imagination. In addition, with Harris onboard as a partner and friend, Kubrick enjoyed a fortuitous and compatible association with a producer who was invaluable in securing the financing for new projects.

Beginning with his preparations for *The Killing* in 1955, now under the aegis of Harris-Kubrick, Kubrick's working habits became more elaborately organized and followed more closely Pudovkin's advice. Hence, Kubrick initiated during this time what would become a standard practice for the rest of his film career. He would carefully work out, often with the help of skilled writers as collaborators, a detailed treatment of the chosen novel's elements that could be broken down and rebuilt into the temporal rhetoric of a film script. He would develop an approach to point of view consistent with his reaction to the story, organize the narrative into a tightly focused dramatic structure, work out a pattern of characterization suitable to his psychological response to the material, devise visual and dramatic ways of developing the exposition essential to story logic and continuity, and work out an appropriate tone for the dialogue and—if required—voiceover narration. Through this process, the emotional and thematic content of a Kubrick film eventually would achieve objective (temporal) realization. But there was one more lesson from Pudovkin that Kubrick took to heart. According to Pudovkin, the director's final task during the production and postproduction phases was to work out what he called the "cinematographic" or "filmic representation" of the action, which for our purposes here might be more suitably designated as the total visual/ musical rhetoric of Kubrick's films.

What this history reveals is not that Kubrick shared with the Soviet filmmakers of the 1920s a film aesthetic based on montage and a didactic interest in certain historical assumptions. Much of what has been described, after all, applies as well to what we know of the working habits of directors as temperamentally disparate as Hitchcock, Bresson, and Bergman. Indeed, Kubrick's thematics are far more complex than Pudovkin's, but significantly his find expression through a methodology that shared Pudovkin's passion for an exactness of temporal and spatial directorial construction. That such a schematic approach to the construction of the scenario exemplifies the workings of a didactic temperament is obvious, especially if one understands Pudovkin's preference for thematic clarity and a total psychological guidance of the spectator. To surmise, however, that Kubrick's intentions were equally didactic because he followed an organizational exactness would be to equate methodology with aesthetics, politics with creative vision. Kubrick's comments on the question of audience manipulation reveal an attitude more in tune with the tradition of Wellesian ambiguity than with the so-called "analytic" and "undemocratic" (to paraphrase André Bazin) tendencies of Soviet formalism. Rather than linking ideological clarity to an overt manipulation of cinematic form, Kubrick's films, as the diversity in the critical response to their thematic content would suggest, embody his belief that "truthful and valid ideas are so multi-faceted that they don't yield themselves to frontal assault. The ideas have to be discovered by the audience, and their thrill in making the discovery makes these ideas all the more powerful." He thought that film should communicate its concepts as subtext, "obliquely, so as to avoid all pat conclusions and neatly tied up ideas." His views on plot and character, from early in his career, suggest a desire to challenge an audience's awareness through indirect and covert means rather than to manipulate them toward a set of didactic intentions:

> I like the slow start, the start that goes under the audience's skin and involves them so that they can appreciate grace notes and soft tones and don't have to be pounded over the head with plot points and suspense hooks.
>
> You let the character unfold himself gradually before the audience. You hold off as long as possible revealing the kind he is. He comes in

like a nice guy, and when the audience finds out, they're trapped. You cast a person as the opposite of what he's really trying to do, so the audience will find out only later.

His avowed fascination for games of deception like chess and for fantastic, surrealist literature characterizes an artist who preferred to unsettle an audience's comfortable acceptance of the familiar—of "life as it is," to quote Kubrick—and to require that they deal with his films in complex emotional and psychological ways. Hardly anything could be further from Pudovkin's didactic clarity than Kubrick's belief that "there's something in the human personality which resents things that are clear, and conversely, something which is attracted to puzzles, enigmas, and allegories."

Between the generations of Pudovkin (1893–1953) and Kubrick (1928–1999), there was an enormous epistemological and aesthetic gulf. Pudovkin and his contemporaries inhabited an intellectual and artistic environment that still clung to a faith in the human ability to break down the world into tidy rational units and thereby impose an understanding on it. Film practice and theory by 1930, for instance, had split into two prominent stylistic and epistemological camps: (1) the realist tradition of Lumière-Griffith-Flaherty-Stroheim, which developed narrative and documentary styles consistent with a nineteenth-century belief that an organic, autonomic reality existed in history and nature; and (2) the formalist tradition of Méliès, German expressionism, French surrealism, and Soviet montage, which affirmed that a more significant "reality" existed in such hidden or unseen areas as poetic imagination, the unconscious mind, and the dialectics of history. Stylistically, this polarity was defined and distinguished by, on the one hand, a fondness for principles of continuity and illusionist verisimilitude (invisible editing, synchronization of image and camera movements, realist mise-en-scène), and, on the other, an expressive and obtrusive manipulation of the spatial and temporal content of what was photographed (decor, lighting, angle, montage). During Kubrick's formative years in the 1950s, this polarity had been validated in the theoretical essays of Rudolph Arnheim and Béla Balázs for formalism, Siegfried Kracauer and André Bazin for realism.

Yet even while this consolidation was taking place (which conveniently can be dated by the publication in 1960 of Kracauer's *Theory*

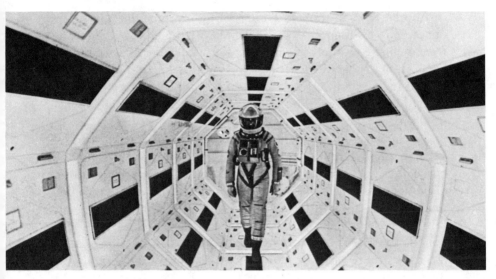

David Bowman (Keir Dullea) of *2001* moving
through a Kubrickian corridor on his way to a
confrontation with his double, HAL

of Film: The Redemption of Physical Reality), the secure status of objective "fact" as a conclusive measure of truth and the dominance of Freudian psychology, with its humanist concept of an internally organized self, had suffered further erosion from the impact of discoveries and theories in a number of scientific disciplines. Quantum physics buttressed Einstein's rejection of the absoluteness of time and space in its demonstration that attempts to map a completely ordered cosmos were futile. Psychologists more often than not asserted that the Self lacked internal coherence and could best be described as a series of identities, splintered into separate roles and masks, seen respectively as either a performer skating across the moving surfaces of life or a Proteus ready to "flow" and embrace new possibilities. R. D. Laing, in particular, had popularized the notion that traditional concepts of madness and sanity could not deal adequately with twentieth-century psychic conditions, and that, in fact, certain schizophrenic tendencies were signs of health rather than dysfunction. In literature, the early modernist reaction to what was perceived as a twentieth-century metaphysical crisis, namely the creation of private mythologies by such writers as Yeats, Pound, Eliot, Joyce, and Lawrence, had been ridiculed by postmodernists as "mythotherapy." In the last decades of the century, the interpretive impulse of any discipline or activity that originated, like Pudovkin's, from inclusive or total assumptive systems had been so devalued that large numbers of college-educated people, living in a growing Culture of Information Overload, searched for "truth" in a constantly changing and uncertain postmodernist landscape of an ideological, psychological, and spiritual shamanism.

At the same time that film realism and formalism developed separate stylistic identities—and that is the way we usually distinguish between, say, Eisenstein and Stroheim—they mined what Kubrick disparaged as their "content" from a similar set of assumptions. Both testify, despite their differing ways, to the durability of nineteenth-century epistemological thinking, which believed in a system of rational correspondence between the structures of phenomena and the structures of the human mind, between private experience and the facts of temporal reality, an equipoise between the self and the world, between depths and surfaces. Eisenstein's and Pudovkin's expressive renderings of film space and time, therefore, share an unlikely epistemological kinship with both the Teutonic stylizations of Murnau and Sternberg, on the one hand, and the naturalistic rigors of Flaherty and Stroheim, on the other. Although the stylistic modes differ—that is, each can be defined by a distinct film language—traditional realist and formalist films have this in common: they assume the existence of "total" or inclusive answers to life's apparent contradictions. Keaton's *The Navigator* (1924) and *The General* (1927), two masterpieces of American silent-film realism, are as "scientific" and logical in their own way as Stroheim's *Greed* (1924), although Keaton posits depth in the sentimental self, while Stroheim favors the determinisms of nature and society. Yet both filmmakers shared the assumption that surface reality attains significance, or depth, through an observable system of laws and correspondences, and that in their films' *total* spatial and temporal structures, a facsimile of the world was represented. Pudovkin's stylistics may distinguish his films from those of his less formalist contemporaries, but his commitment to a totalized worldview does not. As I have discussed, he merely assumed that his cinematographic "reality" attained a thematic clarity by reaching farther beneath photographed surfaces than did the films of the realists. Similarly, the preoccupation of German expressionism with subjective worlds comforts rather than disorients us with its assertion that distinctions between sane and insane are still valid. Witness the psychological dualisms of Wiene and Mayer's *Caligari* (1920), Murnau's *Nosferatu* (1922) and his American *Sunrise* (1927), and Sternberg's *The Blue Angel* (1930). All retain the High German admonition that excesses of the libido must be curbed if psychic and social order is to prevail. While these film traditions express differing political and psychological values, and in so doing adopt appropriate styles, they are unified in their faith in totalized, didactic assumptions, and therefore are appreciated by later viewers as much for their styles of presentation and performance as for their substance. In that respect, Kubrick's evaluation of Eisenstein as "all style" and Chaplin as "all content" could be construed as indicating at once his rejection of Soviet didacticism and his belief in performance (in this case, Chaplin's) as an extension of substance. But I will discuss more of that later (see chapters 3, 6, and 10).

André Bazin's seminal essay "The Evolution of the Language of Cinema"—with its contention that depth of focus in the films of Wyler and Welles, and the absence of montage effects in Italian neo-realism, gave back to cinema "a sense of the ambiguity of reality"— would seem to possess the kind of critical clarity and relevance necessary for an analysis of how Kubrick's aesthetics express a conditional rather than dialectical worldview. Bazin, for instance, described the dangers in those films (mostly examples of formalism) that presuppose a unity of meaning in any dramatic event, and therefore by their very nature rule out ambiguity. Yet, as I have argued elsewhere, Bazin's humanist aesthetic remains consistent with a belief in the "wholeness" of reality—admittedly in this case one that values "complexity" and "ambiguity"—and in the filmmaker's role as a Moses mediating between medium and subject. He believed that for every film subject, from Flaherty's explorations of primitive societies to Welles's Charles Foster Kane, from the complexities of dramatic space in Murnau to the theatrical ambiguities of Renoir, an appropriate (that is, an *a priori*) range of stylistic techniques either was available or would be created. In an excellent biographical study, Dudley Andrew illustrates how Bazin's preferences for certain films and film styles reflect a coherent metaphysical orientation:

> Beneath such concepts as the limitation of perception and the integrity of space lies a belief in the signifying power of nature. When a filmmaker puts a situation under the pressure of a controlled gaze, he

forces "it to reveal its structural depth, to bring out the preexisting relations."

Bazin's often-stated belief that film should "reveal" the order of nature rather than "add" to it becomes a focusing aesthetic principle only in the assumptive context of the sort of dualistic epistemology of the actual and imaginal found, paradoxically, in the film masterpieces of both realism and formalism. And while Kubrick felt strongly that the visual powers of film made ambiguity an inevitability as well as a virtue, he did not share Bazin's mystical belief that the better filmmakers are those who sacrifice their personal perspectives to a "fleeting crystallization of a reality [of] whose environing presence one is ceaselessly aware." For Kubrick, the old-fashioned division of film into the categories of "realism" and "formalism," relegated by the 1970s to a lower-case and qualified identity, merely represented stylistic options for the embodiment of far-reaching speculations about life as it was experienced during his lifetime:

> I have always enjoyed dealing with a slightly surrealistic situation and presenting it in a realistic manner. I've always liked fairy tales and myths, magical stories. I think they are somehow closer to the sense of reality one feels today than the equally stylized "realistic" story in which a great deal of selectivity and omission has to occur in order to preserve its "realist" style.

Could it be that the informational glut created by the electronic communications media after Bazin's death in 1958—a media that Kubrick understood and had a life-long fascination for—eroded all authoritative visions that pretended to encompass what we must describe, in quotation marks and with equivocation, as "modern reality"? Kubrick's films, in fact, reflect one writer's belief that reality in the late twentieth century had become "so extravagant in its contradictions, absurdities, violence, speed of change, science-fiction technology, weirdness, and constant unfamiliarity" that the traditional division between imagination and fact seemed neither definable nor relevant. Perhaps no more accurate description exists for the "normal" experience of film viewing increasingly enjoyed during most of Kubrick's film career—one in which an audience's emotions were constantly assaulted by mixtures of visual/aural style and technique (short- and long-lens perspectives, deep and shallow compositions, naturalist and impressionist colors, the incorporation of wild sound with complex sound mixes); one which demanded that audiences respond with intelligence and understanding to a content that, more often than not, implied that *combinations within the surfaces of reality* (of objects and actors, of sight and focus, of color and shape, of sounds and mood) may be not only more immediate but more "real" than an older faith in *rational correspondences in the depths of reality*. Films then and today present us with a totally contingent universe, where images and sounds mean both nothing and everything, where worlds are erected on the epistemologically shifting sands of total probability and zero signification. And this cinema of contingency found no fuller expression in the second half of the twentieth century than in the films of Stanley Kubrick.

If Kubrick's work cannot be appreciated through the conventions of film realism or film formalism, or as illustrations of a Bazinian séance between an anthropomorphic universe and human meditation, Jean Mitry's encyclopedic and pluralistic approach to film aesthetics may provide a revealing although admittedly synthetic model to work from. In his *Esthétique et Psychologie du cinéma*, Mitry says the following:

> The process of film joins a deep psychological reality and satisfies our desire to understand the world and each other in a powerful yet necessarily partial way. The aesthetics of film is based on this psychological truth and need. And so cinema is the greatest of the arts because it meets this need by showing us the *process* of the transformation of the world. The other arts can show us merely the end result of such transformation, the humanized art world. In cinema human beings tell each other what reality means to them, yet they do so through reality itself, which surrounds their work like an ocean.

If I understand Mitry correctly, he believes that all narrative films both reveal reality (the humanist view) and organize it into significances (the modernist/formalist view), that narrative film by its very nature is both an "open," illusionist form (Realism's Window on the World) and a "closed," artificial form (Formalism's Framing of the World). Mitry contends that while the filmmaker cannot rid his work of reality, he must of necessity insist upon his manipulation of it. Reality has no "totality" that film must serve and represent. Rather than possessing a natural order of surfaces or depths, as both Pudovkin and Bazin assumed, reality, in Mitry's view, stands in a state of contingent readiness for the enrichment of human intervention. As a result, film cannot avoid the aesthetic consequences of the impersonal, concrete nature of reality—its photographic *thereness*—nor can it deny the presence of the human signifier. Mitry's synthesis of the humanist (*psychologie*) and modernist (*esthétique*) traditions is the kind of eclectic but coherent discourse needed to inform our understanding both of a period of stylistic plurality and of a filmmaker of Kubrick's aesthetic complexity.

An awareness of contingency arises whenever there is a loss of faith in teleological explanations, in the inviolability of institutionalized meaning, in the rational structures of nature or the signifying power of mind and language. Once meaning has lost the authority of inherent design and purpose, we then perceive how many different ways there are to create meaning through the expressive extensions of language and form. Yet even while we are acknowledging the subjectivity of perception and the fictiveness of language, our senses continue to record the reality of a sensate and inchoate universe. And if the alliance of modern science and technology can be trusted, one that depends upon our technology to verify the objectivity of the universe in ways impossible for the human mind alone, we inhabit a world that is incredibly complex and vast in its dimensions. No matter if you conceive the universe—its creation or eventual demise—as collapsing, expanding, or oscillating, you are dealing with a temporal and spatial fact that renders puny by comparison the duration of our existence, both individually and as a species. Only then does the human face of contingency show itself, not only as a psychological burden that justifies a retreat into the existential self, but as a challenge to imagination and its potential for humanizing rather than just anthropomorphizing the universe. Anthropology and history, two expressions of that potential, have chronicled our struggles with contingency in their record of the human effort in extending dominion over a universe far more complex than an urge for meaning could possibly hope to embrace. For more than four million years, hominids have projected their conscious and unconscious minds onto nature in an attempt to share its concreteness and its infinitude through forms and artifacts—including the creation of identities, civilizations, the arts—which, like the intelligence behind the monolith in Kubrick's *2001,* survive and define us in a silently indifferent universe.

To say, therefore, that Stanley Kubrick's films reflect a preoccupation with this cosmic and psycho/aesthetic drama would be an understatement. Hans Feldman once wrote an essay in which he discussed Kubrick's profound interest in how human beings create complex extensions of instinctual and psychological conditions through a variety of cultural, technological, and aesthetic forms. He described *A Clockwork Orange* and *Barry Lyndon,* for example, as films that "study the relations between the individual man and the cultural forms through which that individual must achieve the expression of himself." What Feldman's excellent essay touched on but did not fully develop was the recognition that Kubrick's conceptual universe contains more than a simpleminded belief in human corruption, or, as a prominent critic in 1975 so acidly put it, a "message that people are disgusting but things are lovely." Instead, his films repeatedly dramatize the psychological, moral, and aesthetic consequences of contingency: from the efforts of Johnny Clay to control the exigencies of time and space in *The Killing* to Barry Lyndon's entrapment within the psychological and historical forms of his ambition; from the grim axis of trench and chateau in *Paths of Glory* to a nympholept's dreamy retreat from the reflections of his own fate in *Lolita* (1962); from the space odysseys of *2001,* which paradoxically travel backward in time, to the merger of subjectivity and social engineering in *A Clockwork Orange;* from Jack Torrance's journey in *The Shining* through the maze of a collective unconscious to the attenuated structure of order into chaos of *Full Metal Jacket* (1987); from the mad races against time of *Dr. Strangelove* to the surreal dislocations of reality and dream in *Eyes Wide Shut.* They explore the complex extensions of human imagination—its history and its emotion, its forms and its fictions, its grandeur and its triviality—for what they both disguise and reveal about an existence without recognizable purpose amid the myriad stars and worlds. On this subject of our cosmic transience, for instance, Kubrick once said the following:

> If man merely sat back and thought about his impending termination, and his terrifying insignificance and aloneness in the cosmos, he would surely go mad, or succumb to a numbing sense of futility. Why, he might ask himself, should he bother to write a great symphony, or strive to make a living, or even to love another, when he is no more than a momentary microbe on a dust mote whirling through the unimaginable immensity of space?

For Kubrick, contingency provided both a stimulus for filmic expression and a perspective on a wide range of potential "content" embodied in human history and imagination within a variety of forms and ritual activities, in the complex history of artistic expression, in the shapes of societies and histories, and in the struggles of individual consciousness and articulation. Significantly, Kubrick's films stand as complex illustrations of their creator's acceptance of the "challenges of life within the boundaries of death," and as an affirmation of how "our existence as a species can have genuine meaning and fulfillment."

To understand how Kubrick converted an epistemology into an aesthetics, something that will be of practical rather than theoretical concern in subsequent chapters, we might pause to consider his films through a concept known to readers of science fiction as "conventionalization." Kubrick once expressed his conviction that the storytelling requirements of film were an initial step in creating an "objective correlative" for a psychological and emotional content—which means that, in his view, a film's most basic temporal and spatial realization (Pudovkin's twin notions of "action" and "filmic representation") provided the audience with points of reference, the panoply of "conventionalization" we associate with the Aristotelian verities of time and place, while covertly it undermined its own didactic authority and asserted its contingency as a work of art. The relationship that an audience experiences with a Kubrick film, beginning with *Paths of Glory,* resembles Bowman's confrontation with the extraterrestrial intelligence in *2001.* He wanders around in an eighteenth-century room without doors—a temporal and spatial "conventionalization"—while he is being subjected to an experience that will transform him from *Homo sapiens* to Star-Child. Kubrick's films aesthetically embody an analogous principle: they provide us with the familiar terrain of a temporal/spatial coherence—all the features of organizational exactness alluded to earlier, what I prefer to call an overt rhetoric—while they suggest to us, as the room does to Bowman, that viewed from another perspective, one developed through a covert rhetoric, their cinematic corporeality represents an illusion of sorts, something to "fascinate the beholder" while his awareness is being subtly altered. We must remember that the bone which Moon-Watcher, the hominid of *2001,* tosses into the air in a moment of evolutionary victory functions not only as a practical instrument at a given moment in filmic time, but as an artifact, an ur-HAL, that externalizes and expresses a paradox in human nature—it is both a tool and a weapon, at once creative and destructive. For Kubrick, the aesthetics of his medium likewise were tools of expression, mythopoeic extensions for the inner complexities of his vision, an opportunity for converting cinematic form into cinematic meanings.

I hope to trace through the following chapters how Stanley Kubrick's film imagination increasingly took the shape of a series of conceptual and formal paradoxes. As early as the *Look* photographs and *Day of the Fight,* his film work aspired to be both realist and formalist in structure and style. From the time of *Paths of Glory* and *Lolita,* his films increasingly would balance a traditional humanism against the surrealist's fondness for satiric dislocation in their poignant and ironic depiction of the tragicomic nature of human experience. In a personal life that rarely was divorced from his creative life, he had a fascination throughout most of his adult years for the almost daily permutations of American Pop Culture *and* the arcania of philosophy, literature, science, and technology. Even while he was being either absurdly demonized as a misanthropic recluse or spiritualized into a "mystique" by a culture obsessed with personality, he remained by all reliable accounts the American boy from the Bronx who loved to talk sports *and* the British rural intellectual with an insatiable desire to know everything. Ultimately Stanley Kubrick was, in the best sense, a Hollywood moviemaker *and* a brilliant film artist. As you read what follows, it will be for you to determine if this remarkable creative life is worthy of your attention, and particularly of that precious commodity known as time, which Stanley Kubrick used not only well but wisely during the last half of a highly contingent century.

2 THE END OF THE BEGINNING

From *Fear and Desire* to *Paths of Glory*

By the time he had completed his fourth feature film, at the age of twenty-nine, Stanley Kubrick had confronted and in large part resolved a number of narrative, stylistic, and conceptual issues. He had achieved startling success early in the first decade of his career, largely through a process of trial and error. He mastered his craft in the 1950s by doing rather than by being shown how: he served no apprenticeship in either the studios of Hollywood or the classrooms of academe. Like the cinephiles of the French New Wave (*nouvelle vague*), Kubrick moved from watching, discussing, and reading about films to making them. Truffaut and Resnais, like Kubrick, began in the documentary before turning to the greater technical and conceptual challenges offered by feature films. Significantly, *The 400 Blows* (1959) and *Hiroshima, Mon Amour* (1959), two films that, among others, signaled the end of the influence of Italian neorealism and the beginning of a more "personal" and truly authorial approach to film-making, were quietly predated and, from the vantages of hindsight, preempted by Kubrick's first work of consummate skill, *Paths of Glory* (1957). Taken together, Kubrick's first four features contain several stylistic and thematic preoccupations that would be more fully real-ized in his later work. In their rare good moments, *Fear and Desire* (1953) and *Killer's Kiss* (1955) achieve some arresting imagery and develop structural techniques and character ideas that would be worked out with more precision in the next two films. *The Killing* (1956) and *Paths of Glory,* both adapted from competently written but easily accessible novels, show significant advances in artistry as well as in budget and overall production. *The Killing* demonstrates Kubrick's early skill in handling a complex temporal structure, while the visual organization of *Paths of Glory* exemplifies a sustained control and bril-liance not found in his previous work. In addition, these two films show Kubrick departing from the poetic and allegorical styles of *Fear and Desire* and *Killer's Kiss*—which he later would condemn as "pre-tentious" and "amateurish"—and developing an aesthetic capable of assimilating layers of abstraction into a narrative and visual rhetoric characterized by a realistic exactness of time and space.

Fear and Desire and Killer's Kiss lack the narrative intricacy that dis-tinguishes most of Kubrick's work. The scripts are original work (with Kubrick co-authoring *Killer's Kiss*) by Kubrick's friend from high school days Howard O. Sackler, a poet-playwright who later wrote *The Great White Hope* and a clever, surrealist one-act play about American suburban impotence called *The Nine O'Clock Mail.* Both films show a jejune fondness for exploring states of "fear and desire" within loosely conceived and allegorical structures, which, however, provided Ku-brick opportunities for technical experimentation and a thematic overreaching typical of 1950s underground film. (Joseph Burstyn, who distributed films to American arthouses and who was the first to import the work of Rossellini and other neorealists, handled the re-lease of *Fear and Desire.*) *Fear and Desire* begins with a Conradian-sound-ing poem in voiceover, continues with an array of subjective devices as we watch four soldiers wander through an imaginary forest, and con-cludes with a penetration out of a collective heart of darkness into a dawn of new understanding. Lieutenant Corby (Kenneth Harp), the intellectual, discovers the fictitious nature of rationalism as he sym-bolically "kills" himself by killing his double, a Nazi general officer

In the forest of *Fear and Desire*

(also played by Kenneth Harp), while Mac (Frank Silvera), the primitive, fights through his rage and paranoia in a misty raft trip downriver. While the themes of *Fear and Desire* crudely reflect a number of later Kubrickian preoccupations, their expression resembles that youthful grab-bag of 1950s bohemian negativism and existential self-congratulation that the fledgling director no doubt found attractive during the period when he and his first wife lived in Greenwich Village. The film attacks the dehumanizing effects of war and other social institutions, while showing the failures of human reason and the dangers of an unexplored unconscious.* Visually, *Fear and Desire* clearly demonstrates Kubrick's talent for creating mental landscapes that alternate between grotesquerie and surrealistic beauty. Trench knives assault the camera just before we see a view of mangled corpses on which are scattered the leftovers of a meal—a scene that is briefly

---

*When James Mason as Humbert in *Lolita* pretends to be going to Hollywood to make a film about existentialism, which, he ironically tells us, was a "hot thing" at the time, Kubrick may have been commenting on his own early, misguided ambitions.

recalled later in a series of double exposures as the four men flee in a nightmare-like frenzy. Poetic, dreamy states of desire and fear are suggested, respectively, in the sudden appearance of the girl (Virginia Leith) washing in the river and by a raft floating in a state of fog-shrouded suspension. Particularly, the film suggests how repressed sexual desire (Eros) is linked to an unconscious fear of both its psychological disorders and its alliance with the greater dread of personal annihilation and death (Thanatos)—a Kubrickian theme that will dominate such later films as *Dr. Strangelove, The Shining,* and *Eyes Wide Shut.* And because *Fear and Desire* was a low-budget, independent, private operation, Kubrick was able to deal firsthand with many of the problems that later would multiply in scope more than number as he advanced toward commercial and artistic success.

In *Killer's Kiss,* Kubrick continued to explore internal states of nightmare and doubt, but in this case through a commercially viable, derivative narrative form. The story and style of the film evoke both the darkly romantic atmosphere of *film noir* and the melodramatic

The *noir* atmosphere of *Killer's Kiss*

realism of such popular street films as *The Naked City* (Jules Dassin, 1950) and *Panic in the Streets* (Elia Kazan, 1950). On the one hand, the first-person account of Davy Gordon (Jamie Smith), boxer on the lam, shows Kubrick's continuing interest in a psychological subject matter that traffics in basic emotional states (fear and desire, loneliness and entrapment) and allows for a surrealist approach to visual exposition; on the other, its street locations and neorealist flair for random detail (objects and faces in subways, and on the streets and in the shop windows of Times Square) are used to create a chaotic public backdrop at odds with private worlds.

Killer's Kiss contains several narrative and psychological ideas that superficially resemble a sentimentalized version of a *noir* film such as Billy Wilder's *Double Indemnity* (1944). Davy Gordon's first-person flashback account, however, lacks the bite and irony of the tale of sexual attraction and murder that Walter Neff (Fred MacMurray) narrates in *Double Indemnity*. Davy begins his story in the spacious and brightly lit environs of New York City's Penn Station, an early assurance for the audience that he and his girlfriend Gloria (Irene Kane) will answer the train whistle's call and escape to the West. Yet within these unconvincing fairy-tale bookends—no doubt prompted by a young director's hope for a commercial success—the film delineates a world no less menacing than Wilder's. Frank Silvera (as Vincent Rapallo) is again Kubrick's choice to play the bestial man, a kind of modern-day Stromboli who fends off loneliness and feelings of sexual inadequacy by subjugating others to his unpredictable appetites. He controls the shabby dancehall world of Pleasureland, which Kubrick's camera, in two horizontal tracks, characterizes as a languid movement of shapes and shadows, a tableau of faceless people lost to the somnambulant cadences of a tawdry dream. Such scenes merely express in another way Davy's premonitory nightmare of rapid movement down a vertical corridor of city buildings (done in negative image) and suggest that he and Rapallo are psychological doubles, each the other's secret sharer. In one scene, the dream merges with the reality, as Davy's nightmare is penetrated by Gloria's screams from across the courtyard as she resists Rapallo's sexual assault. And while Davy awakes to save her from the ogre, Kubrick has implied a deeper psychological nuance than one normally finds in either the more popular *noir* films of the period or the type of sentimental melodrama that *Killer's Kiss* pretends to imitate.

Much of the psychological and visual logic of the film anticipates the kind of indirect assault on an audience's expectations found in later and more accomplished films such as Welles's *Touch of Evil* (1958) and Hitchcock's *Psycho* (1960). Those films begin by setting up the conventional scenario of young lovers unwittingly ensnared in an evil more complex and profound than their capacity for understanding, while simultaneously forcing the audience to qualify their emotional identification with the characters through a series of maliciously contrived reversals. In Welles's film, for instance, Vargas (Charlton Heston) and his innocuously named wife Suzie (Janet Leigh) become so hopelessly lost in a borderline between good and evil, light and dark, that average viewers experience an unhappy confusion over their own inability to separate themselves from the racist and sexual obsessions of Welles's Hank Quinlan; and in *Psycho* Hitchcock not only teases us into identifying with Marion Crane's fear that her theft of $40,000 will be discovered, but he also teases us, especially the males in the audience, into a voyeuristic longing to gaze with Norman Bates (Anthony Perkins) on the erotically inviting body of Janet Leigh, which Hollywood in its prurience enticingly hid from view for many years. Hitchcock withholds that satisfaction from his audience and instead confronts them with the horror of their own hidden fantasies in the famous knife-rape attack on Marion in the shower. (In *Touch of Evil*, Welles had her symbolically raped in a motel room invaded by the unholy trinity of sex, drugs, and rock and roll.) Both these films, more expertly than *Killer's Kiss*, outwardly work within the popular conventions of an American genre, while covertly they question and even satirize the very values that provide an audience with a familiar bearing and orientation.

The best moments of *Killer's Kiss* combine a voyeuristic and narcissistic definition of character with a surrealist relish for subverting an audience's ready willingness to accept sentimental and commercial film pablum. In an early scene, we watch Davy in his apartment preparing for a fight by examining his face in the mirror (which in its detail recalls *Day of the Fight*), and immediately after, we see it distorted through a fish bowl. As Davy continues this activity, Kubrick switches to Gloria's perspective from across the courtyard, where she, too, goes through the ritual of preparation for another bout with the daily drudgery of her existence. While this scene deftly executes some necessary exposition, and shows a command of visual storytelling not present in *Fear and Desire*, it likewise anticipates later episodes with a voyeuristic content. As Davy has his hands taped and his body rubbed down in preparation for his boxing match, we see Gloria's body on display as well, as she stands in a black brassiere before a mirror getting ready for another night's work as a "hostess" on the dance floors of Pleasureland. The film suggests that both settings—the boxing ring and the dancehall—draw their clientele from the same faceless pool of lonely, vicarious thrill-seekers in search of a private coitus. Next, Kubrick takes us to Rapallo's curiously decorated office (family pictures, which recall Davy's room, mingled with blue jean and circus advertisements), where a television screen illuminates his and Gloria's faces as they watch Davy's fight. Kubrick cuts back and forth from the low angles, zooms, and handheld action of the ring to Rapallo's increasing sexual excitement as he simultaneously watches the fight and mauls Gloria. This suggestion of parallel and doubling actions carries forward something more than the entanglements of a highly contrived and melodramatic plot. It subtly intimates that in the next sequence, as Davy watches a mirror reflection of Gloria undressing while he is talking on the phone to "Uncle George" in Seattle, Kubrick would have us believe that his attraction to the girl in the window is not that different from Rapallo's. Kubrick's wit is especially evident when he shows Davy struggling with the telephone cord in his eagerness to see Gloria directly through the window. His frustration is matched by our voyeuristic disappointment, as our attention wavers between Davy on screen right talking on the phone and Gloria undressing in mirror reflection on screen left. The apartment light goes off, the mirror image turns to black, and the camera holds on Davy, standing and waiting as if he expected his dream in the mirror to magically reappear.

More forcefully depicted than irony, however, is an atmosphere of poignancy and unarticulated emotion that the film visually explores in a series of slow-paced vignettes. In one scene, Davy inspects Gloria's room while she sleeps and discovers both a world of feminine mystery (stockings, music box, doll) and a mirror image of his own loneliness. The camera stays back and interferes only slightly with the almost magical mood of the scene. We watch Davy walking between Gloria sleeping in her bed and the image in her mirror of her sleeping, followed by an intimation of her childlike innocence in close-up, and then a shot of the doll dangling over her head. Such a scene demonstrates Kubrick's early talent for capturing emotional states through an interaction of pace and atmosphere, actors and setting. And the emotion is unmockingly rendered, even though within the film's larg-

A neorealistic moment from *Killer's Kiss*

er narrative ambitions this scene continues an undertone of sexual fetishism and voyeurism. But we must not forget that Professor Rath's fascination with Lola and articles of her clothing in Sternberg's *The Blue Angel* (1930), one of Kubrick's personal favorites, contains as much poignancy as it does irony. The atmosphere of Rapallo's office, more sinister than the dreamlike rooms of the two lovers, likewise captures the pathos of someone trapped in the confusions of a divided self. One brief scene shows him expressing self-loathing and disgust over his own unresolved manhood by tossing a drink at his mirror image. This ability to communicate latent emotional depths through mise-en-scène and performance resonates throughout Kubrick's best work, and eventually evolves into one of his most distinctive but least appreciated signatures in such films as *Lolita, Barry Lyndon, The Shining, Full Metal Jacket,* and *Eyes Wide Shut.*

Killer's Kiss also reveals early signs of Kubrick's skill at developing conflicting narrative lines that at once intensify and work in opposition to the subjective issues of character. The early paralleling between Davy and Gloria, for instance, not only binds them together psychologically but initiates a pattern of narrative crisscrossing through which Kubrick, for the first time, expresses a fondness for the disparities of contingency. The two lovers begin in separate but conjunctive worlds: a high-angle shot records their paths crossing in a courtyard as they leave their apartments, Gloria to Rapallo in a waiting convertible, Davy walking alone down the sidewalk. In one of the film's more inventive scenes, the camera watches—again from above, looking down a flight of stairs going from the dancehall to the street—as Kubrick's narrative weaves a pattern of fate and mistaken identity that will result in the murder of Davy's manager, Albert (Jerry Jarret). Below we see Albert right and Gloria left, each ignorant of the other's identity, and both framed in the windows of a swinging double door. The camera remains stationary and ironic as one of Rapallo's hoods descends and entices Gloria back upstairs while taking her place in the frame opposite Albert, whom he mistakes for Davy. This stairway shot precedes the backlit, shadowy murder of Albert in an alley—a "no exit" dead end—and finds an ironic punctuation in an overhead sign that reads WATCH YOUR STEP. Kubrick reported that the sign was a fortuity of location shooting, an early example of that almost serendipitous use of coincidence which permeates many of the novels that Kubrick, throughout his career after *Killer's Kiss,* would choose to adapt to the screen.

Some of the more intriguing aspects of *Killer's Kiss* involve its often muddled and unrealized approach to character psychology—a flaw, however, that may indicate Kubrick's desire, even at this early stage in his career, to explode the conventions of film narrative. During the boxing match, Davy is characterized by a television announcer as a fighter "long on promise but no fulfillment," whose career has been victimized by a "glass chin" that proves to be "as fragile as ever" when he falls unconscious onto the canvas. We then see a pathetic side to Rapallo's animal brutality in his confession to Gloria that he has always felt "low and worthless," and in the way he begs for her love ("I'll be your slave"). She responds by mocking him as an "old man" who "smells bad," which leads to Rapallo's first attempt on his virile alter ego's life and the coincidence of Davy's being saved by the fortuitous distraction of a passing drunk outside the dancehall and by Albert's inadvertently taking his place. This suggestion of twisted but fragile inner worlds confronting the blindly indifferent punishments and rewards of chance merges with a motif of "faces" that runs throughout the film. Faces are repeatedly reflected in mirrors, seen on playing cards, and on the heads of dolls and mannequins. As Davy inspects his face on the night of the fight, he twists it into the contorted mask of the punch-drunk palooka he might one day become if he remains a boxer. Immediately this touching interlude takes on a curiously sinister quality when Kubrick gives us another view of Davy's distorted face from the other side of a fish bowl. Later, in an old warehouse loft, where he goes to save Gloria from Rapallo, Davy suffers "bad luck" when one of Rapallo's goons throws a deck of cards—with the ace of spades face up—in *his* face. After Davy regains consciousness, we see him face down in profile on the floor, where he stares eyeball to eyeball with a one-eyed jack. Through such oblique methods, Kubrick might be suggesting that our narrator Davy, the sentimentalized *noir* loser who outwardly yearns for the innocence of a horse ranch with "Uncle George" in the West, is nothing more than a "one-eyed jack": a film persona/stereotype unknowingly wearing the mask of "hero" to shield himself and the audience from confronting the face that lives on the other side of both consciousness and commercial film convention. Perhaps it is an early indication of all those contorted and grinning "faces" that increasingly will inhabit—and cohabit—the psychological terrain of Kubrick's films from *Dr. Strangelove* to *Eyes Wide Shut.*

The film's most memorable episode, a fight to the death between Davy and Rapallo in a storeroom filled with mannequins, illustrates Kubrick's fondness for mixing realist and surrealist imagery. This scene is preceded by an extended chase across rooftops with an early morning New York City skyline as background, reminiscent of *The Naked City* and countless other urban crime films. Then suddenly the action drops into a nightmare environment of dismembered and chaotically arranged torsos, heads, and limbs. Rapallo follows his quarry into the room and immediately feels threatened ("I gotta get out of here," he mutters), as if he had unexpectedly stumbled into a Pleasureland located in his nightmares, where the dancing puppets turn on the puppetmaster. In contrast, Davy blends into this world by using the mannequins for cover. In a tracking movement that recalls the film's visual definition of the dancers of Pleasureland (the same warehouse was used for both sets), the camera encourages us to associate Davy with a world without dimension or substance—one in which dreams of happiness with the doll-like Gloria resemble little more than a pleasant but empty world of shop-window dummies. We see

Davy's head poking up in the frame as if unscrewed from its body, framed on each side by two heads facing in the same direction, while arms and hands dangle overhead. He and Rapallo then engage in a struggle of primal intensity, with one wielding a pike and the other an ax. Mannequin heads are severed and torsos punctured, ending with Rapallo falling into a scrap heap of body parts and releasing an animal squeal as Davy drives the pike through his body. This sequence contrasts with the more traditional photo-journalistic handling of the boxing match seen earlier (which recalls Robert Wise's *The Set-Up*, 1949, and Kubrick's short, *Day of the Fight*) and defines a sensibility that continues to thrive on the creation of unsettling visual juxtapositions. Are we to interpret the mannequin scene as Davy's struggle with and liberation from his own shadow self, or as an example of a Kubrickian irony? As Rapallo's death cry merges with a return to the present and the sound of a train whistle, a hackneyed device as old as Hitchcock's *The 39 Steps* (1935), we are left to choose between the flat surfaces of a happy ending and a faint but unrealized satiric distance. It could be that *Killer's Kiss* intimates that in their own unique way, Kubrick's intentions always were closer to the surrealism of Buñuel than to either the baroque self-displays of Welles or the sentimental realism of Kazan.

   Lest my analysis leave the impression that I consider *Killer's Kiss* an undiscovered classic, let me say that it is not a very good film and, all in all, contains more weaknesses than strengths. At the time, Kubrick admitted to the difficulties of writing dialogue, and this film illustrates his point when verbal exposition is required. Consequently, for *The Killing*, his first novelistic adaptation, Kubrick employed the services of crime writer Jim Thompson for additional dialogue. The use of 1950s jazz music, punctuated by loud blasts from a saxophone, and lachrymose violins to express the film's "love" theme suggest low-budget desperation and severely date the film. The acting, except for that of Frank Silvera, is pedestrian (further hampered by post-synchronization), even though Kubrick's camera and eye for visual detail often make it tolerable. The flashback ballet sequence performed by Kubrick's second wife, Ruth Sobotka, is gratuitous and provides neither a satisfactory motivation for the character of Gloria nor a visual coherence for the film. If *Killer's Kiss* were Kubrick's highest achievement, it would not merit much more than a cursory inspection, let alone carry the interpretive baggage placed on it by this discussion. But because it is the early work of a filmmaker with Kubrick's credentials, such consideration seems not only justified but illuminating. Kubrick quickly overcame most of the shortcomings present in *Killer's Kiss:* A year later he released *The Killing*, made on a budget of $330,000 (still below average for a low-budget studio film in 1956), which permitted him to hire a cast of superb Hollywood character actors and for the first time to enjoy some of the benefits of financial certainty. More important, this project gave him the opportunity to resolve the confusions of cinematic point of view that were responsible for much of the tonal inconsistency in the earlier film.

By choosing to adapt Lionel White's *Clean Break* (1955) for his next film, Kubrick seems, at first glance, to have opted for a commercial future rather than to develop further the more abstract and overly poetic tendencies found in an "art film" such as *Fear and Desire* or an existential *noir* such as *Killer's Kiss*. Superficially, at least, White's novel and the outward form of Kubrick's *The Killing* display the fictional incorporation of pseudo-documentary techniques that had been popularized by producer Louis de Rochemont of *March of Time* fame in such films as *The House on 92nd Street* (1945), *13 Rue Madeleine* (1946), and *Boomerang* (1947). These films conferred on the public world of process and fact (i.e., FBI investigative procedures, military commando training) such an aura of epistemological urgency that the basic concerns of individual human beings were made to appear both trivial and irresponsible. White's novel is as clean and lean as its title— precise, economic, transparent—and contains only a few embellishments of style and tone. The characters are clearly defined and, once set in motion, stay on a psychological course as relentless in its logic as Johnny Clay's robbery plan. *Clean Break* is a neat storytelling package, but more important for this study is the part it played in Kubrick's development as a writer—as well as director—of film adaptations.

Beginning with *The Killing*, Kubrick's artistic development moved straight and upward, sidetracked only briefly by the *Spartacus* assignment, and it can be measured in part by his success with adaptation. Unlike Bergman and Fellini, Kubrick was not, strictly speaking, an autobiographical or "personal" artist. With few exceptions, Kubrick's films before *Barry Lyndon* do not draw directly on persons and events from autobiographical experience.* They embody a turn of mind that

*In *The Killing*, Kubrick uses his Greenwich Village chess-playing friend Kola Kwariani (as Maurice), and in *2001* his daughter Vivian has a brief part. See the "Chapter 10" section of "Notes & Trivia" for more on the "personal" in Kubrick.

is more speculative than romantic, where an interest in how human beings give form to or hide from those fears and desires that throb for release inside all of us commands far more attention than what such experiences actually feel like. In *Fear and Desire* and *Killer's Kiss,* Kubrick tried to capture the look and feel of psychic worlds, but at the expense of narrative and tonal coherence. The right novel, therefore, provided Kubrick with a framework of action and character, a kind of ready-made objective correlative, within which he could integrate his own formal and psychological ideas. And more often than not, this process helped him create a tension between exterior and interior space, the demands of novelistic and cinematic form. We shall see that the choice of *Clean Break* and Humphrey Cobb's *Paths of Glory* (1935) represents something more important in Kubrick's career than merely his desire in the late 1950s to be a "commercial" filmmaker. Instead, the adaptation of these two novels accelerated a process of discovery in which a complex personal vision found its own expression through the development of an equally personal and distinctive film aesthetic.

Kubrick screwed the novel's story even tighter than White had, producing a vise of parallel and doubling actions that transform a familiar plot formula into an unexpected philosophic and reflexive treatise. *The Killing,* unlike the novel, begins and ends on a Saturday. It introduces each character, as the narrator explains it, as a "single piece in a jumbo jigsaw puzzle" that has a "predetermined final design," and concludes one week later by showing how these separate human elements come together in time and space to execute Johnny Clay's "foolproof" robbery plan.* Beginning with the credits, the film builds on an involuted structure of simultaneity and repetition. There we see documentary-like footage of San Francisco's Bay Meadows Racetrack and preparations for what will turn out to be the Landsdowne Stakes; later these shots are repeated three times as they are synchronized to the start of the robbery itself. Thus images that at first lack a specific temporal designation—but instead are generalized stock shots of a racetrack—are given significance by virtue of an alignment within

---

*Johnny Clay is played by Sterling Hayden, whose most notable film before this was, of course, *The Asphalt Jungle* (John Huston, 1950), which superficially resembles *The Killing* as another "caper" *noir* film; Hayden's performances in the two pictures are very close. And Elisha Cook, Jr. became a famous American character actor after his role as Wilmer the gunsel in *The Maltese Falcon* (John Huston, 1941), although his portrayal of Harry Jones in *The Big Sleep* (Howard Hawks, 1946), as the "little man" victimized by a typical *noir* bitch, is a better comparative source for the characterization of George Peatty.

the design of both Johnny's plan and Kubrick's film. Similarly, each of the film's principal characters, neatly divided between the inside participants and the outside intruders, attempts through the logic of the robbery scheme to give purpose to an otherwise fragmented and desperate existence. We realize, for instance, that at least two of the five insiders must suppress disorderly psychological factors if the plan is to succeed. The fatherly and homoerotic attachment that Marv Unger (Jay C. Flippen) feels for Johnny remains latent even though it is exacerbated by the presence of Clay's girlfriend Fay (Coleen Gray) and plans of marriage; and George Peatty (Elisha Cook, Jr.) controls his sexual jealousy until after the robbery. In each case, Kubrick extends the novel's implication that the predictable nature of Johnny's plan runs contrary to indeterminable human forces.

Important outside complications described in the novel remain almost intact in the film: Randy Kennan (Ted de Corsia) has troubles with a loan shark, Mike O'Reilly (Joe Sawyer) worries about his invalid wife, Clay has a history of being a small-timer and a loser, and George is sexually enslaved by his wife, Sherry (Marie Windsor). Kubrick, like White, uses the parallel plot of Sherry and boyfriend Val Cannon (Vince Edwards) to represent the one element that endangers both the robbery and the getaway. As the members of Johnny's gang come together to finalize the plan, Sherry and Val initiate what will be a counterplan dependent upon the success of the other. Converging very early in the film, therefore, is the reflexive interaction of schemes within schemes, plots within plots. Kubrick gives the race itself an importance not found in the novel, an activity that focuses the film's complex structure visually, aurally, and conceptually: The Landsdowne Stakes contains the workings of chance within a closed system—one measured in time, organized in space, and presided over by an offscreen deity (Saturday afternoon at 4:25, a mile and a quarter, on a circular track, and responsive to the track announcer's control)—and as a result it can be exploited or disrupted by an outside force not part of its logic. All of which means, of course, that Johnny's plan is equally vulnerable to the unknown activities of Sherry and Val; and by extension, that all three are servants to the temporal/spatial schematics of Kubrick's film, reminding the audience of an artistic design that guarantees its own success at the expense of the others' failure.

Kubrick departed from White's narrative in magnifying the importance of the role of coincidence and chance. Regrettably, he in-

vented a scene in which the sniper Nikki (Timothy Carey) is victimized by a "good-luck" horseshoe that punctures his automobile tire
and leads to his death. In the novel, by contrast, Nikki escapes cleanly
without the interference of poetic justice—indicating, perhaps, that
Kubrick's version was driven by practical considerations (i.e., the ar-
cane morality of the Production Code) and a desire for total narrative
closure. More significantly, the film changes White's ending, which
has George Peatty, bloody from wounds, staggering into the airport
terminal and pumping several bullets into Johnny Clay at the moment
when escape appears imminent. The final passage of the novel explains the irony of its title—an unnamed policeman pulls a blood-
soaked newspaper from under Johnny's body and reads a headline
that declares: RACE TRACK BANDIT MAKES CLEAN BREAK WITH
TWO MILLION. In the novel, it is psychology that destroys Johnny's
plan—not, as in the film, the fateful turns of a contingent universe.
Once he is thrown off his timetable, Kubrick's protagonist must accept with resignation the fortuities and reversals of chance. At first it
appears that luck may save him in the absence of a plan: he arrives at
the assigned meeting place fifteen minutes late, thereby avoiding the
film's second and more grisly "killing," the shootout between his gang
and Val's. But in the end Johnny must flee into a shadowy world gov-
erned by accident, where a faulty lock on a suitcase and a stranger's
poodle determine his fate. Johnny watches from behind a wire fence
as the money, like the gold dust in Huston's *The Treasure of the Sierra
Madre* (1948), wildly dances in a propeller-driven wind in mockery of
all his human striving. Kubrick ends *The Killing* with Johnny Clay turning to face his captors, a man now stripped of plan and purpose, and
admitting to a defeat ("What's the difference?") that the film suggests
is far more profound than merely the consequence of a jealous husband's intervention.

While Kubrick's treatment of story and character displays a thematic clarity absent in his first two features, his structural approach to
narrative and point of view shows early signs of a mastery present in
later works such as *A Clockwork Orange, Barry Lyndon, The Shining, Full
Metal Jacket,* and *Eyes Wide Shut.* The narrator of *The Killing,* in a tone
that resembles the voiceover heard in the *Highway Patrol* television
series, which aired during this time (1955–59), allows Kubrick to
move quickly through potentially tiresome exposition and convey essential information. At the same time, it strikes what Alexander
Walker correctly perceives as an "aural note . . . to which he tunes the

A Kubrickian image of disorder, the second "killing" in
The Killing

rest of the film." The "tune" it plays, in fact, recalls the kind of newsreel authenticity achieved in deRochemont's *March of Time* series,
which Welles so effectively parodied in the "News on the March" sequence of *Citizen Kane* (1941). In *The Killing,* however, this authenticity becomes a near-symphony of reflexive irony. Kubrick's narrator
has an omniscience limited to the external and temporal movements
of character and event. His voice is flat and neutral, although he hints
at unfolding "puzzles" and "designs" that remain ambiguous for purposes of plot suspense. His dispassionate objectivity functions as an
aural timepiece forever ticking off bits of data that have value only
within the design of Johnny Clay's plan. More successfully than the
film's characters, the narrator suppresses the contours of an individu-
alized identity so that he can execute efficiently the temporal plan of
the film. His voice is all surface and no depth, time-bound and blind
to spatial nuances, at once a device for narrative coherence and a foil
to Kubrick's irony. His role in the central action of the film parallels

that of the announcer at the racetrack, another disembodied voice that we hear in repeated cadences, who also puts his faith in the logic of an artificially contrived form. In one of the few surrealistic touches in *The Killing*, we watch Johnny in a dehumanized mask realize the success of his intricately timed and spaced design, just as we hear the racetrack announcer's confusion over the shooting of the horse and his conviction that "exact information" will be forthcoming. Just as Johnny's plan undermines the authority of the race, so does the narrator of the film command an omniscience far more Olympian than that of the track announcer. But just as Johnny's cool and mechanical control turns to frenzy and then despair once it is exposed to a world outside the gameboard of his plan, the narrator plays second fiddle to the subtler intentions of Kubrick's visual narrative.

How Kubrick moves to defeat the authority of his "objective"—or overt—film rhetoric becomes an early example of a temporal/spatial aesthetics that will be an essential element in his development as a master of his medium. The film combines a series of horizontal tracking shots with repeated vertical compositions to create a spatial grid that resembles both a chessboard and a cage. As the narration impresses us with its temporal dexterity, the film's visual exposition shows that in the beginning the characters are more synchronized in space than in time: the camera moves from *left to right* with Marv across the racetrack betting area to Mike O'Reilly's bar, with Randy in the cocktail lounge for a meeting with a loan shark, with Johnny Clay as he walks through the rooms of Marv's apartment to Fay sitting on the bed, with Mike as he goes to the sickbed of his invalid wife, with George Peatty as he walks through his apartment to his wife lounging on their bed. As in *Killer's Kiss*, Kubrick continues to use the repetitions of camera and mise-en-scène to deepen the emotive and conceptual content of his film. The bed motif slyly circumvents the Legion of Decency and, ironically, develops a far more pervasive sexual implication than is found in the novel. The movements of the camera, with far more subtlety than the narration, outline a world that allows the audience to see the bars of a black and white prison long before the characters realize they inhabit a cage without an exit. As the narrator defines the various human pieces that make up Johnny's plan, and then as that plan is executed, the horizontal camera movements stay on a steady left-to-right course. The film's characters enjoy, with the audience, a greater sense of spatial than temporal continuity. Once the robbery is over, the camera movements indicate that escape out of the closed structure of the plan and its inevitable consequences will take a *right-to-left* course. Naturally, Johnny's escape from the track moves in that direction, imitating as it does a concept of film continuity as venerable as Muybridge's experiments with animal locomotion. Interestingly, when Johnny arrives at the airport and moves through the terminal, the camera continues to track with him from right to left; but when he flees from the one thing that might lift him out of his spatial trap—namely, the airplane—he and the camera once again traverse a horizontal course from left to right. But this time Johnny retreats into a maze rather than a controlled plan, where far too many factors, interior as well as exterior, interact for a man with his limitations of vision to succeed.

Johnny Clay, Kubrick tells us, is not quite a master criminal and not nearly an artist. During a scene at the Chess Academy, where Johnny hires Maurice to do the muscle work in his robbery plan, the brawny wrestler indulges in a philosophic reflection on how "gang-

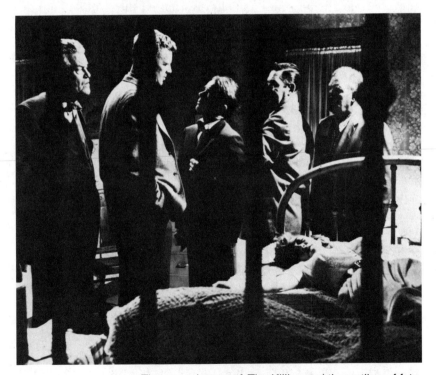

The conspirators of *The Killing* and the outline of fate
(Jay C. Flippen, Sterling Hayden, Elisha Cook, Ted
de Corsia, Marie Windsor, Joe Sawyer)

sters and artists" are alike in the way "they are admired and hero-
worshipped, but there is present an underlying wish to see them destroyed at their height of glory." But when he senses that his words are
falling on deaf ears, Maurice realizes that his friend does not measure
up to such a grandiose martyrdom: "Johnny, you were never very
bright but I love you anyway." Within the film's conceptual scheme,
both Johnny's success with the plan—his brief "height of glory"—and
his failure with contingency become Kubrick's sympathetic portrayal
of an ordinary, unsentimentalized human tragedy.

At key junctures, Kubrick employs a vertical camera movement
that helps to complete the chessboard/cage metaphor. In three
places, the camera moves back in an identical manner as it records
Johnny's movement outside a line of motel cabins. (Undoubtedly,
these three scenes were combined in the film's shooting schedule.)
In the first two scenes, Johnny moves with his usual steady resolution
to the correct cabin, while in his haste to pick up the money on the
third occasion he becomes spatially disoriented (he is fifteen minutes
behind schedule) and almost goes into the wrong cabin. The vertical
camera movement, however, remains the same—it continues to draw
the lines of a cage—as the temporal scheme of Johnny's plan starts to
unravel. The only subjective shot in the film moves vertically with
George Peatty across a grotesquely disordered room of carnage as his
fate comes to resemble the bars of his parimutuel window and the
cage of a parrot that will mock him in death. And in three strategic
places, Kubrick creates a composition of three human figures lined
up and facing the camera: the cardboard G-men targets pointing guns
on Nikki's firing range; the three gang members (Marv, Mike, and
Randy) looking expectantly toward the door through which Val and
another man will come and turn the apartment into a shooting gallery with live targets; and, finally, the three figures (two plainclothes-
men and, to complete the symmetry, an airline employee) who close
in on Johnny during the final image of the film.

From the visual design of *The Killing*, in the way it totally encloses
the world of the film, we can infer that Kubrick wanted to experiment
with a temporal definition of space. Besides the moving camera shots
and vertical compositions, he also uses source lighting to accent a
claustrophobic darkness and an array of objects to suggest psycho/
sexual entrapment. Kubrick, however, transcends the novel's emphasis on the contrary workings of design and disruption by creating a
cinematic equivalent for his avowed fondness for games of deception

and enigmatic works of literature. He extends the novel's *donnée* to include the opposition not only of intellect and passion, design and disorder, but of art and life as well. Yet the style of *The Killing* remains deceptively clean and stark, one in which geometric lines of movement and space are far more evocative than images of density and mass. The tight narrative focus of the novel, with its subordination of psychological depth to complex intersections of plot, offered Kubrick an opportunity to work out a firmer command of film time. And because *Clean Break* clearly defines its interior world, Kubrick, with the help of a professional cast and Jim Thompson's hard-boiled dialogue, was able to move away from the confused subjectivity of *Fear and Desire* and *Killer's Kiss* and develop objective correlatives for a psychological and emotional content. Adaptation, for the first time, provided him with an explicit verbal rhetoric from which he could create a more implicit cinematic one. In the final analysis, *The Killing* may be nothing more than a cleverly executed exercise—Kubrick's "plan"—that reveals, as it entertains, the secrets of a filmmaker whose intentions too often strike us as perversely obscure.

Humphrey Cobb's *Paths of Glory* would seem to be an ideal source for the filmmaker of *Fear and Desire*, *Killer's Kiss*, and *The Killing*. Its style and narration develop an ironic contrast between public and private worlds, the fictions of officialese and the fluctuations of an indeterminate truth. The novel is gorged with passages of hallucinatory intensity depicting the actual and imagined horrors of war, and others showing an empty and formal masking of that truth by characters who are ambitious. Throughout, Cobb's third-person narration remains all-knowing, ironic, and moralistic. In one scene with an obvious appeal to Kubrick's demonstrated interests, the narrator tells us that General Assolant (Mireau in the film), who is obsessed with viewing war as merely a "question of percentages," does not take into account that "a battle is a thing of flux, and that you cannot measure flux by the debris that it leaves behind." Elsewhere, Cobb creates a scene between Assolant and Colonel Dax that contains very cinematic and Kubrickian overtones. Dax feels that the general's problem is one of "seeing," that he is "always looking through lenses, lenses which are made of the insignia of rank." Consequently, Dax tricks Assolant into confronting the human reality of war through a periscope in the trench:

The telescopic lenses seemed to spring the mass of bodies right into his face. The bodies were so tangled that most of them could not be distinguished one from the other. Hideous, distorted, and putrescent, they lay tumbled upon each other or hung in the wire in obscene attitudes, a shocking mound of human flesh, swollen and discoloured.

Cobb concludes his strong indictment of the politics of war with a NOTE at the end of the novel that forces the reader to extend its lessons to life itself and to see the historical truth behind the fictional lie.*

Interestingly, Kubrick's *Paths of Glory* duplicates neither the nightmare landscapes of the novel nor those found in his earlier films. The film contains only two sequences in which subjective camera movements are used, and neither travels over a field of carnage. In places where the novel calls for an expressionistic rather than naturalistic film treatment, Kubrick's style remains objective and realistic, and when he enlarges scenes for which there is little descriptive authority in the novel, such as the attack on the Ant Hill, the court-martial, and the execution, his camera and mise-en-scène become truly impressive. And although he followed the novel's three-part organization (before the attack; the attack and after; the court-martial and execution), Kubrick did not choose to work out its ironic patterns of fate. Cobb, for instance, begins and ends by focusing on two soldiers named Langlois and Duval, the first a veteran and survivor who is convinced that "no German shell or bullet has my number on it," and the other a recruit who dreams of glory and especially admires Langlois's medals, even though they were won in a lottery. At the end of the novel, Langlois (Corporal Paris in the film), as the result of another lottery, is tied to a stake, with his medals on the ground at his feet, and Duval (who is not in the film) is a member of the firing squad that executes him. The novel abounds in such devices, most of which are telegraphed in advance, and which reveal a temporal and psychological straitjacket no less confining than the one Kubrick cre-

---

*Cobb's NOTE (p. 265) to *Paths* reads as follows: "All the characters, units, and places mentioned in this book are fictitious. However, if the reader asks, 'Did such things really happen?' the author answers, 'Yes,' and refers him to the following sources which suggested the story: *Les crimes des conseils de guerre,* by R.G. Réau; *Les fusilles pour l'exemple,* by J. Galtier-Boissiere and Daniel de Ferdon; *Les dessous de la guerre révélés par les comités secrets* and *Images secrètes de la guerre,* by Paul Allard; a special dispatch to *The New York Times* of July 2, 1934, which appeared under this headline: 'FRENCH ACQUIT 5 SHOT FOR MUTINY IN 1915; WIDOWS OF TWO WIN AWARD OF 7 CENTS EACH'; and *Le fusillé,* by Blanche Maupas, one of the widows who obtained exoneration of her husband's memory and who was awarded damages of one franc."

ated in *The Killing.* Kubrick's film likewise downplays the conventional appeal of the novel's manipulation of time—one very cinematic in its parallel "editing" and the "high noon" suspense countdown that precedes the attack and execution—and instead develops a number of spatial complexities through a more deliberate handling of scene exposition. If *The Killing* represents Kubrick's first real success with a temporal film rhetoric, what Pudovkin might have called the "filmic representation" through action (story) and images of a theme (time), then *Paths of Glory* could be considered his early masterpiece of visual storytelling, one that extends the philosophic implications of the novel far beyond the logic of its liberal/moral preachments. Kubrick, in other words, used the temporal and psychological framework of Cobb's novel to develop more fully and more satisfactorily than before an aesthetics of contingency, one which by its very nature requires that the exigencies of any given moment in filmic time (whether psychic or "real") be measured against the larger spatial and ambiguous dimensions of a disparate cinematic universe.*

In *Paths of Glory* Kubrick combined—for the first time—all the elements of a film's soundtrack (language, noise, music) with a visual complexity that illustrates his belief that film narrative can more successfully achieve the ambiguity and "subconscious designating effect of a work of art" through images and music than through a reliance on words. It is evidence of Kubrick's early maturity as a film artist that he uses an offscreen narrator only at the beginning and yet maintains a documentary-like realism of style that develops a complex range of ideas. Following the credits and the playing of the French national anthem, and a title that identifies place and time ("France 1916"), the narrator—his tone anticipating the computer-like voices of *Dr. Strangelove*'s narration and HAL of *2001*—briefly summarizes the beginning years of World War I, first as a series of attacks and counter-

---

*Paths poses difficulties in assigning credit for its verbal ideas, as do a number of later Kubrick films. Undoubtedly, both Calder Willingham and Jim Thompson helped Kubrick with the ironic and literate nuances of the dialogue, although *Barry Lyndon*, scripted by Kubrick with help only from William Makepeace Thackeray, plays with language in much the same way. And the use of narration stands as one of Kubrick's most distinctive film signatures. Kubrick freely admitted that the collaborative experience of putting a film script together is essential to its success, as the significant contributions of Vladimir Nabokov to *Lolita*, Terry Southern and Peter George to *Dr. Strangelove*, Arthur C. Clarke to *2001*, Diane Johnson to *The Shining*, Michael Herr and Gustav Hasford to *Full Metal Jacket*, and Frederic Raphael to *Eyes Wide Shut* testify. However, Kubrick's career illustrated his stated belief that the writer-director who masters both crafts consistently produces the finest work.

The first pathway in *Paths of Glory:* The arrival of
General Broulard (Adolphe Menjou) outside the chateau

attacks, and then as a stalemate of "zigzagging" trenches and un-
changing "battle lines." At the same time, a moving camera records
from a distance the arrival of General Broulard (Adolphe Menjou)
outside a grand eighteenth-century chateau that looks out onto a spacious but formal garden of walkways more appropriate for a ceremonial promenade than for a casual stroll. Two lines of soldiers form a
pathway for Broulard's entrance into a setting of splendor that incongruously, if not anachronistically, houses the headquarters of the
French regiment commanded by General Mireau (George Macready). In this first shot, the narrator's unemotional tone undercuts
the patriotic implications of the *Marseillaise,* while the appearance of
lines and paths anticipates later developments that visually will chart
an elaborate drama of zigzagging political and psychological forces
far more complex than those mentioned in the narration. The execution scene near the end of the film, for instance, will move through
this very setting and bring together the contrary but complementary

worlds of the chateau and the trench. And the film will conclude on an ironic note as a frightened young woman in the bistro sings a sentimental song from the *Musical Memories of Germany.**

The first half of *Paths* (marked by the film's initial fade-out, after the failed attack on the Ant Hill) further develops this ironic structure of oppositions and parallels between the chateau and the trenches, through which Kubrick will turn a system of clearly defined contrasts into a maze of paradoxical associations. A comparison of the aural and visual treatments of the first two sequences effectively illustrates this point. As the first scene begins, Broulard walks between the lines of soldiers and along the pathway into the chateau for a meeting with Mireau in a spacious and ornate room commandeered for his office and apartment. He compliments Mireau on the "pleasant atmosphere" of the room and on his taste in "carpets and pictures." Mireau, obviously pleased, confesses that the room is the "same as when I moved in," and that "I didn't have to do much." Broulard, with no visible indication that he actually appreciates the art of the setting or the unintentional humor of this exchange, proceeds to explain the "top-secret" reason for his visit (it is not, after all, a social call, as Kubrick blurs the distinction between social formality and political manipulation). Mireau interrupts, "reading" Broulard's mind and abbreviating these formalities with his reference to the Ant Hill. After some smiling cajolements from Broulard, and an implied promise of promotion, Mireau slams a fist into his hand and exclaims, "We might just do it!" Kubrick cuts on this sound of fist and voice, first to a bleak panorama of no-man's-land through a horizontal viewer, and then to Mireau, who, like Broulard on his way to the chateau, walks down a pathway lined with soldiers, except that Mireau moves through a trench where the lines are not as formal or exact. And instead of the *Marseillaise* or the voice of the omniscient narrator, we hear shells exploding and see dirt and debris falling from above.

Once again the film shows us a general officer visiting a subordinate, and at the same time implying a vertical line (i.e., chain of command) that ascends (to Broulard and the gods above) and descends (to Dax and the "insect" men below) outside the space of any given frame. Even though Mireau must stoop to enter Colonel Dax's

---

*The song can be found in *Auf zum Oktoberfest* (vol. 2); the German singer is played by Suzanne Christian, née Christiane Harlan, who in 1958 became Kubrick's third wife. They were still married at the time of his death in 1999.

cramped bunker, he does not neglect the verbal formalities of the chateau as he compliments Dax on the "neatness" of his quarters. The colonel (Kirk Douglas), unprepared for this visit, is naked from the waist up, washing from a decorative porcelain bowl (a memento from the chateau, expressive of his desire to stay clean in a dirty world). Even though outwardly he maintains the rules of military protocol by putting on his tunic and addressing his superior officer as "sir," Dax's bluntness of language ridicules these formalities. He plays on Mireau's hollow rhetoric, turning "mice" into "mausers" and "pregnable" into a paradox of birth and death. And when Major Saint-Auban (Richard Anderson) characterizes the fear felt by the huddled men as a herd instinct, an "animal sort of thing," Dax objects, defining it instead as a "human sort of thing." Dax completely asserts his verbal as well as moral superiority when he deflates Mireau's pomposity by citing Samuel Johnson's dictum that "patriotism is the last refuge of a scoundrel." Yet, despite Dax's righteous fervor and humane education, his final comment—"We'll take the Ant Hill"—ironically echoes in its vigor Mireau's statement at the conclusion of the first sequence.

The film's deployment of camera and mise-en-scène, by contrast, provides a larger and more philosophic perspective from which to view and evaluate the psychological and verbal circumlocutions of these early sequences. When Broulard commits a *faux pas* by referring to the paintings in Mireau's apartment as "pictures," Kubrick reveals not just Broulard's artistic illiteracy but his historical and moral illiteracy as well. (When Broulard returns to the chateau after the failed attack, Kubrick shows him traveling left to right on a course parallel to that of a huge painting being carried in the background, but in the opposite direction.) Kubrick's use of the chateau as both primary setting and visual metaphor has little or no precedent in Cobb's novel. There the chateau does not become a factor until the court-martial, and it has little descriptive status, except when the narrator alludes to its history by informing the reader that Napoleon once slept there. In Kubrick's film, it visually embodies an architectural and philosophic period in human civilization and a timeless passion for aesthetic expression. More significantly, it quietly provides a commentary on the efforts of the characters to duplicate in their activities its formal properties while ignoring the beauty of its civilized expression and the implications of its vertical reach.

Throughout the film, characters are shown walking down paths that lead either into a maze of personal ambition and delusion or into

the endgame of death. In sequence one, as the generals circle an ornate round settee in the middle of the room, the camera moves with
them to record the circular logic of both Mireau's thinking and Broulard's persuasion. We notice that Mireau, in his excitement over the
prospect of personal glory, momentarily neglects the formalities of
the occasion and pours himself a cognac without first offering one to
his guest. And when he finally contrives a reason to believe in the
likelihood of the attack's success, the camera stops its weaving motions and watches as the two men move into the background across a
chessboard parquetry. While the vertical spaciousness of the chateau—as well as an implied scope of history and art—belies the horizontal and circular courses of its temporary inhabitants, the visual
definition of the trenches leaves no doubt that their paths take a
deadly straight and narrow course. Not only is no-man's-land visualized horizontally in that shot following sequence one, but literally it is
part of a topography decorated by a series of horizontal trenches that
look more like a surrealist graveyard than paths to glory. Above the
trench line, instead of the spatial expanses of the chateau, we see the
low ceiling of an oppressive white sky, like a coffin's lid, which rains
down shells of death and fills the air with smoke and debris. Kubrick's
first dynamic dolly shot—moving back as it shows Mireau's progress
through the trenches and past the three men who later will be scape-
goats for his failure and vanity—captures a world dramatically in
touch with the extremes of life and death but committed, along with
the planners in the chateau, to destructive and predetermined paths.

Kubrick continues this ironic blending of shown and implied oppositions—of settings and action, words and images, a close-up versus
distanced perspective—during the attack on the Ant Hill. Instead of
prolonging the countdown to battle and extracting its full emotional
and suspense value, as Cobb did, he abbreviates it and stretches out
the attack itself, perhaps to provide his "war" film with at least one
traditional action sequence. Typically, however, Kubrick does not give
the audience an uncomplicated moment of human conflict without
the intrusion of forces far more sinister than those German soldiers
who, if not seen, at least are heard from in the deafening roar of
battle. For one thing, the film never explains until after the fact the
purpose of the attack or the value, strategically, of the Ant Hill (no
such ambiguity exists in the novel). Later, in the last scene between
Dax and Broulard, we learn that the attack was necessitated by political rather than military concerns. Only at the end does the audience,

along with Dax, fully appreciate the extent of Broulard's powers—
that, in effect, he was a political and very corporeal *deus ex machina*
who watched Mireau watching Dax watching after his men, only Broulard mistakenly assumed Dax's motives were as cynical as his own.
Kubrick indirectly prepares the audience for this revelation when he
foils Mireau's activities during the attack with Dax's actual movement
into battle.

For the second time a binocular view of the Ant Hill is shown
from Mireau's always distant perspective, in this instance as he absurdly anticipates victory with smiles, glasses of cognac, and formal
toasts to "France." Kubrick then cuts to the film's first subjective shot,
a bold movement with Dax through a trench lined with soldiers on
both sides and the sounds of bombardment overhead—a movement
that ends inside a ghostly cloud of smoke and dust. For the attack,
Kubrick employed six cameras, including one that he handheld to
bring Dax and the battle into vivid, zoom close-up. The cameras move
primarily on a horizontal path (right to left) with the attack and capture a remarkable three minutes of film. No doubt it is as realistic
and exciting a battle sequence as had ever been put on film prior to
Omaha Beach in Spielberg's *Saving Private Ryan* (1998). But its real
power comes from the sheer magnitude of the disorder and death,
the cacophony and volume of the noise, and that Kubrickian overview which lifts it out of an immediate narrative context into a larger
conceptual one. Kubrick now shows us nightmares taking place in
broad daylight and in "real" moments of film time, in a context where
the faint but insistent sound of Dax's whistle exhorting his men inhabits the same soundscape as Mireau's fulminations against an artillery commander who "humbly" refuses to open fire on his own men.
Each, in its own way, stands as a poignant mockery of both the destruction falling from a godless sky and the verbal and moral corruption descending from the echo chambers of the chateau.

Yet nothing in part one of *Paths of Glory,* not even this stunning
attack sequence, necessarily prepares us for the aesthetic and conceptual brilliance of the last half of the film. The twists and turns of a
psychological/political labyrinth bend in even more sinister directions as the action moves entirely into the chateau. The film's visual
and philosophical emphasis on horizontal and vertical forms, paths
and lines, becomes even more pronounced and intricate as the two
worlds of the film begin to express the paradoxical outline of a single
world. The early scenes of part two, for instance, show that the trench

Colonel Dax (Kirk Douglas) moving into the smoky
nightmare of war and an overhead view of the reality
of its disorder

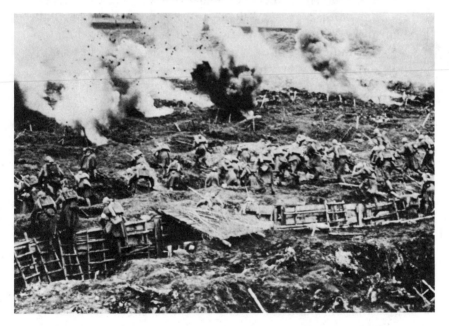

world has come to the chateau and, ironically, that it is not as out of place there as were the formalities of the chateau in the trenches. Dax now visits Mireau in his "quarters," with Broulard present, and brings his moral rectitude and candid tongue into the parlors of euphemism. They sit at the very table where earlier Broulard began to lead Mireau down that path to the ill-fated attack on the Ant Hill. Only now there are three men, and in the framing of the scene Kubrick implies an emerging alliance between Dax and Broulard: a series of two-shots showing Dax left and Broulard right, with a large eighteenth-century painting of an idealized social life between and over them in the background, oppose Mireau's isolation in one-shot. Here Kubrick is suggesting that there are not only deceptive political maneuvers at play but complex cinematic ones as well. Broulard, assuming that Dax's concern for the men is cynical, supports the colonel's request that he be appointed defense counsel, and thereby prepares the way for Mireau to become the scapegoat for the general staff. And while Kubrick is framing this relationship—ironically, one that Dax, like Broulard, misinterprets—he implies another kind of link between them and the "higher" work of art in the background. Not unexpectedly, neither the brutal disorder of the trench nor the Byzantine politics of the chateau acknowledges its status as an emblem of civilized expression and aesthetic beauty. For both, it remains, like the chateau itself, an incomprehensible and unappreciated decoration. For the audience, however, it will be a source for both comprehending and appreciating Kubrick's cinematic artistry.

The three prisoners and the animal stalls that serve as their cell make the presence of the trench felt. Even now, with their humanity so palpable, the soldiers of the trench are viewed by the officers in the chateau as a lower form of life occupying the bottom rung of an imaginary Chain of Being. (And to add insult to irony, their last meal is delivered on an ornate silver tray.) Politically, as the scene involving the killing of the cockroach implies, they have no more status than the insects that crawl over the ground. Here and elsewhere, Kubrick shows their common humanity, their courage and their fears, while, as he did in *Killer's Kiss* and *The Killing,* intensifying a sense of tragic pathos through their ensnarement in a fate at once political and metaphysical: Lieutenant Roget (Wayne Morris) is controlled by a cowardly inability to deal with the stresses of war and its magnification of human mortality, and Corporal Paris is a victim of that inability; Private Ferol (Timothy Carey) is a misfit who does not conform to the military definition of socially acceptable conduct; and Private Arnaud (Joseph Turkel) has been selected by lottery, which epitomizes the trench concept of life as metaphysical crapshoot. Significantly, Kubrick shows us that the same struggles exist, in disguised form, in the corridors and salons of the chateau. Mireau's fear of failure and his desire for an empty glory, Saint-Auban's smugness and sycophancy, Broulard's subservience to unseen forces offscreen, and, yes, even Dax's fervor and naïveté, may not result in their walking down that formal path to an undeserved execution, but they just as surely do not ascend to the more comprehensive understandings embodied in the lessons of history and art that surround them, radiant but unseen. The officers' paths likewise run a horizontal course, as the formal structures of the court-martial and execution make clear.

More than any other scene in *Paths*, or in his earlier films, Kubrick's handling of the court-martial achieves an impressive merger of concept and form. From long shot, the camera shows a detachment of soldiers bringing the three accused men into a vast, elegant room. An enormously large landscape painting hangs high up on one wall, looming above their heads; a white light floods in from tall windows in the rear and to the right; while below, on the floor, are the ever-present chessboard squares of a marble floor. Again, the composition emphasizes the verticals of the chateau, but more strongly than before, while the painting overhead hints at an idealization of the trench landscape and, significantly, provides the one prominent horizontal presence in the shot. While space is enlarged, however, time is compressed. The court-martial proceedings begin at three o'clock in the afternoon and take up very little actual time, even though an elaborate consideration for the formalities of the occasion is evident. The Colonel Judge (Peter Capell) repeatedly chastises Dax for taking up too much of the court's "time" with technicalities that do not bear directly on the case (such as the reading of the indictment!). Formalities, not the "technicalities" of justice, are important here. And in the actual examination and cross-examination of the three men by prosecutor Saint-Auban and Dax, the court makes every effort to deny the reality of time: it will not allow Dax to offer as evidence the past histories of these men as soldiers, only what they did during the three minutes of the attack; and, of course, its primary purpose is to take from the prisoners a right to all future time. Yet this temporal evasion—an avoidance of the existential basis of life—takes on a spatial form as well. For the court to replicate the vertical grandeur of

Three human pawns on an ornate gameboard/
battlefield (Timothy Carey, Ralph Meeker, Joseph
Turkel)

its surroundings would be tantamount to its recognizing its own tragic
absurdity.

Kubrick's audience, however, does perceive this disparity, especially when it realizes that the court-martial itself assumes the formal
properties of a battle on a gameboard. The camera work and compositions leave little doubt about Kubrick's intentions here. On one side
we have the battle line represented by the five judges, symmetrically
composed with the Colonel Judge in the middle, framed by an arch-
way in the background and the French flag overhead. On the other,
the three prisoners sit in chairs, enclosed from behind like pawns by
two lines of guards standing motionless in an attitude of parade rest.
On the flank to their left, and parallel to the windows, is Major Saint-
Auban's table, and behind him sit General Mireau and a line of spectators. And finally, to the prisoners' right is Colonel Dax, opposite
Saint-Auban and clearly outnumbered. This boxlike gameboard
moves along horizontal paths, as the camera reveals when it pans back

and forth behind the line of judges during Saint-Auban's speech and tracks behind the line of prisoners during Dax's. The court-martial, Kubrick implies, formalizes the world of the trenches, not the reaches of the chateau. The scene ends in darkness as the screen fades to black following the Colonel Judge's final words: "The court will now retire to deliberate."

The implication that the politics of the chateau and the horrors of the trench differ only in form and not in substance crystallizes in Kubrick's handling of the execution scene. It begins with a high-angle shot looking across the garden to the massive chateau in the background and down a wide path formed by Mireau's regiment connecting chateau with execution. As the three men and the priest (Emile Meyer) move toward the camera down this ceremonial walkway, the film not only visually links the vertical chateau to the horizontal trench, but reminds us that each side of a chessboard mirrors (and so reverses) the other. The film began with an expansive but formal composition of the area where the place of execution now stands, while in reverse angle it returns to a shot that forms a path to the very entrance where Broulard first traveled down another path into the chateau. Similarly, the second half of the film thematically mirrors the first by demonstrating that an existential struggle with mortality and paradox persists even after the internecine conflicts of state. Kubrick cuts from the prisoners and chateau to a subjective shot moving toward the stakes. In this, the audience's first view of the execution area, Kubrick's camera both creates a sympathetic identification with the three men about to die and recalls Dax's movements into the smoky nightmare of battle—except that now the shot is more generalized and leaves the impression that we, too, move down that same path. Only in this background we are confronted with the ultimate mockery of the chateau's vertical thrust. Three narrow stakes, like the three figures that close in on Johnny Clay at the end of *The Killing,* form a line and rise upward above the sandbags. And while the camera shows in their balanced spacing and proportion that the stakes not only face but imitate the chateau, the time-worn splendor at the other end of the pathway continues to preside over this horizontal labyrinth in silent contempt.

But once its formal mask is defined, Kubrick penetrates the artifice of the execution and reveals a human content that the judges of the court-martial refused to admit as relevant evidence. Tied to the stakes, the prisoners form a line that resembles their position at the

A death sentence read (Richard Anderson) outside
the parlors of splendor

court-martial, only now they are upright and about to face a firing
squad rather than a kangaroo court. Major Saint-Auban stands before
them and reads the formal sentence of the court, only now, in his
hesitations, he expresses an uneasy awareness of death's presence.
Sergeant Boulanger (Bert Freed) pinches the cheek of the mercifully
unconscious Arnaud, who in the trenches had expressed his greater
fear of pain than of dying; while Ferol, no longer confident that he
has an edge over a cockroach, clings to the sacraments—and quite
literally to the rosary—of the priest. And Corporal Paris makes that
final existential choice and struggles to give his death some vestige of
dignity. Lieutenant Roget then walks down the line of prisoners, offering them blindfolds, ironically asking Paris to forgive him. All the
while, the drums continue to roll, and off to one side a cart with three
caskets waits. The last two shots reverse perspective and draw the audience even more deeply into the film's unresolved conflicts: The first
offers a final look at the chateau and the path that connects it to the
stakes, only now the double lines of a firing squad separate the prison-

ers from the spectators; the second reverses this angle and looks over the executioners' shoulders as they fire in unison at the three men. The audience, at once spectator and victim, watches death from afar and confronts it up close—and in the finality of that moment, it perceives that the same pathway that ends in death for Arnaud, Ferol, and Paris encloses the humanist Dax as well as the generals. It is a path beautiful in its symmetry and fearful in its meanings.

Alexander Walker calls *Paths of Glory* Kubrick's "graduation" piece, and no doubt it truly is a masterful film. It provides early evidence of several practices and concepts that later will define the Kubrickian film signature. *Paths* shows the first signs of the passion for exact detail that would come to dominate practically all his films in the future, one that strives not only for authenticity but for a wide range of expressive possibilities. Kubrick clearly wanted to give each scene in *Paths* an interesting visual quality and at the same time to imply a latent coherence of emotion and idea. The imagery of the film blends grainy black-and-white realism and the documentary, handheld camera style of the attack (zooms and telephoto shots) with expressive compositions achieved through extreme deep focus and long camera takes. In every scene Kubrick is careful to preserve an available-light look in the way he always identifies the "source" light, whether it comes from a naked bulb hanging in Dax's bunker, a candle on Roget's table, or the light-flooded windows of the chateau. He repeatedly gives value to unobtrusive objects in the background, either through a brief compositional effect or as counterpoint. When Dax, for instance, meets privately with Broulard just before the execution, Kubrick slyly misleads the audience into thinking that the tables have been turned, and that Dax's humanism may yet prevail over Mireau's vanity. The scene takes place in a library lined with walls of books, a warm fire burning in a fireplace, and carpets on the floor, all of which complement the intimate and politically liberal definition of Dax's character. Dax sips cognac and briefly plays Broulard's game before he plays his trump card—that during the attack, Mireau ordered artillery fire on his own positions. Broulard remains inscrutable and leaves Dax to wonder if, indeed, there exists in the chateau even one spokesman for a humane politics. A china tea set in the background may provide the answer. The library is no different from any other room in the chateau: its books are decorative only, while the tea set at least has the virtue of contributing to the endless rounds of formal bartering which take place there.

In addition, *Paths of Glory* was Kubrick's first film to use music for ironic counterpoint. A typical example, besides those already mentioned, would be the ballroom scene on the night before the execution, which shows a party of French officers and ladies dancing to the "Artist's Life Waltz" of Austrian composer Johann Strauss. Kubrick uses a single shot to suggest an ironic link between the music and its dancers and the horizontal and circular worlds of both the chateau and the trench. His camera tracks an officer moving right to left, passing through the waltzing couples on his way to General Broulard, only to return to its point of origin by following them left to right along the same path as the general exits the room. Another aspect of Kubrick's artistry that is seldom recognized is the superb editing in the best of his work. Because his films give an audience so much to look at and listen for, the artful transitions from one scene to the next often go unnoticed. *Paths,* for instance, shows Kubrick's fondness for merging a thematic approach to sound with an editing style that strives for continuity and juxtaposition within a single cut. Besides the examples already cited, the most notable instance of such a cut in *Paths* is the one that juxtaposes the explosions of the firing squad with the tinkle of silverware from Mireau's breakfast after the execution. (This cut has to do with what will be a leitmotif in later Kubrick films. Like Buñuel, Kubrick has a surrealist's appreciation for both the primal and the ritualistic significance of eating and food, which finds its fullest expression in the futuristic mise-en-scène of *2001*.)*

Paths of Glory marks the full emergence of a distinct film intelligence, and to a greater degree than in his earlier work, Kubrick makes his presence known and felt in the complex worlds of the film. Through a visual definition of conflict, he integrates a series of disparate perspectives through which the audience can respond to the emotional or psychological directions of character and, simultaneously, understand the film's paradoxical blending of irony and affirmation. The conflicting characterizations of Dax and Broulard illustrate this merger of a receptive and generative aesthetics. After their final meeting, when Broulard has used Dax's evidence not to

---

*In the breakfast scene, the tables are turned on Mireau, literally as well as figuratively. He and Broulard each sit where the other sat in the two previous scenes in the apartment, while Dax again sits between them. Mireau's downfall is initiated by Broulard: as he spreads jelly on a croissant, he says casually, "By the way, Paul," and goes on to reveal Colonel Dax's information about the artillery fire. In the library scene, Dax uses a similar verbal tactic ("By the way, General Broulard, did you know that General Mireau . . .").

save three innocent men but to bring down one foolish general, Dax and the audience experience a catharsis of sorts in the scene where the German girl's song turns leers into tears. But by that time, through the library scene and that final confrontation in Mireau's apartment, the film has clearly shown that Dax and Broulard are the victims of equally confining moralities. They, in fact, embody the polarities of the film itself: Dax's character represents that "close-up" and personal view of the trenches found in Cobb's novel, the one that believes in the importance of moral victories in a world without moral order; Broulard's is the impersonal and distant view of the chateau, one that mocks in its vertical politics a defunct belief in an ordered and purposeful cosmos. The first expresses all the right sentiments and glimpses life's contingencies, but lacks an appropriately expressive and objective form, while the second shows an appreciation of form without an understanding of life's existential substance. Each travels in ignorance through the splendor of the chateau, a setting that represents a visual context through which the audience can grasp the tragic and absurd meaning of several narrative moments. In addition, it simultaneously provides an aesthetic, self-referential perspective from which to see beyond those moments and gaze with the film creator into the complex forms of his filmic space.

3 KUBRICK IN NABOKOVLAND
Lolita

If there was a crossroads in the early part of Kubrick's career, it came between the completion of *Paths of Glory* in 1957 and his move to England in 1960 to film *Lolita*. During those years, the Hollywood studios were still adjusting to the economic fallout from the growth of television, and they were beginning to turn to foreign countries, where there were less expensive shooting locations and more lucrative distribution markets. It was a period when Hollywood recycled silent film spectacle into wide-screen puffery, from 20th Century Fox's *The Robe* (1953) to Paramount's *The Ten Commandments* (1956) and MGM's *Ben-Hur* (1959). The appeal of the so-called "small" film, with its social content and intimate treatment, was dwindling, partly because of the competition from television, then in its Golden Age, with its impressive number of dramatic series (*Studio One, Playhouse 90,* and

others). Actor Studio graduates such as Marlon Brando and Paul New-
man were drifting away from human interest films like *The Men*
(1950), *On the Waterfront* (1954), and *Somebody Up There Likes Me*
(1956) to the literary kitsch of *Sayonara* (1957), *The Young Lions*
(1958), *The Young Philadelphians* (1959), and *On the Terrace* (1960). It
was a period when independent production companies proliferated
on the film landscape faster than bug-eyed monsters in 3-D, forcing
the majors to flex their only remaining muscle, namely their control
of the marketplace through distribution. Harris-Kubrick was one of
these independent companies, but one not as well-heeled as those
associated with such established stars as John Wayne (Batjac), Kirk
Douglas (Bryna), and Marlon Brando (Pennebaker). Following *Paths,*
Kubrick and Calder Willingham collaborated for six months during
1958 on a script with Brando, an actor whose name alone could gen-
erate studio money for practically any project he wanted to develop.
Kubrick, by contrast, was only an ambitious pre-*auteurist* director of
Paths of Glory and three low-budget features—and barely thirty years
old, at that. The Brando project, based on a Western novel by Charles
Neider called *The Authentic Death of Hendry Jones* (1956), did not fare
well for Kubrick, primarily because he and Brando had radically different views on how the script should be developed. As a result, Brando rejected the uncompleted script and terminated Kubrick's services
as director. Kubrick was paid off (handsomely, by all accounts), and
Brando eventually became the director as well as the star of *One-Eyed
Jacks* (1961).*

With money from United Artists for *The Killing,* Harris-Kubrick in
1958 purchased an option on Vladimir Nabokov's *Lolita* (1955), an
indication that even during the lengthy work on *Spartacus* (1959–60)
Kubrick was determined to continue an independent course. In February of 1959, Kirk Douglas's Bryna company hired Kubrick to replace Hollywood veteran Anthony Mann as director of *Spartacus* (Universal), which put the young man from the Bronx in charge of a $12
million Hollywood film production. Kubrick, however, was not quite
"in charge." As the firing of Mann suggests, *Spartacus* was Douglas's

*The story goes that the title for *One-Eyed Jacks* was inspired by the rounds of poker-
playing going on at Brando's home during the period when the script was being ham-
mered out. In the film version, the Brando character (Rio) clarifies the title's meaning
when he tells his adversary Dan Longworth (Karl Malden), "You're a one-eyed jack
around here, Dan. I seen the other side of your face." Perhaps it's only a coincidence, but
this use of the playing card as a metaphor for character duality echoes the scene in
Kubrick's *Killer's Kiss* where Davy Gordon goes face to face with a one-eyed jack.

picture, and that included the rather stale leftist sentiments in Dalton Trumbo's script of the Howard Fast novel (in 1962, Trumbo scripted another Douglas-Bryna film, *Lonely Are the Brave*). Later, Kubrick would say that the film had "everything but a good story." Expressing more regret than rancor, Kubrick's description of his role during the 167 days of shooting and months of post-production indicated that he had done what was typical for a Hollywood studio director. He directed the cast, composed the shots, worked with Saul Bass on the design of the film's impressive action sequences, and supervised the editing. Missing from this list, of course, was the total directorial control over the script that was so crucial to the artistry of *The Killing* and *Paths of Glory*, an element that lent distinction to all his films after *Paths*, with the lone exception of *Spartacus* (1960).

Spartacus, however, does exhibit several Kubrickian trademarks, and there is no doubt that the experience taught him a great deal about handling the hundreds of details that go into a large film production. And, as several reviewers noted, compared with other wide-screen spectacles of the period, *Spartacus* is not a bad film at all. Its major weaknesses stem from the often trite, simplistic, and sentimental morality of the script. The scenes between Spartacus (Kirk Douglas) and Varinia (Jean Simmons), for instance, are too insistent about the honesty and intuitive vision of the film's proletarian hero. In contrast to the often gritty realism of the location work, the scenes filmed in the studio take on the overly prettified look that in later years would characterize the television shows produced by the Universal City studios. The epic panorama of battles and armies is well done and reflects Kubrick's skill at showing what he later referred to as the "weird disparity" between the aesthetics of warfare and its human consequences. As the Roman legions commanded by Crassus (Laurence Olivier) move across a large plain toward Spartacus's slave army, a visual dance between Rome's formal grandeur and a solid (if not stolid) mass of humanity changes into a disordered field of death and carnage. The political conflicts of *Spartacus* have clear parallels with those in *Paths of Glory*, but unfortunately they, too, drown in a swamp of Hollywood liberal ideology. The struggle between Crassus and Gracchus (Charles Laughton) degenerates into a war between a sexually insecure militarist (the fascist as impotent proto-McCarthy) and a cunning but sympathetic republican (who, despite his old age, has several loving women in his service). The script glosses over the fact that Gracchus shows no real understanding of the slave rebellion, and that he plays ruthless political games with a young and ambitious Caesar (John Gavin). In a few places, the film does suggest the kinds of irony present in the conflict between the trenches and the chateau in *Paths*. During a fight to the death between Spartacus and a black gladiator (Woody Strode), provided as an entertainment for a Roman wedding party, Kubrick's composition develops as ironic counterpoint a foregrounded exchange between Crassus and one of his political protégés. In a later scene, Kubrick's editing effectively foils Spartacus's address to his army with Crassus's before his legions. But mostly these oppositions reinforce the overly didactic polarities of the script rather than express a paradoxical unity.

Likewise, certain psychological and sexual implications in the story are sidestepped and obscured by a sometimes muddled script. A scene that showed Crassus's homosexual desire for the slave Antoninus (Tony Curtis) was deleted in the original release prints, and in the process the film indulges in reverse censorship by overprotesting the slave brotherhood theme, perhaps from fear that the friendship between Spartacus and Antoninus might be viewed as a Freudian joke. Because the script wants to maintain Spartacus's purity, his character never achieves a convincing sexual identity, which means that Varinia's pregnancy borders on an immaculate conception. This overly hearty depiction of brotherhood without coitus contrasts with didactic precision to the sexual sneers of Peter Ustinov's Batiatus (whose thoroughly despicable character softens into the lovable rogue), the decadent voyeurism of Roman ladies (Nina Foch and Joanna Barnes), and the ambiguous manhood of Crassus. These flaws become especially apparent whenever Olivier is on the screen. His performance confers upon Crassus subtleties that are never fully realized in the film, but which command such attention that the scenes of slave brotherhood appear wooden and insubstantial by comparison.

Because he strove for perfection as a film artist, Kubrick must have felt disappointment and resentment over *Spartacus*. Later films such as *2001* and *Barry Lyndon* clearly demonstrate his talent for matching epic form to an appropriately speculative and philosophic subject matter. In fact, Kubrick's personal critique of *Spartacus* may be present in the film's final scene: In a brief moment of film time, as she holds up her child before the cross on which Spartacus is dying, Varinia conveys more poignancy and meaning than is present in all the bloated speeches about freedom or the addlepated Christ symbolism of the ending. Ironically, it may be Douglas's best scene, and one where he asserts the more profound humanity of silence. Kubrick, in contrast, concludes the film with a composition that recalls the tragic irony of *Paths*. Varinia's cart moves away from the camera, down a path lined on both sides with crucified slaves. In Trumbo's version, of course, the audience is encouraged to believe that she and Spartacus's child are traveling into a democratic future that will give value to his sacrifice. In Kubrick's version, one barely visible to this film's audience, they move into an indeterminate landscape where there exists only the certainty of death. Two years later, in *Lolita*, Kubrick expressed even more strongly his attitude toward the missed opportunities of *Spartacus* when he had Quilty, adorned in a bedsheet Roman toga, utter a parodic response to Humbert's question about his identity: "No, I'm Spartacus. Have you come to free the slaves or something?" And in the last scene, Lolita describes to a despairing Humbert her relationship with the perverse Quilty and how he had promised to take her to Hollywood, where he was to write "one of those spectaculars." Lolita never gets to Hollywood, although Kubrick's *coup de grace* implies that her trip to Quilty's ranch to make a pornographic movie ("art movie") may have been an equivalent experience.

The *Lolita* project began in earnest during the early months of 1960. The previous summer, Harris and Kubrick had asked Nabokov to come to Hollywood and write the script. Nabokov refused, but after a "small nocturnal illumination" later that year and another request from Harris-Kubrick, he accepted the job. On March 1, 1960, Nabokov met with Kubrick for the first time at Universal City (where Kubrick still was working on *Spartacus*), and under the jacarandas of Hollywood, he worked for six months on the *Lolita* script. By midsummer, Nabokov handed Kubrick a 400-page screenplay that included unused material from the manuscript of the original novel. Kubrick asked for a shorter version. In September, Nabokov submitted a script half as long as his first one. Two years later (June 1962), Nabokov saw the film at the New York City premiere, and afterward, in a *Playboy* interview (January 1964), he expressed his admiration for it, while taking no credit for the excellence of its acting or production. One bit of confusion arises, however, when Nabokov's comments in 1964 are compared with those in the 1973 foreword to his published screenplay of *Lolita*. In the earlier interview, he said that his only involvement with the film was the script, a "preponderating portion of which was used by Kubrick," while later he recalled that his first response to the film was "that Kubrick was a great director, that his *Lolita* was a first-rate film with magnificent actors, and that only ragged odds and ends of my script had been used." In the *Playboy* interview, Nabokov very graciously concluded that Kubrick's cinematic approach to the novel was merely different from his own, while recognizing the unique demands, both artistic and those of the Production Code, placed on Kubrick by his medium. Regrettably, later critics have been less understanding about Kubrick's considerable achievement in adapting to film one of the most difficult and brilliant novels of the twentieth century. Alfred Appel, Jr., for one, claimed that Kubrick used only twenty percent of Nabokov's submitted screenplay and, through innuendo more than argument, deprecated the film. Rather than considering the film an adaptation and transformation of both the novel and the screenplay—and seeing them as sources of stimulation to Kubrick's creative interests—Appel (as do others) looked at the film through his vision of the novel and proposed scenarios for what it should have done. Nabokov's comments, on the other hand, indicate that he clearly perceived Kubrick's talent (and the talents of the cast) and his rightful assumption of artistic license.

An examination of Nabokov's published screenplay (1974) reveals three very important factors: the screenplay includes scenes from the 400-page version that were deleted from the shorter version Kubrick accepted; in its overall structure, the film uses considerably more than twenty percent of the final 1960 script; and Kubrick created several visual and verbal translations of effects suggested in the Nabokov script, which is more theatrical and poetic than cinematic. For Nabokov, adapting *Lolita* to the "speaking screen," as he calls it, involved the staging of a complex network of verbal revelations punctuated by an occasionally obtrusive camera. Nabokov's cinematic ideas—some of which probably interested Kubrick—would, if strictly followed, have announced an authorial film presence in tones louder than Kubrick preferred. The screenplay's description of camera movements in the first scene illustrates this point: Nabokov has the camera gliding around and through Quilty's mansion like a theatrical invader (it "locates the drug addict's implementa on a bedside chair, and with a shudder withdraws"), which he probably visualized as an equivalent for the many assertions in the novel of his ironic presence as counterpoint to the distortions of a first-person unreliable narration. If Kubrick had adopted such a strategy, his *Lolita* would have

pleased those critics who felt that the baroque stylizations of an Orson
Welles provided the best model for a cinematic translation of Nabokov's prose style. But if my consideration of his earlier films has revealed anything, it is that Kubrick manipulated cinematic point of
view in ways that are far more covert (but not necessarily any more
complex) than Nabokov's. Ironically, in the hands of an expressionist
such as Welles or even Sternberg, the subtle and intricate style of the
novel might have been transformed in the film into the kind of cloying and pretentious seriousness that Nabokov disparaged throughout
his life. Kubrick's version, instead, strives to find its own expression
for both the subtlety and the playfulness of the novel. And it should
not be forgotten that *Lolita* represents Kubrick's first effort at adapting to film the novelistic convention of the unreliable first-person
narrator, an understanding of which will illuminate the narrational
ironies of *A Clockwork Orange* and *Barry Lyndon*, two other films based
on novels that confuse point of view in much the same way that *Lolita*
does.

For Kubrick, *Lolita* represented an important advance in the development of a psychological film style. Nabokov's *Lolita* gave him, for
the first time, a novelistic source that constructed its world from
inside the mind of a single fictional intelligence. And even though
Humbert's imagination can mesmerize the reader with its richness of
invention and distortion, Nabokov uses the ironic and often parodic
intrusions of his third-person "voice" to undermine and transcend his
narrator's clever special pleadings. No such rhetorical strategy exists
in either White's *Clean Break* or Cobb's *Paths of Glory*. There, the po-
tentials of psychological conflict are either harnessed or suppressed
within the impersonal order of a demanding objective activity (robbery plan, war), one in which a degree of anonymity is not only a
virtue but a necessity. Consequently, Kubrick was able to develop a
dramatic tension between repressed psychological forces and the requirements of a temporal mechanism in the one film (*The Killing*),
and between the human reality of war and the antiquated structures
of a military politics in the other (*Paths of Glory*). In each film, external contingencies combine to create a fate that ultimately overwhelms
and frustrates the aims of a very elemental psychology. Nabokov's
novel, by contrast, generates its narrative conflict from within Humbert's solipsistic universe, which is at odds not only with itself but also
with the larger ironies of the novel. For the psychological world of his
Lolita, Kubrick squeezed his style down into a more pinpoint, less ex-

pansive focus than the one conceived for *Paths of Glory,* where the puny ambitions of character are measured against grandeur, both historical and spatial in scope. He moved from the openness of location shooting to the interiority of performance and the studio, where, as he mentioned while making *Lolita,*

> everything is inky darkness and the lights are coming from an expected place and it is quiet and you can achieve concentration. . . . I think that too much has been made of making films on location. . . . For a psychological story, where the characters and their inner emotions and feelings are the key thing, I think that the studio is the best place.

Kubrick's avowed admiration for Chaplin's films, which also depended to a great extent on the studio for their psychological effect, reflects the importance that Kubrick attached to the actor. Despite a lack of cinematic sophistication, Chaplin developed a subtlety and complexity of performance that became a creative alternative to Eisenstein's greater range of film styles. *Lolita* shows that, for Kubrick, performance could be as crucial to the expressive substance of a film as camera and mise-en-scène.

In Pudovkin's *Film Technique,* Kubrick would not have found a very far-reaching critique of the film actor's role. For Pudovkin, the actor was subordinated to the director, and performance to filmic construction. He did stress, however, how the actor could focus a film's emotional manipulation of the spectator, while the director, through editing and images, worked on his mind. With the possible exception of *Spartacus,* Kubrick's films do not contain highly emotive performances of that kind, although beginning with *Lolita* they increasingly exhibit a variety of subtly expressive and emotional acting styles. Kubrick often mentioned that early in his career he had found Stanislavsky's ideas about working with actors to be helpful, and he continued in later years to recommend Nikolai Gorchakov's *Stanislavsky Directs.* During the formative years of Kubrick's career, Stanislavsky's theories already had influenced and helped shape the so-called school of method acting brought to the Broadway stage by Elia Kazan and Lee Strasberg of the New York Actors Studio (founded 1947). The Stanislavsky method was especially important for the expression of psychoanalytical themes found in the plays of Arthur Miller and Tennessee Williams. Interestingly, this theatrical movement coincided with American film neorealism (1945–55) and its treatment of "controversial" social issues. At times, however, the intimate, interiorized performing techniques of "method" actors would conflict with a less stylized visual realism (e.g., Brando's performance in *The Wild One*, 1953, or James Dean's in *Rebel Without a Cause*, 1955). Not until *Lolita* did Kubrick work with a cast capable of the kind of intuitive approach to performance recommended by Stanislavsky, which specialized in oblique psychological revelation through a manipulation of gesture, mannerism, and voice. In *Killer's Kiss*, he had the right kind of script for such a treatment, but not the right kind of actors. Consequently, he experimented with a highly expressive visual style in order to suggest psychological complexities beyond the abilities of his actors, while *The Killing* and *Paths of Glory* required their professional performers (with the exception of Kirk Douglas, veteran Hollywood character actors dominate both films) to give functional life to roles that rarely strayed from convention or stereotype.

Perhaps one reason why *Lolita* remained for years after its release Kubrick's most unappreciated and misunderstood early film—why so many critics failed to notice that, like Buñuel's *Viridiana* (1961), for example, it develops a surrealist mise-en-scène through a deceptively sparse naturalism—is the strength of its performances. The film's cast develops and improvises so many revealing details of character that its subtle manipulation of mise-en-scène might go unnoticed. Peter Sellers's spellbinding transformations, as well as the performances of James Mason, Shelley Winters, and Sue Lyon, command such attention that filmic complexities may travel through a receptive consciousness like so much visual Muzak. And besides its almost perfect expression of a Nabokovian verbal playfulness, Sellers's conception of Clare Quilty parallels an attitude toward the unreality of conventional social personas that Kubrick described in an interview as early as 1958:

> The criminal and the soldier at least have the virtue of being against something or for something in a world where many people have learned to accept a kind of grey nothingness, to strike an unreal series of poses in order to be considered normal. . . . It's difficult to say who is engaged in the greater conspiracy—the criminal, the soldier, or us.

The other principal performers strengthen not only the film's satiric assault on the "normal" but, more important, its strong emotional subtext. Shelley Winters plays a perfect foil to the comic exaggerations of Sellers's Quilty and the vulgarity of Sue Lyon's Lolita. In that delightful tour of the Haze home early in the film, through a mannered control of hands (which wave a long cigarette holder around in assertive flourishes) and voice, she comically expresses Charlotte's social and sexual aspirations. Later, she shows the child in Charlotte's character, the "lotte" Lolita, as she sits in the midst of a Kubrickian soft-textured close-up, smiling like a plump fairy princess and delicately ringing a bell for her maid to serve dinner. And even while we laugh at her vulgarity, Winters suggests a sadness in Charlotte's character, one that glimpses but does not understand its own pathetic desperation. (As she cries and embraces the urn, she yells at "Harold," her dead husband: "Why did you leave me? . . . I didn't know anything about life!") James Mason and Sue Lyon repeatedly play off each other, and likewise communicate both the satiric and the poignant truth of Humbert's obsession with Lolita. Mason develops a series of facial and gestural mannerisms to express Humbert's European archness and his terrible vulnerability. When Humbert experiences moments of emotional exposure, for example, Mason's face twitches uncontrollably as his hands move frantically to restore order to his facial landscape; and by the film's end, the character's formal mask cracks under the internal pressure from a growing despair that releases an almost unbearable poignancy. Especially moving is the scene in the hospital where Humbert, his entire physical being shattered by an incalculable emotional and psychological loss, discovers Lolita gone and himself surrounded on a dark corridor floor by four figures in white who interrogate him as if he were a candidate for an insane asylum. In the car with Humbert, just after they have made love for the first time at the Enchanted Hunters Hotel, Lolita displays that harmonious relationship with the objects of her teenage environment which eludes Humbert, as she erotically sucks a straw in a Coke bottle and wraps her tongue around potato chips in a bag. Meanwhile, Humbert—the ever-present voyeur—drives the car and slyly glances at his nymphet now sitting next to him like a "date" prepared for an evening of heavy necking and petting. Significantly, the very next scene shows Lolita, childlike, curled up in Humbert's arms on a motel bed, crying over Charlotte's death and the loss of her "normal" existence. At Beardsley, in an argument with Humbert over her lies and deceptions, and dressed as an elfin princess, she chews gum and blows bubbles as Humbert's entreaties grow more desperate. He pathetically rubs his hand on his pants leg and kneels in a gesture of total submission before his now frigid princess, while Lyon maintains Lolita's teenage imperviousness to his suffering. Not until the performances within the elegiac mise-en-scène of *Barry Lyndon,* the nightmarish mazes of *The Shining,* and the surreal dislocations of *Eyes Wide Shut* will Kubrick's actors again lend such a tragic pathos to his larger and more ironic look at the disparities between the forms of social normality and the truths of an unarticulated but real psychological disorder.

Kubrick did fault his *Lolita* on one important count: Because of pressures from the Production Code and the Catholic Legion of Decency, he could not sufficiently dramatize the erotic aspect of Humbert's obsession with the nymphet. And even though Sue Lyon was thirteen when shooting began, she plays Lolita closer to fifteen than twelve. (In the novel we are told that the nymphet exists on an "enchanted island" between the ages of nine and fourteen.) Kubrick, however, did provide in the film a definition of the nymphet (it is different from the one in Nabokov's screenplay) and of Humbert's attraction that indicates the film's altered sexual and psychological focus. In voiceover while writing in his diary, Humbert defines the "twofold nature" of this nymphet as a mixture of "dreamy childishness" and "eerie vulgarity," thus suggesting that his obsession with Lolita has nothing to do with the unsuccessful retreat of Nabokov's Humbert into that timelessness lost in the "princedom by the sea" of his childhood. Instead, James Mason's Humbert starts as a whimsical satyr who, as he flees from the omnivorous clutchings of predatory American matrons, becomes enslaved to a tragic fascination for the iridescence and triviality of a child-woman. And in this movement from satire to poignancy, Kubrick weaves a pattern of sexual innuendo and implication that imitates the playfulness and pathos of the novel more than its eroticism. Brandon French, in an essay on the film, points out a few examples of Kubrick's attempt to give his *Lolita* a dense sexual subtext: In the first scene, Humbert's phallic gun (called "Chum" in the novel, forever eager to discharge its bullets, which Humbert fears will go "stale" from disuse) opposes Quilty's impotent ping-pong balls, while later we see Charlotte fondling the same gun as she reminisces about the "late Mr. Haze." Humbert's introduction to Charlotte and Lolita initiates his early entanglement in a relationship where double entendres fly back and forth in a vulgar American mating ritual. Charlotte's falsetto laugh trumpets her first advance on Humbert's dark European handsomeness when she tells him that he couldn't get more "peace" [*sic*] anywhere than in her home. She then takes him into her bedroom to show off *her* collection of "reproductions" (Dufy, Monet, Van Gogh) after mentioning how "stimulating" Clare Quilty, a TV playwright, had been in his lecture on Dr. Schweitzer and Dr. Zhivago. (She, of course, had a pre-Humbert affair with Quilty, who also uses Charlotte to capture the nymphet.) In the hallway, Charlotte apologizes for the presence of a "soiled" sock, which, it is assumed, belongs to Lolita and prepares for Humbert's discovery, post–Camp Climax, of his nymphet's sexual precocity. Nabokov especially must have delighted in the ending of this scene, where Humbert has his first vision of Lolita in the garden and instantly decides to stay and enjoy Charlotte's promise of "late snacks" and "cherry pies."

The film develops the ultimate sexual irony when it shows Humbert's involvement in an American *ménage à trois* that subtly disguises Quilty's presence and the more sinister outlines of a *ménage à quatre*. In an early montage, Kubrick shows the comic drama of Humbert's naiveté as his advances toward the nymphet are checked by the moves against him by Charlotte and Lolita. As Humbert peeks over a book at Lolita hula-hooping in the garden, Charlotte's blowsy sexuality and flash camera break the spell; as Charlotte ponders a move in a game of chess with Humbert (a favored Nabokovian device, as well), Lolita slides in and gives him something more than a goodnight peck on the cheek ("You're going to take my Queen," moans Charlotte); while at a drive-in theater watching a Hammer horror film that shows the monster turning on his creator (*The Curse of Frankenstein,* 1957), Humbert is trapped between the clutches of mother and daughter; and finally, Charlotte moves against Lolita in a conspiracy with the Farlows (Jerry Stovin and Diana Decker), which puts Charlotte in the house alone with Humbert. Ironically, Kubrick casts Humbert in these early scenes as a sort of Daisy Miller in reverse: the innocent rather than decadent European who becomes a chessboard queen to Charlotte and Lolita's knights. This sardonic look at the American Peyton Place reaches a climax in the scene where Charlotte, dressed in a leopardskin pants suit, mixes the rumba and pink champagne in her primal assault on Humbert's European reserve. Lolita unexpectedly returns (her "move" against Charlotte), because, she says, "salty fish eggs" were being served at the Farlow slumber party. What follows is a marvelous scene of Humbert, nervously cracking walnuts, caught between Charlotte's pink champagne and Lolita's turkey and mayon-

naise sandwich. He eventually gives Charlotte the cracked shells rather than his gonads, which anticipates his later comment during their brief conjugality that she leaves him as "limp as a noodle."

This bourgeois bacchanal within the pastoral simplicity of New England America turns darker whenever the film brings in the surrealist presence of Clare Quilty. Kubrick said that he and Nabokov agreed to have the film begin with Humbert killing Quilty without explanation, so that a narrative interest could be sustained after Humbert and Lolita are coupled at the Enchanted Hunters Hotel. But it also lends an atmosphere of impending menace to the lightly satiric quality of the early scenes. During the school dance, for example, Charlotte anticipates Humbert's walnut shells when she hands him her hot dog to dance with John Farlow; and later she skitters across the dance floor to say "hello" to Quilty, who, in a tuxedo and wearing horn-rimmed glasses, looks more cherubic than decadently spent. She whispers in his ear (as Lolita will in Humbert's just before she seduces him), and only then does he associate Charlotte with the beautiful, lilting name of Lolita. Quilty then joins the film's game of playful sexual innuendo when he knowingly smirks over Lolita's having a "cavity filled" by his Uncle Ivor, the local dentist. In this context, Quilty seems harmless enough, although the constant companionship of the darkly exotic and slightly lesbian Vivian Darkbloom (in the novel, an anagram for Vladimir Nabokov) hints at something kinkier than just another American suburban rendition of hide the salami. (Lolita will later extol Quilty's "beautiful Oriental philosophy of life," which explains the "Tokyo" poster on her bedroom wall in Ramsdale.) In another scene, Humbert sits on Lolita's bed and reads Charlotte's "confession" of love, which turns his despair over losing Lolita forever into a gleeful appreciation of life's unexpected twists (his laughter begins when Charlotte asks him to "link up" his life with hers and "be a father to my little girl"). Just as he tearfully celebrates his good fortune, however, Kubrick's camera reminds us of darker forces waiting in Humbert's future as it ominously pans to Quilty's picture on a cigarette poster. Eventually Humbert, Quilty-like, will add incest to his sins, and so begin a journey into a nightmare in which Quilty's presence, alternately spectral and corporeal, will provide a mirror image for both his own sexual degradation and Lolita's triviality.

While in *The Killing* and *Paths of Glory* Kubrick sacrifices complexities of character to the rigors of temporal and spatial structures, his

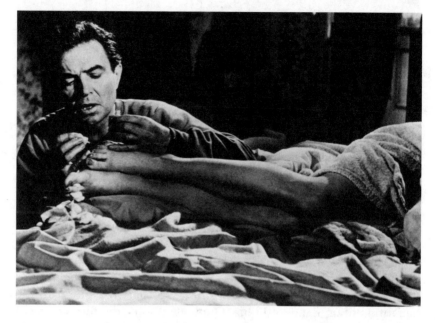

Lolita examines interior worlds with a delicacy of tone and distance that eluded him in *Killer's Kiss*. The imagery and decors of *Lolita* merge an ethereal softness of texture with a surreal dissonance in deep focus to create a style of presentation that, overall, develops a deceptive naturalism. The film starts with a girlish foot descending into an unfocused blur and the melodic piano music of Bob Harris's romantic "Lolita" theme, followed by a pair of male hands coming into the frame and delicately administering a pedicure behind the film's credits. Completely removed from context, this initial shot creates an imagery that both gives form to Humbert's dreamy obsession with Lolita (including, perhaps, the wedding ring on the left hand) and satirizes his demeaning subjugation. Later, the first sequence at Beardsley will put this image in a dramatic context and reveal Humbert's sexual enslavement as he comically vacillates between the roles of whining lover and nagging father. Throughout the early part of the film, Kubrick tends to define Humbert's interiority through images and space, while Quilty, his alter ego, is associated with objects and temporality. After the credits, the camera floats toward Quilty's medieval castle; once inside, the imagery sharpens into deep focus and delineates a mise-en-scène that, in its surreal merger of Classical and

Camp, parodies Humbert's loving embrace of the illusory. This Humbert/Quilty doubling overshadows, in the film, the novel's focus on Humbert's desire to "fix once and for all the perilous magic of nymphets." Nabokov begins and ends Humbert's narrative with the word "Lolita" ("Lolita, light of my life" and "This is the only immortality you and I may share, my Lolita"), while Kubrick verbally frames his film with Humbert's call for "Quilty," a name that assumes, for Humbert as well as the audience, both an exclamatory ("Quilty!") and an interrogative ("Quilty?") meaning. Who or what is Quilty? And what do his various appearances tell us about the psychological and conceptual ambitions of Kubrick's film?

When Humbert first enters Quilty's Xanadu, we hear the ghostly ripplings of a harpsichord, which later will signal all of Quilty's menacing reappearances. Humbert moves through a bizarre clutter, unaware that it defines not only Quilty's physical domain but an inner sanctum: a three-dimensional surrealist canvas in which an ornate harp mixes with a ping-pong table, Shakespeare's bust with boxing gloves, Venus de Milo with Victorian bric-a-brac, a tiger's head with an

eighteenth-century portrait. Quilty, swathed in a sheet, rises from his chair and plays both Spartacus in drag and resurrected spook to Humbert's indignant civility. His invitation to play Roman ping-pong—"like two civilized senators"—mocks Humbert's urbane and scholarly mask, that pose of normality that conceals a mind as darkly cluttered as Quilty's. He mistakes Humbert for one "Jack Brewster," who, we find out backstage at Beardsley, is one of Quilty's groupies ("Brewster, go buy me some Type A Kodachrome film"). This highly stylized encounter continues as Sellers improvises, in masterly fashion, a series of perverse impersonations that anticipate and parody the movement of the film into the "normal" social and psychological landscape of Ramsdale. He sprinkles his language with clichés like the Boy Scout motto, as he pulls from a robe pocket beneath his toga an endless supply of ping-pong balls. He playfully prepares us for games to come when he responds to Humbert's brandished pistol with "it's not who wins but how you play." He goes through a repertoire of B-movie character parts (an old Western codger who reads Humbert's painfully

precious poem as if it were the "deed to the ranch"; a boxing cham-
pion who wants to settle differences "like two civilized people") that
indirectly mock Humbert's fatuous assumption of moral outrage.
Even when he realizes that he cannot playact his way out of the situation, Quilty still satirizes the formal and civilized exterior of Humbert's Europeanism and, indirectly, later examples of suburban cultural pretense. He tells him to "stop trifling with life and death," and
that, being a playwright, he knows all about this sort of "tragedy and
comedy and fantasy." Yet Humbert does not see his face in the reflexive mirror of Quilty's impersonations: he does not see that his romantic infatuation with an image rather than the reality of Lolita finds its
demonic incarnation in Quilty and the obscure objects of his desire.

Instead of expressing this important scene through the flourishes
of a Wellesian chiaroscuro, as Nabokov's screenplay invites, Kubrick
chooses to materialize the dreamy evasions of Humbert's character
through a realistic depiction of Quilty's nightmare world. He gives
the surreal a palpable shape and sound, thereby preparing the audience for a flip-flop in scenes to come, one where a surreality shines
through the transparent facade of middle-class normality and cinematic naturalism. In this remarkable scene, Sellers's performance
transforms the Evil One—Quilty's Shadow to Humbert's Persona—
into a pathetic creature trapped in a black comedy he did not com-
pose, futilely striving to find in Humbert a wit and humanity that
could save Quilty's life. But to no avail. His comic rendering of both
Chopin's *polonaise* ("Do you think it will make the Hit Parade?") and
his own death ("You really hurt me . . . my leg will be black and blue
tomorrow," he says after the first bullet strikes) does not dissuade the
solemn avenger. He tries to bribe Humbert by appealing to his voyeurism—"I could fix it for you to attend executions, just you, do you
like watching, Captain?"—but instead the executioner chooses to
watch Quilty die. Kubrick concludes this prologue to his *Lolita* (Nabokov's novel begins with a parodic foreword by psychologist "John Ray,
Jr., Ph.D.") with Quilty seeking cover behind a portrait of a child-
woman who resembles one of Gainsborough's eighteenth-century
·"ladies," and whose beauty is violated by the bullets that extinguish
the life of the hidden monster. The portrait introduces a metaphor of
Humbert's tragic obsession with Lolita—a neoclassical serenity masking the grin of death—one that will serve as a backdrop to the film's
titled epilogue: "Humbert Humbert died in prison of coronary

thrombosis while awaiting trial for the murder of Clare Quilty." This demure image twice seen, and the repetition of the call for "Quilty" that immediately precedes it, provide the film with an aural and visual Rosebud which, like a recurring dream-nightmare, frames Humbert's loss of vision in the dark obstacle course of the self.

Within this prologue and its ritualization of both Humbert's enslavement to Lolita (pedicure) and his execution-killing of Quilty, Kubrick establishes a third-person detachment from the subjective (first-person) narration that begins just afterward in a flashback to "Four Years Earlier." By materializing the surreality of Quilty's character and linking it, through the eighteenth-century portrait, to Humbert's romantic fondness for images rather than objects, Kubrick is able to wrest the film from Humbert's subjective perspective and imply that, from the moment he steps into Charlotte's garden, his course inexorably leads to Quilty's mansion. Throughout the film, Humbert's attachment to the illusory is juxtaposed with various objects and characters that, in a different way, illustrate Quilty's view that people are interchangeable with furniture (he knows a man "who looks just like a bookcase"). In his first tour of the Haze domain, Humbert runs a gauntlet through the obscure objects of Charlotte's desire as he crosses a chessboard foyer into an interior that shows signs of a mental landscape almost as disordered as Quilty's: In every room, decorative wallpaper—vertical lines of a cage downstairs, flowers in the bedrooms, sailboats in the bathroom, fish on the shower curtain, and a clutter of table settings in the kitchen—clashes with a rococo collection of objects. Charlotte takes him into her bedroom and shows off a shrine to her late husband, which includes an urn holding his ashes (on which Humbert inadvertently rests his hand), the gun that will kill Quilty (a "sacred" treasure wrapped in silk), and Mr. Haze's picture voyeuristically gazing down from the wall onto the bed where the future Mr. and Mrs. Humbert will play at marital bliss. The upstairs hallway is cluttered with ghastly Mexican art and a porcelain cat, and downstairs various *objets d'art* fill out a world of cultural poverty and sexual desperation. (Lolita later will play with a bronzed hand holding a phallic arrow as she traces the sculptured outlines of an African head in the scene where she undermines Charlotte's rumba lesson in leopardskin.) Kubrick concludes this sequence, and its doubling of Charlotte's home with Quilty's Pavor Manor, by giving cinematic form to Humbert's dreamy idealization of Lolita. We first see Lolita in the garden, from Humbert's point of view: bathed in soft light and an aura of sensuality, mysteriously abstracted from time and linked to the imagery behind the credits and the portrait in Quilty's mansion, she is shown wearing a bikini, a sun hat, and heart-shaped sunglasses. Once again, Kubrick immerses his audience in Humbert's imagination and simultaneously inserts an ironic complication: first a pedicure, then a bullet hole through the face of the portrait, and now the sounds of a vapid teenage song ("yah-yah") playing on the nymphet's radio that firmly locate Lolita in time and objectify an existence on the other side of the mind's eye.

Throughout, Humbert has trouble dealing with the material and mechanical substance of a world that frustrates his every move. Characters close in on him as he fumbles with a plate of cake and a cup of punch during the dance; he investigates the gun in Charlotte's bedroom, and the bullets fall out; and at the Enchanted Hunters he is as intimidated by the mechanics of a folding cot as by Quilty's impersonation of a policeman. Humbert prefers, instead, the private sanctuary of words in his diary and the elusive sounds of "Ulalume," written by "the divine Edgar." He fails to deduce Quilty's identity partly because it exists in a dark and very corporeal part of the imagination, the one that emanates from the loins rather than the cerebral cortex. Kubrick's Humbert, given a more sympathetic form by James Mason's performance than in the dense forest of Nabokov's prose style, wants to glide through space rather than tread the ground of primal instinct. In one of the film's most inventive and original scenes, Kubrick shows that Humbert, balancing a drink on his chest and listening to the faint sounds of Lolita's "yah-yah" garden music playing in his mind, is more at home in the dreamy and masturbatory delights of a hot bathtub than in the clutches of Charlotte's voracious libido.* Humbert relaxes in the very bathwater that Charlotte had been drawing for herself just before reading his diary and fleeing to her rain-

---

*Humbert in the bathtub might be an ironic allusion to Jean Paul Marat, the eighteenth-century French revolutionary who was stabbed in his bath by a Charlotte, Charlotte Corday. In Nabokov's novel, Humbert refers to Marat's tub when he recounts his unfortunate marriage to Valeria, an ur-Charlotte. Nabokov especially associates Quilty with bathrooms and Humbert with beds: Quilty flushes the toilet ("waterfalls") all night long in the room next to Humbert's at the Enchanted Hunters Hotel; Humbert finds Quilty at Pavor Manor coming out of the bathroom and finally kills him in bed, where "a pink bubble with juvenile connotations formed on his lips," which is another of the many signs linking Quilty and Humbert as fellow nympholepts.

soaked death. And in a devilish joke at the expense of his protagonist, Kubrick has Humbert's position in the bathtub duplicate Charlotte's in the street, including the supplicatory presence of one Mr. Beale (James Dyrenforth), whose son's car ran over Mrs. Humbert, and who moves from sitting on the curb next to her covered body to sitting on the toilet seat next to Humbert's submerged one.

Scenes in bedrooms and bathrooms abound in *Lolita,* as they do in Nabokov's novel, and indicate the film's highly developed use of studio-bound settings to express the comic and tragic modalities of a psychological/sexual content. Within these private chambers of an otherwise public domesticity, where the guilty and repressed secrets of suburbia find both release and purgation, Kubrick develops a visual and musical coherence that binds setting to both character fate and film concept. Throughout much of the film, bedrooms and bathrooms come together in an expression of primal irony. Charlotte, just before she escorts Humbert into her bedroom, makes a point of illustrating her home's old-fashioned plumbing by pulling the toilet chain and synchronizing her vulgar laughter to its flushing. Later, on the morning Lolita leaves for camp, Humbert crawls from his bed and, with the bathroom visible in the background as counterpoint and the theme music rising in pitch, receives Lolita's embrace as she winks and tells him not to forget her. He then goes into Lolita's room to sit on her bed, flanked by innocence on one side (a teddy bear) and vulgarity on the other (Quilty's picture on the cigarette poster), as he reads Charlotte's confession of love. In marriage, Humbert escapes from Charlotte's bed into the bathroom, where he scribbles his secrets in a diary and is pursued by her pouty snoopings into his private life. And in that same bed, Charlotte starts to tell him about her "most ambitious fantasy" as he simultaneously makes love to her body and *his* fantasy embodied in Lolita's picture on an end table. When he discovers that Charlotte's fantasy also involves Lolita— sending her off to boarding school so that she can have him all to herself—Humbert rolls over and contemplates the gun lying opposite Lolita's picture. At the Enchanted Hunters, Kubrick creates a sense of *déjà vu* as he delivers Humbert and Lolita into a room that mirrors the decor of Ramsdale, with flowered wallpaper in the bedroom and a bathroom in the background with a chessboard floor. Humbert comes out of that bathroom and hovers in a state of cleansed readiness over the sleeping beauty, but alas, she wakes up and sends him scurrying to the cot. The next morning, Lolita bends over a tired and unshaven Hum-

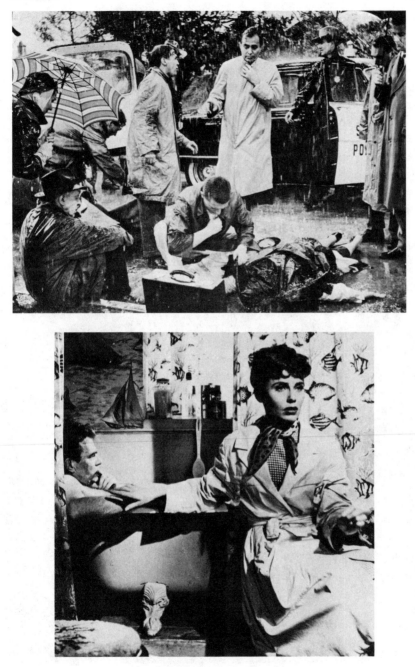

bert lying in his "collapsible" bed and whispers *her* dirty secret into *his* ear.

    In later scenes, this comic movement within a maze of private passions takes darker and more poignant courses. And more successfully than in any of his previous films, Kubrick demonstrates in *Lolita* a remarkable talent for directing his actors and developing a profound emotional content within the larger structures of an ironic distance. In a motel, he shows a tearful Lolita walking through another bathroom, this one separating her room from Humbert's, to seek comfort (Humbert has told her of Charlotte's death) on a bed in semi-darkness, illuminated from behind by the light from the bathroom. Humbert consoles her with promises to restore her life to normality and never to leave her ("cross my heart and hope to die") as we see the child in Lolita break through the mask of teenage precocity. In a moment that is both touching and satiric, Lolita clings to her middle-

Lolita's final descent into normality (Sue Lyon and Gary Cockrell)

class belief that normality can be measured in the continuity of such objects as records and record players, while we fully appreciate the tragicomic nature of Humbert's obsession. Despite his failure to find Dante's Beatrice in Ramsdale's Eve, he eventually must comfort and love the real Lolita, who later will double back and become another Charlotte. Even at the end, with Quilty gone ("the only man who I was ever really crazy about") and Humbert wasted and herself facing the tawdry prospect of her existence as Mrs. Richard T. Schiller (in Nabokov, the middle initial is "F"), Lolita still takes refuge in the enduring value of things and resists both Humbert's vision and his love. In their last scene together, Humbert faces a new Lolita—no longer dreamy or magical, but bloated by pregnancy and wearing horn-rimmed glasses like Quilty—and sits with her on another bed (on which, ironically, there is a copy of *Seventeen*), this time in a living room cluttered with domestic junk and the ubiquitous decorative wallpaper. He tearfully begs her to come away with him, "to live and die" with him, only to be rejected by her in her newfound morality and her tragic triviality. She accepts from Humbert only a last gift, in the form of money and property settlements. He flees in despair to confront Quilty, as we hear the last chords from the theme music, which now express pathos rather than satire. And Lolita sends him on his way in a cascade of clichés ("What's past is past" and "Keep in touch," as she waves hand and money in a gesture of farewell) and documents the ultimate shallowness of her character and the futility of Humbert's dream.

But as the film sympathetically records Humbert's loss, it visually develops his entrapment on a gameboard far more deadly than he ever imagined. Kubrick creates a cinematic chess game, reminiscent of both his earlier films and Nabokov's novel, that opposes Humbert's White to Quilty's Black. Chess, of course, superbly objectifies a state of paranoia and the themes of deception and entrapment; it demands from each player a constant vigilance lest he become the butt of an opponent's malicious joke. In *Lolita,* Kubrick allows his audience to watch the game from his vantage point by providing both privileged glimpses of Quilty's moves and, long before it dawns on Humbert, the knowledge that Lolita longs to be Quilty's Black Queen rather than Humbert's White. Not only is Humbert's first view of Lolita cast in soft light, but throughout the early part of the film all their encounters are brightly and realistically lit. Thus, Humbert has the illusion that his dream of Lolita might take shape in the daylight of a "normal" world. Quilty disguises his true role at first, although Kubrick brings him into the high school dance, where Humbert's white dinner jacket opposes his black tuxedo; of course, Quilty travels with his Dark Queen, Vivian Darkbloom (Marianne Stone). And on the soundtrack, blasts from Humbert's romantic piano oppose the subtle but sinister sounds of Quilty's harpsichord. Kubrick initiates a visual shift in the film at the Enchanted Hunters, even though the mood remains lightly satiric as the lighting becomes darker. On the hotel veranda, the camera is positioned so that the audience watches Quilty's face while Humbert, sitting in the background, remains ignorant of his identity (which, incidentally, parallels the camera's independent pan away from Humbert to the picture of Quilty in Lolita's bedroom). Quilty dominates the frame, while Humbert tries to maintain his composure despite a latent paranoia about policemen and his anticipation of incest with his "daughter" Lolita. Quilty fidgets with his glasses and speaks in nervous, broken phrases about how he wishes he had a "lovely, pretty little girl" and indirectly mocks Humbert's pretense of familial normality (one "normal guy" to another) by expressing a concern that their "accommodations" (read "bed") might not be comfortable enough; at one point, he ironically says that Humbert should have the "bridal suite." He surrealistically objectifies for the audience Humbert's internal disorders, and when he asks to have a look at the room so that he might use his influence with the hotel desk clerk, Humbert beats a hasty retreat to the sleeping Lolita and a battle with an intractable cot.

Humbert next confronts his sinister incubus in the form of Dr. Zempf, sitting in the dark of Beardsley ("to save you electricity," he tells Humbert). By now, Humbert's cultured and cool exterior shows signs of cracking as he imagines sexual competition from nonexistent forces (the "Rexes" and "Roys" of Lolita's adolescence) and misperceives the true nature of Quilty's game. And while the audience could appreciate Quilty's earlier pranks as forms of poetic justice, they surely must feel an uneasiness about his Zempf impersonation. The game now takes on sinister and cruel tones, as Sellers twists his conception of Quilty toward that neo-Nazi monster who will roll out of the cavernous shadows of *Dr. Strangelove*. First as Zempf, and then as a voice on the telephone, Quilty throws a diabolical light into the darkness of Humbert's soul and forces him to experience the nightmare that lurks beneath his dream, the one facing him on the other side of the gameboard. Zempf's psychological profile of Lolita ("a sweet little child" who suffers from an "acute repression of the libido") denies

Humbert's love for Lolita and ridicules his debasement. Zempf exaggerates Humbert's European pomposity through his psychobabble and his Germanic anality, his thick glasses and the efficient row of pens protruding from his breast pocket. And Kubrick, as before, has Quilty acting out an inside joke for our benefit—and at "Dr. Hombart's" expense—when Zempf offers Humbert a Drome cigarette (the poster in Lolita's bedroom) and maliciously tells him to "keep the pack." Humbert's final contacts with Quilty, before Lolita's escape from the hospital, are nightmarishly disembodied ones. Quilty's car follows him across the barren Southwest ("the designation of doom"), and as he contemplates a rear-projection image through the window of his car, Humbert's daylight world begins to match his nocturnal one. Sick and obviously dying, Humbert drags himself out of bed in a darkly lit and ominous motel room to answer the call of a telephonic nightmare: Quilty refuses to identify this impersonation by name ("My name is really obscure and unremarkable") and more successfully than before exposes Humbert's comic fear that policemen and faceless civil authorities have formed a legion of decency against his quest for the dream of Lolita. Tragically, Humbert never sees the twofold truth Kubrick shows us: Quilty mirrors the perverse underside of that dream, and Lolita never embodies its romantic substance.

4 THE DESCENT OF MAN

Dr. Strangelove

During the months following the early summer release of *Lolita* in 1962, Kubrick began work in his New York City apartment on a screenplay with an ex-RAF officer named Peter George. In 1959, Harris-Kubrick had purchased the film rights to George's novel *Red Alert* (1958), which dealt with the subject of a thermonuclear accident. (It had been published in Britain as *Two Hours to Doom* by "Peter Bryant.") This project would eventually lead Kubrick to move with his family to England in the fall of 1962, and to sever his partnership with James B. Harris. At the time, his move abroad was necessitated by the deal that Harris-Kubrick had worked out with Seven Arts, who put up the original money for *Lolita* with the stipulation that it be spent in England. Thus, *Red Alert* was scheduled to start production in October of 1962 at Shepperton Studio just outside London. Kubrick's wife

Christiane and their three daughters went on ahead to England to find a home, while Kubrick remained in New York City working on the script with George and casting the film with Harris. It was at this time that Harris-Kubrick dissolved their nine-year partnership, primarily, it seems, because Harris wanted to direct and did not want to relocate to England. Harris went on to direct his own Cold War nuclear film, *The Bedford Incident* (1965), which remains one of the best film treatments of that subject from the 1950s and 1960s. After moving to England, Kubrick formed his own independent production company, Hawk Films, which would be the holding company through which almost all of his remaining films would be released. By 1964, he and his family had moved into a house (Abbots Mead) near the Borehamwood studios in the suburbs north of London, where they would reside for the next twenty-three years. Stanley Kubrick would never again live in America or make a film in his native land.

Kubrick had been preparing for a number of years to make a film like *Dr. Strangelove; or How I Learned to Stop Worrying and Love the Bomb* (1964). Consistent with an interest in the aesthetic and moral implications of forms and plans, he began during the 1950s to read books and journals on the subject of nuclear warfare and strategy, with titles like *Nuclear Tactics, Aviation Week,* and *Bulletin of the Atomic Scientists.* He was struck by "people's virtually listless acquiescence in the possibility—in fact, the increasing probability—of nuclear war." Moreover, in his 1950s films he indirectly expressed this fascination through film structures that thrived on the tensions between a human world of design and the unexpected intrusions of contingency. In many ways, *Dr. Strangelove* merely exaggerates and externalizes the satiric irony of *Paths of Glory* and expands the temporal complexities of *The Killing* toward more profound philosophic conclusions. As he had once decided to move from the interiority of *Killer's Kiss* to the disparities of plan and accident in *The Killing,* so Kubrick in the early 1960s moved from the psychological focus of *Lolita* to the broader, mythopoeic expression of *Strangelove.* Yet he did not forget to incorporate the satiric lessons learned in adapting Nabokov's novel to film. Despite its temporal and spatial limits—the film has a running time of ninety-four minutes, which closely approximates the fictional time it dramatizes, and almost all the action takes place in three confined settings—*Strangelove* is a much more expansive and ambitious film than *Lolita.* It clearly advances beyond *Paths of Glory* in its development of complex ideas within a film rhetoric that mixes a realism of detail with a surrealist visual and verbal stylization. More important, it provided Kubrick with the opportunity to refine a film aesthetic that would, in the years to come, increasingly blend satiric irony with cosmic speculation.

In Peter George's *Red Alert,* Kubrick found a novelistic source for his belief in the possibility of an accidental nuclear war. Interestingly, the novel is written in an explicit prose style reminiscent of the dramatic and thematic clarity of White's *Clean Break* and Cobb's *Paths of Glory.* Its tight, economical structure recalls White's manipulation of time, and although it is organized in a more straightforward manner than White's book, the course of its development is equally relentless. George, like White, creates a sense of temporal urgency as his characters grapple with the vicissitudes of chance and barely avert impending doom. His use of parallel and isolated settings—Sonora Air Force Base (Texas), the B-52 bomber ("Alabama Angel"), the War Room in the Pentagon—is structurally comparable to Cobb's development of the conflicts between the intimate world of the trenches and a more distant military hierarchy. And like both those novels, George's adopts a third-person omniscience that intensifies its apocalyptic content through an impersonal style of reportage. Consequently, George makes every effort to impress his reader with the very real possibility of nuclear war by accident rather than design. He carefully delineates the technology of nuclear politics and its complex tangle of procedures, communications, and security safeguards, as well as the presence of basic human elements that conspire to turn this "fail-safe" system into a weapon of global destruction. He scrupulously motivates the decision by General Quinten (Ripper in the film) to launch an unprovoked attack against Russia through the character's sincere belief in the Red Menace and the fact that he is dying of a terminal disease. The book, in contrast to the film, shows how Quinten's nuclear paranoia has a rational basis in fact as he persuasively counters the objections of his thoughtful and humane executive officer, Major Howard (Mandrake in the film). George's novel contains very few descriptive flourishes, except in its elaborate and convincing network of technical detail. He instead invests the novel's events with an empirical authority that confronts the reader with the real possibility of nuclear war. In the end, however, George retreats from the seemingly implacable logic of his story by ending it on a note of liberal/moral fortuity. The H-bomb dropped by the "Alabama Angel" does not fully detonate, which leads to the possibility of détente between a forceful and competent American president (an idealized Adlai Stevenson type) and the Russian ambassador.

Initially, Kubrick viewed the project as a "straightforward melo-drama," but early on he and Harris, while Kubrick and George were working on the script in New York, would facetiously entertain them-selves during off-hours by discussing the prospect of nuclear holo-caust in satiric ways. Even after he left for England, Kubrick contin-ued to struggle with the serious approach used in George's novel, as the absurdity of nuclear politics repeatedly reared its comic head. Eventually, he began to change his thinking about how to make a "truthful" film about thermonuclear war: "the things you laugh at most are really the heart of the paradoxical postures that make a nu-clear war possible." The most acclaimed "serious" nuclear war film before this time was Stanley Kramer's *On the Beach* (1959), which, in its Cold War liberal morality, thematically resembles George's *Red Alert* in ways that Kubrick's film never does. And, coincidentally, in the same year that *Dr. Strangelove* came out, Columbia released *Fail-Safe* (Sidney Lumet, 1964), a realistic but ponderous depiction of the same thesis. In the Lumet version, Henry Fonda plays an American president who is faced, like the president in George's novel, with de-ciding whether to allow the Russians to retaliate in kind and with-out interference after an American bomber accidentally drops an H-bomb on a Soviet target. Both these films are highly dramatic and appropriately sober, but from Kubrick's perspective they were not nec-essarily "truthful" or even "serious" renderings of the nuclear theme. Kubrick's comments about how he eventually gravitated toward the comic style of *Strangelove* not only clarify this point but reveal a film imagination that strives for the widest possible scope:

> But after a month or so I began to realize that all the things I was throwing out were the things which were the most truthful. After all, what could be more absurd than the very idea of two mega-powers willing to wipe out all human life because of an accident, spiced up by political differences that will seem as meaningless to people in a hun-dred years from now as the theological conflicts of the Middle Ages appear to us today?

For Kubrick, the filmic expression of something "truthful" about a given subject required first an aesthetic and philosophic detachment, and then an appropriate dramatic context and perspective to direct an audience toward new or unexpected discoveries. From what point

Kubrick lining up a shot for *Dr. Strangelove*

of view, for instance, should nuclear destruction be considered? How
can a film embody both its immediate (political and moral) and its
theoretical (historical and philosophic) implications? Kramer's and
Lumet's films adopt approaches as limited as they are predictable.
Nuclear war is a serious business, their films say, one that demands a
naturalistic film treatment, with primary characters who impress the
audience with their humanity and sense of responsibility; for in the
end, it is a problem that we all must share and for which we all must
be held accountable. Like Dax amid the madness of *Paths of Glory*,
films such as *On the Beach* and *Fail-Safe* play it both earnest and safe.
They would rather be on the "right" side of a morally complex issue
than transform or unsettle an audience's perception by showing how

such a problem, more often than not, originates from deep inside the structures of a social mythology and the paradoxes of human nature.

That Kubrick, in December of 1962, brought in comic novelist Terry Southern to help with the development of satiric ideas for *Strangelove* is not surprising. Beginning with *Killer's Kiss,* Kubrick's films increasingly show signs of a satiric distance that, in part, opposes the humanity of their characters. Before *Lolita,* his interests were focused on temporal and spatial structures that enveloped the characters in a blanket of speculation and irony, even though he always gave them internal dimension. But in *Lolita,* his first "comic" film, Kubrick complicates a sympathetic identification with Humbert, Lolita, and Charlotte through satiric performances and a control of point of view that force the audience to see authorial ironies at work which expose either a perverse or a trivial underside to character. In Peter George's *Red Alert,* Kubrick worked with a novel oriented toward plot and message, where two primary questions dominate, one immediate and the other implied: Will the B-52 be stopped? How can a nuclear accident like the one depicted be prevented? George's characters, as a result, are not very interesting, except when they or their psychology becomes a factor in either the main plot device or the story's thematic single-mindedness. What Kubrick did, in collaboration with George, Southern, and a fine cast, was to redirect and expand the novel's psychological/thematic emphasis. *Strangelove* is not only a highly satiric and exaggerated treatment of a madness that far too many people accept as "normal." Unlike *Red Alert* or the other nuclear films of the period, it also matches every plot suspense device with a set of ideas and speculations that reveal Kubrick's mythopoeic intentions. The film not only shows how a nuclear accident could happen (something that George's novel does just as well), but deals with the less visible causes and implications. Kubrick shows a more profound interest in origins, both psychological and philosophical, than does George's novel, which indicates that *Dr. Strangelove* more properly should be seen as occupying a middle ground between the historical ironies of *Paths of Glory* and the cosmic speculations of *2001.*

By characterizing the subtext of *Strangelove* as "mythopoeic" and cosmic, I mean to separate its satiric ambitions from those conventionally associated with normative satire. Kubrick's films rarely outline a model of individual or social behavior through which an audience can measure and evaluate psychological aberrations. Like most traditional satire, however, they do throw light into the spaces that

exist between illusion and reality, between the splendor of the chateau and the chaos of the trenches. But for Kubrick, that middle space
where design and disorder intersect forces one to acknowledge the
presence of an inexplicable universe that any definition of the "truthful" must also ponder. Kubrick's satire has no immediate corrective or
utilitarian purpose, unless its exploration (both ironic and sympathetic) of a human tendency to create myths and reinvent the universe through form and structure constitutes an "arm against fantasy."
Instead of resolving the opposition between illusion and reality, Kubrick's films before *Strangelove* suggest an ever-present paradox that
involves three primary factors: the existential but dynamic terrors of
life experienced in time and in the self (i.e., Johnny Clay's "what's the
difference?", the trenches of *Paths,* Humbert's despair); the attraction of aesthetic form, which embodies a contrary movement away
from life as it is experienced in time toward *either* an expressive release into the sublime *or* a deadly, often dehumanizing enclosure (i.e.,
Johnny's plan, the chateau, Humbert's dream of Lolita); and finally,
the presence of a contingent universe that quietly and almost invisibly
presides over this cinematic world in conflict, and that in its vastness
and duration both diminishes the efforts of its fictional inhabitants
and inspires the achievement of its actual creator. If *Strangelove* continues Kubrick's indictment against humanity for preferring fantasy
to reality, especially a fantasy that could result in the ultimate evil of
self-genocide, then it also indicts itself. His film is also a fictional con-
struct, and, whether or not we succeed in destroying our planet, who,
in the twenty-first century, or on some distant world, will care that one
film or one book signaled an alarm? All that a film aesthetic based on
a recognition of contingency can do is speculate and entertain both
disparities and possibilities and, in the absence of a total belief system, be true to itself in the act of creation.

As was the case in *Lolita,* Kubrick depended on both performance
and dialogue to carry, at least overtly, most of the satiric weight of *Dr.
Strangelove.* Almost all his primary actors use exaggerated postures,
facial contortions, and idioms that externalize their respective characters into recognizable comic types. Slim Pickens (as Major "King"
Kong), cast against type as a B-52 bomber pilot, is enough in himself
to inspire laughter and incredulity. But after his first words when told
about Wing Attack Plan R—"I've been to one World's Fair, a picnic,
and a rodeo, and that's the stupidest thing I've ever heard over a pair
of earphones"—the film, along with his cowboy hat, his redneck men-

tality, and the sounds of "When Johnny Comes Marching Home," ac-
celerates a satiric style that grows more absurd and surrealistic as
Kong's plane nears doomsday. George C. Scott develops an array of
facial and postural gestures that define Turgidson as the blockheaded
jingoist. He chomps down on his chewing gum like a cud, prowls
around the War Room with the same grunting intensity he employs in
the bedroom, and obscures nuclear war through a mixture of military
euphemism and homespun verbosity (destroying the Russians becomes "catching them with their pants down," and causing the deaths
of 20 million Americans "getting our hair mussed"). Sterling Hayden
portrays the mad Ripper as the prototypical 1950s right-wing general
eager to bomb the world back to the Stone Age in order to preserve
the American Way of Life ("Better Dead Than Red"). His absurd phallic cigar and machine-gun in a golf bag give comic tangibility to his
babble about Communist infiltration and "precious bodily fluids."
And Peter Sellers, in three brilliant impersonations, gives us a gamut
of character types who collectively express humanity in the grip of a
hilarious and deadly madness: as President Merkin Muffley, the bald-
headed and ineffectual man of reason in a world of madness—a Ste-
vensonian egghead satirized—who worries as much about decorum
as he does annihilation ("I have never heard of such behavior in the
War Room"); as Group Captain Lionel Mandrake, whose civilized English reserve foils Ripper's impenetrable American obsessiveness; and
as Dr. Strangelove, the mad scientist with a mechanical arm that assumes an independent life in its repeated salutes of "sieg heil," whose
madness becomes animated only when the prospect of death and
darkness looms near.

And Kubrick gives his audience a great deal to consider, more
than in any of his previous films, while they are being assaulted with
the ambiguities of a visual style that lends an unfamiliarity to the real
and an empirical life to the surreal. During the early 1960s, by his own
admission, he wanted to develop such a style, one barely glimpsed in
the films before *Lolita:*

> The real image doesn't cut the mustard, doesn't transcend. I'm now
> interested in taking a story, fantastic and improbable, and trying to get
> to the bottom of it, to make it seem not only real, but inevitable.

In the three settings of *Strangelove,* internal and external worlds com-
mingle so often that each not only distorts but comments on the
other. In the B-52, once the "go" code is received, fantasy should take

The machine in space, traveling toward Doomsday

a backseat to both the hard reality of the machine and Kubrick's *ciné-ma vérité* camera, which, in a cramped atmosphere illuminated only by source lighting, works close-in through quick zooms and jerky motions to document the intricacy of instrument panels and attack profiles. Yet the satiric exaggeration of Kong's character turns realism toward the fantastic, as Kong acts out a private drama in an Old West showdown with civilization, while his crew, drawn in more naturalistic terms, suppress forces from within as they work in harmony with the plane. Without Kong, the scenes inside the B-52 would assert the kind of technical and mechanical authenticity found in *The Killing* and, incidentally, Peter George's novel (characters in both join to execute a plan). But in *Dr. Strangelove,* Kubrick externalizes the inner/outer conflicts of the earlier film and shows how a plan or machine can be an extension of an instinct or obsession rather than an agent that directs such dissonance underground. The earlier film, for instance, stresses the dramatic ironies between the presence of George Peatty's sexual jealousy and the rigors of Johnny Clay's plan, while *Dr. Strange-*

love develops the mythopoeic paradoxes of a Ripper/Kong pathology finding expression through the orderliness of Plan R.

In Ripper's office, Kubrick allows the audience to see and consider everything within the frame through long camera takes and depth of field. From a distance, the wide-angle lens pulls this enclosure into sharp focus and exaggerates its low ceiling and horizontal geometry. It reveals all the details that make up Ripper's world and, as a parallel to Mandrake's role within this setting, challenges the audience to decode its meaning. While almost everything we see has a vivid but surreal clarity, what we hear transforms that imagery into the logic of a nightmare. In the early scenes, Kubrick alternates between medium shots that place Ripper within the symmetry of balanced compositions and low-angle close-ups that blur out surrounding space and visually reinforce the madman's verbal muddle. Later, Ripper's organized world is demolished by both the machine-gun fire from outside and his rapid mental deterioration from inside. In each case, Kubrick uses the arrangements of setting and object in both literal and expressive ways. He constantly reminds us of the existence of a material world, that it is concrete and real, and that when its inanimate substance becomes confined or organized, and in the process removed from a place in contingent space, it can assume the properties of a dream or nightmare. All the things that envelop and define Ripper—i.e., the "Peace Is Our Profession" slogan behind his desk, a tool/weapon for clipping cigars, his guns and model airplanes—in another film might play only a functional role in a credible visual landscape. But here and elsewhere, Kubrick reaffirms his talent for taking everyday minutiae and, through context, charging it with a conceptual and surrealist energy. He leaves the audience no choice but to explore the imagery of *Dr. Strangelove* by undermining its faith in the inviolability of surface reality. As a result, the viewer's position in relation to this film is like that of those soldiers who are defending Burpleson and Ripper's madness from an advancing "enemy" (American troops). The defenders, who are themselves part of the film's most documentary-like sequence (shot in the grainy telephoto realism of Orthochrome), temporarily question—as does the viewer in another way—the evidence of their senses: "You sure gotta hand it to those Commies, those trucks sure look like the real thing."

Throughout the film, Kubrick characterizes the War Room as a place where civilization appears to make a last stand against an encroaching barbarism, only to reveal that the attention given there to a verbal and formal aesthetics springs from a source not far from the deadly logic of Plan R and Dr. Strangelove's devotion to the perfection of the Doomsday Machine. Everywhere one looks there is a visual geometry. The room itself is triangular (designed by Ken Adam, who worked on several James Bond films), with the Big Board and its square displays tilting above a world of circles (the large conference table with its ring of lights overhead) on a metallic black floor. Kubrick brings the visual style of Burpleson into this more formal realm when he blends incredibly sharp and deep wide-angle imagery with close-ups in which the edges of the frame lose resolution and adumbrate an ever-present mental disorder. From a high angle, the camera reveals a world encircled by darkness but internally organized, suggesting from the beginning that it already resembles the insides of a mine shaft. Strangelove, in particular, is isolated in close-up and medium shots, enveloped by darkness and patterns of light from the Big Board. At first he is separated from the rational processes of the table, only to be sought out like an alter ego once an emerging madness begins to break down the illusion of formal order. When he cuts to shots around the table, Kubrick shows another kind of paradox, both in the collapse of language as tool and in the tangible objects that exist within the formal patterns admired from a distance. We see the lettering on Turgidson's top-secret notebooks—"World Targets in Megadeaths" and "War Alert Actions Book"—which coexist with his gum wrappers. We notice the careful place settings on the table (pitchers of water, recessed phones) that are duplicated in a circle like reflections in a trick mirror. And finally, we notice how ordinary human distinctions are blurred through either a sense of uniformity (the characters wear suits or military uniforms, and with few exceptions maintain placid expressions) or the exaggerated and dehumanized postures of a Turgidson and Strangelove. In such ways does Kubrick visually link the surreal atmosphere of the War Room with both the B-52's steady course toward death and Ripper's mad asylum.

Strangelove, more than anything else, demonstrates Kubrick's genius for translating ideas into narrative and visual film structures. And because the film defines character satirically, thereby subordinating psychology to concept, Kubrick was free to play with the forms of his medium in ways that earlier scripts made impossible. Even the humor relies almost as much upon the use of narrative and visual contexts as it does upon language, contexts that, according to Kubrick, place everyday human behavior within nightmarish situations:

> like the Russian premier on the hot line who forgets the telephone number of the general staff headquarters and suggests the American president try Omsk information, or the reluctance of a U.S. officer to let a British officer smash open a Coca-Cola machine for change to phone the President about a crisis on the SAC base because of his conditioning about the sanctity of private property.

Such a strategy recalls the way *Lolita* develops a surreality and absurdity beneath the bland surfaces of normality, only here the stakes are higher (the ultimate endgame) and the cinematic contexts more expressive. In one reflexive moment, for instance, Kubrick seemingly parodies the sexual fantasies and bathrooms of *Lolita*. Buck Turgidson is introduced through his "private" secretary, the aging nymphet Miss Scott (Tracy Reed), wearing a bikini and sunglasses, whom we first see sunbathing, not in a garden, but under a heat lamp on a hotel bed in her best centerfold pose. Buck, in the bathroom off-camera, grunts and complains as she simultaneously talks to him and another general on the telephone. Besides being an indication that the film's libido, as well as Buck's, has escaped from the closet of *Lolita*, this scene illustrates Kubrick's definition of *Dr. Strangelove*'s comic method:

> Confront a man in his office with a nuclear alarm, and you have a documentary. If the news reaches him in his living room, you have a drama. If it catches him in the lavatory, the result is comedy.

The sexual content of *Dr. Strangelove*, what one critic labeled a "sex allegory" and another an example of "erotic displacement," represents the most discernible and widely discussed mythopoeic element in the film. The progress of the film from "foreplay to explosion," to quote one critic, is clearly and almost too neatly connected with the satiric characterizations. Consider the following:

1. General Jack D. Ripper is named after history's most notorious sex offender. He disguises his loss of potency by raving about fluoridation as a Communist plot to poison our vital bodily fluids. He launches a phallic retaliation against the Russians in the shapes of B-52 bombers, a jutting cigar—which, before his death, has burned down to a stub—and the machine-gun that he fires at his own countrymen. Defeated and spent, he takes a pearl-handled pistol into the bathroom and kills himself rather than endure the "torture" that his

madness envisions as his fate. Later, Colonel "Bat" Guano (Keenan Wynn) will look at Mandrake's "suit" and peg him as a "prevert"— suggesting that he confuses transvestites with soldiers in a foreign military service—rather than a man trying to save the world.

2. Aboard the B-52 bomber, Major "King" Kong is introduced reading *Playboy* and admiring the film's parody of Fay Wray, namely Miss Scott, who is Playmate of the Month. Her pose in the centerfold photo is identical to her pose in Buck's hotel suite, only here a magazine (*Foreign Affairs*) rather than a bikini covers her backside. Inside the door of the safe containing packets outlining the procedures for Plan R, we see girlie pictures. We then discover that the name of the primary bombing target is "Laputa" (Spanish for "whore"), and we hear Kong detail over the intercom the contents of a survival kit, which includes silk stockings, lipsticks, and prophylactics ("Shoot, a fellah could have a pretty good weekend in Vegas with all that stuff"). Later, Kong goes into the bomb bay, where sexually suggestive salutations adorn the tail-end of two H-bombs—"Hi There" and "Dear John" (Peter George's novelization of the screenplay names the second bomb "Lolita"). He straddles a bomb as if it were a bronco, and in the process grows a gargantuan phallus moving toward the ultimate score, a doomsday orgasm.

3. When we first meet General "Buck" Turgidson—whose name

decodes as "swollen male animal who is the son of a swollen male animal"—he is on the toilet and in the company of his Playmate of the Month. As he goes off to either save or help destroy the world, he tells her in the language of the occasion to start her "countdown" and be ready to "blast off" when he returns (in George's novelization, Buck instead talks about "reentry"). And in the War Room, just before the final explosions, Turgidson's jaw hangs open in stupefaction as he envisions the demise of monogyny in Strangelove's brave new world of mine-shaft cohabitation.

4. In the War Room, the presiding figure is President Merkin Muffley, whose name Anthony Macklin has identified as a reference to the vulva, and even though both "merkin" and "muffley" suggest a "covering," he is bald, which makes his head look like a phallus. Muffley's prissy and effeminate manner stands between Turgidson's overly erect postures and Strangelove's crippled impotence. He talks on the hotline to the Russian premier, named "Kissoff," who is both drunk and with his mistress.

5. Finally, through the title character, Dr. Strangelove, whose real name is "Merkwuerdigichliebe" (which decodes as "cherished fate"), the film directs this sexual satire into thematic implications that go beyond the lighter antics of Turgidson and Kong. Dr. Strangelove brings Ripper's madness into the "rational" world of the War Room and links it to man's intercourse with the machine and a sinister love affair with death.

While the narrative logic of *Dr. Strangelove* may indicate that the world goes up in mushroom clouds because of one general's madness or as a result of sexual malfunctions and transference, its aesthetic and thematic texture says that there is more. Consequently, the film's "sex allegory" is only one of several conceptual levels that are interconnected and hold this fictional world together. Everywhere you look in the film, for instance, there are hints of primal and infantile regression that suggest a reverse descent not into space but into time. There is Kong's Neanderthal Man and the primitivism of Turgidson, who slaps his hairy belly while standing over his mistress and in the War Room repeatedly assumes apelike stances. There is Ripper crawling on all fours as his mind degenerates to the same level as those juvenile scrawls on his notepad that contains the recall code. There are the opening images of the film, a B-52 bomber being refueled in midair, suggesting both copulation and a mother giving suck, while on the soundtrack we hear "Try a Little Tenderness" and on the screen we read pencil-line credits that resemble a child's graffiti. Kong's bomber assumes the characteristics of a womb (once he tries to sleep and let the plane fly itself), from which he is dropped screaming and bellowing into a cataclysmic world. Ripper's base is called *Burp*leson, and it houses a character who yearns for a world of neo-platonic "purity" and "essence" where ice cream cannot be contaminated, and who is humored by a nervously smiling Mandrake. In the War Room, Turgidson, who is forever chewing gum like a masturbatory adolescent, clutches his top-secret notebooks to his chest and whines about security when informed that Russian ambassador de Sadesky (i.e., the Marquis de Sade, played by Peter Bull) will be allowed to see the "Big Board." In every setting, language breaks down and characters revert to either the antiquated clichés of a primitive value system (Ripper's "the Redcoats are coming," Kong's "*nuculur* combat, toe to toe with the Rooskies," and Turgidson's "prayer" of deliverance before the Big Board) or the conversation of children (Muffley's baby talk with Kissoff and Turgidson's with Miss Scott). And in the end, Dr. Strangelove becomes both sexually erect and childlike as he learns to walk in preparation for a descent into the mine shaft.

Kubrick gives food and eating a primal importance almost equal to that of sex. The first scene in the B-52 shows several members of the crew eating, and when Lieutenant Goldberg (Paul Tamarin), the radio operator, reports to Kong that he has received the code for Wing Attack Plan R, his words are obscured by a sandwich he is stuffing into his mouth. At Burpleson, Ripper never eats, no doubt so he can maintain a purity of bodily fluids, and he drinks only branch water and grain alcohol. When Mandrake is collecting a transistor radio from inside a computer printout machine, we see that someone has left behind an uneaten sandwich and two pieces of fruit (an apple for the Garden, a banana for the Jungle, and the Machine). In Turgidson's hotel suite, through a mirror reflection behind Miss Scott, a table covered with dirty dishes is prominent, as this long camera take visually decodes as the recurring cycle of food, sex, a lavatory purgation, and sleep. And in the War Room there is a large buffet of gourmet food and pastries displaying the ritualization of a primal function and an absurd attention to pre-apocalypse formality. (Kubrick shot a custard-pie fight, which originally was to conclude the film, but he deleted it before final release.) At the very end, after all is lost, the president sits next to the buffet, drink in hand, and calmly considers Strangelove's mine-shaft computations, which include, among other things, green-

houses for plant life (food and oxygen) and breeding places for animals to be *slaughtered* (with particular emphasis on that last word). As
civilization descends into a new Dark Age, another survival kit provides for the nourishment of the body as well as the libido.

Dr. Strangelove recalls *The Killing* in the way its plot and settings are
geared to the clock. The narrator's soothing, documentary voice in a
prologue alerts us to the possibility of time's end in his comment that
"ominous rumors" continue to circulate about the "ultimate weapon,
a Doomsday device." Then a few minutes later (in his final intrusion),
he tells us that the SAC bombers are "two hours from their targets
deep inside Russia." The "fail-safe" system itself—defined by manuals,
decoding books, and attack profiles—represents a human obsession
with the mechanics of time and the hope of anticipating both the
designs of a known enemy and the unseen courses of fate. Once trig-
gered, the relentless logic of the fail-safe system meshes with the
doomsday machine to complete a timetable as inexorable as a mathematical formula. In the War Room, attempts are made to thwart this
clockwork doom through the improvisation of counterplans that,
ironically, try to circle back and frustrate what was originally envisioned as the ultimate contingency plan (Plan R was invented in case

all other nuclear safeguards failed). While Muffley conspires with the
Russian premier to foil both the Doomsday Machine and a plan de-
vised to destroy Russia, Mandrake decodes Ripper's mad doodles.
However, a third factor—chance—intervenes, not only knocking out
Kong's receiver, but, even worse, causing a fuel loss that directs the B-
52 to the "nearest target opportunity," where there will be no Soviet
missiles waiting to intercept and destroy (chance is not nearly so inventive in George's novel). Meanwhile, in contrast to the B-52's mechanical and efficient pace, the War Room's "rational" deliberations
become comically inert as Kubrick shows us a world that has reduced
the vastness of space to the smaller dimensions of human time. The
huge circular table and its halo of fluorescent light visually embody
the processes of reason, while overhead the Big Board arranges space
into finite expressions of time (its lights and geometric shapes outline
the "fail-safe" system on a "map" of the world). In these patterns of
circularity, Kubrick visually anticipates the film's ending, where we
hear the temporal mockery of Vera Lynn's "We'll Meet Again" and
see a doomsday shroud form another halo around the billowing cloud
of a hydrogen bomb and the extinction of life.

Within the involutions of this temporal/spatial paradox—of plans
and counterplans, a cinematic world circling back on itself in both
time and space—Kubrick employs straight cuts to go back and forth
between settings and to intensify a narrative pace that confers an om-
nipotence on the rule of time. The film shows that once the exercise
of free will and choice becomes overly formalized in the machinery of
"fail-safe" systems and "human reliability" tests, options and possibilities are diminished as characters fall victim to the ceaselessly creative
and unpredictable intervention of either human psychology or
chance. Ripper's telephonic communication to the War Room, the
one read aloud by Turgidson, not only captures his comic madness
("This man is obviously a psychotic," says the president) but verbal-
izes a temporal condition that leaves little room for human choice.
Ripper dictates a doomsday morality when he institutes Plan R and
tells them, "My boys will give you the best kind of start, fourteen hundred megatons worth, and you sure as hell won't stop them now."
Turgidson then talks about the "moment of truth" and the necessity
of choosing "between two admittedly regrettable but nevertheless dis-
tinguishable post-war environments; one, where you got twenty million people killed, and the other, where you got one hundred fifty
million people killed." The president, who always believes "there are

alternatives still left open to us," eventually faces both the logic of Buck's argument and a world caught between a Doomsday Auschwitz and Mine Shaft Dachau.

Consider, finally, these examples of simultaneity and juxtaposition, which link the film's temporal rhetoric to the ethics of endgame:

1. While Kong is reassuring his men that he shares their "strong personal feelings about *nuculur* combat" and promising them "promotions and citations" once their mission is over, Turgidson is likewise assuming the existence of a future of "normal" human activity when he tells Miss Scott to keep her sexual clock ticking until he returns.

2. As Kong reads aloud the lock-step procedures for Plan R to his men, Mandrake becomes a prisoner in Ripper's office and listens to a recitation of how that plan will determine life and death on a global scale ("while we are chatting so enjoyably," says Ripper).

3. As de Sadesky and Strangelove explain the purpose of the Doomsday Machine as ultimate deterrent, one designed as an "automated and irrevocable decision-making process that rules out human meddling," Ripper details for Mandrake his paranoid delusion that fluoridation represents an insidious and invisible evil ("on no account will a Commie drink water").

4. Once Kong's CRM 114 is destroyed, he and his crew have no choice but to drop the bomb, which they do at the same moment that Dr. Strangelove is reassuring the president that computers are better equipped than mere mortals to make the difficult decision of who goes into the mine shafts and who stays behind to breathe the deadly Cobalt Thorium G.

Paradoxically, in a film that carefully details a twentieth-century descent of man, the machine, for the first time, plays a prominent role in Kubrick's work. *Strangelove* predates *2001* and remains his darkest vision of what an emerging "machinarchy" could mean to humanity and human civilization. The presence of machine technology dominates the visual landscape in each of the film's three settings and ironically complements a human world that symbolically moves back in time almost as fast as Kong's B-52 flies through space. In some respects, this machine environment resembles the merger of World War I barbarity and eighteenth-century neoclassicism in *Paths of Glory:* it provides both a context for evaluating the human madness within the film and a perspective on where that madness comes from and where it may be going. Each setting becomes a dark cave or womb, where characters are surrounded by machines that once served as tools of communication and progress, but now function as weapons of destruction and descent. Ripper cuts off all telephonic communication with the outside world, and as he closes the venetian blinds in his office, he wraps himself in the artificial illumination of fluorescent lights and the psychic darkness of a primitive mentality. The antique guns mounted on the wall, the model airplanes on his desk, an aerial photo of Burpleson, and photographs of bombers frozen in space define his alignment with the technology of death. One of his last contacts with the outside is the cryptic FGB code, which mechanically clicks into the B-52's CRM 114 and turns an instrument for receiving messages into one that cuts off all communication (except with Ripper's mad OPE code prefix), directing the plane on a predetermined course toward death. Our first sight of Mandrake is as a figure obscured by a large printout sheet, in a computer room where machines outnumber people. He then sits down at a console and talks with Ripper on the phone (it is the only phone at Burpleson that is still working, except for the pay phone that he will use in the Coca-Cola machine scene), as computer tapes move back and forth in circles behind him. Kong's B-52 becomes a machine that not only seems capable of flying itself, but in the intricacy and fineness of its craftsmanship (a set based on a photograph from a British aviation magazine) lends a grossness to the human beings who give it direction. This machine, which moves forward through space (horizontally, not vertically) and propels its inhabitants backward in time, cannot be recalled because a Russian missile, first seen as a blip on a radar scanner, destroys the CRM 114. At almost the exact same moment at Burpleson, Guano reluctantly shoots off the lock of the Coca-Cola machine so that Mandrake can get the change to use the pay phone to communicate the recall code to the president. Kubrick had a huge triangular set especially built for the War Room that is both realistic (it resembles a similar complex in NORAD's Cheyenne Mountain near Colorado Springs) and highly expressive. In this setting, the Big Board's sophisticated machine language and brightly lit, complex displays tower over the increasingly trivial and primitive verbal intercourse below. Here, as elsewhere, Kubrick shows a world cut off from reason and outside contacts, both actual and imaginative, cut off, indeed, from everything that might enable it to see the ironic truth of its dependence on the machine. The very technology that assists the human dream of order and duration—nuclear deterrents, "fail-safe" systems,

The Monster patiently waits in the darkness

and a "contingency" plan like Plan R—works on principles of repetition and predictability, and once set in motion, it has no choice but to
fulfill its logic. Thus, once committed to their course, and no longer
subject to rational intervention, Kong and his plane find a target and
fulfill not only their mission but the Doomsday Machine's as well.

Yet Kubrick implies that this merger of madness and machine
originates as much in a human passion for beauty as it does in the
primal darkness of the Id. The first image of the film, from high above
the clouds over the Zhokhov Islands, shows us the pure beauty of
space from the machine's (or God's) vantage point, even though,
paradoxically, it is linked to the "ultimate weapon" and the regressions of time both here and in its resemblance to the doomsday imagery of the ending. Throughout, Kubrick uses the machine to embody

not only an efficiency (a temporal value) lacking in the psychological
and political worlds of the film, but a sense of harmony (a spatial
value) as well: the imagery behind the credits of planes mating in
midair may prepare for sexual themes to come, but it also literalizes a
principle of conjunction that repeatedly eludes the time-bound characters. In those opening images, Kubrick reminds us that in space,
harmony and conjunction are functional requirements, not merely
the formal adornments of a civilized life or the abstract goals of artistic expression. In *Dr. Strangelove,* however, the machine assists a descent into time rather than an ascent into space, one where the perfection of its logic and the beauty of its form paradoxically objectify a
human retreat into fantasy and death. It stimulates Ripper's desire to
play God and turn the clock back to a world of purity and the stasis of
death. It creates the illusion in the War Room that mini-universes can
be created and insulated from existential truths (i.e., death no longer
is even real) outside computerized gameboards. And finally, Sellers's
performance as Strangelove provides Kubrick with both a human
form and a marvelous conceit for the futuristic tool–as–primitive
weapon: in his love of the Doomsday Machine's invulnerability to human interference and his perversion of scientific discourse (he refers
to future survivors as a "nucleus of human specimens"), in his means
of locomotion (wheelchair) and mode of animation (a mechanical
arm that turns against him), and in his doomsday "rebirth" as the New
Man who will lead the chosen people into darkness.

5 THE ULTIMATE CINEMATIC UNIVERSE

2001: A Space Odyssey

None of the available evidence regarding the conceptual and technical beginnings of Kubrick's next film indicates that he fully anticipated the enormity of its scope and impact. Even now, from the vantage of the twenty-first century, *2001: A Space Odyssey* (1968) stands not only as one of his most important and controversial films, but as a landmark work in the history of cinema. Yet it was not suddenly born full-grown like Athena from Zeus's skull: What began in 1964 as a harmless and intriguing speculation about what might happen if contact were made between human beings and an extraterrestrial intelligence evolved into a creative and logistical leviathan that eventually took years to complete, involved hundreds of people and an incalculable number of details, consumed hundreds of thousands of man-hours and millions of dollars, and succeeded primarily because of the indelible stamp of one man's creative film sense. Like *Dr. Strangelove,* this film started as an embryonic idea, which in the process of creation grew and expanded well beyond the explanatory boundaries outlined by Kubrick himself:

Man must strive to gain mastery over himself as well as over his machines. Somebody has said that man is the missing link between primitive apes and civilized human beings. You might say that that idea is inherent in *2001*. We are semi-civilized, capable of cooperation and affection, but needing some sort of transfiguration into a higher form of life. Since the means to obliterate life on Earth exists, it will take more than just careful planning and reasonable cooperation to avoid some eventual catastrophe. The problem exists, and the problem is essentially a moral and spiritual one.

Whether one reads the numerous accounts of the making of *2001* or Arthur C. Clarke's description of how the script developed from short story to novelized screenplay (*The Lost Worlds of 2001*, 1972), or whether one considers the technical exposition of experts such as Douglas Trumbull (a supervisor of special effects) and Kubrick's own extensive commentary in countless interviews, one cannot help but be awed by the achievement of *2001*. But awe is a poor substitute for understanding, and for that we must turn, first, to Kubrick's cinematic past, and consider how it is as much a part of the evolution of *2001* as any of the factors described in the accounts of the various stages of the film's production.

As early as *Paths of Glory*, Kubrick sought to express in a visually coherent way a conceptual conflict between a closed world of time and intimations of an open world of space. He used the ambience of the chateau to embody a "higher" perspective from which to view the circular and horizontal courses of a human world moving toward political and moral extinction. He suggested to his audience that outside the closed systems and formal compositions of *Paths*, there existed a world so vast and mysterious that even the filmmaker must acknowledge it as a creation greater than his own. In such ways did Kubrick imply rather than fully dramatize a belief in the possibility of an expansion and even transformation of human consciousness. While *Paths* positioned its audience in the middle of a paradox between irony (execution) and hope (the German girl's song), *Strangelove* forced viewers to contemplate the *reductio ad absurdum* of humanity's infatuation with mechanical perfection at the expense of life itself. In that context, *2001* could be viewed as *Dr. Strangelove* in reverse, a Kubrickian mirror that reflects his vision of a perfect harmony of substance and form rather than just another image of madness dressed in the guise of beauty. During the twenty-one months (April 1964–January 1966) in which they worked on the script, Kubrick repeatedly directed his and Clarke's thinking toward a conceptual design that ultimately would journey through irony on its way to wonder and magic. Originally, Clarke conceived of the project as an extension of Kubrick's previous film (jokingly titled "Son of Strangelove"), to include a climax in which the Star-Child detonates a ring of nuclear bombs orbiting the Earth in an act of cosmic purification (a conclusion that remains intact in Clarke's novel). But Kubrick steered the film version away from the Swiftian satire of *Dr. Strangelove* toward an emphasis on mythic journeys and transformations (the Homeric title was Kubrick's idea; it replaced the original title, *Journey to the Stars*). And prior to final release, he removed from the film both a ten-minute prologue of scientific "background" material and a narrator's voiceover in "The Dawn of Man" section, thereby completing his ultimate goal of turning *2001* into a "mythological documentary" rather than a more conventional blend of science-fact and film-fiction.*

Before creating the evocative visual structures of *2001*, however, Kubrick again turned to what he considered the objectifying powers of the word. By this point in his career, Kubrick's success in developing a cinematic organization of images and sounds can be measured in part by how a fully novelized and explicit script provided him with the essential temporal outlines of story and character. Between 1964 and 1980, from the making of *2001* to the release of *The Shining*, Kubrick's output would diminish to an average of one film every four years. During those years, he increasingly spent more time than ever before on all the separate phases of a film's creation—script development, pre-production, shooting, editing, and scoring—and would come to view the early and late stages of this process as the most creative. Two specific reasons why *2001* took so long to complete are its epic scope and the necessity of creating a full novelistic treatment from a ten-page short story (Clarke's "The Sentinel"). Significantly, Kubrick and Clarke spent as much time on the screenplay as Kubrick and a battery of technical advisors took to create the 205 special-effect process shots required by the futuristic landscapes of *2001*. The shooting schedule began in December 1965, even as Clarke continued to

---

*Here is how Kubrick compares the film and novel versions of *2001:* "The novel, for example, attempts to explain things much more explicitly than the film does, which is inevitable in a verbal medium. The novel came about after we did a 130-page prose treatment of the film at the very out-set. This initial treatment was subsequently changed in the screenplay, and the screenplay in turn was altered during the making of the film. But Arthur took all the existing material, plus an impression of some of the rushes, and wrote the novel. As a result, there's a difference between the novel and the film" (Gelmis, *The Film Director as Superstar,* p. 308).

struggle with alternative endings for the screenplay. More than two years later, in April of 1968, the film was released, followed in the summer by the publication of Clarke's novel, which even today remains an extremely lucid version of the film's story and an exposition of some of its more explicit themes. But more important for our purposes is its value as a source for understanding the cinematic intentions that took shape in Kubrick's mind between 1965 and 1968, long after Clarke had completed his work and gone home to Ceylon.

Clarke's "The Sentinel" (1950) and his novel (*2001: A Space Odyssey*) provide further evidence of how Kubrick worked as a filmmaker. They especially illuminate an aesthetic that developed its conceptual complexities through a masterly manipulation of an inherent tension that exists between the temporal rhetoric of a film (i.e., plot, character, narration) and its visual/musical rhetoric. In its most basic form, this tension involves a conflict between the causal logic of linear thinking, in which the world is organized into straight lines and rationalized forms, and the associative logic of a creative interiority, in which the world is assembled into parallel planes and imaginative shapes. The first is objective and pseudo-scientific, like Johnny Clay's robbery plan and *Strangelove*'s "fail-safe" systems. The second is dreamy and internal, like Humbert's vision of Lolita or the nightmare surrealism of the War Room. As we have seen, Kubrick liked to turn his audience's expectations inside out by challenging the authority of the "real" and elevating in importance intimations of less visible worlds more resistant to easy categorization. Thus he must have been particularly struck by two passages in "The Sentinel" that describe the meaning of an alien moon-machine (a pyramid, not a rectangular monolith) and speculate about its ancient creators:

> The mystery haunts us all the more now that the other planets have been reached and we know that only Earth has ever been the home of intelligent life in our Universe. . . . It was set there upon its mountain before life had emerged from the seas of Earth.

> Think of such civilizations, far back in time against the fading afterglow of Creation, masters of a universe so young that life had as yet come to only a handful of worlds. Theirs would have been a loneliness of gods looking across infinity and finding none to share their thoughts.

Throughout the novel, Clarke combines these evocations of exploration and wandering amid the lonely expanses of space with an elaborate substructure of explanatory material that ultimately has the effect of subordinating "mystery" to the speculations of science. The film, by contrast, is more open-ended than Clarke's novel, perhaps because Kubrick realized that mystery, whether futuristic or historical, becomes trivialized on the screen once it assumes a definable, objective shape. Consequently, his *2001* is less dependent on narrative exposition than the novel, and more committed to the development of its ideas through the free play of image and sound.

While Clarke built a series of clear connections between the six parts of his novel, Kubrick took a more audacious course. The film's elliptical structure compresses the action of the novel by omitting expository scenes and narration, a tactic that ultimately requires the audience to fill in the resulting narrative gaps through a combination of visual attentiveness and subliminal penetration. An obvious example of this method is the famous match cut that spans four million years of film time between parts one and two, a transition that associates Moon-Watcher's bone with an orbiting satellite. In contrast, Clarke concludes his first section ("Primeval Night") with a chapter that briefly develops the "ascent of man" and his tools following an alien visitation—and only then does he move on to the year 2001 and Dr. Heywood Floyd's trip to the Moon (titled "TMA-1," for Tycho Magnetic Anomaly-1, identifying the monolith and the moon crater where it is found). Kubrick does not title this part of his film, and through the visual association of Pleistocene bone and twenty-first-century space hardware, he initiates an important doubling pattern in *2001* that has no source in Clarke. The novel maintains its linear and connective structure when it moves from the moon excavation scene to the Jupiter mission. In a chapter called "The Listeners" at the end of part two, Clarke explains how signals from the monolith are picked up by space monitors on the dark side of Mars. He then moves the action into part three ("Between Planets") and the journey of the spaceship *Discovery* on a course toward Saturn and the receiving end of those signals. Kubrick, by contrast, cuts from the piercing sounds emitted from the monolith and a conjunctive image of monolith, Earth, and Sun to a title on a black screen that identifies part three of his *2001* as "Jupiter Mission: 18 Months Later." As before, he leaps over time into space (the darkness behind the titles, into which *Discovery* moves from screen left) and, in an image of conjunction reminiscent of "The Dawn of Man," continues to build an associative rather than strictly logical visual structure. The film does not "explain" the purpose of the monolith or the mission to Jupiter until the end of part three, just after Bowman performs a lobotomy on HAL's Logic Memory Center. In the process, Kubrick enlarges the role of the monolith and its value as object and symbol far beyond the role it plays in the novel, where it functions primarily as a teaching device and cosmic burglar alarm.

When he moves to the fourth and last part of the film ("Jupiter and Beyond the Infinite"), Kubrick employs the same type of abrupt transition used between parts two and three. He shows Bowman suspended in the space inside HAL's brain room, watching a small screen and listening to Floyd's "explanation" of the mission and TMA-1, which, Floyd ultimately admits, remains a "total mystery." As György Ligeti's unearthly music once again is heard, the film cuts to the blackness of space both behind the titles and in a shot that precedes the camera's downward tilt to reveal yet another conjunction, this one between Jupiter, its moons, and a huge monolith in orbit. Finally, during Bowman's transformation into Star-Child and the film's movement out of an eighteenth-century enclosure (what Kubrick calls a "hospital room"), he repeats the music from Richard Strauss's *Thus Spoke Zarathustra*—associated earlier with planetary conjunction, the monolith, and an important evolutionary moment. He then pushes the camera through the blackness of the monolith and back into space for the Star-Child's journey toward Earth. In ways that are reminiscent of both *Paths of Glory* and *Dr. Strangelove,* the film converts the familiar (in this case, the room) into the surreal and transports the viewer into a world where the ordered memories of time oppose the mysteries of contingent space.

Kubrick internally organizes *2001* in ways that likewise combine a minimum of explanatory clarity with a maximum of visual ambiguity. Clarke's third-person narration, for example, clearly defines the life cycle of a near-extinct tribe of ape-men on an African savannah, and how Moon-Watcher, the one hominid with a spark of sentient intelligence, senses the significance of the monolith's lessons. Clarke tells the reader what this moment means and provides a cosmic perspective from which to evaluate its importance to subsequent chapters. Kubrick, on the other hand, plays a malicious joke on his audience and simultaneously challenges them to develop more perceptive film-viewing habits. On one level, he makes the monolith as much a mystery for us as it is for the ape-men, unless we perceive an almost subliminal connection between the film's opening image of conjunction (Moon, Earth, Sun) seen from the Moon, significantly accompanied by the Strauss, with the longest-distance reverse angle in the history of cinema, the one that looks up from the base of the monolith and shows the Sun and a partially eclipsed Moon as seen from the Earth. While Kubrick directs his audience toward a visual rather than verbal definition of the film's complex structure, Clarke works in a medium that requires that even the notion of mystery be circumscribed within a system of temporal and verbal logic. In the novel, for instance, the monolith "means" several things (otherworldly machine, teaching device, cosmic alarm, and gateway to a universe of "pure energy"), while in Kubrick's film its value is defined by its shape (rectangular), its color (black), and the sound of Ligeti's monolith music, all of which associatively blend with other shapes, colors, and sounds into a cinematic symphony in space. As an element in Kubrick's objective narrative, the monolith has the same "meanings" it does in Clarke's novel. But in the context of an alternating and expanding cinematic paradigm, it becomes an otherworldly version of such artifacts and extensions as bone, fountain pen, satellite, spaceship, computer, eighteenth-century room, and crystal glass.

The narrative and visual ambiguities in *2001* would seem to have even less precedent in Kubrick's earlier work than in Clarke's novel, although certain revealing comparisons can be made. With the exception of *Lolita*, the films before *2001* are restricted in both time and place. *Fear and Desire* develops a single action of about twenty-four hours in one setting (forest). *Killer's Kiss* takes place in New York City, covers no more than a few days, and focuses on Davy's rescue of Gloria and escape from an alter ego (Rapallo). *The Killing* isolates a handful of settings and characters within the mechanics of a single plan in a time span of one week. *Paths of Glory* telescopes three highly dramatic events (battle, court-martial, and execution) within two settings and a time period of about four days. And *Dr. Strangelove* deals with the ultimate endgame within three enclosed settings during a two-hour countdown to doom. Each of these subjects provided Kubrick with a dramatic situation in which he could compress a great deal of psychological and thematic material without sacrificing the continuity or logic of film narrative. With few exceptions, the films achieve their conceptual and aesthetic effect through a structure of juxtapositions and repetitions from one setting and scene to another, while they avoid a more deliberate method of exposition or development that would confer autonomy onto individual narrative segments. Kubrick's film universe before *2001* thrived on associations and connections, no matter how paradoxical or surreal, and the workings of separate elements within larger and more ambiguous wholes. Johnny's plan and the racetrack become inseparable parts in a larger thematic and aesthetic game; the trenches and chateau project different forms of the same paradoxical truth; and the three worlds of *Dr. Strangelove* are variations on a single global madness. *Lolita,* even though its story spans four years, develops the same kind of involution through settings that mirror one another (Quilty's mansion and Charlotte's home; bedrooms and bathrooms) and through patterns of psychological doubling (Humbert and Quilty; Lolita and Charlotte). In significant respects, Kubrick's films always put the "cinematic" (images, sounds) in opposition to the "novelistic" (story, language, character), even though at times such a conflict functions on a level of implication rather than assertion. What particularly distinguishes *2001* from these earlier films is its frontal assault on the traditional conventions of Hollywood narrative filmmaking. The temporal range of *2001* spans infinity rather than days or years, yet the film omits explanatory background and transitional connectives. And spatially, it embodies a kind of ultimate cinematic universe, where all the assurances of "normal" perspective are literally turned upside down, and "settings" project either an eerie remoteness despite their authenticity or a disturbing lack of contextual and historical definition.

Unlike the novel, in which thematic elements merge with both the intricacies of a good story and the psychology of its characters, *2001* stages its emotional and intellectual drama within a visual and musical framework. Clarke, for instance, not only goes inside the mind of Moon-Watcher, but in moments of narrative drag, such as Floyd's trip to the Moon or Bowman and Poole's trip to Saturn, he does the expected thing by fleshing out the psychological texture of the novel. Although the film has been faulted for what some see as a "dehumanized" or minimal treatment of character, it could be argued that its space psychology is entirely plausible. Kubrick's ironic point that a highly intelligent computer—programmed to operate the spaceship and provide "companionship" for astronauts on journeys covering vast expanses of space and time—could assume an expressive humanity superior to that of sentient travelers separated from the familiar domesticities of Earth seems probable enough. What may be lacking in *2001*—and could explain this critical stir—is the abundance of earthbound "human drama" that we are conditioned to expect from most films. More important than a debate between "dehumanization" and authenticity, however, is how Kubrick departs from the novel's illusion of psychological depth and aligns character with the film's mythological aspirations. In each of the four parts, Kubrick places his characters in psychological situations that alternate between wakefulness, sleep, and awakening. Moon-Watcher (Dan Richter) huddles in a darkness illuminated by the Moon (an appropriate presence in a film about suprarational consciousness and transformation) and a leopard's glowing eyes while watching for the terrors of a primeval night. Only after he has touched the monolith does Moon-Watcher, over the pile of bones, show an awakening of consciousness. Dr. Heywood Floyd (William Sylvester), a twenty-first-century man with his primitive instincts well in hand, sleeps while his "bone" (fountain pen) floats in the weightless air of a shuttle carrying him to the space station. Yet when he is awake on the Moon, we discover that, as with Moon-Watcher, his childlike reaction to the presence of the monolith seems almost preconscious. Aboard *Discovery*, David Bowman (Keir Dullea) and Frank Poole (Gary Lockwood) take turns sleeping, and even in their wakefulness they seem lethargic and remote; their only companions are three figures in coffin-shaped hibernacula and a computer whose red and yellow eyes seem to never sleep. Only after HAL reasserts the primitive's instinct for survival by killing Poole and the three hibernators does Bowman begin to show indications of an internal "awakening." And in a journey through the Star-Gate's slit-scan corridors and in a scene on the bed of an eighteenth-century room, the film makes its final evolutionary leap and shows us, in Bowman's rebirth as Star-Child, the awakening of a new form of human consciousness.

Again, some significant comparisons can be made between the psychological structure of *2001* and Kubrick's earlier films. Beginning as early as *Fear and Desire* and *Killer's Kiss,* his first two features, Kubrick consistently showed a greater interest in states of mind and emotion than in character itself. Although the second film provides a backstory of guilt and frustration for the characters of Davy and Gloria, its best psychological moments—visualized in dreamlike and nightmarish imagery—suggest forces at work on the other side of consciousness. *The Killing* traffics in the very basic emotions of sex, greed, and a pathetic desperation, all of which endanger a "rational" plan, while *Paths* defines character within a more abstract conflict of politics and morality. In each of these four films, psychological issues are subordinated to Kubrick's development of ideas and perspectives beyond the comprehension or expression of any single character. And it is to his credit that these films contain several moving and poignant scenes, even as they encourage the audience to see the workings of larger cinematic designs rather than engage in a full emotional identification with any one of their fictional inhabitants. Only *Lolita* confers on character a function equal to more inclusive thematic and aesthetic concerns, mainly because its primary subject is psychological rather than philosophic. Even there, however, Kubrick offers his audience the means to escape Humbert's subjectivity and perceive both its self-deception and its pathos. And *Dr. Strangelove,* in a more exaggerated fashion than *2001,* totally subordinates "character" to satire and mythopoeic speculation. Perhaps, therefore, it is not so much that Kubrick's conception of Floyd, Bowman, and Poole is "dehumanized" or represents a radical departure from the humane sensibilities of *Paths* and *Lolita.* Instead, it could be that his conception of these characters—in its realistic particularity within a context of a dominating mythic generality—seems inappropriately small compared to the gargantuan dimensions of *2001*'s technological and spatial mise-en-scène. But, of course, that is one of the film's more obvious points.

While the concept of character assumes an almost nascent definition in *2001,* language becomes a tool as obsolete as Moon-Watcher's bone would be to a scientist of the future like Dr. Heywood Floyd. In order to make the film as complete a visual and musical experience as possible, Kubrick not only deleted narration and an introductory prologue but assigned dialogue a minimal expository function. The film is 141 minutes long, but only about 40 of those minutes include scenes where language has any importance. Consequently, the formal and laconic emptiness of the film's dialogue develops subtle thematic ironies as much as it illuminates the workings of plot or character. About thirty minutes into the film, after four million years have elapsed, *2001* picks up Floyd moving through space toward a meeting with the monolith and carrying with him an archaic and earthbound verbal baggage. At Hilton Space Station 5, in the Howard Johnson Earthlight Room (printed language makes similar statements, but with less circumlocution), Floyd's empty ritual of sounds in the presence of Russian scientists has hardly any more value as communication than Moon-Watcher's grunts of bewilderment or screams of triumph. At this second waterhole, Kubrick shows how battles for territory and tribal dominance persist even in the rarefied air of space. We learn, for instance, that the Moon, a dead and arid world, has been divided into American and Russian sectors, and that language, at least in its political and social functions, has evolved into a polite and banal mask (e.g., the "cover story" of a Clavius epidemic) for Pleistocene struggles.* Suggestions of other worlds and other universes elude these travelers as the evolutionary and linguistic gravity of Earth pulls them back toward moral and spiritual extinction. Ironically, as Floyd goes "up" to Clavius, Smyslov (Leonard Rossiter) and Elena (Margaret Tyzack) go "down" to Earth, where, she tells him, her husband works on ocean floors ("underwater research in the Baltic") while she travels in space. At no time does anyone comment on the wonder of their spatial environment or imply that it has stimulated an exploration or expansion of psychic or sensory experience. Significantly, the first spoken words in the film reveal that the one tool that could assist such an endeavor—language—has not kept pace with a technological entry into a universe far beyond the boundaries of Earth. The flight stewardess's "Here you are, sir" and Floyd's "See you on the way back" illustrate the kind of time-bound, linear vocabulary repeatedly used by the characters of *2001*. They ignore the fact that in space, directional terms such as *forward* and *backward* or *up* and *down* no longer have the same meaning as they do within Earth's gravity. Likewise, positional definitions of place and time seem primitive in their insistence that concepts such as *here* and *there* or *now* and *then* continue to have a Newtonian authority. Throughout the two middle sections of the film, where all the spoken utterances are concentrated, characters persist in the illusion that the verbal contours of Earth can chart a journey through the infinitude of space.

One scene in particular illustrates how language in *2001* works in opposition to a cinematic form of communication that constantly rearranges spatial perspective and spatial relationships. At Clavius, the American Moon base, Floyd tries to "beef up morale" during a briefing that takes place in a small room, around a horseshoe-shaped table,

---

*At Space Station 5, just after the Picturephone scene, Smyslov tells Floyd that the telephones at Clavius have not worked for ten days, which later can be explained as part of an American "cover-up." Paradoxically, communications are broken off at the same time that an extraterrestrial machine (the monolith) makes contact with an earthbound intelligence. The telephones of Burpleson AFB (*Strangelove*), it seems, were still dead.

illuminated by rectangular fluorescent wall panels. In this boxlike enclosure, where geometry commands a higher status than understanding, Floyd reenacts Moon-Watcher's role as bone-carrier and tribal leader in his polite but authoritative enforcement of an ancient pecking order.* As before, language conspires with politics and a primitive social hierarchy to conceal the discovery of the monolith, a discovery so immense that potentially it could provide the means for humanity to escape its bondage to those very instincts that now threaten rather than guarantee survival. For this scene, Kubrick not only used a small and sparsely decorated room to complement a sense of verbal and moral regression, but employed his camera in a textbook manner to visually outline the stasis and circularity of this world's thinking: He structured the scene by first making a "master" shot, used to introduce and conclude the action, and then by shooting a number of angles to be either inserted into the finished film or discarded in the editing room. In a long take (the "master" shot), we look over the conference table from Floyd's empty chair (which he occupies only in the beginning) toward the podium, where he is introduced by Halversen (Robert Beatty) to the polite applause of an audience. Only then do we hear his words about the scientific importance of the "discovery" and the necessity for both a "cover story" and "secrecy oaths" (to preclude culture shock on Earth). As the scene verbally unfolds, the camera neither clarifies nor adds to Floyd's "briefing" as it routinely cuts back and forth from one standard setup to another before it predictably returns to the original "master" shot. Significantly, unlike the scenes in space that precede and follow, where shifts of camera position and angle signal possible changes of perception and apprehension, these remain as conventional in their failure to communicate any "new" visual information as do Floyd's verbal responses to the mystery of the monolith. Later, aboard *Discovery*, Kubrick will punctuate this scene when he links the death of machine intelligence with the last words in the film, appropriately spoken by Floyd in another "briefing," this time on a tiny screen in the narrow corridor of HAL's defunct brain before Bowman's speechless gaze:

---

*The rectangular geometry of the conference room (fluorescent wall panels in the form of horizontal rectangles; a horseshoe table; a white podium resembling a small monolith) is complemented by the circular movements of the characters: Halversen moves to the left around the table and introduces Floyd, then circles to the right when he returns to his seat as Floyd walks left.

Good day, gentlemen. This is a prerecorded briefing made prior to your departure and which for security reasons of the highest importance has been known on board during the mission only by your HAL 9000 computer. Now that you are in Jupiter space and the entire crew is revived it can be told to you. Eighteen months ago, the first evidence of intelligent life off the Earth was discovered. It was buried forty feet below the lunar surface, near the crater Tycho. Except for a single, very powerful radio emission aimed at Jupiter, the four-million-year-old black monolith has remained completely inert, its origin and purpose still a total mystery.

Only when Bowman leaves the spaceship—and the almost irresistible tugs of Mission Control and HAL's 9000 twin on Earth—does he move through interior space into outer space and escape the tyranny of words.

Beginning with *The Killing*, his first novelistic adaptation, Kubrick's films repeatedly express an ambivalence toward language. We know how much his success as a film artist depended on written sources to provide a framework of action and character prior to the creation of ambiguous visual structures. Yet he constantly undermined and even ridiculed the authority of these verbal "objective correlatives." Excluding *Fear and Desire* and *Killer's Kiss*, which are based on original scripts, the films before *2001* satirically devalue words at the same time they rely on their temporal assertiveness. Lest we forget, *The Killing*, *Paths of Glory*, and *Dr. Strangelove* are full of "talk" and narration, even though it could be argued that much of it lacks substance or quality equal to its formal expression. In *The Killing*, Kubrick gives language a deceptively authentic and "objective" ring, only to reveal its limitations: the narrator knows something about time, but nothing about space; and the racetrack announcer expresses confusion over the killing of a horse, while we know the hidden truth. Here and elsewhere, Kubrick's film worlds suggest that understanding and mystery are matters of visual context and perspective, and not of words. A great deal of talk bounces off the interior walls of the chateau in *Paths*, but none of it reaches the ceiling. Instead, characters clothe a smallness of vision in an inflated suit of euphemisms, moral axioms, and hypocritical platitudes, while the visual music of the chateau and the grim symmetry of the execution, like the exploding shells over the trenches, metaphorically drown out these verbal encounters. In *2001*, several scenes of dialogue inside spaceships are shot silent and then enhanced by musical selections such as Herbert von Karajan's version of "The Blue Danube" (aboard the flights of

Orion and *Aries* with Floyd) and the adagio movement of Aram Khatchaturian's "Gayne Ballet Suite" (aboard *Discovery*). Very little, however, drowns out the complex verbal exchanges of *Lolita,* although in an appropriately Nabokovian manner they tend to nullify the authority of language as explainer or clarifier. Puns, innuendo, and double entendres function as a perfect linguistic expression for Kubrick's earlier tendency to oppose words with images. They aurally embody the kind of punch and counterpunch found in the opposition in *Paths* between politics as conversation and the chateau's visual splendor. *2001* imitates the word/image disparities of *Paths* more than it does the verbal involutions of *Lolita,* probably because the second is both too civilized and too decadent a mode for a psychological world that vacillates between insentience and a birth into a post-linguistic consciousness. In *Dr. Strangelove,* Kubrick shows the last orgasm of language in an explosion of bombastic clichés, overwrought euphemisms, and a strangulating jargon very much like the Mission Control "Technish" of *2001,* all of which accelerate the devolutions of Eros and Thanatos rather than the ascending flights of Reason and Imagination. The Earth world of *2001* may have dodged the apocalyptic consequences of Ripper's madness, but it clearly inherited the banality of his language.

What makes *2001* such a fascinating and enduring film is the sheer emotional and conceptual appeal of its spatial aesthetics, one that vibrates with a plurality of universes within universes. Throughout, Kubrick combines the linear demands of narrative with an associative and repetitious system of images, activities, and sounds to unfold a cinematic world moving on parallel but opposing courses. It is a world that not only ascends into space and descends into time, but collapses from within in gestures of reflexive mockery as it expands outward toward implied realms of the imagination beyond even its own 70mm Cinerama frame. In parts one and two, Kubrick links a prehistoric and eroded dwelling place with excavations on the Moon, and intimates that while Floyd moves up in space, he descends in time. Parts three and four parallel HAL's regression from machine logic to primitive instinct with Bowman's trip to an eighteenth-century memory room, as we perceive that journeys through space also involve backward glances toward both "real" and psychic time. Patterns of psychological doubling reappear throughout the film—the metamorphosis of Moon-Watcher into Floyd, the pairing of Poole and Bowman, and their symbiotic relationship with HAL and his twin on Earth—as Kubrick explores inner worlds that shuttle between extinction and renewed vision. Repeatedly, characters engage in ritual activities and inhabit settings that double back on the past and point to a new future in space: (1) in the celebration of birthdays on a primeval Earth, on screens and ships in space, and in a neoclassical room that magically appears and disappears; (2) in the evolution and regression of eating from an act of survival (the primate as vegetarian) and relish (the ape-man as carnivore) on an African wasteland to one of synthetic functionalism in the spaceships of the future, only to climax in yet another ironic reversal in the eighteenth-century formalism of Bowman's last meal; (3) in the development of those patterns of sleeping and awakening mentioned earlier, particularly the hominid's terrified gaze into a waking nightmare, the implied link between Floyd's weightless sleep and Poole's description on a BBC newscast of the dreamless voids of hibernation, and in the implied connection between HAL's death and Bowman's "awakening" as the astronaut completes the monolith's ancient mission by becoming a luminous beacon moving toward Earth and a new generation of Moon-Watchers and sleepers. Shapes of the past merge with and comment on shapes of the future. In the first shot of the film, the camera tilts up from the Moon to reveal a partially eclipsed Earth, and in "The Dawn of Man" it shows the Moon in a similar waning phase as seen from the Earth. In the process, one cannot help but notice that planets are enclosed circles within other circles, and that each occupies a place in a boundless darkness. Moon-Watcher's bone goes up in space only to descend, while a bone-shaped satellite orbits in circles. Spaceships create the gravity of Earth within large centrifuges, which provide a treadmill for Poole's jogging and primitive shadow-boxing, as well as wombs for hibernators in the twenty-first century. Externally, these futuristic machines resemble the fossil remains of the technological and psychic evolution of an ancient race. Everywhere one looks, there are eyes and shapes of eyes, either framed within a larger geometry or themselves framing and reflecting what is seen, just as Kubrick and his special-effects crew repeatedly create within the wide-screen frame an impression of screens within screens, of inner worlds within outer worlds. Overall, *2001* invites its audience to "see" beyond the earthbound (and film-bound) limits of time and self, and to experience a cinematic imagination that gives form to its own dreams of duration in the amorphous expanses of contingent space.

Within the four-part structure of *2001*, Kubrick creates a maze of visual and narrative motions that develop this paradoxical tug of war between centripetal (collapsing) and centrifugal (expanding) forces. Consider, for instance, these examples of how the film associates planetary conjunction with narrative doubling in parts one and two: (1) In a prologue behind the title of the film, the vertical alignment of planets (Moon, Earth, and Sun) and Richard Strauss's *Zarathustra* not only anticipate an evolutionary event but provide a cosmic perspective that both looks "up" (the camera tilt) and descends to Earth ("The Dawn of Man"). Ironically, the "space odyssey" of *2001* begins in darkness and time (Earth), and in this film universe "up" sometimes means "down," and backward movement in time precedes forward leaps in space. (2) In "The Dawn of Man," Kubrick alludes to the first alignment in the vertical imagery of that low-angle shot showing monolith, Moon, and Sun, only there an extraterrestrial artifact assumes a status equal to a planet's and locates a cosmic intelligence within the film that stimulates a sense of impending revelation in both the minds of the hominids on the screen and the audience in the theater. From this reverse angle, Earth is "down" and Moon is "up," just as the narrative declines in time only to advance in space. The monolith and its blackness become part of a vertical symmetry that points toward the darkness of space and opposes the horizontal and static contours of an African landscape littered with bones and projected in a series of still photographs, augmented only by the sounds of a desolate wind. (3) Part two concludes with a repetition of both Ligeti's music—including sounds of alien "voices"—and a second vertical alignment of monolith, Sun, and Earth, as the film comes full circle. Indicating that involution more than evolution is the theme of this scene, Strauss is not invoked either before or after six figures imitate their primordial doubles by descending into an excavation to encircle, touch, and photograph the Earth monolith's Moon twin, their humanity obscured by spacesuits rather than the hairy disguise of Pleistocene primates. Some four million years in film time after that initial tilt-shot from the Moon, Kubrick shows Floyd and his generation doubling back on Moon-Watcher, weaving concave circles of time in the convexities of space.

Especially prevalent in part two, therefore, are the first signs of a cinematic *déjà vu* that prompts viewers to jog their memories and participate in both the film's dreamlike reflection on its own past and its vision of things to come. It is not only the match cut from bone to satellite that stimulates such a responsive process, but an array of other associations as well. The camera, as before, initiates the second movement of this film symphony by tilting up and revealing a visual alignment of Sun, Earth, Moon, *and satellite,* just as the silent grace and harmony of the camera's slow and deliberate motions are complemented by the sounds of "The Blue Danube." This shot not only recalls earlier conjunctions, particularly the one anticipating Moon-Watcher's slow-motion expression of evolutionary victory, but also introduces several intriguing complications: (1) the initial monolith-conjunction of the film expressively announced the presence of an unseen but superior intelligence, while the satellite imitates the bone (another tool/weapon) and signals the existence in space of Moon-Watcher's legacy; (2) ironically, this shot's visual harmony represents a by-product of technology and space travel rather than a necessary enlargement of vision, as—perhaps—the nineteenth-century music (from Johann Strauss) in a twenty-first-century environment implies; (3) the bone and satellite are not only artifacts but extensions of the human race in time and in space, respectively, while the monolith ultimately functions as a gateway to a realm of consciousness where such objects, like language, dissolve into the void once their purpose has been served; (4) and finally, the monolith is a highly expressive film device that functions as an emblem, more than as an artifact, of the Mystery Beyond, while the space hardware of *2001* both asserts an authentic science-fiction landscape and expresses Kubrick's concept of humanity as Tool-Maker.

Floyd's trips to Hilton Space Station 5 aboard a Pan Am shuttle (the *Orion*) and to Clavius Moon Base aboard a spherical spaceship (the *Aries*) provide two additional sequences in part two where images of conjunction reinforce the film's early emphasis on visual and narrative circularity. In the first, Moon-Watcher's bone assumes a more streamlined and expressive shape in *Orion*'s arrowlike and phallic movement toward a conjunctive rendezvous with another ancient tool duplicated in space. From close up, the rotating wheel of the space station rivals in size a luminous Earth, while the diminutive *Orion* completes another harmonious trinity of artifacts and celestial bodies. More so than before, Kubrick's camera now travels in space on conjunctive paths and creates a *ballet mécanique* among itself, *Orion,* and the wheel, but not without reminding us of the presence of enclosed human spaces. Inside the shuttle, the camera implies a satiric alignment between the bone/satellite outside and Floyd's fountain pen inside. As the pen floats in harmony with his levitating arm, he sleeps before a "movie" screen that trivializes humanity's sexual instincts in its depiction of a banal love scene in a futuristic car. Through this pairing of external beauty and internal reflexivity, Kubrick, as he did in *Dr. Strangelove*, suggests the disparities between a technological aesthetics in space and evolutionary factors that create a counter-motion toward descent at the moment of ascent. But while Floyd sleeps like a baby before a screen, dreaming the memories of his race, the pilots of *Orion* watch computer readout screens that both visualize a complicated docking procedure and record through a system of coordinates and grids the perfect conjunction of two human artifacts disguised as futuristic machines.* Following the film's second "waterhole" scene, the one inside the wheel between Floyd and the Russians, Kubrick returns the film to space and conjunctive visions complicated by temporal and psychological disorders. Initially, we can't help but notice how the spaceship *Aries* resembles a planet as it keeps company in a single shot with the Sun and Moon, while inside the spacecraft it is another story. There we see Floyd reenacting the ancient cycle of sleeping, eating (through straws from a tray that pictorially identifies what he's "eating"), and elimination ("Zero Gravity Toilet"), and flight stewardesses walking upside down and watching on screens the formalized aggression of judo wrestlers. Floyd's two-part journey concludes with another docking maneuver—this one between *Aries* and the Clavius Astrodome—that resembles the union of a descending seedpod and a flower/vulva opening its petals in a rite of outer-space pollination.

Particularly through the use of screens and windows in part two, Kubrick develops a conflict between, on the one hand, temporal inversion and spatial reduction and, on the other, breathtaking 70mm visions of harmony and expansion. The space travelers in the early scenes are confined in a series of enclosures that prevent direct access to space itself. They inhabit spaceships, space stations, Moon bases, and spacesuits that frame through window screens the infinity of space. By contrast, Kubrick's camera—through its "inside" and "outside" trips, its angles and reverse angles—records these enclosed per-

---

*One particular shot and composition during the *Orion*/Wheel sequence recall an earlier film. Kubrick's camera, from inside the Wheel's docking area, moves back to frame outer space within the narrow confines of a horizontal mail slot, recalling the way in which no-man's-land is first visualized in *Paths of Glory*. For Floyd, as well as the viewer, space in *2001* represents a different kind of "no-man's-land."

spectives as it contends with the boundaries of a Cinerama frame that both registers its aesthetic presence and, as if to acknowledge the Mystery Beyond, encircles itself in a rim of darkness. In the space station, Kubrick brings Floyd into a setting that at once suggests an antiseptic cage and resembles the interior of Moon-Watcher's bone. It is long and narrow, curved slightly at both ends, blindingly white, and decorated with ghastly pink chairs shaped like surrealist rock formations; and along each wall are windows containing small-screen, fragmentary images of an enormous Earth and a boundless space far more at home within the film's Cinerama frame. Inside the Picturephone booth, Floyd has a "screen" conversation with his daughter (Vivian Kubrick), which in its banality (it recalls the love scene on an *Orion* screen) evokes not the mystery of the monolith, but a drama closer to man's dawn. It contains such revelations as a mother not being home, a babysitter in the bathroom, and a daughter's birthday and request for a "bush baby" doll. At no time does Floyd turn away from these domestic trifles to look through the window on his left, which partly frames a brilliantly luminous image of Earth. Rather than beauty and spatial expanses, his mind responds to the murky involutions that unfold on small screens, in polite conversation, and during top-secret briefings. Following the conference at Clavius, in an enclosed room with no windows or screens, Kubrick places Floyd inside a bone-shaped "bus" that transports him to the Tycho excavation and TMA-1. Again, exterior wonders conflict with interior comedy: Outside the moonbus and its horizontal movement over a ghostly but stunning lunar surface, we hear the faint sounds of the Ligeti monolith music and see a partially eclipsed Earth hovering in a dark sky. Inside, Floyd and two men discuss the mystery of a four-million-year-old monolith and the difficulty of distinguishing a "real" ham sandwich from a synthetic one. As he has done so often before, Kubrick places the familiar within surreal or remote contexts and forces his audience to acknowledge worlds unaccounted for by those conventions that dominate both psychological frames of reference and what we see on screens in a movie theater.

Reminiscent of *Dr. Strangelove,* parts one and two assume the characteristics of an involuted surrealist comedy: (1) A series of four fades, from the *2001* title to the discovery of the first monolith, mark the different phases of "The Dawn of Man," which describes a cycle, beginning with signs of the ape-men's near-extinction on an arid landscape of bones and sparse vegetation, to territorial struggles around a waterhole and the terrors of the night, and finally the sudden appearance of an alien artifact before a "magical" evolutionary event. (2) Part two begins by showing another silent landscape littered with "bones" (satellites) and illuminated by a dawn (the sun appears from behind a dark Earth), then goes into the wheel for a second "waterhole" encounter; it follows with people eating food no more appetizing than those roots foraged earlier, and ends with the appearance of another monolith and lunar dawn. Significant differences, however, indicate the film's satiric attitude toward its futuristic tribe of civilized humanity. As mentioned before, at no time does Floyd gaze into his world in an expression of terror or awe, partly because his vision is framed and enclosed, while Moon-Watcher's directly confronts his world. Technological man, the film tells us, exchanges vision for a self-satisfied security, and while he sleeps better than his primitive ancestors, he also loses the capacity to dream. When Floyd descends into the crater containing the monolith, he is not as well prepared as is Kubrick's audience to deal with its mystery. He remains locked into his spacesuit and frames of ignorance, while the theater viewers, with the help of some highly expressive film techniques, both transcend this reflexive content and detect promises of release from the film's circularity. Earlier, for instance, Kubrick used the subjective powers of slow-motion to suggest Moon-Watcher's elation and escape from extinction, while here the handheld camera that follows the six figures introduces an element of mental disorder into an atmosphere previously dominated by slumber and stasis. Lights around the monolith and Ligeti's music combine with camera movement and composition to enhance the importance of this scene. As in a recurring but incomplete dream, six indistinguishable figures move in circles around a rectangular totem. Then, in one striking shot, Kubrick blackens half the screen with a close-up of the monolith's impenetrable surface and shows Floyd emerging from behind its darkness on screen right; his gloved hand reaches out, like Moon-Watcher's tactile one, and ritualistically confirms its reality. Ironically, these men turn magic into farce when five of them line up in front of the monolith so that it can be framed and trivialized as a backdrop for a photographic memento. Kubrick completes this surreal moment by interrupting their efforts with the light of a lunar dawn, an event that not only triggers the monolith's piercing alarm but provides the necessary element (the

Sun) for his camera's low-angle conjunction shot and a transition to unfinished journeys into the mysteries of space.

Khatchaturian's desolate and lonely music sets the tone for part three and the actual beginning of *2001*'s "space odyssey." In the first half of the film, Kubrick's primary emphasis was ironic and time-bound, even to the point of linking technological evolution in outer space to a process of psychological regression. But in parts three and four, perspectives change as interior and exterior space finally come together and express a harmony found in earlier scenes only between machines or planets. In part three, the most complex psychological situation of the film occurs in an environment that recalls part two and internalizes the death-into-life paradox of "The Dawn of Man"—only now, a computer with human characteristics assumes control over a self-sufficient technological universe and threatens to reverse the parable of *Genesis* by destroying its creators. The fossil-like shape of spaceship *Discovery* reasserts Pleistocene landscapes as it floats through dark, empty space like a prehistoric leviathan. Inside this colossus, human consciousness inhabits a twilight world somewhere between insentience and a traumatic new life, one in which the involutions of part two pull against the expansive journeys of part four. Bowman and Poole become extensions of Moon-Watcher and Floyd, while HAL's "death" climaxes the film's treatment of humanity as Tool-Maker and provides a necessary step toward the symbolic implications of an eighteenth-century room and the birth of Star-Child. Visually, "inside" enclosures dominate "outside" worlds, and the use of subjective camera devices and disorienting angles signifies the presence of an important internal struggle. Images of circles and corridors convert the interior of *Discovery* into a well-lit womb of death where hibernators are aborted, and one character, from the darkness of space, gains reentry to destroy the tool–turned–Doomsday Machine and begin a new evolutionary cycle.

To fully appreciate the conceptual complexity of this section of *2001*, the viewer must recognize how it evokes shapes and images seen earlier. Throughout, Kubrick has emphasized eyes and shapes of eyes to complement themes of visual blindness and perceptual awakening. "The Dawn of Man" matches the leopard's inhuman yellow eyes against both Moon-Watcher's look of terror and his dawn of awareness. Floyd either sleeps too much or uses his eyes to express the ratio-

nal man's detachment rather than the space traveler's sense of wonder; he looks at and touches the monolith's blackness, as Moon-
Watcher does, but he fails to explore its mystery.* In contrast, Kubrick
assaults his audience's gaze with an array of shapes that convert aesthetic beauty into evolutionary paradox. The hominid's bone is transformed from a primitive tool/weapon into a graceful, bone-white satellite. Together with *Orion*'s imitation of a phallus and *Aries*' of a
head/planet (with glowing white eyes), it gives form to Kubrick's futuristic vision of technological man filling the lonely expanses of
space with artifacts and rivaling both the duration and the harmonics
of planetary bodies. Initially, for instance, the film teases the audience
into believing that HAL represents the ultimate tool for a human exploration of space. His manual dexterity (he opens and closes doors,
operates pods, and keeps the spaceship on course) and the rational,
mathematical precision of his electronic brain would seem to provide
an ideal environment for human discovery. Instead, Bowman and
Poole are HAL's tools, servants to his omniscience, and inevitably, like
Moon-Watcher's bone, nothing more than artifacts to be contemplated or objects to be tossed into space once their function has been
fulfilled. HAL's madness climaxes the film's thesis that machines, as
physical extensions of the human mind, merely sublimate rather than
transcend Moon-Watcher's instincts, while aesthetically they express
the rule of imitation over the struggles of vision. The outer space of
2001, like the Big Board of *Dr. Strangelove*, represents a mirror universe in which humanity shrinks infinity to the more manageable contours of mechanical form. Rather than toys, machines in this context

---

*In "The Dawn of Man," the hominid's sentient eyes contrast with the yellow glow of
the leopard's eyes. In part two, the detached or cool expressions in human eyes contrast
with the glowing white "eyes" of Aries and the glowing red eyes of the moonbus. In part
three, HAL's single eye, with its red iris and yellow pupil, seems more alive than the remote, glassy expressions seen in Bowman and Poole's eyes. HAL has eyes throughout the
spaceship—and always flanked by the screens of monitoring boards to reinforce the sense
that he "sees" and controls everything on a technological gameboard. In the birthday
scene, orange goggles enlarge the significance of Poole's eyes, even though they continue
to show only an eerie disengagement. The pods have a cyclops eye with two white lights
on each side that, when activated, make the machine look like an alien monster. During
Bowman's conflict with HAL, Bowman's eyes come alive and are framed in color and
light. In part four, Bowman's blinking eye fills the screen several times during the Star-
Gate sequence, and our first view of the eighteenth-century room is framed through the
pod's eye. When Bowman, as aging gentleman, looks toward the bed to acknowledge his
dying twin, he noticeably *squints*. And the Star-Child's distinguishing feature is his huge
eyes, which, in the last image of the film, look directly into the camera.

become our children, inevitably growing to gargantuan proportions and turning on us in acts of self-sufficiency. They perpetuate our instinct for survival even at the expense of inner growth; our love of beauty and passion for order; and, tragically, our secret longing for the immortality of the Inanimate. Only the shape and color of the monolith deviate from this anthropomorphic geometry, primarily because its mode is transcendent and futuristic rather than imitative and nostalgic. In part three, *Discovery*'s skeletal shape anticipates the demise of technological man, while HAL's distorted vision, which envelops everything inside but understands nothing outside, indicates that Reason, some four million years after its escape from primeval barbarity, has evolved into another defunct tool, one blinded by its own arrogance and mechanical certainty.

The psychological content of part three recalls the doublings of *Lolita*, but in *2001* Kubrick shows a character shedding his *doppelgänger* and opening his eyes to new perceptions. Poole's physical and earthbound activities balance Bowman's slightly more dreamy and spatial definition. Poole jogs and shadowboxes, wears gym shorts, sunbathes under a heat lamp (like Miss Scott of *Strangelove*), and watches his birthday celebration over a screen transmission from Earth while reclining between two coffin-shaped hibernacula. Bowman, in contrast, prefers to draw pictures of figures, like himself, who sleep away time in anticipation of an awakening in deep space. Overall, however, Poole and Bowman represent mirror twins more than true doubles, especially after it becomes apparent that a computer, not Poole, will play Quilty to Bowman's Humbert. Not only does Kubrick choose two actors with a significant physical resemblance, but he repeatedly places them in visual or comparative contexts that create a mirroring effect. Bowman is left-handed and Poole right-handed, and both eat the same food while narcissistically watching, on separate newspad screens, a BBC telecast (ironically titled "The World Tonight") in which their images, along with HAL's eye, are duplicated. Poole loses a game of chess to HAL (a foreshadowing of his death) while Bowman sleeps, and Bowman displays his simple drawings of the hibernators before one of HAL's appreciative fish-eyed lenses while Poole sleeps. In most two-shots, normally seen through one of HAL's eyes, Bowman occupies screen right and Poole screen left, while in one-shots an empty space or chair recalls the missing twin. When Bowman shows HAL his drawings, for instance, Bowman is framed to the right and an empty chair is prominent on the left; at the end of this shot,

Bowman brings the pictures closer to HAL's eye so that they fill the screen-left position. Later, when they talk in the pod just before the lip-reading scene, Bowman (right) and Poole (left) are profiled as twins, while between them Kubrick frames HAL's eye within the pod's oval eye. Included in this shot is the empty red helmet of Bowman's space suit, surrealistically staring, along with HAL, into the pod. In this single image, Kubrick both twins Bowman and Poole and doubles HAL and Bowman. Poole and Bowman each take an extravehicular trip outside the spaceship while the other watches on a screen from inside; and finally, after Poole is murdered by HAL's "bone" (the pod), Bowman uses another pod in an attempt to rescue his twin from the darkness of space. Both serve HAL in a janitorial capacity and depend on him for companionship, for knowledge of their world's status, and for the very air they breathe. In addition, HAL has a 9000 twin on Earth (the Jekyll to his Hyde), and his "character" is defined by shots of his eye, which recall both the hominid's watchful look and the leopard's yellow stare,* and by the sound of his voice (Douglas Rain), which imitates Floyd's language of calm reason. Through visual and dramatic associations, Kubrick both doubles Bowman and HAL and recalls the pairing of Moon-Watcher and Floyd. Bowman is first seen as a revolving and distorted reflection in HAL's eye (as he "descends" and rotates from the ship's hublink), and both experience a journey into memory at the moment of "death." HAL's life expires in the middle of a song called "Daisy," and Bowman, while reaching his hand toward the monolith, dies on a green and gold bed in an eighteenth-century room. Symbolically, HAL reenacts both Moon-Watcher's primitivism, when he becomes the first killer in space, *and* Floyd's blindness, when he denies knowledge of the monolith. Bowman, by contrast, both reaffirms the humanity of that first struggle for life in a hostile environment and transcends the earthbound limitations of Floyd's vision.

Consider the following rearrangement of the narrative logic of part three and how it reveals the importance that the film attaches to the HAL/Bowman doubling: (1) On numerous occasions, HAL expresses pride in his infallibility and that of his 9000 counterparts, even

*Herb A. Lightman (*American Cinematographer*) claims that the yellow glow in the leopard's eyes was an accidental effect caused by the front projection innovation. In Clarke's novel, the leopard is described as having "two gleaming golden eyes" (p. 31) that stare out from the night at Moon-Watcher. Clarke did see some of the early rushes before he finished the novel, but in his version HAL's pupil is not yellow, as it is in the film.

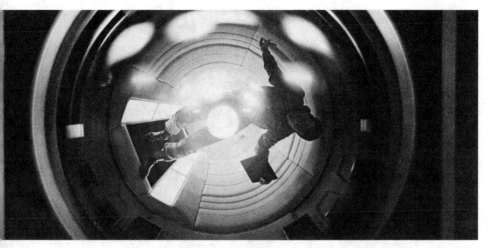

Bowman as a reflection in HAL's eye

though he knows that in the event of a malfunction his Earth twin will take control of *Discovery.* (2) In the Logic Memory Center, Bowman learns that, from the outset, HAL and the three hibernators knew about the monolith and the ultimate purpose of the Jupiter mission. (3) Earlier, just after he has looked at the drawings of the hiberna- tors—and we experience his distorted, subjective point of view—HAL expresses a latent insecurity about his "secret" knowledge when he asks "Dave" if he has any "second thoughts" about the mission. (4) Immediately thereafter, HAL detects a fault in the AE-35 communica- tions unit that connects the space travelers with Mission Control and himself with a 9000 twin. (5) When the tests on the AE-35 prove nega- tive, HAL finds it "puzzling" and attributes it to "human error," while Mission Control tells Bowman and Poole that the 9000 twin confirms it as computer error. (6) Bowman and Poole go into a pod, cut off all outside communication, and discuss HAL's "strange" behavior, and how, if the AE-35 does not fail as predicted, they will have to discon- nect (kill) him and let the Earth twin take over his electronic func- tions. Ominously, another subjective shot then shows HAL reading their lips through the window of the pod. (7) Finally, HAL murders Poole and the three hibernators and denies Bowman access to the interior of the spaceship, only to be violated by a forced reentry and disconnection. Quite correctly, most interpretive responses have cited this sequence of events as evidence that HAL's hubris combines pride and guilt, but neglect to comment on its importance to Bowman's

Discovery's twins (Gary Lockwood and Keir Dullea)
separated by the eye of madness

eventual transformation into the Star-Child. Why, for instance, does
HAL make such a simple and uncharacteristic mistake about a well-
functioning AE-35 unit? Could it be an expression of insecurity about
his role in the Jupiter mission and a desire to cut off communication
with Earth? After all, only Mission Control, the 9000 twin, and the
hibernators know the truth: that HAL's infallibility as a machine and
benevolence as a deity are compromised by his part in one of Floyd's
Earth-inspired conspiracies. Once programmed to be "human," HAL
loses the machine purity that, no doubt, his Earth twin still possesses.
He becomes imbued with a consciousness of his own autonomy and
denies his function as a tool. Therefore, his unconscious mind—
where, like a hibernator, the truth sleeps—associates Bowman's drawings with his own fallibility and initiates a plan to break contact with
Earth and the threat of his "perfect" twin. Later, when Floyd's screen
image and voice are brought into the Logic Memory Center, Kubrick
"explains" not only the mission but HAL's behavior, as that play of
light and sound represents the last flickerings of the computer's unconscious mind and the secret that drove it to madness. Bowman, on
the other hand, succeeds at the expense of HAL's failure. Symbolically, once Poole—Bowman's Earth twin—is murdered by his "ratio-

nal" and mechanical alter ego, Bowman undergoes a traumatic awakening even more dramatic than Moon-Watcher's discovery of the bone. He forces himself back into *Discovery*'s fossilized womb, destroys HAL, and frees technological man from the tyranny of his own tools.

In this showdown between man and machine, Kubrick creates one of his most evocative cinematic encounters. While the distortions of angle and HAL's fish-eyed lens define interior scenes and give visual shape to latent psychological disturbances, deep-focus clarity and symmetry outside *Discovery* reinforce the ambiguity of spatial darkness. More so than before, he characterizes space travel as a frightening and mysterious equivalent for the monolith itself. Rather than visions of planetary conjunction or luminous images of other worlds, he shows only a surreal spaceship or occasional meteor moving through this black universe. In the three extravehicular pod trips, the film takes its characters into this spatial context and, for the first time, creates a psychological syntax at war with the past tense. Each trip begins with a shot of the pod emerging from behind and rising over *Discovery*'s enormous head, an image of "dawn" and conjunction involving two man-made machines, but not the "magical" association seen earlier between planets and monolith. Such an image, however, does reenact a pattern from "The Dawn of Man" and anticipates the reappearance of the monolith. Later, *Discovery*'s head will assume the characteristics of a partially eclipsed planet (repeating an image of Earth in the film's credits) as it enters Jupiter's space and the alignment of planet, moons, and orbiting monolith. Inside the pod, Bowman and Poole's faces are animated by the distortions of red and blue lights from the control panels, and both look out through a window shaped like an eye. Each emerges from the pod like a fetus from a womb—with helmet tops shaped like heads and decorated with two "eyes"—and each drifts upside down in space toward the hull of *Discovery* like a newborn child in search of its mother's body. While Poole works to replace the AE-35 and the ship's link with Earth, the pod moves toward him with its dexterous arms extended like claws—its empty eye intercut with a zoom shot of HAL's eye inside the ship— and severs his umbilical cord, sending his body swirling into space. Inside the spaceship, as Bowman confronts the loss of his Earth twin, his placid mask starts to break up as Keir Dullea indicates the first signs of his awakening and transformation. In his anxiety to rescue his twin, Bowman figuratively loses his head (he leaves his red helmet behind), the one that protects him from an airless space but insulates him from perception. From inside the pod, his face changes color, and his eyes are framed in light as he searches the darkness and becomes the first character in the film to look through a window/eye in an act of spatial exploration.

Symbolically, Bowman now searches for himself, that earthbound twin whom he must shed before his eyes can open and experience the colors and shapes of the Star-Gate. He eventually finds Poole—now an object more like *Discovery* than like Bowman, floating in space like the remains of an extinct species—and cradles Poole's body in the motherly arms of the pod. But now he is denied entrance into a technological womb that aborts its children (hibernators), turns pods into weapons, and creates the sterile perfection of a reflexive universe. Bowman has no choice but to release Poole's body into the darkness and use the pod's explosive bolts to force his way through the red, uterine corridor of the ship's emergency air lock. Not since Moon-Watcher has a character in *2001* taken such a life-affirming action, although paradoxically Bowman's involves an act of divestment rather than accumulation. Once he chooses to survive and battle his way back into *Discovery*, Bowman begins a process in which he will shed a sense of self-identity (Poole as twin), the extensions of Reason and technology (HAL as alter ego), and the temporal reservoir of memory (eighteenth-century room). His prenatal breathing on the soundtrack and Kubrick's handheld camera internalize Bowman's last struggle against HAL's verbal authority ("Look, Dave. I can see you're really upset about this. I honestly think you should sit down calmly, take a stress pill, and think things over"). Significantly, as he disconnects HAL within the vertical red enclosure of the Logic Memory Center, Bowman speaks only once in reply to HAL's childish desire to sing a song ("Yes, I'd like to hear it, HAL. Sing it for me"). He then gazes in wonder before the innocence of creation ("Daisy, Daisy, give me your answer true, / I'm half crazy all for the love of you") and the experience of time (Floyd's prerecorded briefing). It represents a backward journey for the film as well, a return to Moon-Watcher's legacy, one that not only reverses but nullifies time.

Of all the sequences in *2001*, Bowman's journey through the Star-Gate represents both the most "cinematic" (visual) and the least enduring part of the film. When first seen, it was as dazzling for the audience as it was for Bowman, but I suspect it was not entirely unexpected. Throughout the film, Kubrick indirectly promises such a development, a pushing out into the world of the monolith and away from the languid Newtonian movements of a clockwork universe. Science-fiction films of *2001*'s scope normally require at least one pyrotechnic orgy, and an audience most assuredly demands it. Once *Discovery* enters Jupiter space and is dwarfed by a conjunction of orbiting monolith, planet, and moons—and the camera repeats the kind of upward tilt that began the film—the audience expects something "magical" and momentous to occur. And Kubrick delivers: The Star-Gate shows Bowman's escape from earthbound forms through both a screen bombardment of shapes and colors not seen before and the repetition of familiar images in new visual contexts. Bones, satellites, spaceships, and the previous predominance of black and white are superseded by slit-scan, multicolored corridors of light, crystal diamonds, explosions of worlds, fetal shapes, intimations of new dawns, and the sensation of rapid movement. Time and space acquire a plasticity not realized before, just as Bowman's face, through a series of freeze frames, undergoes a radical transformation. His blinking eyes become a huge and repeated presence which, as they come to life in colors not seen before in the film, recalls HAL's multiple distortions of interior space, except that now, like Moon-Watcher's, his eyes look outward in an expression of wonder. Earth-like landscapes pass below (Scotland's Hebrides and America's Monument Valley) but are visualized as color-filtered negative images of a universe on the "other side" of reality. Like the surface of an oversized camera lens where the refractions of inner and outer space intersect, it is a world of unbridled perception and "seeing" in which anything is possible and nothing is certain.

But in part four ("Jupiter and Beyond the Infinite"), as Bowman confronts new visions and new worlds, both Kubrick and his audience grapple with an aesthetic problem that, in all probability, has no satisfactory solution. How does a filmmaker give form to something "beyond the infinite" without a loss of thematic integrity or narrative consistency? For a start, he can undermine the authority of "objective" temporal structures—that is, the continuities of plot, character, dialogue, narration—and require, as Kubrick does, an audience to scan his images and sounds for an associative or symbolic logic. He can refuse to "explain" in conventional film terms such things, for instance, as why Dr. Heywood Floyd has less psychological dimension than either a hominid or a computer. To a certain extent, Kubrick plays all these cards, and sometimes he even does more. He turns a computer into the calm, impassioned voice of reason for a journey into the unknown, and then, in a flashback to the narrator of *The Killing*, uses him to parody the very concept of omniscience and detachment. HAL "knows" everything aboard *Discovery*, but, for purposes of "morale," he pretends (or is programmed to pretend) ignorance so that an illusion of "democracy" can remain intact. His role resembles Floyd's at Clavius and Kubrick's in *2001:* all seemingly give direction to the events in their respective worlds and ensure an audience (at Clavius, aboard *Discovery*, in the theater) that the rule of reason functions even during moments of mystery. Eventually, HAL's omniscience breaks down in a fit of paranoid uncertainty and then expires in the sounds of an electronic meltdown that expose this god as man-made creation. But Kubrick is no fiction; his reality is palpable, and although his presence informs every scene and image in *2001*, his omniscience is more imaginative than authoritative. In a gesture of creative fallibility, he all but announces through the film's conclusion that the Mystery Beyond eludes his grasp as well, that—like Moon-Watcher and Floyd standing before the monolith—he touches it without fully apprehending it. Just what are the aesthetic implications of a film, or a work of literature, concluding on such a note of uncertainty? Is it not an admission by the artist of his own insufficiency? While he and God create worlds with beginnings and endings, which by their very nature assert some form of cognitive order, an indeterminate universe never ceases to create itself in the silent expanses of infinity.

By his own admission, Kubrick did not settle on an ending for *2001* until just before he had to shoot it. In the original screenplay, he and Clarke concluded Bowman's journey in an extraterrestrial cage or observation tank resembling a hotel suite from the space traveler's earthbound memory. Bowman was to wander around in a room tricked out with familiar artifacts (a Washington, D.C. telephone directory, modern furniture, a ceiling television screen) and then witness the monolith's final appearance. According to Clarke's account (in *The Lost Worlds of 2001*), the Star-Child transformation became a factor in the script about two months before shooting began. Evidently, Kubrick was enthusiastic about this ending but had not decided how to reconcile it with Bowman's entrapment in an alien zoo made to look like a "modern" hotel room. Clarke's novel partially clarifies the ending of the film, although it does not explain why Kubrick decided to give the room an eighteenth-century definition. In an ending that resembles an episode in the novel *The Man Who Fell to Earth* (1963), Clarke's Bowman realizes that his mysterious hosts have duplicated a hotel room seen on a television transmission from Earth; he even goes so far as to characterize it as a "movie set." He eventually connects the room with the discovery of TMA-1 and assumes that it has some purpose beyond his understanding. In a chapter called "Recapitulation," after Bowman goes to sleep on the "hotel" bed, Clarke describes the room "dissolving" back into the mind of its creators as the astronaut recalls his past and finally is drained of identity: "As one David Bowman ceased to exist, another became immortal." On the simplest narrative level, Kubrick's ending does not depart all that much from Clarke's: The orbiting monolith, Bowman's Star-Gate journey, the Ligeti "voices" within the room, the reappearance of the monolith, and Strauss's *Thus Spoke Zarathustra* continue visual and aural patterns developed throughout *2001*. They tell the film audience that something "magical" is happening, and that Bowman as homo sapiens is evolving toward some form of spatial/planetary consciousness. Here is how Kubrick explains it:

> No, I don't mind discussing it, on the *lowest* level, that is, straightforward explanation of the plot. . . . When the surviving astronaut, Bowman, ultimately reaches Jupiter, this artifact [monolith] sweeps him into a force field or star gate that hurls him on a journey through inner and outer space and finally transports him to another part of the galaxy, where he's placed in a human zoo approximating a hospital terrestrial environment drawn out of his dreams and imagination. In a timeless state, his life passes from middle age to senescence to death. He is reborn, an enhanced being, a star child, an angel, a superman, if you like, and returns to earth prepared for the next leap forward in man's evolutionary destiny.

But why, for instance, does he use eighteenth-century period decor or have Bowman witness his aged counterpart breaking a crystal wineglass? What are the implications of this ambiguity? Does this mysterious scene have a legitimate conceptual function and complete the film's explicit as well as implied intentions?

While the experience of seeing represents the meaning of the Star-Gate, understanding what is seen defines the ambiguity of the film's last sequence. Subjective/framing devices, associative reoccurrence, and a sense of spatial/temporal dislocation merge the enclosures of memory and the involutions of cinematic structure—namely, the initial shot of the room through the pod's window/eye, the return of breathing sounds, as well as a mirror and doorway, the reappearance of the monolith and the disappearance of the pod, a handheld camera in the bathroom, jump-cuts and temporal ellipsis, the Ligeti and Richard Strauss musical themes. As Bowman sheds his earth-bound identity, as both astronaut and man in time, *2001* meditates on itself and, before its final odyssey into an undefined future in space, invites the audience to integrate the images and activities of the room with the film's "past." Bowman, minus his Earth twin and mechanical double, assumes an anthropological and historical generality before he "dies" and evolves into a mythic progenitor of a new race of man. Once again a setting resembles the inside of a bone or artifact, as Moon-Watcher's life cycle and Floyd's territorial regressions are for-malized in the room's stark white fluorescent floor, complete with chessboard squares and pale green and blue walls. Pleistocene water-holes and twenty-first-century space stations become indistinguish-able from a nostalgic eighteenth-century mise-en-scène, a process that encloses the astronaut Bowman in the primal and ritualized processes of human time. Odysseys and cycles seen earlier are now compressed into a universal human coda that travels from cleansing and a solipsis-tic contemplation of self (Bowman's aging mirror twin) to eating (for-mal table setting), from a final sleep and awakening (large bed) to death. Only the slightest hint of green (the walls, a dressing gown, a headboard, bed sheets, and paintings) suggests the presence of "veg-etation" on this landscape of death and the possibility of survival through rebirth. History and identity are merged and nullified as Bowman wanders through this surreal dream of innocence and expe-rience—his "Daisy"—and divests himself of temporal and mechanical form. He escapes the artificial enclosures of technology (pod and spacesuit) and the formal remains of pre-mechanical man (an eigh-teenth-century gentleman eating dinner and breaking the crystal glass), that missing link between the hominid/bone and Floyd/ma-chine. As he reaches out in death toward the monolith, like Moon-Watcher and Floyd before him, he escapes their legacy of ignorance before the mysteries of infinite space.

2001 brings the human race to the limits of its growth, where, like the bone, it is converted into an artifact that turns to crystal and shat-ters from the weight of evolutionary gravity. Bowman's last form be-fore death resembles that of a shrunken and fossilized chrysalis, trans-formed into a luminous and transparent bubble containing the Star-Child, who, with Kubrick's camera, penetrates the blackness of the monolith, escapes a room without windows or doors, and moves through space as a world unto itself. Earlier, Moon-Watcher's bone

ascended in space only to descend, Floyd's machines moved forward
in space while Floyd regressed in time, and Poole died in space where
now the Star-Child lives. This enhanced being carries no tools, speaks
no tongue, and contemplates space without the mediation of the
primitive's instincts or the rationalist's machine logic. The mirror
world has been broken, and beyond its reflexivity awaits the unknown
and unexplored. In the final images of the film, the camera shows the
Moon before it tilts down to reveal Earth on screen right—reversing
the upward movement of the camera in the opening titles—and suggests the beginning of a new cycle, only now the Star-Child assumes its
cosmic perspective. He enters the frame from the left to create the
film's only conjunction between human (not machine) and planet.
The Star-Child's bubble rotates like a planet, and his huge eyes look
not only toward Earth below, its home and destination, but directly
into the camera, like a humanized monolith mutely imploring the
audience to ponder its mystery.

6 THE PERFORMING ARTIST
A Clockwork Orange

As it often does in the film business, economics in the late 1960s put the squeeze on artistic grandiosity and forced Stanley Kubrick, at the moment of a great achievement, to postpone an ambitious project on Napoleon. No doubt it would have been an impressive sequel to *2001*, dealing with the paradoxes of history as inventively as *2001* had dealt with the mysteries of space. But a rollback in film production—particularly at MGM, which had agreed to finance the Napoleon film—dictated other choices and other directions. In the summer of 1969, Kubrick read Anthony Burgess's *A Clockwork Orange* (1962), a Swiftian fable and linguistic *tour de force*, set in the future, about the loss of ethical choice through psychological conditioning. Not only was Kubrick excited by the novel—"the narrative invention was magical, the characters bizarre and exciting, the ideas brilliantly developed"—but for the first time in his career as an adapter of novels to film, he could start with a *finished* story:

the story was of a size and density that could be adapted to film without oversimplifying it or stripping it to the bones. In fact, it proved possible to retain most of the narrative in the film. . . . Some of my films have started with the accumulating of facts, and from the facts narrative ideas seemed to develop, but of course *A Clockwork Orange* started with a finished story, and I was quite happy to skip the birth pangs of developing an original narrative.

The language of the novel, a Slav-based invention called Nadsat (Russian for "teenage"), is chiefly oriented toward sound (onomatopoeia) rather than concept, and the limited use of it in the film blends well with Kubrick's musical selections. Alex, the first-person narrator, prefers action and fantasy to the pontifications of abstract reasoning, and therefore inhabits an interior world accessible to the image-making powers of film. Burgess's plot structure emphasizes picaresque movement and fairy-tale coincidence, what Burgess characterized as a "moral parable" and Kubrick as a "psychological myth," where the central thesis is stated by at least three characters in different contexts. Alex constantly repeats his call to action—"What's it going to be, then, eh?"—which, in the moral framework of the novel, suggests his intuitive exercise of free will, while the prison chaplain and F. Alexander (in the film, Mr. Alexander) extend this theme into theological and political areas. By January 1970, the script was completed (Kubrick's first solo as a screenwriter), but the real work was just beginning. Here is how Kubrick defined his intentions in the film:

> I'd say that my intention with *A Clockwork Orange* was to be faithful to the novel and to try and see the violence from Alex's point of view, to show that it was great fun for him, the happiest part of his life, and that it was like some great action ballet. It was necessary to find a way of stylizing the violence, just as Burgess does by his writing style. The ironic counterpoint of the music was certainly one of the ways of achieving this. All the scenes of violence are very different without the music.

Most discussions of the novel center on Alex's character and his Nadsat dialect, and how they express Burgess's Christian belief in original sin, the importance of moral choice in a fallen world, and the dangers of behaviorist application. As a Catholic, Burgess accepted the reality of human evil—that human beings are more inclined to the bad than the good—while he believed in the redeeming grace of free will. If inherent evil is denied, as it is in the works of behavioral psychologist B. F. Skinner, and relocated in an external function such as environment, Burgess argues, our definition of human nature becomes dangerously simplified and life morally empty—"one in which everything is made easy, in which you shall be wound up like a clockwork machine and be good all the time and not worry about making ethical choices." Alex may be nasty and completely despicable as an ethical or social being, but in Burgess's ethos he is undeniably human: "He has the three human attributes—love of aggression, love of language, love of beauty." When the novel begins, he is young (fifteen years old) and does not understand the significance of his freedom; he exists in an imaginative Eden or Hobbesian state of nature, and only after he falls from a window in a suicide attempt does he show signs of moral awareness. In the original British ending (Heinemann, 1962), which is not included in the American version (Norton, 1963), Alex "chooses" this other course: at eighteen, burned out by teenage amorality, he longs for the domestic order of marriage and family. Although it was much debated, as well as openly condemned by Kubrick himself, this conclusion docs conform to Burgess's belief that human beings and societies are part of a cyclical process moving back and forth in time between goodness and evil, totalitarianism and freedom. In the novel, Alex eventually exercises a choice (like a *man*) in response to an organic and natural instinct (like an *orange*), rather than lose that unique human attribute through the mechanical (clockwork) imposition of goodness through aversive therapy (the Ludovico Technique). In the final analysis, he is neither a machine nor an orange, for in that last act of denial and choice he moves toward a more complete embodiment of Burgessian humanity.

A *Clockwork Orange* could be read as Anthony Burgess's "modest proposal," except that in its original form (no longer available even in the British edition) Burgess breaks from the novel's satiric style and overtly asserts a cyclical affirmation. Like Swift's essay and its outrageous analogy between political oppression and cannibalism, however, Burgess's work masks its serious intent through metaphor, satiric exaggeration, and ironic misdirection. It employs an unreliable first-person narrator—an ironic "persona"—who both shocks the average reader's sensibilities and illustrates the novel's satiric thesis. Alex's love of "ultraviolence" and his passion for Beethoven, especially the "Glorious Ninth," join together to express Burgess's view that cultural or artistic sensitivities are no guarantee of moral elevation; instead, they spring from the same source as Alex's anti-social behavior—human nature—and one does not exclude the other. Alex's Nadsat casts a futuristic spell over the action of the novel and provides a linguistic alternative to the tiresome slogans articulated by the proponents of social and moral order, whether from the Right (prison chaplain and minister of interior) or the Left (F. Alexander, author of another *Clockwork Orange*). The prison chaplain may believe in free will ("Goodness is something chosen. When a man cannot choose he ceases to be a man"), but his hellfire and brimstone oratory is far too severe for either Alex's pleasure principle or Burgess's irony. Moreover, while F. Alexander may deplore the clockwork State, in both his radical zeal and his belief in human goodness ("a creature of growth and capable of sweetness, to ooze juicily at the last round the bearded lips of God") he opposes his creator's more conservative and humane Catholicism. In such a fictional world, understanding comes to the reader covertly, through the intricacies of style and rhetoric, rather than in the direct assertions of character or narrator. In fact, not everything in Alex's story is as clear as his "unmuddied lake or azure sky of deepest summer." As Nabokov does in *Lolita*, Burgess creates a system of literary/cultural allusion—the subtext as text—that frees the alert reader from Alex's perverse grip and allows an appreciation of the novel's merger of artifice and thesis, its "choice" of creative mode. Alex lacks not only conscience, like an innocent, but knowledge as well. His sense of history is personal and solipsistic, extending no further than the three-year period of his "memory" story, a story in which he converts English history and literature (for instance, Queen Victoria, Disraeli, Shelley, Joyce) into the idiom of private myth. But Burgess is no Alex, and ultimately his tale addresses those readers who love language and beauty more than physical or psychic violence, which ironically forces them into identifying with Alex, and not with the behavioral engineers and political fanatics. He speaks to those who have struggled with their natures, made choices, and accepted, in the positive spirit of irony, the challenges of a fully expressive life.

In discussing B. F. Skinner's *Beyond Freedom and Dignity*, Kubrick revealed how his thinking paralleled and, in significant respects, departed from Burgess's rigidly dualistic philosophy. He agreed that any utopian view of man's goodness is a "dangerous fallacy," and he especially objected to the notion that human nature could be "explained" or rationalized in behaviorist terms. Skinner, it should be noted, opposed any form of negative (aversive) reinforcement, but instead wrote enthusiastically about how humans can change environment and inevitably control both stimulus and response—"Behavior can be

The artist behind the cameras of *A Clockwork Orange*

changed by changing the conditions of which it is a function." Somewhat mysteriously, he contends that such changes are mandatory if human beings are to survive as a species, that we all must shed the illusion of autonomy and go "beyond freedom and dignity" (that is, beyond romantic concepts of innate goodness). Kubrick, who in *Dr. Strangelove* and *2001* had considered the subject of civilization and its discontents, offered a thoughtful critique of Skinner's book when he described how

> it works on the premise that human freedom and dignity have become inconsistent with the survival of our civilization. It's a very startling and sinister and not totally refutable contention, and *Clockwork Orange* is very concerned with this sort of idea.

Notice the "sinister" and "not totally refutable": typically, he remained both skeptical about and open to a variety of ideas and speculations, no matter what their consequences or how they might have gone against the grain of his own philosophic leanings. Burgess, on the other hand, flatly rejected Skinner on the basis of a personal commitment to historical cycles and moral order, while Kubrick displayed an artist's fascination with the enigmatic and unknown. He opposed Skinner's concept of human beings as stimulus-response creatures for the same reason that he pushed Bowman as Star-Child through the monolith into space. For Kubrick, the inner universe potentially harbored as much mystery as the outer one, while in their own way both behaviorism and Burgess's Augustinian brand of Catholicism (in which evil is the norm and goodness a happy surprise) function best in argumentative rather than imaginative contexts. Hence, Burgess's *A Clockwork Orange* not only is didactic but develops a theme far too simple for the brilliance of its literary invention. Like other "modernist" works (including Eliot's *The Waste Land* and Joyce's *Ulysses*), it illustrates the thesis of moral/cultural decay through an ironic opposition between style and statement.

But human nature and civilization are not the only issues here. Kubrick, it must be remembered, brings the shifts and surprises of a contingent universe into any conceptual situation, while Skinner maintains that "contingencies" are subject to scientific control, and Burgess accepts them as a necessary element in an essentially Manichean world view. From *The Killing* onward, Kubrick's films repeatedly dramatize the intersections of choice and contingency, and how each works on the other to produce a series of paradoxical "responses." In their psychological tangle of conscious and subconscious acts, in the proximity of design and accident, these films embody his belief in the inextricable unity of choice and fate. Johnny Clay chooses to follow the logic of his plan, even after the intrusions of inner and outer forces far too complex for his rational design to handle. Colonel Dax in *Paths of Glory* discovers that in the man-made labyrinth of World War I politics, and in the absence of real choice, what matters is the pretense of civilized behavior, of moral form without function. Humbert searches for his dream of Lolita and instead finds the perverse Quilty, an objectification of his own degradation and a disguised fate. In *Dr. Strangelove,* the creation of "fail-safe" systems and Doomsday Machines represents the ultimate choice—a kind of behaviorist dream turned nightmare, in which a passion for control eliminates not only contingencies but life itself. By *2001,* Kubrick considered the possibility that in a future dominated by machine intelligence, human beings might lose both the commitment to and the instinct for moral choice. Moon-Watcher's discovery of the bone/tool is viewed as a magical occurrence, one in which inner awareness and outer mystery come together in a single moment of time, while Floyd imitates the hominid's territorial instincts, but not his capacity for inner growth. He and the travelers aboard *Discovery* have almost lost those essential human attributes that were as important to Kubrick as they were to Burgess. The love of aggression, the love of language, and the love of beauty have been transferred to machines, while human consciousness hibernates in a kind of pre-evolutionary void. HAL's "humanity" (his madness) forces Bowman to rediscover his own, and to contemplate the presence of an outer universe that paradoxically defies understanding as it stimulates growth.

Separating novel from film, the novelist from filmmaker, represents an essential step in estimating Kubrick's achievement in *A Clockwork Orange* (1971). If he had been a writer and not a film artist, Stanley Kubrick might very well have composed such a novel, except that his would have been less theological and more speculative. But consider these Kubrickian echoes in Burgess's work: (1) The narrative invention and doubling—as in the coincidental repetitions of part three, in which Alex suffers retribution at the hands of his previous victims—could be compared to both *Killer's Kiss* and the more sophisticated *Lolita.* (2) The reflexive intrusions that remind the reader of the truth of fiction and the lie of reality, such as F. Alexander's political novel within Burgess's fantastic one, resemble the involutions and self-reference of Nabokov's *Lolita* as well as Kubrick's film. (3) Burgess's ironic reflection on civilized pretenses, even to the point of diminishing the moral authority of its own linguistic instrument through Alex's Nadsat ("civilized my syphilized yarbles"), recalls the devaluation of words and forms in *Paths of Glory, Lolita, Dr. Strangelove,* and *2001.* (4) The blending of the ordinary and bizarre, of social reality and private truth, resembles the kind of surreal mise-en-scène that increasingly would dominate the Kubrick films of the 1960s. Significantly, the novel's first-person narration provided Kubrick with a psychological and narrative focus even more subjective and nightmarish than the one in Nabokov's *Lolita.* No character as important as Clare Quilty challenges Alex's insidious control or vision; indeed, Alex is the alter ego incarnate, the Evil One, who gleefully mocks the masks of normality worn by both the Humberts in his fictional world and the readers in Burgess's real one. But like Humbert's account, Alex's narration maintains a past tense (his "flashback"), and even though it moves forward in time from episode to episode, its content remains subjective and associative rather than objective or logical.

Kubrick described Alex's adventures in the film as a psychological myth about "natural man in the state in which he is born, unlimited, unrepressed" and likened him to Richard III:

> Alex, like Richard, is a character whom you should dislike and fear, and yet you find yourself drawn very quickly into his world and find yourself seeing things through his eyes. It's not easy to say how this is achieved, but it certainly has something to do with his candor and wit and intelligence, and the fact that all the other characters are lesser people, and in some ways worse people.

But his Alex (Malcolm McDowell) is a simpler version of both Burgess's protagonist and Shakespeare's diabolical villain. He is a character of intuition and instinct, a mythopoeic extension of human nature, one who does not think as much as he dreams and acts. He drinks "milkplus" in the Korova Milkbar in order to sharpen himself for "a bit of the old ultraviolence." He and his droogs beat up an old tramp (Paul Farrell) drunkenly singing a song, a scene that expresses not Burgess's theme of youth versus old age, but Alex's gratuitous love of violence. (It likewise prepares for later coincidences and dream-like recurrences—in part three, the tramp and his friends beat up Alex.) He orchestrates a battle with Billyboy (Richard Connaught) and his gang, not to settle an old score or to claim the devotchka (girl) being raped, but because it is an activity that gives him an intense pleasure. And he speeds through the night in a stolen car, with no specific destination in mind (one "home" is as good as another), only to revel in the visceral sensation of machine and body—"The Durango-95 purred away real horrorshow—a nice warm vibratty feeling all through your guttiwuts." As in the novel, the operative word here is *horrorshow*. For Alex, it expresses the good (from the Russian root *khorosh*, for "fine" or "splendid"), and, in the thematic context of the film, it represents the union of violence (horror) and aesthetics (show)—as demonstrated in Alex's impromptu rendition of Gene Kelly's "Singing in the Rain" (a detail not in the novel) while he prepares to rape Alexander's wife (Adrienne Corri). Particularly in the early scenes of the film, Kubrick characterizes Alex's dreamlike reverie in terms more of space and sound than of time, of seeing and hearing, of being seen and heard. Alex, for instance, rarely strays from his obsessive egocentricity to editorialize about sociopolitical matters (as he often does in the novel) or to satirize the corruption of other characters (as Richard III does). Instead, he ruthlessly demands the right to look at the world in his own way—even through one eye with a false eyelash—and to choreograph scenes for his own amusement. His dresser drawer contains several stolen watches, but his wrists are adorned only with decorative bleeding eyeballs on each cuff. Unlike his droogs, he shows no interest in profit ("pretty polly"), social position, or efficient planning, all of which are practical and time-bound concerns; instead, he searches for moments of private ecstasy, of "gorgeousness and gorgeosity made flesh." Alex wishes to render "gravity all nonsense now" by escaping into a world of "lovely pictures" (fantasy), sounds (Ludwig van), and physical sensation (action as performance). In Kubrick's version, he is the Star-Child of the Id, who, like an adolescent Quilty, explores and acts out the dark secrets of interior space as an alternative to "growing up" in a clockwork society:

> Our subconscious finds release in Alex, just as it finds release in dreams. It resents Alex being stifled and repressed by authority, however much our conscious mind recognizes the necessity of doing this.

In a wry twist, Kubrick turns his audience into voyeurs (Quilty's "Do you like to watch, Captain?" echoes in Alex's "Viddy well, little brother"), closet Humberts who watch in the dark and inevitably celebrate the monster's rebirth on an illuminated screen.

If the generic niche for *2001* is "mythological documentary," then *A Clockwork Orange* may be nothing less than a psychological "case study." However, its investigative method works from the inside and documents an imaginary world even stranger than the one that ushers Bowman through the Star-Gate to a final meeting with the monolith. As a first-person narrative—what Bruce F. Kawin in his excellent book on the subject would call Alex's "mindscreen"—it far surpasses anything attempted in *Lolita,* Kubrick's only other first-person film. Additionally, Burgess's prose style is more cinematic than Nabokov's, and neither the setting nor the subject matter of the novel posed problems in 1970 comparable to those that had troubled the *Lolita* project in 1960. The Production Code and the Legion of Decency were not significant factors, which meant that the violence and the sexual content of the novel could remain intact, while the setting of the action in England, in the near future, encouraged Kubrick to shoot on location for the first time since leaving the United States. In addition, it allowed him the opportunity to develop more fully a surreal style of narrative development that reversed the studio-bound tendencies of his three previous films. By bringing Alex's unique and distorted imagination into contact with perfectly credible environments, Kubrick's *Clockwork* gives the impression that the private nightmares of Quilty's Pavor Manor and Strangelove's Mine Shaft walk the streets of the real world and inhabit the domiciles of social normality—that psychological disorder and cultural madness are one.

Paradoxically, the film seems more "realistic" and contemporary than Burgess's novel, even though it derives much of its visual and aural power from the techniques of cinematic distortion. In opposition to Skinner's view that environment acts upon the "perceiving person," Kubrick's film, through images and sounds, shows how Alex and others transform objective reality into the contours of psychological obsession. For Alex, place or setting has no real significance in itself—whether it is the sanctum of his own bedroom (a "real" room) or the Korova Milkbar (one of the film's four sets), Alexander's living room (an actual home in Radlett) or his bathroom (set). Instead, each serves as a stage on which he actualizes his theater of instinct. All the tangibles of a random and concrete world—people, places, objects—become his props and backgrounds, which means that Alex, perhaps more than any other "perceiver" in literature or film, is a ready-made cinematic concept. His field of vision changes according to his psychological condition or conditioning, just as the filmmaker uses reality as plastic material, responsive to both the control of predetermined factors (that is, script and budget) and the unexpected directions of creative inspiration. Especially in his "natural state" (pre–Ludovico Technique), Alex's psychological world lends itself to the kind of expressionistic rhetoric that characterizes Kubrick's film:

1. exaggerated acting styles and pop-cult costumes;
2. stylized sets to suggest symmetry and doubling (Korova Milkbar, a mirrored hallway with a chessboard floor, a mirrored bathroom);
3. the use of unusual or ironic locations for symbolic purposes (a derelict casino for a fight; an audio-visual theater for Alex's "treatment");
4. severe backlighting for night scenes shot on location (near the Thames Embankment) and photolamps in lighting fixtures for

interior scenes, both of which incorporate the devices of *cinéma
vérité* (night for night; "available" light; ultra-fast lenses) into a
coldly modern and eerie photographic style;

5. odd-angled close-ups and an extreme wide-angle lens (9.8mm)
   for interior scenes to create foreground distortion (of faces and
   prominent objects) and tunnel-like compositions and pathways;

6. the use of a handheld Arriflex camera and a variety of subjective
   shots, including those of characters looking into the camera (as
   in the opening shot of the film and in the HOME rape scene);

7. the formalizing of violence through editing, choreography, and
   music (the casino fight), speeded-up motion and music (at two
   frames per second for Alex's satiric "orgy" with two teenyboppers), slow-motion and music (Alex's attack on Dim; Dim's later
   retaliation with a milk bottle; Alex's last fantasy);

8. an obtrusive editing style in moments of joy or crisis (for instance,
   when Alex is masturbating to Beethoven and during the killing of
   the Cat Lady);

9. the electronically realized sounds and music of composer Walter
   Carlos on the Moog synthesizer.

But *A Clockwork Orange* does more than record the mental landscape of a highly unusual character. Its narrative field includes not
only what Alex says (voiceover), what he sees (subjective camera), and
what he thinks (mindscreen), but also a provocative series of images
and actions that originate in the iconography of Kubrick's earlier
films. In that respect, the film becomes a *trompe l'oeil*, Kubrick's reflection on his cinematic past, one that puts an audience, like Bowman, in a strange room and demands that they look for signs of an
unseen intelligence. The opening shot, for instance, bizarrely links
the endings of *2001* and *Paths of Glory* to the beginning of *Clockwork*—
except that Alex's gaze into the camera more closely resembles the
leopard's stare over a Pleistocene wasteland or HAL's fish-eyed surveillance of a futuristic deathship than it does the Star-Child's look of
evolutionary awakening. And the world that Alex contemplates is
as black as the walls around him. The camera, instead of moving
through that darkness, as it does when the Star-Child escapes the eighteenth-century room, zooms back to reveal the symmetrical outlines
of a path in the middle of a world (Korova Milkbar) no more inviting
than the one that concludes *Paths of Glory*. But in this film we will
witness a life-and-death struggle between Alex's instinct for free ex-

pression and a social environment that prefers the efficiency of machines to human imagination, that creates HALs instead of Star-Childs, and that builds enclosed trenches rather than spacious chateaus. Throughout the film, the imagery recalls the corridors, paths, and tunnels down which so many of Kubrick's characters have traveled, toward either a waiting death or a dazzling rebirth. Early in the film, Alex and his droogs are seen as stationary figures against the darkness of the Korova Milkbar and as silhouettes at the end of a tunnel (inside a pedestrian underpass, where they assault the tramp). These images recall the terror awaiting Davy Gordon in *Killer's Kiss* at the end of his nightmare corridor-ride, the execution stakes looming before the three prisoners of *Paths,* and the three figures that close in on Johnny Clay at the end of *The Killing.* In a scene reminiscent of earlier Kubrickian travelers, Alex moves freely through the aisles of a music bootick while the camera prepares his way with a 360° turn; in another, he experiences his own version of the Star-Gate as he seems to fly through a multicolored night in the Durango-95.

Suggestions of primal struggle and evolutionary regression, of civilization moving in reverse, link *Clockwork* to the mythopoeic structures of *Killer's Kiss, Dr. Strangelove,* and *2001.* At the beginning, Alex is the bone-carrier and tribal leader who asserts his supremacy over Dim (Warren Clarke) beside another Kubrickian waterhole (a marina) and even imitates Moon-Watcher's apelike gestures of victory in slow motion. Later, the bone assumes the ironic shape of a milk bottle as Dim and the droogs turn on Alex and undermine the autonomy of this primitive raiding party disguised as juvenile night-gang. The fight between Alex and the Cat Lady (Miriam Karlin) resembles the one in *Killer's Kiss* between Davy and Rapallo in the mannequin factory, except that in *Clockwork* the antagonists are surrounded by a surreal blend of erotic art, black and white cats, and athletic equipment in a period home. And instead of such primitive weapons as an ax and pike, they use the tools of a decadent civilization—a sculptured penis and a gilded bust of Beethoven. Alex's fantasies of orgasmic explosions and death seen early in the film recall the apocalyptic ending of *Dr. Strangelove,* while in later scenes Alex becomes the victim of an impotent lunatic in a wheelchair (that is, his Strangelove), so obsessed by a desire for revenge and political power that he is more machine than man. Certain settings repeat the enclosures of *Dr. Strangelove* and *2001,* particularly the bone-white interior of the modernistic HOME (the White side of the board to Korova's Black) and its resemblance to Space Station 5. In this setting, Alex initially plays the primitive in his assault on the writer and his wife, only to return later and become the victim of a savage retribution at the hands of his "civilized" double (Mr. *Alex*ander).

That all this should be taken in the spirit of self-parody—as Kubrick's first-person reprise through the trick mirror of Alex's mindscreen—becomes a likely possibility when the conclusion of *Clockwork* appears to mimic *2001*'s pattern of cosmic death and rebirth. When Alex, wet and beaten, is carried into HOME, it initiates the familiar Kubrickian motif of *cleansing* (in Alexander's bathtub), *eating* (on Alexander's glass table), and *sleeping*. Only now, there are no flushings offscreen or Zero Gravity Toilets, no nympholept scribbling his dirty secrets in a diary, no crystal glass breaking on a fluorescent floor or regenerative green beds. Sitting at a table and eating, at first alone, with the sound of tinkling silverware recalling the generals' breakfast in *Paths* and Bowman's last meal in *2001*, wearing the red and white robe worn by his double during the HOME rape scene, and drinking drugged red wine rather than milkplus, Alex unceremoniously falls face down into a plate of spaghetti. Like Bowman, he awakens as a prisoner in an unfamiliar room (French Provincial decor), but unlike the Star-Child in his movement through the monolith, Alex and the camera go into space through a window, only to crash-land on the earth below. Ironically, this suicidal descent prepares for Alex's "rebirth" into a post-Ludovico world (or so he comes to believe), one that culminates with an "awakening" on a hospital bed and the discovery that he has been "cured." It is not only Alex's capacity for violence that has been restored—a point crucial to the film's ironic affirmation—but the possibility that someday he may choose to follow his love of beauty. Alex may not be ready for the mystery of the monolith, but he does escape his HAL (Alexander as double) and "re-evolve" into a human condition where inner growth and a free imagination remain two measures of hope for the future.

A Clockwork Orange was Kubrick's most culturally assertive film before *Barry Lyndon, Full Metal Jacket,* and *Eyes Wide Shut*. It evokes a formal and dehumanized atmosphere closer to the disco Seventies than the psychedelic Sixties. In part one, particularly, Kubrick draws as much attention to the psychological origins of a cultural malaise as he does to the specific aberrations of Alex's character. In the association of psychic enclosure with the demise of civilization, the film resembles the drama that takes place in *2001* after HAL murders Poole, aborts the hibernators, and denies Bowman access to *Discovery*. HAL assumes control over a lifeless world of mechanical objects like himself in order to preserve an illusion of machine infallibility. In *Clockwork*, characters inhabit equally artificial environments—mirror worlds—in which they sacrifice the complex plurality of the self for the simple perfection of mechanical form. Appropriately, Kubrick uses an extreme wide-angle lens in almost all these settings (Korova, HOME, the Cat Lady's), thereby creating another version of HAL's fish-eyed madness. Long before Alex becomes the Frankenstein monster of a clockwork state, social communication has degenerated into an impersonal and sterile intercourse—masculine with masculine, feminine with feminine, objects with objects. Alex disturbs this reflexive seance—and becomes the only regenerative force in the film—because he embodies the concept of the Other, society's shadow rather than child, more *doppelgänger* than twin.

The classical symmetry of the Korova, for instance, not only stands as High Camp mockery but expresses as well a conditioned society's transference of sexual fantasy and function to the solidarity and harmony of machines disguised as art objects. White female statues perform machine functions (as tables and dispensers of milkplus) and assume postures in a humiliating, sadomasochistic Grand Guignol. They can be either contemplated from afar, as Kubrick's camera invites us to do at the end of the opening reverse zoom, or "used" as machines. In one scene, Dim reaches between the legs of one figure ("Pardon me, Luce") to pull the phallic lever that dispenses milkplus through the nipple of a jutting breast, while the arms, in chains, extend backward in a gesture of erotic submission. In the first HOME scene, Kubrick creates a domestic version of the same world. Mr. Alexander (Patrick Magee), in his red and white robe, is first seen as a figure behind a prominent red IBM Selectric, just before Kubrick's camera records a conjugal distance in a track right that shows his wife, in a red pajama suit, engulfed by a white modernistic chair shaped like a lopsided egg and upholstered in the assertive hues of Korova purple. As before, decor—the arrangement of shapes and colors within a confined space—absorbs people as well as things into the configurations of a clockwork aesthetic. In the hallway, as Alex and his masked droogs invade this museum advertised on an illuminated sign as the archetypal HOME, mirrors on each side of a chessboard floor create a triptych that recalls the static duplications first seen in the Korova Milkbar. Yet seemingly none of this affects Alex, the only original in a world of machine reproductions. At the Korova, his sinister glare and his Nadsat bring a highly charged consciousness into an otherwise inhuman and somnambular mise-en-scène, while in HOME his improvisations resemble those of an unruly but creative child turning the tables on parental authority. Alex not only disrupts HOME's Korova-like stasis, but forces Alexander to watch as his wife is twisted into an animated version of a Korova sex-machine (except that her pubic hair is natural red). Although, like an adolescent, Alex first goes for the breasts (milkless, not milkplus), his sexual mode is phallic rather than oral. He wears a mask with a long red nose, which he pokes toward the camera and into Alexander's face; he carries a cane harboring a knife; and, as if to exaggerate his genital authority, he wears a large codpiece in which he stores rubber balls. Because this scene is inventive as well as shocking, Kubrick's ironic point is made. In the context of the Korova's sexual postures and its unnatural colors (bright oranges and purples) in the midst of a predominantly black and white world, as well as HOME's heterosexual sterility (the Alexanders spawn objects instead of children), Alex's rape of the wife/mother has the virtue of being a "normal" (even if Oedipal) expression of an unrepressed libido.

Alex's killing of the Cat Lady extends this sexual allegory even further. When first introduced, the Cat Lady is an upside-down figure in a landscape of erotic paintings showing women in various states of sexual excitement, either masturbatory or lesbian. Overall, she assumes a character and definition several steps higher on the aesthetic ladder than Alex's own Mum, making her the decadent rather than pathetic mother-figure. Em (Sheila Raynor), for instance, decorates her home in a ghastly combination of colors (electric blue and pink in the living room; yellow, orange, and silver reflective checkers in the kitchen), with discount-store paintings of darkly exotic women who all look alike. Moreover, she wears brightly colored Orlon wigs (like the statues in the Korova) and vinyl miniskirts to disguise both her age and her maternal status. Even her bedroom—seen only once, when Deltoid (Aubrey Morris), Alex's "Post Corrective Adviser," plays the role of surrogate father/castrator (he punishes the truant in the crotch)—exemplifies the same kind of dehumanized nightmare found elsewhere. The pink walls and green bedspread attest to her bad taste, not to visions of rebirth. And the presence of white wig forms without eyes or mouths, and dentures without a head in a glass

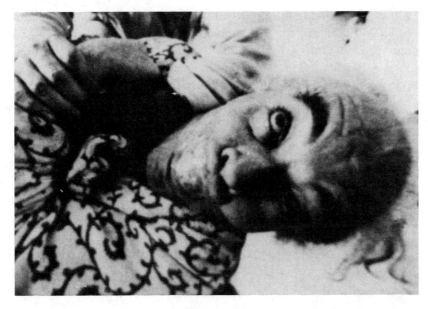

The victim as voyeur (Patrick Magee)

of water—respectively staring and grinning toward the camera in unison with Deltoid on the bed—aligns this lower-middle-class domicile with the Korova's and Cat Lady's more decadent aberrations. But the Cat Lady totally denies her procreative function (one which Em, like Charlotte in *Lolita,* symbolically denies). She lives amid lesbian self-portraits (including a face with mouths within mouths, and teeth to link her with the grinning dentures), colors herself like an art object (heavy lipstick on a large mouth, red-tinted hair, green and white leotards), and twists her body into contortions as if to replicate an abstract piece of sculpture or her own "health farm" exercise equipment. This psychosexual landscape, like the Korova, suggests not only that sexual function has been replaced by sexual extensions, but that human beings, machine-like, imitate the objects of their own creation. As a female masturbatory nightmare, the Cat Lady's room both opposes the masculine fantasies of the Korova and symbolically castrates them. In one shot, for instance, a boot being caressed by a woman in one of the paintings appears to kick the sculptured penis, on the table below, in the testes. And before Alex brings his decidedly phallic sexuality into this domain, we notice that only two objects— the penis and Beethoven's bust—have a male association, and each, to quote the Cat Lady, is a "very important work of art." Alex (and

Kubrick's handheld camera) disrupts this narcissistic world, which the Cat Lady identifies as a "real" person's house, and turns an object of contemplation into a tool/weapon when, in an act that is simultaneously murder and oral copulation, he crashes the bone-white phallus into the Cat Lady's mouth. Symbolically, he actualizes his culture's almost extinct unconscious (she uses the bust as weapon), gives its artifacts a renewed function (albeit a violent one), and increasingly assumes the role of life-force as well as scourge.

During Alex's nocturnal adventures in the early scenes of *Clockwork*, from Korova to private orgasm, Kubrick builds a progression of music, images, and events into a mock-heroic preamble. Alex, like Moon-Watcher, inhabits a wasteland littered with bones, only here they are the aesthetic remains of a mechanical civilization of the future. He is a child of darkness, a satiric spirit of life, who awakens from the sleep of the dead to act out his worst dreams and bring a renewed vitality and function to the people and things of his world. Notice, for instance, how the following outline of Alex's journey through the night evokes the resonance of such a myth:

1. The film begins with the dark, processional sounds of Purcell's "Music for Queen Mary's Funeral" on the Moog, an appropriately surreal rendering in the context of both the Korova's decor and Alex's Nadsat. Alex's face and eyes fill the screen, just as the glaring countenance of Beethoven on a window-blind will dominate his room during a triumphant masturbatory fantasy, while from long shot, he and his droogs seem to slumber inside the womb of a cultural death-chamber.

2. Next, Alex and his droogs appear as shadows in a uterine tunnel, quadruplets ruling the night, while the only sounds heard are the tramp's nostalgic "Sweet Molly Malone" and Alex's mockery in voice-over. Spotlighted from behind, Alex and the droogs applaud the tramp's efforts before descending on him like a pack of carnivores from man's twilight more than his dawn.

3. Rossini's "Thieving Magpie"—a lighter piece than the Purcell—ushers us into the derelict casino for an invigoratingly satiric showdown between rival gangs. The camera zooms back from a flowered landscape in pastel and a gilded proscenium arch with a Zeus-like head at its apex—relics of a more romantic age—to reveal below a stage "spotlighted" in a purple glow, surreal heads of laughing dummies against the wall, and, *in medias res,* the rape of a young woman with large breasts. A piano, a broken roulette table, and debris strewn

on the floor before the stage complete the decor. The fight itself, a surprisingly bloodless affair, is a graceful ballet of music and movement (stunts and fast-paced editing) that effectively captures the reverie of Alex's mindscreen and its merger of instinct and performance.

4. After the nightride in the Durango-95, Rossini gives way to HOME's doorchime (a chord from Beethoven's Fifth) and Alex's "Singing in the Rain," staged as a parody of Gene Kelly's song and dance from the 1952 MGM musical. In place of an umbrella, Alex uses his cane as both dance prop and weapon, for as the song says, he has that "glorious feeling" and is "ready for love." He overturns Alexander's bookshelves and writing desk, emblems of a humane past as extinct as the aesthetic traditions and games of chance found in the derelict casino. On a white wall hangs a modern landscape painting, which becomes especially prominent as a backdrop to the rape itself and recalls the artwork that presided over the fight with Billyboy's gang. In the end, Alex's grotesquely masked appearance and Alexander's face—distorted in close-up by the wide lens and a ball protruding from his taped mouth—form complementary images of Alex the performer and Alexander the voyeur.

5. Then, all "shagged and fagged and fashed," Alex and his band of merry players return to the Korova and hear a woman (a "sophisto" from a TV studio), with a gold frame highlighting her eyes like a proscenium arch, sing a fragment of Schiller's "Ode to Joy" from Beethoven's Ninth. Alex is an appreciative audience, while Dim exercises the privilege of the unenlightened by moronically blowing a raspberry (for which he receives a rap from Alex's cane).

6. Finally, Alex walks home to the music of Purcell, through the clutter of Municipal Flatblock 18A (a Thames architectural project), passes a blandly idealized socialist mural ("The Dignity of Labor") decorated with juvenile graffiti, and relieves himself in his bathroom. With the sounds of the scherzo from Beethoven's Ninth filling his bedroom, the camera prepares for Alex's orgasmic climax through a series of startling images. Successive zooms move closer and closer to Beethoven's face on the shade, until his eyes stare directly into the camera, then to a painting of a nude woman blissfully smiling in a pose of sexual invitation and a pan down to Alex's snake, Basil, curled around a branch, seemingly about to enter the vaginal opening. Then, within the same shot, four Christ statues on Alex's dresser, joined in a passion of celebration (crown of thorns, nails in wrists, red hair, genitals, right fists raised in defiance and left feet extended in

dance), convert crucifixion into performance. The faces of Christ, Alex, and Beethoven then come together in a prelude to that imaginary ride through a private Star-Gate dominated by a repeated close-up of Alex/Dracula, bloody fangs and all, presiding over a B-movie apocalypse of hanging figures, avalanches, and doomsday explosions.

As these sequences demonstrate, Alex works from the inside out —from fantasy to performance—as he transforms the lifeless settings and cultural mythology of an overly conditioned society into a new order of truth. Not content to remain a slumping figure in the static decor of the Korova or to become lost in a sentimental and boozy journey into the past (the tramp, like Alex, leans against a darkened wall), Alex gives form to his imaginative life through action and performance. The derelict casino symbolizes the decline of imagination (theater) and a belief in chance, which intersect in an act of creation and oppose the repressive aims of a clockwork state. And this setting perfectly suits Alex's dreamlike character. He travels through the night impulsively, seizes the moment and spins the wheel, and envisions action as a theatrical mixture of dancelike movement and music. He does not separate mind from body, reflection from action, the unconscious from social reality; nor does he transfer his sexual or violent urges onto objects and become, like others, a voyeur of his own degradation. Instead, he forces Alexander to watch the rape of his wife—a primal scene in reverse, where the father watches the Oedipal moment—and to confront a complex humanity which, by part three of the film, Alexander and his madness share with Alex. Significantly, Alexander does not close his eyes or avert his gaze—it is a *horrorshow* that holds the same fascination for him as it does for his adolescent double. Alex may stand and watch, even applaud, the tramp's song or Billyboy's gangbang, but ultimately he is a performer, not a voyeur, and he gives his inner world both a violent substance and an aesthetic form. Performance rather than sublimation defines his mode. Similarly, he transforms the Christian idea of the Fortunate Fall (that Adam's sin bestowed on humanity the moral freedom of choice and the possibility of redemption) into a celebration of pleasure, the liberation of the libido from the restraints of perfection, the bestowing onto humanity of the gift of multiplicity. Alex's Eve (in the painting) opens her legs for Basil because in this futuristic parable, Eden represents the original clockwork state, and the snake, like Alex, becomes a sign of the Other. Kubrick's Alex reverses the Freudian notion that multiplicity in the human personality often leads to psychosis, that repression is not only inevitable but necessary and benevolent. His character exhibits a wholeness of mind and body absent in such mechanical caricatures as Pee (Philip Stone) and Em, Deltoid, and Alexander. Rather than fetishizing Beethoven's music and Christ's suffering as aesthetic or spiritual objects, he experiences them as emotional and physical realities. Beethoven's face, like Alex's, confronts the audience in close-up with the artist's interiority, while Alex's Christ is both pluralistic (four in all) and an entertainer with balls, one who mocks the passive glory attached to religious suffering and defiantly celebrates the triumph of body over spirit. Because he lives in a decadent world, in which the mechanics of sublimation are so pervasive that the conscious mind not only rules the body and its instincts but turns it into a machine, Alex's humanity can be expressed only through violence and creative improvisation.

Not surprisingly, this journey through the geography and iconography of Alex's mindscreen has several ironic complications and stands in sharp relief to Kubrick's omniscience. Alex's originality as an artist/performer exists on a primitive level, in that Alex takes received images and sounds—cultural systems—and rearranges them into an egocentric paradigm that is more preconscious than intuitive, parochial rather than catholic. In parts one and two, especially, he fails to express a *chosen* middle ground between his enslavement to instinct and a forced acquiescence to the dictates of a clockwork society. The music of Rossini, for instance, both inspires his violent improvisations ("lovely music that came to my aid") and functions as an integral component in their enactment ("Thieving Magpie" for the casino/marina fights and the killing of the Cat Lady, "William Tell Overture" for the orgy), while Beethoven's Ninth sweeps him into a state of private ecstasy ("Oh, bliss . . . bliss and heaven. . . . It was like a bird of rarest spun heaven metal or like silvery wine flowing in a space ship") and triggers an internal *horrorshow*, Alex's Cinema of the Id. He experiences the fight with Billyboy's gang as a stylized barroom brawl, reminiscent of the choreography found in a musical such as *West Side Story* (1961) or a classic Western such as *Dodge City* (1939). Inside this mental screening room, Alex transforms himself into a Hammer horror film performer (in this instance, Christopher Lee's Dracula) who incongruously directs a series of deaths and stock-footage disasters reminiscent of the 1960s Hercules epics from Dino de Laurentiis. Ironically, this "outer-space" reverie resembles a subspecies of a midnight horror-camp classic like *The Rocky Horror Picture Show* (1975)

more than it does the extraterrestrial visions of *2001*. Alex's imagination repeatedly asserts a juvenile fondness for creative parody and re-
structuring of a Hollywood-induced film mentality. His mindscreen
reverses the sentimental and melodramatic formulas associated with
popular film storytelling, just as Kubrick's film not only frustrates
conventional expectations and sympathies but undercuts a mindless
identification with Alex, its nominal "humble narrator" and resident
cinéaste. In that context, part one of *Clockwork* portrays the rude beginnings of Alex's artistic evolution—his "dawn"—in which a creative
vitality is threatened with extinction by the clockwork intrusions of a
highly mechanical and repressed society. And finally, we should not
neglect to mention Malcolm McDowell's brilliantly innovative but
controlled performance. Through a blending of facial expressiveness
and body kinetics, McDowell fully objectifies Alex's progress from the
enfant terrible of part one, through the ordeal of conditioning and
mechanical transformation in part two, to the struggles of rebirth in
part three. His is one of the most underrated performances of the
1970s in one of that decade's least understood films.

Parts two and three of *Clockwork,* characterized by the slow movement
from Rossini's "William Tell Overture" and Alex's voiceover as "the
real weepy and tragic part of the story," show our "friend and humble
narrator" moving from artist/performer to victim/voyeur. For Alex as
well as film viewer, it represents a symbolic descent from the mysteries
of inner space into the real but sinister order of exterior time. It is as
if we had traveled through a surreal landscape of wonders and nightmares, a Star-Gate in reverse, only to double back and discover that
we had never left the gravity of temporality—of causal logic and mechanical process, the "science" of stimulus-response psychology and
the art of linear filmmaking. In Kubrick's vision, as far back as *The
Killing,* the clockwork state (of mind, as well as that of the body poli-
tic) prefers to take that which is complex or otherwise intractable and
diminish it to a level of predictability compatible with any one of several process-systems. The state always prefers such reduction to exploration and speculation. In the prison scenes, Alex's identity is quickly
reduced from "Alexander de Large" (the Great) to a number
(655321) by the chief guard (Michael Bates), the film's most amusing
example of mechanical man. Alex toes the white line in a prison reception center decorated with horizontal rows of shelved boxes (civil-
ian clothes in mothballs), a desk for personal inventories (Alex's be-

gins with half a bar of chocolate and ends with a "Timawrist" watch),
tables for stripping and physical identification (where Alex bends
over for a rectal), and tubs for cleaning the body. For his soul, Alex
confronts the dubious *choice* between the prison chaplain's (Godfrey
Quigley) "incontrovertible evidence that Hell exists" (from his "visions") and the biological conditioning of the Ludovico Technique.
On a platform/stage in the prison chapel, Alex becomes the object of
"leering criminals and perverts" while he turns an overhead projector
that displays the ironic words of a hymn ("I was a wandering sheep")
about the evil of straying from the fold ("I was a wayward child / I did
not love my home") and the necessity of *control* ("I did not love my
shepherd's voice / I would not be controlled"). Later, he is bound in
a straitjacket inside a theater—his head wreathed by the straps and
electronic plugs of a Frankenstein crown of thorns, his eyes held open
by lidlocks—and forced to watch, but not participate in, hackneyed
film versions of his past history, namely droogs tolchocking a man
(the tramp scene) and raping a devotchka (the casino). In each case,
he finds himself defined within the time-bound category of incorri-
gible sinner/criminal, and thereby falls victim to an institutional monolith (State/Church/Science) that would deprive him of *his* visions
(of violence and beauty) by transforming him into the ultimate Clockwork Man, a two-way mirror, at once an object for others to contemplate and a voyeur.

Even as he brings Alex down to earth and adjusts the visual/aural
style of the film to a more "objective" and less expressionistic mode,
Kubrick continues to develop associative details that provide the audience with sources of understanding independent of his protagonist's
first-person manipulations. In other words, *A Clockwork Orange* illustrates the dangers of psychological conditioning in both a social context (Alex's plight) and a cinematic one (Kubrick's film). On one
level, Alex's screen duplicates our own, which means that it can mesmerize as well as brainwash us into a condition of total identification.
If we fail to escape Alex's control, we become *his* victims and voyeurs
of *our* psychological disorder. Yet when we *choose* to acknowledge Kubrick's dreamlike presence—the "real" performing artist—through a
recognition of the symbolic or associative structure of the film, we
throw ourselves into a contingent world where almost anything is possible and nothing is certain. Consider how the following visual and
aural patterns reveal this disparity between Alex's mindscreen and the
filmmaker's intentions. In Alex's single fantasy in part two (from pris-

on reception to Ludovico release), a biblically inspired vision of Sodom and Gomorrah (the scourging of Christ, the cutting of throats in
battle, and the despoiling of Jewish handmaidens), Kubrick once
again draws attention to a primitive cinematic imagination. Alex's simulacrum is satiric, certainly—his fantasy assumes a cliché-ridden film
style reminiscent of the biblical movie epics of the 1950s, complete
with the bombastic chords of Rimsky-Korsakov's "Scheherezade"
(Rimsky-Korsakov is the Miklos Rozsa of classical music), while his
focus suggests the inspirations of a Marquis de Sade rather than a
Cecil B. DeMille.* And, no doubt, the scene offered Kubrick another
opportunity to exorcise some private demons having to do with
Spartacus, his only film mounted in Alex's "height of Roman fashion."
Of greater significance, however, are the parallels between this scene
and others. The Christ figure, with his wooden cross and crown of
thorns, recalls the statuary in Alex's bedroom, although here his passion is given a more old-fashioned ("realistic") film treatment, even
down to the obviously painted blood on his forehead (a throwback to
the days of the Production Code). Later, in an audio-visual theater,
Alex wears the Ludovico crown of thorns and watches a man being
beaten in a film that likewise clashes with the visual originality of
Kubrick's film. Alex, however, likes what he sees, particularly the
blood on the victim's face ("the red, red vino on tap"), and even expresses the aesthetic judgment that "the colours of the real world only
seem really real when you viddy them on the screen." Yet the blood on
the screen-victim's face is blatantly artificial and contrasts with an earlier scene in a police interrogation room, where Alex's blood (on his
face and a white wall) seems far more "real" *on our screen* than what is
seen on the screen in the Ludovico facility. Finally, after Alex is beaten
in part three by Dim and Georgie (James Marcus), who are now policemen in Her Majesty's Service, Julian (David Prowse, who plays
Darth Vader in three *Star Wars* films), Alexander's strong-man com-

---

*Anyone who grew up watching the American *film noir* of the 1940s and 1950s, as
Kubrick himself did, would be familiar with the sounds of Hungarian-born Hollywood
composer Miklos Rozsa. His distinctive form of invigorating musical bombast enhanced
an impressive number of *noir* films—*Double Indemnity* (1944), *Spellbound* (1945), *The Killers* (1946), *Brute Force* (1947), *The Naked City* (1948), and *The Asphalt Jungle* (1950). What is
particularly interesting, however, given the parody implied in Kubrick's selection of
"Scheherezade" for Alex's scourging-of-Christ fantasy, is the fact that during the 1950s
and 1960s, Rozsa scored a number of biblical or epic behemoths, among them *Quo Vadis*
(1951), *Ben-Hur* (1959), *El Cid* (1961), and, most appropriate of all, the atrocious *Sodom
and Gomorrah* (1962). One of his last credits was for the music in Resnais's *Providence*
(1977), where, as in *Clockwork,* one can hear the chords of musical parody.

panion, carries Alex into HOME as if he were a child. Significantly, Alex's bloodied face is identical to the one in the Ludovico film, only once again the color red is far more "realistic."

More than anything else, such authorial maneuvers show Alex becoming the victim of Kubrick's irony. Because he cannot see the unreality and contrivance of those films, or put aside his instinctive reactions in the interest of imaginative freedom, Alex's responses are conditioned even before the injection of aversive serum by Dr. Branom (Madge Ryan). He does not see, for instance, the differences between his fantasies and those projected on a movie screen, whether in a commercial cinema or in the laboratories of *Clockwork*'s mad scientists. He characterizes the first Ludovico film as "a very good, professional piece of sinny, like it was done in Hollywood," indicating that Kubrick—not Alex—asks *his* audience to associate the sentimental or visceral responses induced by the archetypal Hollywood product with those created by the Ludovico Technique. What Alex fails to notice about such films, of course, is that they encourage (or force) an identification with victims rather than victimizers. But as a Hobbesian primitive (who is both free and innocent), he lacks the moral awareness to understand such intentions. Whether it be a film or life itself, he responds to experience instinctively, not ethically. Thus the Ludovico Technique ultimately represents in the ethos of the film, as well as that of the novel, the horrors of an enforced social contract, even one that occurs on the decadent landscapes of a near but imaginary future. Yet Kubrick knows beforehand that his viewers in present time will have those responsive and "civilized" codes plugged in at the moment he assaults them with the surreality of both Alex's mindscreen and his own. Ideally, his audience will *choose* to engage the parody (as the midnight-cult audience has done for decades) as well as the aesthetic/conceptual density, and will, to quote the film's Minister (Anthony Sharp), who is standing before *his* audience in yet another theater, be sufficiently stimulated to "observe all." To observe, for instance, that the post-Ludovico Alex falls from a private Eden into a world where he must not only identify with life's inevitable victims but become one himself. To observe that Alex's crown of thorns and bloodied face have no more "reality" on our screen than do his internal horrorshows or the Ludovico images of a man being beaten. To observe that, symbolically, his suffering is the primitive retribution of a clockwork society. And finally, to observe the workings of a Kubrickian parable that brings the audience into an illusory world of cinematic "normality" (stylistically as well as morally) only to demonstrate that Alex as passive victim of the Good has far less expressive value as a human being *or* as a film character than does Alex the scourge and performing artist.

But images are not the whole story. When Alex's imaginative world is flushed out into the open and brought under the temporal authority of science, his aural sense also loses contact with that part of his humanity—a love of beauty—which might someday allow him to choose a creative rather than violent form of expression. Beethoven's Ninth (the "Turkish" march, fourth movement) is not only an inadvertent casualty in Alex's treatment when it serves as "background score" (to quote Dr. Branom) for a Ludovico newsreel film showing goose-stepping Nazis and World War II battlegrounds. Such an inappropriate musical selection causes Beethoven to degenerate into a type of decorative Muzak on the same order of inspiration as a fatuous tune like "I want to marry a lighthouse keeper," heard on a radio when Alex returns home and discovers that Pee and Em have replaced him with a surrogate son (Joe the lodger, played by Clive Francis). Throughout parts two and three, Kubrick frequently uses musical associations and repetitions to complement Alex's experience as victim, all contained in a series of nightmarish recurrences in the broad daylight of cinematic realism. The fourth movement of the Ninth, for instance, is first heard in part one, when Alex marches through the music bootick and dazzles us—as well as two teenyboppers licking phallic ice-sticks—with his satiric majesty. At the same time, Kubrick's dynamic 360° camera movement and a brief glimpse of a *2001* soundtrack album (listed under the heading "Underground Records") alert us to the filmmaker's presence. Inevitably, that music is associated in the Ludovico theater with film propaganda (synonymous with "art" in a conditioned society), clockwork armies marching to the tunes of war, and a shot of children in a statuary dancing hand in hand on a devastated landscape. To make the pop-culture charts, both Beethoven and Alex's musical gifts would have to undergo the same Anglo-Slavic vulgarization, as evidenced by one teeny's preference for "Googly Gogol," "Johnny Zhivago," and "The Heaven Seventeen."

Aside from such incidental or satiric purposes, Kubrick uses musical associations to support and deepen the film's ironic account of Alex as life-force. In perhaps the most striking scene of part two, Alex stands on a stage, spotlighted in a dehumanized blue color, to demonstrate before an audience the curative wonders of the Ludovico Technique by playing the part of victim/voyeur in a stimulus-response

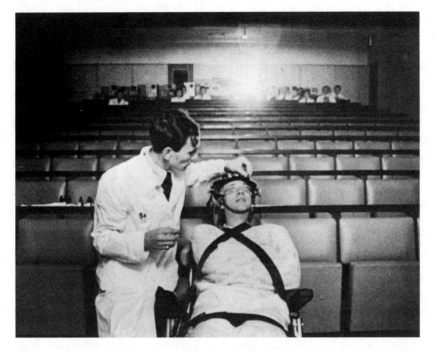

entertainment. First, he is humiliated and brutalized by a stage actor (John Clive) in a vaudeville routine that mixes farce (face-slapping, nose-tweaking, ear-pulling) and subjugation (Alex pushes out his "red yahzik [tongue] a mile-and-a-half to lick the grahzny boots"). For ironic counterpoint, Kubrick on our soundtrack plays the Elizabethan-inspired music of Terry Tucker's "Overture to the Sun." Following polite applause and bows by the actor, a partially nude blonde actress (Virginia Wetherell) appears from behind a dark curtain and confronts Alex, the audience in the auditorium, and the viewers of *Clockwork* with an erotic objectification of a collective unconscious. She moves out of the darkness toward us as well as Alex, who ironically describes her as "like light of heavenly grace" before feeling the Ludovico sickness—not the tugs of conscience—and wants to "have her right down there on the floor with the old in-out, real savage." This scene connects with those earlier occasions in which Alex was the performer and others were his foils or victims, while the sounds of Purcell's "Music for Queen Mary's Funeral" on the Moog associate it with the visual and conceptual milieu of the Korova Milkbar. Only now Alex remains a slumped and lifeless figure, not a spirit of renewal awakening to prowl the night. He kneels before the now stationary and impassive girl, reaches up toward her beautiful breasts, and cups his hands in midair around nipples jutting outward like one of those grotesque machine-dispensers of milkplus in the Korova. But like others, he has been conditioned to look, not to touch. Later, the Purcell will return when Alex is taken into the woods and beaten by his former droogs. They submerge his head in the muddy water of an animal trough (an ironic replay of his attack on Dim in the water of a marina) while the electronic sounds of the Moog are synchronized to blows from Georgie's nightstick. In such ways does Kubrick portray Alex's retreat into a womb of death.

In part one, the scherzo (second movement) from the Ninth provides Alex with inspiration for that mock-heroic display of masturbatory imagination, while in another bedroom (the French Provincial room of part three) it becomes an instrument in Alexander's revenge. As Alex pounds the floor of his eighteenth-century "cage" and pleads with unseen forces below to turn the music off—in itself an inversion of 2001's final vision of a Bowman/monolith symbiosis—his double looks up and smiles in a mask of grotesque beatitude that mimics Alex's facial ecstasy whenever he nears an orgasmic epiphany. The camera zooms back from Alexander in close-up and, from a distance, centers him in a symmetrical arrangement of machines (stereo equipment) and people (the other three conspirators) that forms a pathway down a green billiard table to a lovely tapestry hanging on the far wall. Even though the colors (predominantly greens) and the music are regenerative and heroic, the optical movement and composition recall the imagery of that opening shot in the Korova. But here Alex's look of malign creativity dissolves into the crazed look of another Dr. Strangelove spiritually resuscitated by the prospect of death.* As an element in Clockwork's narrative repetitions and visual/aural associa-

*Throughout Clockwork, as in all his films, Kubrick creates some interesting associations through visual geometry. The Cat Lady's room, for instance, represents a surreal blend of aesthetic and temporal associations at the same time that it functions as a psycho/sexual enclosure. Besides those items of decor already mentioned in the text, the room contains a Persian rug (on which she exercises), gold drapes (the same color as Alexander's clothes in the last HOME scene), white wallpaper with a gold fleur-de-lis pattern, and a green ceiling. Through various low camera angles and the wide lens, Kubrick creates the geometry of a rectangular box with a green lid (ceiling)—one that resembles the compositional lines in a later scene showing Alex in a prison exercise yard, only in that enclosure an over-exposed sky creates a blindingly white "ceiling." And Korova's narrow tunnel shape (again, enhanced by the lens) is repeated in the contours of the prison reception center, both of which were sets built in the same warehouse. Overall, the film not only exhibits a strong visual coherence but demonstrates Kubrick's remarkable ability to abstract emotional and psychological meaning from color and shape.

tions, this scene not only reasserts the Korova's deathscape but asks the audience to compare our narrator's midnight fantasies (satiric, vital) with a daylight nightmare that turns Beethoven (now the author of the "dreaded Ninth Symphony") and a generative art (the tapestry) into unwitting accomplices in both Alex's suicidal despair and a culture's Dance of Death.

This scene also marks the culmination of the elaborate doubling of Alex/Alexander that has been developing. Alex/Alexander can be paired in several polarities: youth/age; "primitive" adolescent/"civilized" adult; performing artist/writer; visual imagination/verbal manipulation; Beethoven as inspiration/Beethoven as decoration (HOME's doorchime); phallic virility/mental impotence; movement and dynamism/inertia and sitting (either behind a typewriter or in a wheelchair). In the two HOME sequences (parts one and three), the following repetitions/pairings occur: (1) In both sequences the same camera position is used outside—in the first, when Alex and his droogs in the stolen car stop on the other side of the illuminated HOME sign, and in the second, when Alex arrives in the rain, alone and beaten. (2) The first shot inside the house in both sequences uses the same camera position and movement—from Alexander seen behind an IBM Selectric (red in the first, light blue in the second) to a track-right and a sitting figure in red (his wife, reading a book, in the first; Julian, wearing briefs and exercising with dumbbells, in the second). (3) In each scene, Alexander responds to the doorchime with "Who on earth could that be?"—a question that assumes a special kind of resonance in a film by the director of *2001*. (4) The camera position in the mirrored hallway with a chessboard floor is repeated, the first sequence showing an invasion by the droogs in clown masks and the carrying of the wife, and the second sequence showing Julian picking up and carrying the bloody-faced Alex. (5) In the first sequence, Alexander is forced to watch as victim the "Singing in the Rain" performance/rape; in the second, he listens from the opposite side of a bathroom door to the ghostly echoes of Alex singing the same song while taking a bath. (6) In the first, Alexander wears a red and white robe; in the second Alex puts on the same robe after his bath and wears it during the scene at the table where he is drugged by the wine.

Almost mummified in white plaster from head to foot, Alex awakens from the sleep of the dead on a hospital bed and begins his "recovery" from the Ludovico Technique and the madness of his "civilized" HAL. To complement this ironic resurrection, the film shows the return of Alex's violent/creative instincts in a scene where he "interprets" a series of slide-projected drawings on a small screen. The artwork in these comic-strip Rorschachs is even more primitive than the style of the Ludovico films, although Alex's psychic/aesthetic responses remain those of a performer rather than a voyeur. That is, his imagination translates them into the same kind of satiric or adolescent "meanings" found in the more expressive imagery of his fantasies. Even the camera movement and colors of this sequence suggest Alex's eventual restoration to a state of psychological and physiological "normality." A long, fast-moving dolly shot, like the one in the music bootick of part one, ushers a female psychiatrist (Dr. Taylor, played by Pauline Taylor) into his hospital room, where she (and later the minister) is greeted with sneering majesty. However, the appearance of bright but natural colors (e.g., an EAT ME basket of fruit, Em's red vinyl, Dr. Taylor's orange and blue dress) offsets the hospital's resemblance to prior institutional settings. And in that final rapprochement between Alex and the minister, Kubrick slyly binds the formal hypocrisies of the state to an unruly primitivism in an exchange where paternal authority both solicits the savage's blessing and pops food into his demanding jaws. Of all the ritualized eating scenes in Kubrick— the post-execution breakfast of *Paths,* the buffet in the War Room in *Dr. Strangelove,* Moon-Watcher's first carnivorous meal, and Bowman's last meal—this scene from *Clockwork* best captures a Buñuelian conjunction of civilization and its primitive discontents.

Appropriately, Kubrick ends *A Clockwork Orange* in a flurry of images and sounds. Photographers and a stereo unit with two enormous speakers rush into the hospital room to record and celebrate an alliance between two smiling and cynical droogs, one satisfied that his time-bound needs are secured (good job, good salary), and the other prepared to turn that proverbial other cheek in a gesture of political survival. And yet, for all one knows, Alex may wake up from his newfound bliss only to discover a clockwork Mephistopheles waiting to demand his payment. But for now, Kubrick invites his audience to revel in Alex's victory as both Alex's imagination and Beethoven's Ninth are liberated from the tyranny of time's engineers. In what becomes the last image of the film, on our screen as well as Alex's, Kubrick for the first time visualizes Alex's exultation ("I was cured all right") as a play of fantasy *and* performance. In slow motion, Alex cavorts in a field of artificial snow with a nude woman in black gloves and stockings, while two lines of spectators dressed in the Ascot fashions of a *fin-de-siècle* British aristocracy form a pathway and applaud the two performers. Unlike previous visions, in either Alex's imagination or Kubrick's mindscreen, this image implies an evolution toward a paradoxical but encouraging future, one that exists on the other side of the Korova's black wall. The backgrounds are a luminous white, the activity blends Victorian formality and sexual freedom, at once the enclosures of time and the expanses of inner space. We are left to hope, perhaps with Kubrick as well as his cinematic double, that this path into an empty white space leads somewhere other than back into the involuted circles of time. Perhaps it leads to the *tabula rasa* of a movie screen, waiting for the performing artist and the light of his creation.

7 A TIME ODYSSEY
Barry Lyndon

For his next film, Stanley Kubrick undertook the difficult task of adapting to a large screen canvas William Makepeace Thackeray's *The Luck of Barry Lyndon* (1844), a rambling, digressive first-person novel written in an eighteenth-century picaresque form. Unlike Burgess's *A Clockwork Orange,* this novel did not provide him with a "finished" story, nor, despite its first-person style, with an intriguing subjective focus. In writing the screenplay, Kubrick eliminated at least half the episodes in the novel, but he retained most of its temporal sweep. His story of the rise and fall of Barry Lyndon covers more than twenty-five years (ca. 1760–1789) and, unlike Thackeray's account, attaches fully as much significance to the historical/cultural milieu as it does to the more transparent concerns of character. In the context of Kubrick's previous films, *Barry Lyndon* (1975) fits more comfortably into the philosophical and aesthetic constellation of *Paths of Glory* and *2001* than into the first-person mirror worlds of *Lolita* and *A Clockwork*

Orange. In addition, it probably represented for Kubrick a less expensive ($11 million) alternative to making a film about Napoleon, while it satisfied an apparent desire to match *2001*'s epic vision of mankind in future space with an equally ambitious film odyssey into past time.

Thackeray's novel spans at least five decades (ca. 1760–1811), develops a historical backdrop that includes the Seven Years' War and the American and French Revolutions, and chronicles not only the fictional life and death of Barry Lyndon (who dies in Fleet Prison of "delirium tremens") but the end of one era and beginning of another. As a counterpoint to Barry's first-person "memoir," told from the nostalgic and distorted perspective of "gouty old age," Thackeray creates a temporal organization that blends the "murderous work of kings" (for instance, Frederick the Great) and the extravagances of social vanity into a mock-epic treatise on human irrationality. Thus the novel is psychologically coherent as well as reductive, while structurally it is large. Because Thackeray wished to parody a nineteenth-century fondness for "personal" history (diaries, memoirs, letters, ecstatic poetry) through the guise of an eighteenth-century rogue novel, his "Romance of the Last Century"—to quote the subtitle—re-creates the moral seriousness of the Enlightenment more than it imitates the social or psychological realism of a Charles Dickens or George Eliot. Unlike the first-person involutions of Nabokov's *Lolita* and Burgess's *A Clockwork Orange,* Thackeray's use of the unreliable narrator turns into a thinly veiled disguise for a more encompassing satire directed against the excesses of the romantic imagination. His novel mourns the loss of an eighteenth-century dream of order rather than his narrator's shallow ambitions or personal tragedy. But, of course, between Thackeray and the works of Nabokov and Burgess—as well as the films of Kubrick—an epistemological and aesthetic evolution occurred that replaced an older faith in the rational order of both nature and the individual self with a twentieth-century universe of relativity, randomness, and psychological pluralism.

Thackeray's novel must have presented Kubrick with problems of adaptation and cinematic translation unlike any he had ever encountered. Distinct from *Lolita* and *Clockwork,* its first-person style, through a method of rhetorical disengagement, quickly diminishes both the importance and the appeal of Barry's subjective peculiarities. No unique or startling "mindscreen" can be extracted from these pages. Barry's verbal posturings become as obvious as they are trite, so that one soon learns to measure what he *says* against what Thackeray *means.* As George Savage Fitz-Boodle, the spurious "editor" of Barry's memoirs, Thackeray repeatedly deplores his protagonist's self-serving distortions of the truth and his shoddy moral character:

> We beg here respectfully to declare that we take the moral of the story of Barry Lyndon, Esquire, to be—that worldly success is by no means the consequence of virtue; that if it is effected honestly sometimes, it is attained by selfishness and roguery still oftener; and that our anger at seeing rascals prosper and good men frequently unlucky, is founded on a gross and unreasonable idea of what good fortune really is.

Even in the absence of such intrusions (in the 1856 edition, Thackeray deletes Fitz-Boodle's commentary), Barry's penchant for self-aggrandizement and his skill at blarney quickly make the reader suspicious about the truthfulness of his confidences, especially in his oft-repeated claims of nobility for the "house of Barry of Barryogue":

> Truth compels me to assert that my family was the noblest of the island, and, perhaps, of the universal world.

Barry, one learns, is a very inventive storyteller who fabricates both his legal and his moral history in order to justify on a grand scale, *ex post facto,* a life of cheating, lying, and wife-beating. Note, for instance, how hyperbole (Barry's "voice") and indirect disclosure (Thackeray's irony) merge in an early description of his father:

> My father was well known to the best circles in this kingdom as in that of Ireland, under the name of Roaring Harry Barry. He was bred like many other young sons of genteel families to the profession of the law . . . and, from his great genius and aptitude for learning, there is no doubt he would have made an eminent figure in his profession, had not his social qualities, love of field sports, and extraordinary graces of manner marked him out for a higher sphere.

What this actually means is that "Roaring Harry Barry" preferred gaming to learning, and the "higher sphere" of social vanity to eighteenth-century enlightenment. Like father, like son. Throughout his "memory" account and mock confessional, which is quite different from the dreamlike reveries of Humbert and Alex, Barry remains steadfast in his belief that wealth, titles, and fashion—the *appearances* of value—give substance to humanity's journey through time:

> We wore silk and embroidery then. . . . Then it took a man of fashion a couple of hours to make his toilette, and he could shew some taste and

genius in the selecting it. What a blaze of splendour was a drawing room, or opera, of a gala night! What sums of money were lost and won at the delicious faro-table! . . . Gentlemen are dead and gone. The fashion has now turned upon your soldiers and sailors, and I grow moody and sad when I think of thirty years ago.

No clear understanding of the incalculable sorrows of human life within the relentless processes of time liberates Barry's perspective from a nostalgic faith in the importance of a socially objectified morality. For Thackeray, as well as the reader, Barry Lyndon remains a comic figure with a tragic fate.

But in keeping with another picaresque convention, Thackeray invests his protagonist with certain redeeming graces. Barry's naiveté and ready courage—particularly evident in the first half of the novel—lend his character an emotional integrity that tragically disappears amid the ephemera of Vanity Fair. He falls in and out of love too easily and too often, violates the rules of decorum in the interests of passion (e.g., by throwing a glass of claret in Captain Quin's face during a contest for the hand of Nora Brady), and is far too eager to fight for love, honor, and country. Because he lacks the ability to harness these instincts into an enlightened moral or intellectual understanding, Barry Lyndon becomes a victim of a deceptively attractive *haut monde* as well as his own shallow character. By the time he moves into that "higher sphere" of fashion, fictional claims have been converted into personal truths, just as moral substance defers to painted surfaces. When he first encounters the Chevalier de Balibari—who, it turns out, is nothing more than an Irish gambler and pretender like Barry himself—his emotional largess transforms itself into social aspiration:

> It was very imprudent of me; but when I saw the splendour of his appearance, the nobleness of his manner, I felt it impossible to keep disguise with him. . . . I burst into tears.

What Barry sees is a splendor that he desires for himself, and, ironically, one attainable only through the art of disguise. By the end of part one, Thackeray's hero has not only learned the rules of the game—and the first one is that honest emotion must curtsy before the demands of decorous formality—but acquired the skills of an accomplished player. No longer swayed by romantic notions of love or honor, he ruthlessly pursues Lady Lyndon for a year to obtain "the style and title of Barry Lyndon," and he later strives for a peerage that ultimately eludes his grasp. In the final pages of the novel, with his life

in a state of personal and financial ruin, Barry's unwitting self-expo-
sure becomes complete. He eventually acquiesces to the romance of
his own inventions, which earlier were nothing more than studied
responses to the accidents of fortune and his ambition for social rank.

While Thackeray requires the reader to dismiss Barry's manipula-
tive, unreliable account and appreciate both Fitz-Boodle's editorial
morality and his own irony, Kubrick asks his film audience to follow
Barry's story from the distanced perspective of an omniscient narrator. Having a storyteller (Michael Hordern), whose voice is steady and
deliberate in its ironic and sympathetic reflections on the rise and fall
of Barry Lyndon (Ryan O'Neal), allows Kubrick to condense a great
deal of the story's objective and psychological exposition. The narrator both explains the historical ambience (the Seven Years' War) and
interprets the inner workings of character (Barry quickly recovers
from a tearful farewell with his mother because "no lad who has lib-
erty for the first time and twenty guineas in his pocket is very sad").
He creates in part I an atmosphere of comic fate and irony, while in
part II his comments become increasingly sympathetic and support a
growing mood of tragic irony. He alerts us to patterns of fortune and

chance that the characters, especially Barry himself, fail to comprehend. Kubrick's protagonist in part I accepts fortuity with confident,
unreflective self-assurance, while in part II the narrator anticipates
for us the death of Barry's son and our hero's eventual ruin. In such a
manner, Kubrick structures a narrative vise of irony and fate, comic in
part I and tragic in part II, and reminds us of that broader historical
context from which no character, not even the narrator himself, can
hope to escape. The titled "Epilogue," taken from chapter 1 of Thackeray's novel, stands as Kubrick's most noticeable intrusion into the
temporal structure of the film. It transcends the narrator's limited
frame of reference and reminds us of time's irrevocable obliteration
of the personal struggles of an entire era. "They are all equal now," we
read, as most of us shall be sometime in this new century. Except, of
course, for the relative few, such as Kubrick, who leave behind compelling, material reminders of their brief human presence in the irre-
versible annihilation of time.

Not only the Epilogue of *Barry Lyndon*, but the film's narration
and dialogue, as well as the titles for parts I and II, either come directly from or appear to be inspired by Thackeray's novel. Yet Kubrick,
by not allowing Barry to tell his story as Thackeray does, further diminishes his character's perceptual range and freedom of choice. In
the novel, for instance, Barry makes observations and voices opinions
about his historical milieu, even though his authority in such matters
is challenged by Thackeray's ironic presence and his own admission
of shortcomings as a "philosopher and historian." Rather than have
his protagonist tell his own story, as Humbert and Alex are allowed to
do in *Lolita* and *A Clockwork Orange*, Kubrick chooses a strategy that
creates a disparity between the film's "objective" structure (i.e., its
temporal rhetoric) and a brilliantly conceived visual/musical form.
On the one hand, the narrator gives the impression that *Barry Lyndon*,
to use one critic's description, is a "documentary on eighteenth-century manners and mores," while on the other his temporal authority
is undermined by the part it plays in Kubrick's more expressive cinematic ambitions. Like those disembodied voices of objectivity in *The
Killing, Paths of Glory,* and *Dr. Strangelove,* and like HAL in *2001,* the
narrator of *Lyndon* knows something about time but nothing about
space. He offers us a comfortable and ironic detachment from Barry's
rise and fall, while he fails to see Barry's emotional complexity or
moral growth. He provides a historical awareness that strengthens the
sense of fate in the film, but he fails to comprehend its larger philo-

sophic or aesthetic meaning. His is the voice of reason and wit, to be sure, a mixture of eighteenth-century urbanity and Thackerayan bonhomie, but one confined within the temporal frame of the film. He has access to knowledge of Barry's ultimate ruin and sorrow, to the complexities of eighteenth-century European politics, and in general to the basic dynamics of social intercourse. Beyond the level of story, that rudimentary urge to tell a tale, the narrator has little or nothing to say. Significantly, he does not comment on most of what we *see* and *hear.* He has no access to the cinematic order of images and sounds of which his narration is but a small part. Like others in the film, his existential presence metaphorically turns to dust and becomes absorbed into an expressive film art that looks backward in time and outward toward the duration of cinematic space.

Yet the narrator's importance in the film should not be underestimated. Both his detachment and his sympathy serve to make the tone elegiac rather than nostalgic. As a narrative time machine, his voice mournfully ticks off the tragic foibles and petty strivings of an ordinary humanity ensnared in the processes of life itself. In part I, for instance, the narrator's commentary on Barry's first taste of battle and the folly of the Seven Years' War reaches far beyond a single moment in time:

> Though this encounter is not recorded in any history books, it was memorable enough for those who took part.

In this "skirmish" with the French, Barry loses his friend Captain Grogan (Godfrey Quigley), who dies, with countless others, on one of history's innumerable forgotten battlefields. And in part II, the narrator sadly recounts Barry's decline into debtorship and the social disgrace and banishment that result from his stepson's revenge on him. The narrator foretells the death of Barry's son—"fate had determined that he should leave none of his race behind him"—and even tells us that he will finish life "poor, lonely, and childless." Kubrick, unlike Thackeray, literally frames his *Barry Lyndon* within both an atmosphere of transience and the finality of death: The film begins and ends with formal white titles and end-titles on a black screen, while on the soundtrack we hear the elegiac grandeur of the main theme from Handel's "Sarabande." Part I begins and ends with death, while part II moves from the resplendence of a marriage in scene one to the dissolution of that bond and the scene where Lady Lyndon (Marisa Berenson) mournfully signs an annuity made out to Redmond Barry.

In the first part, Kubrick frames the film's rising action by going from a long-distanced view of Barry's father being slain in a duel to a close-up of Sir Charles Lyndon (Frank Middlemass) struggling vainly to stay alive. As we witness this second invasion by death, with its hideous shrieks and twitchings, the narrator's unemotional reading of the old man's obituary reduces him to just another forgotten entry in the endless rolls of history:

> From a report in the *St. James Chronicle:* Died, at Spa, in the Kingdom of Belgium, the right honorable Sir Charles Reginald Lyndon, Knight of the Bath, Member of Parliament, and, for many years, His Majesty's representative at various European courts. He has left behind him a name which has endeared to all his. . . .

As the reading of the obituary slowly fades out and the screen cuts to black, we anticipate that shortly Sir Charles's esteemed name will be usurped by one Redmond Barry. Ironically, part II—in its journey from marriage to estrangement—shows Barry losing the name of Lyndon and returning to a tragic obscurity (as Redmond Barry) for which posterity keeps very few records.

Throughout, Kubrick strives to lift the events from Thackeray's novel out of period time (that is, the eighteenth century) into a realm of emotional and conceptual film time. The temporal fabric of his film is made up of not only marriages and deaths but births and birthdays, old families and new families, first loves and last loves, friendships and sibling rivalries, quarrels and duels, games and debts—that is, an elaborately ritualized parable of journeys begun and journeys ended. He compresses and arranges the content of the novel into a formal tapestry that brings together the archetypal delusions of youth and the sorrows of time—the trivial within the sublime—while the pace of the film resembles a stately procession moving through vanity fair on its way to tragic pageantry. Barry's father dies in a formal pistol duel over, the narrator informs us, "the purchase of some horses"—and not, as is the implication in Thackeray, of cardiac arrest while gaming at the Chester Races. Later, Barry's purchase of a horse—for his son Bryan's ninth birthday—will lead to a death whose poignancy is untainted by comic irony. In part I, Barry fights a duel with the braggart Quin (Leonard Rossiter) for a prize—Nora Brady (Gay Hamilton)—who is being auctioned off to the highest bidder, ignorant of the fact that her family has rigged the contest as insurance against losing the Captain's £1,500 a year. In part II, Barry confronts the hatred of his stepson Bullingdon (Leon Vitali) in another duel with pistols, only now he gives the ritual the substance of moral courage by refusing to fire on his wife's sole remaining heir. During his first journey from Ireland and eventually to England, Barry is initiated into the perils of the road by an amusingly polite but efficient highwayman named Captain Freny (Arthur O'Sullivan), while in part II, crippled and on crutches, Barry takes his last journey to a carriage that will transport him out of England into permanent exile. In part I, Barry cynically woos Lady Lyndon over a Belgian gaming table and prompts this example of our narrator's ready wit: "to make a long story short, six hours after they met, her ladyship was in love." In part II, following several infidelities with maids and concubines, Barry's arrogance turns into a loyal affection for his "vaporish" (neurotic) wife and an abiding love for his doomed son. In such ways does Kubrick's *Barry Lyndon* transport its audience both backward in historical time (the eighteenth century) and forward in narrative time through a credible but distanced landscape. In the end, however, it becomes an odyssey that, in its canvas of humanity, embodies a pattern not only close to us all but one for all time.

In the language and music of *Barry Lyndon,* one can chart Kubrick's development as a complete film artist. From the beginning, even within the crude narrative mythology of *Fear and Desire* and *Killer's Kiss,* he demonstrated a visual talent commensurate with the spatial complexities of such later films as *Paths of Glory, Dr. Strangelove, 2001,* and *A Clockwork Orange.* But not until *2001* did a Kubrick film realize a sound aesthetics equal to its temporal and spatial brilliance. *Paths* dabbles briefly in musical counterpoint (e.g., a Strauss waltz before an execution) and the euphemisms of power politics, while *Dr. Strangelove* balances laughter and surreal terror in a handful of popular tunes ("Try a Little Tenderness" and "We'll Meet Again") and a grimly amusing Doomsday jargon. *2001,* by contrast, develops a paradoxical alignment of language and classical music by characterizing the first as an extinct fossil (e.g., HAL's primitive regressions) and the other as conjunctive with the evolutionary mysteries of outer space (e.g., *Zarathustra* and the monolith). And in *Clockwork,* Alex's Nadsat symbolizes a verbal conduit to a highly intuitive inner life, one that opposes the assembly-line slogans and knee-jerk politics of the Clockwork State, while the music of the film mixes parody with creative improvisation. In adapting *Barry Lyndon* to film, Kubrick used the subtly ironic and formally measured syntax associated with Thackeray's "voice" rather than Barry's first-person hyperbole. As a result, the language suggests Barry's psychological entrapment within the formal properties of a verbal maze that an outsider may imitate but will rarely understand. Just as he perceives the mechanical workings of fate, however, the narrator commands this language and thereby aligns his voice with Barry's eventual victimization in a decorous and formal labyrinth disguised as an eighteenth-century mise-en-scène. Unlike Barry, however, the narrator gives the impression that he has escaped the painted cage and now, from above, muses over its splendor with a fascination that belies his stance of urbane contempt. Perhaps Barry's tragedy can be explained, in part, by the faith he invests in not only titles but words—in an assurance that once he takes up the King's English, his future, like that of any gentleman, will be secured and ordered. In part II, for instance, his quest for peerage brings him to one Lord Wendover (André Morell), whose patronage and balanced syntax envelop Barry in a cocoon that stimulates the illusion that chance curtsies before the whims of human design:

> When I take up a person, Mr. Barry, he or she is safe. There is no question about them anymore. My friends are the best people. I don't mean they are the most virtuous, or indeed the least virtuous, or the cleverest, or the stupidest, or the richest, or the best born. But the best. In a word, people about whom there is no question.

And besides, Lord Wendover explains, "any gentleman with an estate and £30,000 a year should have a peerage." By the end of the film, Barry's vocabulary has declined to an occasional whisper—and little more—just as he begins to show an emotional and moral strength of character that eludes the explanatory powers of the narrator's Word.

Kubrick's musical choices for *Barry Lyndon*—primarily baroque rather than purely classical, with the heavy elegance of Handel's "Sarabande" providing the central musical theme—reinforce the film's elegiac structure as well as its narrative and tonal disparities. The brief selections from Bach (a concerto for two harpsichords played in a recital at Castle Hackton) and Vivaldi ("Cello Concerto in E Minor," which first appears after the marriage scene of part II and later blends into the "Sarabande-Title" music for Bryan's funeral) suggest minor harmonic progressions common to the baroque, while the lighter piece from Mozart ("March from Idomeneo," played during Barry's brief tenure as a spy for Captain Potzdorf) and one from Schubert (a "German Dance," heard during the period of Bryan's eighth birthday celebration) blend with the simpler and more traditional melodies associated with Barry's romantic entanglements with Nora and a young German girl (e.g., "Women of Ireland," "Lilliburlero," "British Grenadiers"). Together these selections form a baroque whole that supports the film's visual mixture of lyrical simplicity and formal artifice, its narrative merger of the comic and the tragic, its emotional subtext of the trivial and the sublime, a vanity fair and an epical grandeur. As part of a system of aesthetic analogy (to several forms of seventeenth-, eighteenth-, and nineteenth-century art and music), the music contributes to the historical dimension within the film that both documents and universalizes the end of an era.*

Throughout his career, Kubrick repeatedly expressed his fascination with the classical style and forms associated with an eighteenth-century sensibility, even though *Barry Lyndon,* his tenth feature film, was the only one placed in that period of history. On the simplest conceptual level, a classical mise-en-scène in a Kubrick film accentuates the tension between the enclosures of time and the expanses of space discussed throughout this study. In highly formal environments, whether they are defined through aesthetic or mechanical imagery, Kubrick's characters become separated from both the unresolved conflicts of inner space (resulting in sublimation and repression) and the irreducibility of outer space. Consequently, within the Kubrickian mythos, they have less access to mystery, creativity, and the possibility of future hope. Moreover, Kubrick expressed throughout his career a strong but sometimes latent surrealist temperament through the placement of an eighteenth-century formalism within a variety of dissonant film contexts. Johnny Clay's robbery plan in *The Killing,* for instance, matches the precision of classical design against the ubiquity of chance. In *Paths of Glory,* an eighteenth-century chateau provides a "civilized" battleground for World War I barbarity, while Quilty's mansion in *Lolita* represents a Gothic parody of classical order, and the Gainsborough-like portrait behind which he dies suggests an image of lost innocence. The inhabitants of *Dr. Strangelove's* mad enclosures cling to a faith in an eighteenth-century Clockworld, which they assume will run forever and carry them beyond Dooms-

---

*Other musical selections in the film include Schubert's "Piano Trio in E-Flat" (discussed more fully in the latter portion of chapter 7), an adaptation of Paisiello's "The Cavatina" from *Il Barbier di Siviglia* (used in two card-cheating scenes involving Barry and the Chevalier), and Frederick the Great's "Hohenfriedberger March" (ironically associated with Barry's desertion and his movement through Prussian lines).

day, while the travelers of *2001* organize the infinity of space into a technological harmonics as an alternative to vision. And *A Clockwork Orange* visualizes the death throes of civilization as a dislocated eighteenth-century nightmare (e.g., the Korova's symmetry and statuary) taking place in an imaginary future. Not until Bowman's final excursion into past time (his "memory" room) did Kubrick begin to clarify the role that neoclassical formality plays in his film iconography— and it is more than just a belief in the tragic entrapment of one historical period within a rational and mechanical formalism. It stands for a memory as much as for a historical fact; a dream of order and beauty, not just a period of time; a human artifact, not merely a museum collection of paintings and music, great homes and palaces. It is a vision of people in their created world, of a civilization with its discontents hidden from view, one that in some parts of the globe still surrounds *our* creations like a radiant but alien presence. Yet like the characters of *Barry Lyndon,* we frequently gaze at its strangeness and splendor as voyeurs of time, imitating its surfaces while misapprehending its complex meanings.

Within the two-part structure of *Barry Lyndon,* and its balancing of comic and tragic irony, Kubrick develops additional narrative comment through a series of ritual activities. Among these dramatized motifs, four stand out—dueling, wooing, card-playing, and debt-paying—as evidence of his desire to visually objectify the conceptual and emotional content of the film in ways beyond the narrator's compass. All four of these activities include in their formal order the workings of fate or chance, and each, in its own way, dramatizes a Kubrickian conflict between human design and contingency. As the characters pursue either their instincts or the mediated goals of "civilized" ambition, they become absorbed within a larger temporal and cinematic process. As they duel with one another over the ephemera of love and honor, we comprehend their losing battle with fate. As they idly pass the time playing cards, or attempt to fulfill selfish ambition by cheating at these games of chance, we realize that their time is short and running out. And while the Chevalier (Patrick Magee) and Barry may cheat and win with the cards or in the game of love, in the film's larger order of moral reference they must inevitably pay up. In part II of the film, Kubrick isolates the piling up of debts and the signing of bank drafts as another ritual activity performed at a table—on two occasions with three present (Barry, Lady Lyndon, and a bookkeeper), as in the games of Ombre seen earlier—and again portrays in micro-cosm the thematic and psychological content of the film.

A close look at how Kubrick shapes and patterns these narrative motifs in part I ("By What Means Redmond Barry Acquired the Style and Title of Barry Lyndon") reveals something more complex than the narrator's irony or the simple mechanics of fate. The film's initial scene, shot from afar and explained by the avuncular yet detached narrator, links the death of Barry's father to the contrary designs of nature and human artifice. A spectrum of natural color (from top to bottom: gray, blue, brown, green) captures in portraiture the ro-mance of eighteenth-century dueling (isolated figures integrated into a stunning landscape), while the narrator's exposition functions as ironic counterpoint to the painterly appeal and verbal formality of the dueling scene. As the narrator tells us about the father's promis-ing legal career ("no doubt he would have made an eminent figure in his profession"), we hear a countdown to death ("Gentlemen, cock your pistols. One, two, three") and the popping sounds of exploding gunfire, while we notice the lone figure on the left falling to the ground at the same moment that the narrator completes his com-mentary ("had he not been killed in a duel over the purchase of some horses"). Immediately, Kubrick forces us to look at such human struggles from a distance, at once historical and cinematic, and to note the disparities between form (a duel) and content (a human life sacrificed to a quarrel over horses).

Barry's duel with Captain Quin, drawn out sufficiently by Kubrick to capture the ritual and aesthetics of an eighteenth-century barbar-ity, likewise has an ironic substance. In a later candlelit scene, Captain Grogan informs both Barry and the audience of the film that the pis-tols were loaded with harmless pluckets of tow, and that the cowardly Quin fainted from fright. During the duel itself, the audience remains as ignorant of the Brady family's machinations as Barry does (al-though a clue is provided to both when Barry notices that Grogan, his second, has handed him someone else's pistol), just as it fails to per-ceive a sordid truth (a family's avarice) within the forms of ritual. In this instance, the narrator's silence links him to the filmmaker's de-ception. A slow reverse zoom and the steady rhythm of Handel's "Sara-bande-Duel" take us from a close-up view of the pistols being pre-pared by Grogan and Ulick, Barry's cousin, to a long shot of five figures (as in the first duel) in a lovely natural setting of blue water and green trees. Barry, like his father before him, occupies screen left, although here it is the duelist on the right (Quin) who falls to an apparent death. Significantly, Kubrick cuts back and forth between emotional close-up (of Barry's foolhardy courage and Quin's coward-ice) and a pleasingly attractive distance, thereby providing his audi-ence with both a source of psychological identification and an aes-thetic distance. Within the film's thematic aspirations, it indicates how the forms of things can be manipulated and the courses of fate mo-mentarily postponed. By the end of part I, following his and the Che-valier's disconnected wanderings through the courts of Europe, Barry has learned how to thrive on guile and good form as he develops an art for dueling as well as for lovemaking and card-playing.

In the three love/wooing scenes of part I, through a pattern of visual and aural repetition, Kubrick enlarges the significance of Bar-ry's moral progress from Irish primitive to rakish gentleman. In the ribbon scene between Barry and Nora, he captures both the charm and the triviality of romantic love by slowing down the pace and al-lowing the action to play itself out, to assert a temporal and emo-tional integrity that solicits from the audience both responsive feeling and circumspect understanding. Here, as elsewhere, a reverse zoom moves from something particular (i.e., the statue of a child) to a more generalized composition of human figures, colors, and light. Sitting at a table playing cards ("Killarney"), with the pleasing sounds of a spring rain and the music from "Women of Ireland" blending into a soft-textured imagery, the two performers embody familiar sentimen-tal gestures, a subtle turn of the head or closing of the eyes too stud-ied to be profound. Even though the narrator intrudes with his usual sardonic advantage ("First love!" he intones. "What a change it makes in a lad . . . the tender passion gushes instinctively out of a man's heart!") and subsequently deplores Nora's shallow emotional charac-ter and her family's greed, Kubrick—by means of the integrity of the scene—forces us to apprehend a world at odds with that commentary and to acknowledge a fuller human content.

During another rainstorm complemented by music from "Women of Ireland," Barry sits by candlelight with his Lischen and her baby (Diana Koerner gives a remarkable performance as Lischen) at an-other table, only this one serves for eating rather than card-playing. Again Kubrick preserves the internal coherence of the scene, allow-ing it a full emotional and visual exposition and communicating nu-ances of character beyond those already apparent in Barry's disguise (in deserting the English army, he has assumed the identity of one

"Lieutenant Fakenheim") and soldierly pretenses ("I'm an officer and must do my duty," he says in response to Lischen's concern about the dangers of war). Kubrick (and Ryan O'Neal) reveals how simple and human it is for Barry to become enveloped in the magic of his own invention, and how, for a brief moment of time, we, too, share that magic. This sequence completes itself the next morning with the two lovers in close-up—their heads tilted together in a static tableau of bright light and soft focus—as we relish the visual charm and innocence of the exaggerated sentiment. In contrast, the narrator's game calls for him to get the last word ("This heart of Lischen's was like many a neighboring town, and had been stormed and occupied several times before Barry came to invest it") and to announce, somewhat condescendingly, an explicit verbal formulation of Barry's tragicomic attempts at circumventing both fate and his own emotional character.

For Redmond Barry, this scene foreshadows his movement into a "higher sphere" of fashion more commensurate with the narrator's civilized detachment than with his own naiveté, a sphere where spontaneity loses its way in a labyrinth of psychological disguise and social formality. Barry's wooing of Lady Lyndon over a Belgian gaming table recalls his earlier contest with Nora, only now the mask of bold ambition replaces youthful ardor, and the measured elegance of Schubert's "Piano Trio in E-Flat" replaces the more lyrical "Women of Ireland" as the musical love theme. Dressed in silk and lace, manicured, painted, and coiffured like a figure from an eighteenth-century wax museum, Barry ruthlessly pursues Lady Lyndon to a blue moonlit terrace, where she turns to receive his advances in a ritual of love that pleases the eye but chills the heart. Soon afterward, Barry, with his newly acquired arrogance and cruelty, enters an ornate candlelit room where he confronts Lady Lyndon's crippled husband with his sexual advantage, while the old man, sitting at his card table, rails and dies in a losing game with time.

Besides the light it casts on Barry's development, this progress in the mise-en-scène of the film from natural beauty to formal artifice contains the paradoxical merger of economics and aesthetics. When he flees from the mercenary deception of the Bradys, Barry takes the twenty guineas that belong to his mother (Marie Kean) on a journey through a series of beautiful rural settings to an unexpected rendezvous with a highwayman and his son. This brief exchange is ironically polite and formal: Barry keeps his boots but not his money or his horse, as Captain Freny demonstrates both the ethics and the aesthetics of his profession. He takes Barry's horse out of practical considerations ("With people like us, we must be able to travel faster than our clients"), while he leaves him his boots out of sympathy and, more important, an appreciation for proportion and balance (to take them would be excessive, an act of bad form more than of cruelty). Stripped of money to support his trip to Dublin, Barry becomes seduced by the simple blandishments of an English recruiting sergeant seeking to enlist cannon fodder for the European wars. He offers promises of money (one shilling a day for life) and honor (to those "ambitious of becoming gentlemen"), as well as an opportunity for Barry to wear the uniform he earlier had enviously admired while watching Quin parade and strut with his regiment. Once he takes the bounty, however, Barry becomes imprisoned within a military geometry that recalls the horizontal lines and pathways in *Paths of Glory*. Several zoom/telephoto shots of Barry marching in an army of multitudes or leading a man through a brutal Prussian gauntlet reinforce this sense of entrapment, while the first battle scene in the film—a brilliantly staged affair in a rural orchard between stationary (the French) and advancing (the English) lines—shows how eighteenth-century warfare maintained its formal aesthetics even at the expense of human life and tactical sense. Barry carries the fatally wounded Grogan into a muddy, smoke-filled trench similar to the one that directs Colonel Dax's movements in *Paths*. But this soldier weeps over the body of a friend, who ironically has willed him a portion of the money (100 guineas) earned from his part in the Quin/Nora marriage (meaning that Grogan, his friend and second, was party to Barry's deception). Significantly, this money represents what is left from Grogan's losing battle with the cards on the night before his death. In such ways does truth emerge from a tangle of commerce and decorum, ambition and artifice, the civilized mask of war and its lethal absurdity.

In still other ways, Kubrick opposes the forms of a rigid military aesthetics with complicating internal factors and prepares his audience for Barry's eventual absorption into a highly artificial cultural milieu. Barry's fistfight with a belligerent soldier named Tool both conforms to specified rules and takes place inside an enclosed regimental square, while Kubrick's handheld camera not only records the violence of the fight but counterpoints its formal outline. The second battle of the film is framed initially through a square farmhouse window—surely a visual allusion to the horizontal viewer through which

we first see no-man's-land in *Paths of Glory*—before all is scattered into
confusion and exploding cannon fire. During the most frantic and
disordered moments of the battle, Barry instinctively risks his life to
save Captain Potzdorf (Hardy Kruger). Later he is castigated by a
Prussian colonel for immoral conduct off the battlefield, as well as
rewarded for his courage with two *Frederics d'or* during a ceremony
that takes place within a formal regimental horseshoe. Appropriately,
this fortuitous intersection of courage and profit enables Barry to escape military service and advance even closer to the gentlemanly
splendor that he privately covets. In Berlin, in an ornate and classical
palace that resembles the chateau in *Paths,* Barry assumes another
disguise, in this instance the double one of Potzdorf's spy and the
Chevalier's confidant.

     Yet the film intimates that even though these games of state func-
tion on a scale grander in their formal properties than Barry's puerile
involvement in a romantic triangle and a family's greed, they lack a
correspondingly noble substance. In one scene, for instance, Barry
stands between symmetrical gold pillars in the palatial office of the
Minister of Police, reporting false information about the Chevalier,
while the camera, positioned behind the minister, tracks back and
forth (left to right, right to left) on a horizontal course that opposes
Potzdorf's pacings. Visually, this scene recalls the court-martial in
Paths and its paradoxical suggestion of horizontal entrapment in a
setting of vertical reach and aspiration. In Barry's first meeting with
the Chevalier, Kubrick visually prepares for a movement from one
world into another, from the clockwork machinations of military formality to an environment of aristocratic self-indulgence; and in terms
of cinematic self-reference, from the chateau of *Paths* to that extraterrestrial room in *2001.* He begins the scene in the Chevalier's palatial
apartment from a distance and behind a figure on screen-right who,
like Bowman as eighteenth-century gentleman, sits with his back to
the camera and eats breakfast at a formally prepared table. After Barry
enters through a door centered in the background and framed by
white pillars, a reverse angle reveals the Chevalier's startling appearance—a white wig, a powdered and rouged face, a black patch over
his right eye, and beauty marks both above and below his left eye—as
well as the presence of a red canopied bed in the background. Appropriately, there are no rebirths or moral transformations here—only
Barry's exchange of one disguise and patron (as Potzdorf's spy) for
another (as the Chevalier's protégé), as well as the illusion that the

splendor of this painted rogue will transport him out of a world of horizontal intrigue into a realm inhabited by ethereal beings who seem as enduring as the attractive *objets d'art* that surround them.

To complement the contrary tendencies of verbal narration and visual narrative, what upon reflection could be termed the disparities of film content in *Barry Lyndon,* Kubrick employs an impressive technical strategy that binds the film into an aesthetic and philosophical whole. His use of camera and lens, composition and mise-en-scène, and a musical score of recurring baroque cadences produces a grandiosity of form that someday may help redefine the concept of the film epic. *Barry Lyndon* exemplifies many of the characteristics traditional to a genre first developed by Griffith and the Italians, refined by Eisenstein and Russian theories of epic montage, and exploited for its full commercial value through bravura technical feats by such filmmakers as Abel Gance and Cecil B. DeMille. It is characterized by a display of innovative visual and technical effects, impressive formal compositions, rhythmic editing, and an actual or pseudo-historical ambience. Yet, as Kubrick himself has noted, while such films historically resulted in significant advances in the areas of film technology and film language, they rarely embodied a content equal to their formal pretensions.* Kubrick's often stated belief that "Eisenstein is all form and no content, whereas Chaplin is content and no form"— combined with his following comment—articulates what I take to have been his primary goal as a film artist and his actual achievement in *Barry Lyndon:* "Obviously, if you can combine style and content, you have the best of all possible films."

In part I of *Barry Lyndon,* for instance, Kubrick's use of the reverse zoom allowed him to move into and away from a given scene without fragmenting the harmonious appearances of space or compressing the realities of time. More important, it allowed him to create an ironic juxtaposition between Barry's gradual rise and a complex mise-en-scène, one that supports the film's spatial/musical rhetoric as it transcends its temporal content. As the love tryst involving Barry, Nora, and Quin develops in time, Kubrick slowly zooms back from the particulars of film content (e.g., Barry chopping wood, Nora's and Quin's hands joined, pistols being prepared for a duel) to assert open

---

*Exceptions to this observation would include David Lean's *Lawrence of Arabia* (1962), arguably the greatest historical epic ever made, and perhaps Bernardo Bertolucci's *The Last Emperor* (1987) in its restored form.

landscape compositions similar to those found in the paintings of
Gainsborough and Constable, a lyrical ordering of the rural setting,
which dwarfs the conflicts that unfold inside that world.* Because
Barry fails to perceive such basic disparities as those between his
rather ordinary ambitions and an expressive natural environment, he
lacks the necessary imagination to transcend his own fate. Instead, he
abandons the open expanses of rural space for the attractive enclosures of social space—an alignment of choice and chance that takes
him into a world far closer to the formal gardens and internal mazes
of Resnais's *Last Year at Marienbad* (1961) than the exuberant eighteenth-century gregariousness of *Tom Jones* (Tony Richardson, 1963).
Correspondingly, Kubrick's camera reverses its earlier tendencies and
becomes more static (with even less optical movement), especially in
those impressive candlelit scenes (made possible by a Zeiss still-camera lens) at the Belgian spa in part I and at Castle Hackton in part II
that visually resemble the incandescent paintings (and re-creations)
by Adolf Menzel of Frederick the Great's concerts at Sans Souci.

By the end of part I, the camera often starts off by establishing a
distant and static tableau in which characters artfully blend into a generalized period setting, before it then cuts into the specific details
of such internal narrative developments as Barry's wooing of Lady
Lyndon or her husband's death. Paradoxically, the film implies that
Barry's attraction to this world comes from his seeing it, as the narrator does, from afar rather than close up. Such a development reverses
Barry's earlier failure to escape a subjective response to his rural im-
broglios by viewing them—objectively and imaginatively—from the
expanded distances afforded the film's audience by the zoom lens. In
a larger aesthetic sense, Kubrick suggests how painting and film cor-
respond as visual media wherein the artist both reshapes personal
experience into the contours of imagination ("subjective," like Alex
of *Clockwork*) and universalizes the processes of time for a receptive
audience ("objective"). The aesthetic of the zoom lens allowed him to

---

*Painterly sources for the imagery of *Barry Lyndon* probably include the works of
Thomas Gainsborough (1727–1788), known for his lyrical rural landscapes and his rather
ethereal portraits of women; John Constable (1776–1837), whose landscapes are remarkable for the beauty they attach to the everyday and mundane; William Hogarth (1697–
1764), whose paintings of eighteenth-century social life are less idealized and more satirical than the above; and Adolf Menzel (1815–1905), a German lithographer and painter
whose primary claim to fame is his renderings of Frederick the Great's court. No doubt
the list goes on and includes several other names.

capture close up the triviality, absurdity, and tragedy of various human entanglements, some of which collectively add up to what we call history, while from a distance it stimulates, through an integration of spatial form and temporal content, a release made possible by the perspectives of art. In that respect, Barry Lyndon unknowingly imprisons himself within a painted cage because, unlike the performing artists of *A Clockwork Orange* (Alex *and* Kubrick), his is an imitative rather than creative imagination.

More than ever before in a Kubrick film, time becomes a felt presence in part II of *Barry Lyndon*—"Containing an Account of the Misfortunes and Disasters Which Befell Barry Lyndon"—even as the action moves into a plush aristocratic society that makes every effort to slow it down and deny its existence. Reverend Runt (Murray Melvin), flanked by two large candles, presides over a regal marriage ceremony in which he affirms the sanctity of marriage and moralizes about "man's carnal lusts and appetites" (sternly looking at Barry), while the narrator provides the first specific date in the film, June 15, 1773. At the "pitch of prosperity," Barry exudes a confident glow in keeping with the symmetry and resplendence of his new setting, one which

Kubrick characterizes as a formal dream in slow time. Throughout the early scenes of part II, life at Castle Hackton proceeds as if it were floating in suspended animation, a world of rarefied figures brushed onto an idealized canvas or carved into the stone of a Grecian urn, a world that assumes the appearance of motion without the finality of consummation. From a distance—and that is apparently how Barry initially sees it in his mind's eye—its pleasing formalities express a cultural/period harmony while they lack specific definition. In truth, of course, the film's characters rarely occupy their generous allotment of leisure time with practical duties or concerns, but rather indulge in such ritual pastimes as dwelling at their toilette (with servants to hold ornate mirrors and washbowls), selecting from a tailor's collection the fabrics necessary to proper fashion, walking in gardens and riding in carriages, boating and fishing, playing lawn games by day and cards at night, and lingering over sumptuous meals prepared with great care and served by ubiquitous well-liveried servants. For Barry, it gives him time to master the rules of the game, to learn that if one wishes to indulge in sexual infidelities or bribe a willing member of the nobility in the pursuit of peerage, it must be done within the bounds of decorum (i.e., over a game of cards, during a formal dinner party, or in the guise of collecting works of art).* Lady Lyndon, on the other hand, passes time with her two children, plays cards with her ladies-in-waiting, polishes her skills with the harpsichord in the company of the Reverend and Lord Bullingdon, dresses herself like an art object to be admired, and, as Barry's obsession with a title increases, sits at a table with Graham (Philip Stone), her bookkeeper, and tirelessly signs bank drafts to pay for that extravagance. But time does not stop or

---

*In a brief satirical episode in which Barry bribes an unnamed nobleman by purchasing works from his art collection at exorbitant prices, he fatuously admires one painting ("I love the use of the color blue by the artist"), which the nobleman explains is by one "Ludovico Corday, a disciple of Alexandro Allori, and shows 'The Adoration of the Magi.'" Kubrick, I suspect, creates an inside joke here. For one thing, no such painter as "Ludovico Corday" ever existed, as far as I know, but the first name, of course, recalls *Clockwork*'s Ludovico Technique (which, then, decodes as an imitative and mechanical art). Alexandro Allori (1535–1607) was known for his mediocre anatomical drawings; he was an imitator of the Florentine school, which means that the fictional "Ludovico" is an imitator of an imitator. Moreover, the Adoration of the Magi has to be one of the most hackneyed and overdone subjects in the history of art, something of an obligatory piece for the artists of the Renaissance (Botticelli's is probably the most renowned example). The color blue that Barry admires is, of course, associated with the Virgin, and in several scenes he wears that color. And finally, the nobleman—like General Broulard in *Paths*—refers to the painting as a "picture" ("this is one of my best pictures"). I suspect that Kubrick's wife Christiane, herself an accomplished painter, had a hand in this scene.

slow down, even if the emotional and spiritual life of Castle Hackton does. The lugubrious chords of a Vivaldi cello concerto become a prominent musical theme and represent a variation on Handel's "Sarabande" and its march toward death, while the sounds of numerous ticking clocks (for instance, as Barry reads Bryan a book about birds, or as Mrs. Barry dismisses Runt) and the ringing of church bells acknowledge time's passage. All of which prepare for the death of Barry's son—that "contest with the grim invincible enemy," to quote the narrator—and its disruption of this dreamy immobility. Bryan's death forces Barry and Lady Lyndon to experience a tragic loneliness so inconsolable that the durable but uncomprehended art that has embellished their leisure now serves as a mockery of their transience.

While the characters in part II live in an illusory slow time, the audience experiences in rapid succession the following: a marriage, a birth, the gradual dissolution of a marriage, a birthday, Barry's fervent quest for peerage and another title, a second birthday, and a death. One cannot help but recall the birthdays of *2001,* touchingly absurd in their expression through the gargantua of space-age technology, and their foreshadowing of Bowman's rebirth as Star-Child. In *Barry Lyndon,* however, the birthdays blend in with other ritual activities and support a parable of time rather than an odyssey through space. A pattern of touching and tragic irony is captured by the sight of Bryan's ornate white coffin leading his world in a procession of regal sorrow. It is transported by the carriage and lambs that had been his birthday present the year before, and which now carry his body after his death in a fall from the horse that his father gave him as another birthday present. The boy's bed provides a setting for two birthday scenes. The first is one of charming innocence, with father and son by candlelight, as Bryan holds a stuffed toy lamb and Barry tells a highly embellished story from his military past (about his assault on a fort with "rampaging he-devils" and the cutting off of heads). In the second scene, the bed serves as Bryan's deathbed and the site of Barry's greatest loss as he breaks down in tears while repeating the same story about the fort. More than anything else, Bryan's innocence represents Barry's single perception of something fine, a brief glimpse of a tangible human beauty within the grasp of his appreciation. We are allowed to sense, through Kubrick's enforcement and compression of time, an emotional growth in Barry's character beyond that found in Thackeray, but one that, tragically, comes too late. Barry no longer plays at sentiment as before, but now suffers a tragedy so profound that not even the narrator's explanatory genius can do it justice. Kubrick lets us read it in the hands that clutch at Bryan's fragile life and on the faces of the two people left behind to ponder their sorrow and isolation.

As wooing and card-playing were appropriate to the rising action of part I, debt-paying provides Kubrick in part II with an expressive activity enacted at a table, one that capsulizes not only Barry's personal decline, but that of an entire culture. Since the characters of *Barry Lyndon* lack sufficient imaginative resources to mitigate the harsh rule of time, they fatalistically bow to its authority and probably repay more than a fair share of their accumulated debt. In Kubrick's moral universe, Barry and Lady Lyndon pay for their shallowness, for their passive willingness to be absorbed into the formal and mechanical hypocrisies of their social milieu. In three of the four debt scenes, the scratching sounds of Lady Lyndon's quill pen and the rustling of paper complement the methodical signing of her name to endless stacks of notes and checks, while Kubrick embodies in a single human activity a culture's fall into the morass of its own triviality and petty entanglements. As "H. Lyndon" (her Christian name is "Honoria") increasingly becomes a dominant visual motif, the film reminds us that such documents are all that survive as the record of a myriad of ordinary human struggles, in our own time as well as eighteenth-century time. Barry and Lady Lyndon leave behind no art or beauty to express their sorrows or their fondest dreams. Barry's hope for futurity, his son, dies, as do his ambitions, in a tangle of debts and writs. In that respect, Kubrick's *Barry Lyndon* is one artist's attempt to capture a human pathos that, more often than not, becomes lost in both the temporal progress of history and the spatial distances of art.

Especially through Barry's conflict with Bullingdon, Kubrick infuses *Barry Lyndon* with that mythopoeic subtext that dominates the structures of *Dr. Strangelove, 2001,* and *A Clockwork Orange.** While Barry is an Irish "ruffian" and "upstart" who assumes the disguise of an English gentleman, Bullingdon's "civilized" character exhibits a wide range of cultivated language and social form at odds with his latent barbarity, which expresses itself in an attack on Bryan and the revenge directed against his stepfather. Just as part I shows Barry rising in fortune and declining in character, part II matches him against Bullingdon as a way of objectifying Barry's moral growth during his

*For a discussion of the "mythopoeic" in Kubrick, see chapter 4.

fall into misfortune. In a scene not found in Thackeray, Bullingdon disrupts a formal gathering during a musical recital (Bach) at Castle Hackton (the shoes scene with Bryan), just as Barry in part I threw a glass of wine in Quin's face rather than submit to a code that required him to play the gracious loser in a contest for Nora Brady. There is a difference, however: Barry's violation of decorum (amid formal toasts of marriage at a dinner table in the Brady home) was the spontaneous act of a lovesick adolescent, while Bullingdon's act is a calculated move in a young nobleman's revenge. As Bullingdon artfully castigates Barry with his verbal superiority, the recital audience remains politely inert, as if to demonstrate the extent of their civilized restraint. No one moves in his chair or raises an objection until Barry counters Bullingdon's words with his own violence. In his savage attack against his "noble" stepson, in full view of those he seeks to impress with his claims of peerage, Barry offends this society's sense of form and decorum, rather than arousing its moral indignation. Unlike Bullingdon, he has not learned to express his malice through an acceptable verbal disguise or social form. Significantly, Kubrick's camera departs, for the first time in part II, from its polite and almost static objectivity when its handheld commotion records the confusion of the fight. The entire gathering scatters into emotional disarray as several men slip and fall on the polished wood floor in an attempt to restrain Barry's ferocity, while the women flee in horror from such an uninhibited exhibition of human aggression. And even though this scene reaffirms the existence of the "wild" Redmond Barry, it also shows that Bullingdon, his "civilized" double, has no more claim to that title than Barry does. Just as Bowman sheds HAL, his mechanical alter ego, before he moves through the Star-Gate to an awaiting rebirth, or the "primitive" Alex escapes the madness of Alexander before awakening into a post-Ludovico world, Barry paradoxically emerges as a character with moral substance only after he falls from the heights of fortune and overcomes his callow fascination with those "civilized" formal surfaces now embodied in the style and title of Lord Bullingdon.

During the period after Barry's attack on Bullingdon and Bryan's funeral, Kubrick gradually moves his protagonist out of a world characterized by formal beauty and inner ugliness through a series of scenes in which the film's mise-en-scène declines in artifice (which reverses the pattern of part I) as Barry undergoes an emotional and moral transformation. The final scene with Barry at Castle Hackton places him in a candlelit room, drunk and slumped in a chair. His pose recalls an almost identical pose assumed by a man seen on screen left in the candlelit room at the Belgian spa where Sir Charles Lyndon died. In this case, however, the scene begins and ends with a shot of a symmetrical and ornate wall (a door framed by two candelabras, two large vases, and two larger paintings), which frames Barry being carried out by two servants. In an early morning setting of static and composed sloth, which is invigorated only by the most extensive camera movement of the film (a long reverse dolly shot), Bullingdon marches through a gentlemen's club, past several slumping figures, and confronts Barry—also slumped asleep in a chair—with his demand for "satisfaction." Throughout this scene, Handel's "Sarabande-Duel" plays, as it did in part I during the duel with Quin, while in the background several paintings on a blue wall are metaphorically duplicated by "real-life" card-players watching the scene unfold, seemingly frozen in place, cards suspended in their hands, like figures in a Hogarth painting. Then the action moves, still with Handel's music, to what appears to be an abandoned church or tithe barn (with cross-shaped windows and a cathedral ceiling) for the climactic duel of the film— the one between Barry and Lord Bullingdon—in a setting that recalls Barry's rural beginnings (straw and sacks of grain on the floor, pigeons fluttering and cooing) but here serves as backdrop for his one noble act. Finally, the film goes to a small room in a local inn, where Barry lies in bed and silently plays cards with his mother, the only sounds coming from distant church bells, as he sadly contemplates the loss of his leg and the ruin of his life.

If nothing else, this sequence of events reaffirms Kubrick's remarkable talent for abstracting the resonance of myth both from the narrative demands of his medium and from its almost epistemological faith in the inviolability of "real" space (in narrative terms, "setting"). Here he implies that once Barry suffers public exposure—not as one lacking good character but as one lacking good form—and loses his son, he eventually reenters the existential context of time and exhibits a capacity for moral choice. Like Bowman and Alex before him, Barry comes out of a deadly hibernation—embodied here in a dreamlike but stillborn eighteenth-century formalism—and metaphorically "awakens" from his slumber (as a collapsed figure in a chair). Stimulated by the intervention of fate (Bryan's death) and instinct (his attack on Bullingdon), Barry escapes a world where human beings deny their moral complexity and creative potential by imitat-

Bullingdon moves down a formal corridor of
slumping figures on his way to "claim satisfaction"

ing the painted and decorative art that surrounds them. Kubrick repeatedly transfers the frozen imagery of wall paintings onto his moving screen creations (in makeup, costumes, formal poses and gestures) as a way of objectifying a psychological stasis in which the
wellspring of consciousness becomes immobilized rather than animated by the visions of art. Barry himself becomes a figure in such a
landscape (for instance, when he sits with Bryan under an enormous
and idealized painting of eighteenth-century social life, or when he
slumps in Hogarthian inebriation) as the film visually associates the
palaces of civilization with the regressions of self. Consequently, Bullingdon's return "to claim satisfaction" links the demands of gentlemanly honor to a primitive code of revenge, just as part I binds
the rituals of honor to one family's meretricious greed and an Irish
gambler's skill in cheating at cards. But now chance regains the upper
hand and proves to be a far more instructive tutor than all the patrons
and formal activities that audaciously strive to circumvent it. In the
last scenes of the film, Barry no longer cheats at cards for profit or
gain, but now, in a small room, plays with an already dealt hand as he
faces the unembellished presence of his fate.

Kubrick climaxes the film's treatment of ritual activities in the final duel between Barry and Lord Bullingdon. Significantly, he nullifies both the narrator's voice and Thackeray's inspiration (no such scene occurs in the novel) as he returns to a form of stylistic exposition associated with Barry's rise rather than his fall. Although in more extensive terms than in part I, Kubrick once again draws out a scene and preserves its temporal and emotional integrity, while indicating complex disparities between form and human content. The scene takes up almost 9 of the film's 185 minutes, and for the first time in *Barry Lyndon,* screen time and "real" time are brought into conjunction. Barry's journey through the byroads of his ambition and into the dreamy parlors of splendor now ends in the existential actuality of time. An old church, now functioning as a tithe barn or storehouse, provides a complex setting for the deliberate exposition of this scene. One might say that for Barry Lyndon, part II begins and ends in a church: the first, cast in a brilliant social and aesthetic symmetry; the last, closer to his rude beginnings yet ironically appropriate for his only freely chosen moral act. Psychologically, Barry comes full circle and confronts himself in the person of Bullingdon, his "noble" double.

The scene begins with a close-up of hands preparing a pistol, although here the camera does not zoom back as it did in the duel with Quin, but instead cuts to a shot that establishes a moral rather than natural landscape. Once again Barry duels with someone else's pistols (a "matched pair" belonging to Lord Bullingdon), and he occupies the screen-left position associated both with his father's death in the first duel and with his own apparent success in the duel with Quin. But now the rules are more rigid in their mechanics and formality. Instead of a duel in which each man fires simultaneously after a count of three, this one incorporates chance or luck into its formal order: being the "offended" party, Bullingdon enjoys the privilege of calling the coin toss to determine who will fire first. As pigeons incongruously coo and stir about the barn, one man (identified only as "Sir Richard") administers to both the duel's formal requirements (tossing the coin, marking off ten paces between the two men) and its credible but absurd verbal procedures ("Mr. Lyndon, are you ready to receive Lord Bullingdon's fire?"), while three others function as seconds and witnesses. Barry's refusal to fire on Bullingdon after Bullingdon's pistol misfires—a moment apparently structured by Kubrick to indicate Barry's capacity to act independent of a fortuitous turn of chance—is one instance in the film where the elaborate mechanics of social form embody a correspondingly significant moral and emotional content. Unfortunately and ironically, such gestures are not enough to save Barry or his world from the consequences of their folly. Rather than displaying *noblesse oblige* and accepting Barry's act of conciliation, Bullingdon insists on "satisfaction," just as he has violated decorum by vomiting in fear right before he was "to receive Mr. Lyndon's fire" (and the gentlemen in attendance register frowns of disapproval). In the end, Bullingdon concludes his shabby performance by firing on his opponent before Sir Richard even completes the count of three. In quick succession, therefore, Kubrick invests two human acts with the substance of existential truth, even though they are partly obscured by the mechanics and formality of ritual. Perhaps it is significant that Barry's only utterance during this long scene is a repeated "yes."

The final two episodes of *Barry Lyndon* unite Barry's tragic fate and Lady Lyndon's private sorrow, while they express, more succinctly than in any film before or since, both Kubrick's artistic intelligence and his personal vision. He concludes *Barry Lyndon*'s story with the only freeze frame in the film, with the sounds of Schubert's "Piano Trio in E-Flat" returning for the first time since the wooing of Lady Lyndon in part I, and with the narrator's last words ("He never saw Lady Lyndon again"). The camera reveals Barry from behind (probably a one-legged double for Ryan O'Neal) as he enters a carriage, artlessly suspended in midair without the support of either good fortune or good form. This series of frames, repeating and freezing the same image, visualizes Barry's personal decline within the informality of contingent space, just as the last scene of the film shows Lady Lyndon's sorrow within the static enclosures of formal space. To reconstruct this brilliant conclusion is to appreciate the mastery of *Barry Lyndon:* (1) Cut to interior shot, a large room at Castle Hackton. From a distance the setting appears static and painterly, with a large window on the left and light flooding in; a table stands in the right background on a polished wood floor, with three people sitting and one standing. The balanced spatial composition suggests a general cultural/period form, but not a specific human content. The Schubert music from the previous scene continues to play. (2) Cut to close-up view (there is no dialogue or narration) of Lady Lyndon slowly and methodically signing bank drafts. We hear the scratching sounds of her pen, a moment's hesitation as Bullingdon, to her right, places another one before her to be signed. The camera concentrates more on her face than on the activity itself. (3) Cut to slow zoom shot of a bank draft made out as follows: "Pray pay Redmond Barry for Annuity 500 guineas, and debit to my account." As she signs her name ("H. Lyndon") to the right, we see a date in the lower left corner of the frame, "Dec 1789." (4) Cut to close-up of Lady Lyndon's distracted and sorrowful stare. Following a moment's delay and an expression of muted emotion, she continues the ritual of signing her name to the remaining documents. (5) Cut back to long shot, static composition as before, as the last piano note strikes. (6) Screen cuts to black as Handel's "Sarabande" plays during the film's end-titles.

In the film's temporal structure, this remarkable three minutes of film completes the domination of time in part II (which begins and ends on specified dates), while it reaffirms an eighteenth-century society's entrapment within its own forms and rituals, its own folly and moral irrelevance. As before, Kubrick's method of visual exposition delincates how the particular human content of one era becomes tragically lost in time and absorbed into the aesthetic distances of its art. By selecting 1789 for the terminating date of the story (no such date exists in Thackeray), with its allusion to the French Revolution and the beginning of a new age in Europe (which might explain the Schubert selection and serve as an indirect reference to the postponed Napoleon film project), Kubrick asks his twentieth-century audience to consider the passing glories and tragic failures of nineteenth-century heroic individualism. Perhaps, he implies, the disparities between one period of history and another may not be disparities at all, but particular instances of a universal condition—of that Kubrickian odyssey through time in which mankind evolves in fits and starts on its way to a civilized humanity waiting in space on the far side of 2001. In the end, however, Kubrick's *Barry Lyndon* leaves its audience with something less tangible but far more enduring: the haunting memory of those last frozen images of Barry and Lady Lyndon, he with his back to the camera and falling into space, she lost forever in a distant mise-en-scène, and both imploring us to gaze with feeling and understanding at two film portraits that refuse to eviscerate humanity in the formal pursuit of art.

8 REMEMBRANCE OF THINGS FORGOTTEN

The Shining

After *Barry Lyndon*, his least commercially successful but one of his most artistically satisfying films, Stanley Kubrick turned to a contemporary American horror novel by Stephen King. As interesting a potboiler in its own right as Thackeray's obscure nineteenth-century picaresque adventure, King's *The Shining* (1977) represented for Kubrick something more than just a ready commercial property for a filmmaker rebounding from a financial setback. What's surprising is not his choice of the novel but the fact that he waited so long to make his first "horror" film. Here is how he described the popular mythology of the genre as well as its psychological and emotional appeal:

> One of the things that horror stories can do is show us the archetypes of the unconscious; we can see the dark side without having to confront it directly. Also, ghost stories appeal to our craving for immortal-

ity. If you can be afraid of a ghost, then you have to believe that a ghost
may exist. And if a ghost exists then oblivion might not be the end.

As early as *Killer's Kiss,* through the intertwined characters of Davy
Gordon (a paradigm of homogenized, repressed manhood) and Vincent Rapallo (the dark beast), a Kubrick film crudely embodied the
horror genre's most enduring device: the psychological allegory of
the *doppelgänger,* alter ego, or double. In an excellent essay on the
subject, Robin Wood describes the classic horror film formula as one
where "normality is threatened by the Monster," and the *doppelgänger*
motif as one "where normality and the Monster are two aspects of the
same person." Throughout his career, however, Kubrick employed
psychological doubling in ways that increasingly resembled the twists
and ironies of a Nabokovian blend of play and metaphysics more than
a *locus classicus* like Stevenson's *The Strange Case of Dr. Jekyll and Mr.
Hyde.* His films repeatedly mix the grotesque and banal, the conventions of Gothic confessional morbidity (for instance, De Quincey's
The Confessions of an English Opium-Eater or Poe's "William Wilson")
and the self-conscious involutions of modernist parody. Humbert
reads the "divine Edgar" (Poe), confesses his libidinous yearnings for
Lolita in a diary, and becomes ensnared in a dark fate disguised as the
protean Quilty, who, like the Monster seen on a drive-in movie screen
(played by Christopher Lee), slowly unwraps himself before his urbane creator/double. In *Clockwork,* Alex plays the "humble narrator"
of a tale that forces the audience to accept his violent freedom as a
chosen alternative to the monstrous creations of the State. And in *Dr.
Strangelove,* normality itself becomes indistinguishable from Peter Sellers's brilliant conception of Strangelove as mad scientist and resurrected monster, while *2001* develops a futuristic parable of mankind
awakening from an evolutionary slumber to reclaim its destiny from
the polite but murderous control of a monster/machine.

Like Buñuel, who satirically incorporated the iconography of horror into such films as *The Exterminating Angel* (1962) and *The Discreet
Charm of the Bourgeoisie* (1972), Kubrick had a surrealist fascination for
the dark archetypes of an unruly unconscious, where, to quote Robin
Wood, "the Monster is normality's shadow." That nightmare journey
through the forest of *Fear and Desire* and Davy Gordon's battle in a
mannequin factory with a relentless Shadow figure anticipate later
doublings that locate the primitive in the formal disguises of civilization and, paradoxically, the traces of civilized evolution in the savage's

aggressive disorder. *Lolita*'s Humbert becomes less European and more sympathetic as he wanders through Quilty's devious maze, just as Barry Lyndon shows a capacity for moral choice only after he falls from the graces of civility and faces Bullingdon's ritual vengeance. Muffley's imperturbable sanity merges with Strangelove's madness, and both are nurtured by the same darkness, while in *2001* Bowman loses himself in an eighteenth-century memory room that encloses him within the decor of civilized aspiration and temporal reduction. Colonel Dax of *Paths* waits too long before he sees the Monster in the chateau's splendor, while Alex, *Clockwork*'s primitive artist, both animates Alexander's latent savagery and reverses a culture's decline into the stasis of voyeurism and sublimation.

Such paradoxical complications rarely inform the more conventional pleasures of King's novel, although an appreciation for its psychological and thematic logic does illuminate some of the more complex intentions of the film. Unlike the script written by Kubrick and American novelist Diane Johnson, King's work does not locate its mystery or its ambiguity in the characterization of Jack Torrance. King's omniscient style allows the reader to figuratively "shine" and rationalize practically every nuance of character, even though it never explains how or why Jack's five-year-old son Danny acquired his precognitive/extrasensory powers, nor the sources of the haunted-house "shinings" at the Overlook Hotel. Danny's powers and the shinings are merely two horror-fiction givens which support the conventional wisdom of Reason's impotence before the mysterious workings of Mind and Nature. (This "more things in heaven and earth" idea is partly expressed in the epigraph of the novel, Goya's "The sleep of reason breeds monsters.") And even though Jack stubbornly resists both his and Danny's unwelcome gift of "shining," his steady descent into madness resembles a psychological case study as much as a journey into the heart of darkness. The novel associates Jack's lapses into murderous rage with a pattern of father/son doubling, with his own father's frustration and drunken failures, and with a latent wish to punish his wife and son for his inadequacies as a man and his incompetence as a writer/teacher. (Early in the book, for instance, we learn about Jack's violence against a former student and how he once broke Danny's arm, while he barely controls a sadistic urge to hurt his wife, Wendy, during lovemaking.)

King enlarges and complicates this psychological drama through a symbolic structure that inventively mixes the pulpy cliché of Pop

Culture Gothic horror (the novel's primary analogues include Poe's "The Masque of the Red Death," Shirley Jackson's *The Haunting of Hill House,* and Don Siegel's 1956 film version of *Invasion of the Body Snatchers*) with an implicit critique of the post–World War II American character. (Jack's "shinings" in the novel return him to a masked ball at the Overlook on the night of August 29, 1945; in the film, it is a 1921 dream party.) In that context, Jack's history becomes symptomatic of an American withdrawal from Cold War uncertainty into apocalyptic self-indulgence and a denial of the social/existential imperatives of conscience. The Overlook, like some impersonal and Kafkaesque corporate state, claims Jack's soul and signs him to a lifetime contract as its caretaker and official biographer. He loses interest in the humane focus of his own writing (he comes to "loathe" the characters in his unfinished play) and in the intimate bonds of family. In the end, he becomes the alter ego of King himself, who was so fond of the characters in *The Shining* that he killed off only Jack Torrance and the Overlook's spooks. As he explores the history of the Overlook in a scrapbook, not only does Jack become absorbed into its demonic past, but his madness resuscitates both its ghouls and his father's legacy. Thematically, King suggests that this symbiotic link between hotel and man represents America's secret longing for a timeless escape (like the revelers in Poe's story), where the complex moral demands of the so-called nuclear family are abrogated by a mindless devotion to technocratic "work" (Jack's obsession with "doing his job") and by the lure of visceral pleasure. If nothing else, Stephen King's *The Shining* reminds us that Hawthorne's New England morality and Gothic sensibility can be translated into the fictional idiom of more than one American generation.

Central to the effect and fascination of King's novel is the conflict between Family and Monster, between the norms that Jack's moral education teaches him to revere and his urge to destroy those restraints and release a diseased libido. An implicit reference in both novel and film is those sudden outbursts of inexplicable violence on the placid landscapes of American family life, of husbands butchering loved ones and killing themselves, those real-life tales from the American Crypt. In King's version, the Family—that bedrock of normality, continuity, order—is threatened from within by both the Father (creator/destroyer) and the Hotel (America's recent past), while the son functions on an allegorical level as Redeemer rather than Antichrist. Danny's ability to "shine" enables him to read thoughts (e.g., he dreads the word "divorce" whenever it appears in Wendy's mind), to locate missing objects, and to "see" things from both the past and the future. Initially, King misleads the reader into believing that his character may be another Satanic Child, when in fact it is the Overlook which is possessed and which needs both the boy's powers and Jack's madness to revive a dormant evil. Since he does not always understand his visions, Danny creates a fifteen-year-old alter ego named "Tony" (in the book, Danny's middle name is Anthony), who not only "tells" and "shows" him things but glimpses their meaning. Near the novel's ending, when the integrity of the family confronts its greatest danger, Danny experiences a vision/dream in which he falls through a Poe-inspired ballroom clock into a nightmare world akin to Lewis Carroll's *Alice in Wonderland*. In that imaginary journey, Danny confronts in "Tony's" face a composite of his and Jack's visages. After Jack and the hotel are destroyed and evil is purged by an exploding boiler, the novel does not completely resolve this second father/son doubling. It quietly suggests that the father's heritage survives in some hidden corridor of the son's mind, even as a new family order forms around Hallorann (Overlook's black cook), Wendy, and Danny.

As the above indicates, King's novel provided Kubrick with a reasonably accessible group of characters and numerous opportunities for either conceptual/symbolic enlargement or alteration. The director of *Dr. Strangelove, 2001,* and *A Clockwork Orange* must have been particularly intrigued by a narrative tendency to subordinate conventional linear surfaces to a symbolic or dreamlike logic, one in which the rational dualities of normal/abnormal, sane/insane cohabit in the imaginative terrain of a modern Gothic fairy tale. Needless to say, Kubrick's *The Shining* (1980) offers little evidence that he "believed" in such things as "shinings" and paranormal close encounters, but it does reveal a film aesthetic that continued to confound audience expectations at the very moment it appeared to fulfill them. For a start, Kubrick eliminated many of the supernatural episodes found in the novel, especially those that bordered on horror-film cliché and that —in an era before Computer Graphic Imaging (CGI)—would have been impossible, optically, to conform to his stylistic preferences. For the director of *Dr. Strangelove, 2001,* and *A Clockwork Orange,* the psychological archetypes common to the horror genre could be rendered on film only through a realist/surrealist style, which requires that the unconscious assume a palpable and empirical life. Besides the explosive ending, which King telegraphs from the beginning,

Kubrick deleted these significant details from the novel: (1) an empty wasps' nest that mysteriously revives and attacks Danny; (2) an animal topiary (rabbits, dogs, lions) that keeps moving and guards the entrance to the Overlook Hotel; (3) a fire hose that becomes a snake and threatens Danny; (4) an elevator that moves by itself and contains signs of the 1945 ball (a mask, confetti); (5) a roque court (roque is a form of croquet) from which Jack gets the short-handled mallet he uses as a murder weapon in the novel; and (6) a model playhouse/ replica of the Overlook Hotel in which Danny feels a malign presence.

Elsewhere, Kubrick and collaborator Diane Johnson altered both the impact and the meaning of several key episodes found in the novel. In the novel, Room 217 is where Danny first sees REDRUM (written on the bathroom mirror) and a bloated female corpse in the bathtub. In the film, room 217 has become 237, the locus of a psycho/ sexual event for Jack Torrance (who, in the novel, never sees the woman). The film retains most of Jack's conversations with Lloyd, the ghostly bartender, as well as his dialogue with Delbert Grady, the hotel's former caretaker, but places them, respectively, in an authentic Jazz Age mise-en-scène and a startling red bathroom. In both instances, the film enlarges and complicates the doubling patterns found in the novel. Instead of a masked ball, the film re-creates a formal party, which, it turns out, takes place at the Overlook on July 4, 1921, and which includes an old song ("Midnight with the Stars and You") about romantic dreams and recollection. And in the film's climax, Jack kills Hallorann with an ax (in the novel, the Overlook cook recovers from a roque-mallet attack), then later suffers a lonely, frozen death (rather than an explosive, infernal one) after Wendy and Danny escape in a snowcat.

But this is not to say that the film neglects all the expected trappings of horror fiction and horror filmmaking, although at times it uses them facetiously or buries them so deeply that they pass unnoticed. Jack (Jack Nicholson) tells hotel manager Stuart Ullman (Barry Nelson) that his wife is a "ghost story and horror film addict" after he listens to a foreshadowing story about one Charles Grady, the caretaker in 1970, who ran amok and killed his family with an ax before blowing his brains out with a shotgun. We learn from Ullman that the hotel's season runs from May 15 to October 30 (a change from the novel), which means that the Torrances move in on Halloween. During her initial tour of the kitchen with Hallorann (Scatman Crothers),

Wendy (Shelley Duvall) remarks that it is like a maze, and she later characterizes the fast-emptying hotel as "like a ghost ship." On their way to the Overlook, the Torrances discuss the Donner party and cannibalism, a subject that Danny (Danny Lloyd) knows about from TV and that Jack characterizes as a necessary means of "survival." During the closing-day tour, however, Hallorann shows Wendy that they will have more than enough provisions for the winter, which anticipates the film's thematic concern for psychological/spiritual cannibalism and survival through Jack's eventual descent into madness. In a scene in which Hallorann discusses "shining" with Danny, knives hanging from a kitchen rack become prominent only after the boy asks him if he is "scared" of the Overlook, which foreshadows both Wendy's clutching one of the knives after she locks Jack in the pantry and her later slashing of his hand as he attempts to force his way into their bathroom with an ax. Not only the knife but suggestions of birds and birdlike menace recall a primary motif in another film about the American family and schizophrenia, Hitchcock's *Psycho*. The opening camera movements swoop through the Rocky Mountains and pass over Jack's yellow Volkswagen like birds of prey; strange bird sounds accompany several exterior transition shots of the Overlook; and shrieking music accentuates certain moments of terror. A model of a dark eagle with its wings spread in flight rests on a windowsill in Ullman's office, and Jack wears a green sweatshirt adorned with a large black eagle ("Stovington Eagles") in the scene where he eats breakfast in bed, discusses *déjà vu* with Wendy (he feels that he's been in the Overlook before), and playfully mocks her haunted house fears. Ullman passes on the apocryphal story that the hotel was constructed (1907–1909) on an old Indian burial ground, which misleads us into believing that the spirit dancers in the enormous imitation Navajo sand painting over the fireplace in the Colorado Lounge (the main room where Jack types his "book") will come to life and haunt the Torrance family. Another foreshadowing occurs in a kitchen scene where Wendy prepares supper while watching a Denver television newscast about a convicted murderer being given a "life sentence" (an indirect allusion to Jack's subsequent desire to join Overlook's immortals), an "Aspen woman" who has disappeared during a "hunting trip with her husband," and the progress of a snowstorm that will isolate both her and Danny during Jack's animal-like transformation. When Jack and his ax move through the hotel and into the snow-covered hedge maze (appropriately, its hedges are thirteen feet high), his exaggerated limp and foot dragging (the result of a fall down the staircase) recall all those horror-film cripples and hunchbacks of the 1930s, just as Wendy's vision of cobwebs and skeletons (including the humorous remains of Delbert Grady, standing with a tray in his hand and serving his "customers") in the hotel's "reception" area revives one of the horror genre's hoariest devices.

In almost every respect, Kubrick's *The Shining* challenges both an audience's expectations and its conceptual understanding of narrative events in ways that King's novel rarely does. In the early scenes, Kubrick develops Jack's character from a deceptively "objective" point of view, except for that moment when Jack "shines" over a model in the reception area of the hedge maze and the camera (from Jack's perspective) slowly zooms down on the tiny figures of Wendy and Danny arriving in the center of the "real" hedge maze outside. Before his first conversation with Lloyd the bartender (Joe Turkel), Jack's interiority remains largely a mystery (in marked contrast to the novel's method), as the film requires the audience to "shine" by interpreting his character through either Danny's subjectivity or other visual details. Many clues are offered:

A light moment on the set of *The Shining* (Jack Nicholson, Stanley Kubrick)

1. Through Danny's imaginary friend "Tony" (a voice who lives in his mouth and hides in his stomach) and his "shinings"—the elevator of blood, the two Grady girls standing hand in hand and facing the camera, REDRUM—*The Shining* not only visualizes three images of horror but provides a symbolic conduit (visual and aural) into Jack's unconscious mind as well as its demonic reincarnation within the collective unconscious of the Overlook Hotel.

2. The Grady sisters, who look like twins but are actually doubles (their ages of eight and ten are established in Jack's interview with Ullman), link Jack to the caretaker (Charles Grady) who axed his family in 1970 (in one bloody "shining" Danny sees the girls' bodies and the ax lying on the floor in one of the hotel's corridors), while the elevator of blood first appears to Danny through a bathroom mirror in the Boulder apartment just after "Tony" tells him that Jack has accepted the Overlook job and is about to phone Wendy.

3. Subsequently, both the elevator/blood vision and REDRUM appear as "shinings" (through parallel editing) whenever Danny reacts in terror to a dramatic increase in Jack's anger or madness (for instance, when Jack blows up at Wendy's suggestion that they leave the hotel, and during the scene in which she holds a baseball bat and retreats from his threatening advances).

4. In the film, the hotel scrapbook—a critical and fully explained property in the novel—becomes not only a subtle narrative device but a significant visual motif. Jack, for instance, starts to write his "book" only after the scrapbook appears on the table next to his typewriter, and it is on prominent display in the foreground of a wide-angle shot when he becomes angry with Wendy for interrupting his work ("We're going to make a new rule. When I'm in here, and you hear me typing, or whether you don't hear me typing, or whatever the fuck you hear me doing in here, that means don't come in"). In such a way does the film imply that his obsessive and lonely typing (he yanks the paper out of the carriage when she arrives), his bursts of violent temper, and his trancelike states are connected with his discovery and exploration of the Overlook's secret past in the scrapbook.

5. The large brown scrapbook not only looks ancient but contains pasted newspaper clippings that assume the shape of a maze's internal design.

6. Later, in the meeting with Delbert Grady (Philip Stone) in the red bathroom of the Gold Room, Jack claims to recognize him from

newspaper photos (in the scrapbook) as Kubrick creates a doubling effect not found in King. In the film there are not only two Grady daughters but two Grady fathers—Delbert Grady, a waiter/butler type (called "Jeevesy" by Jack) at the 1921 party, who says that his wife and daughters are somewhere in the hotel, and Charles Grady, the caretaker who killed himself and his family in 1970.

7. The various doublings imply that there are two Jack Torrances, the one who goes mad and freezes to death in present time and the one smiling out of a 1921 photograph that hangs on the gold corridor wall inside the Overlook Hotel.

Instead of the novel's animal topiary, its replica playhouse, or its roque court, Kubrick's film uses a hedge maze (100 yards long in the script, but reduced to a smaller scale on Elstree's backlot) to metaphorically focus the meaning of Jack's madness as well as visually embody larger conceptual aspirations. Mazes—like games of chess—combine design and deception, paths and choices, fate and cul-de-sacs—all of which, in various guises, play significant thematic roles in almost every Kubrick film. Mazes are highly artificial human contrivances whose orderly and complex sense of purpose involves a twofold conceptual game in which the player must not only search for the center but *remember* how to get out. Thus a maze embodies the reverse spatial idea of movement toward enclosure (self-contained, formal art uncontaminated by life) and movement toward freedom (chaos, infinity, contingency). In the fiction of Jorge Luis Borges, for example, characters repeatedly search for the "center" of their existence, only to discover that life has no essence, but that it does contain an appealing multiplicity and complexity within its mazelike exchange between objective and subjective worlds. Kubrick's chateau in *Paths of Glory* resembles a labyrinth (corridors, uncertain turns, spatial design from afar and dislocation from within), but only General Broulard moves through it with assurance, and even he answers to unseen forces off-screen. More often than not, Kubrick's characters get lost in a tangle of ambition and desire: Davy Gordon's romantic infatuation with a ballroom dancer becomes confused by the obscure objects of his desire and the deceptive moves of Rapallo, while both Humbert and Barry Lyndon briefly attain the "center" of their respective quests (nymphet, wealth/title), only to realize that it resembles an empty room without doors.

In *The Shining*, the maze concept encompasses the film thematically and aesthetically (i.e., both within the film itself and with respect to the audience watching it). It not only helps explain Jack's madness (that is, the unconscious as a labyrinth in which the conscious self gets lost) but inspires the Overlook's floor plan and decor (for instance, the maze pattern of the carpet outside Room 237), as well as the events that occur there. In addition, the film contains a maze-within-a-maze (the model inside the hotel) that doubles with the "real" maze outside. Significantly, Jack wants to stay inside the hotel's maze rather than explore its surroundings (after closing day, he is not seen outside until that final chase through the snow into the hedge maze), to control its center (the Colorado Lounge) like a madly inspired God writing his book of Creation. Symbolically, he wants to "forget" himself (Jack Torrance in present time), and to "remember" not how to escape from the center of the maze but how to command its static and enclosed timelessness. In contrast, the film associates both Wendy and Danny with "outside" worlds, with contingency and movement, which means from the beginning that they will either escape Jack's madness, if they "remember" how to retrace their steps, or be cornered in a no-exit hallway if they choose the wrong path. Early in the film, for instance, they learn how to negotiate the corridors of the hotel ("to leave a trail of breadcrumbs," to quote Wendy), and in one scene Danny moves in a circle around the Colorado Lounge on his Big Wheel tricycle, while Jack tends to remain stationary within its center. Wendy and Danny explore the hedge maze and complete a circular journey that travels into and out of its diabolical design. Jack, on the other hand, imitates what Borges characterizes as the death-in-life of the "North" (that is, northern European intellectualism)—that yearning for a totally rationalized world without those crevices of unreason that arouse despair in some and imagination in others—rather than the "South's" desire to traverse the maze and engage its multiplicity, to confront fate and choice, and to outface oblivion in an act of creation. To covet the center of the maze as permanent resting place leads not only to death but to madness.

Within the mazelike designs of *The Shining*, Kubrick develops a series of doubling/mirroring effects that go far beyond anything found in King's novel. And because the film so completely integrates these doublings into a narrative and visual labyrinth, the viewer-turned-critic needs a descriptive map before daring to chart any interpretive course. We must see what is there, before asking what it means. With that in mind, as well as the summary already provided, consider the following:

1. Jack's interview with Ullman, whose confident affability contrasts with Jack's unconvincing nonchalance, pairs off with the meeting between Wendy and a woman doctor (Anne Jackson), whose sober and professional womanhood reacts in stunned disbelief to the housewife's offhand but slightly cowed explanation for an old injury (a separated shoulder) inflicted on Danny by his drunken father.

2. For the interview, Jack and Ullman are joined by a hotel employee named Bill Watson (Barry Dennen), whose only real distinction (and function) is his striking physical resemblance to Jack Nicholson, especially when seen from behind (they pair off into chairs opposite one another and facing Ullman); and on closing day Watson completes a double pairing of four figures walking in single file (Ullman, Wendy, Jack, Watson) through the Colorado Lounge and past the hedge maze on their way to the snowcat, where they divide into twos (Wendy and Watson on the left, Jack and Ullman on the right).

3. Interestingly, this grouping resembles the four horizontally placed figures inside the "circle" of the Navajo sand painting over the fireplace, with Wendy and Jack occupying the privileged "center" position, and Ullman and Watson framing them on either side.

4. On two occasions, Ullman says goodbye to two young female employees, and just as the Torrances are ushered into their hotel living quarters, Jack noticeably glances after them in a gesture of sexual interest.

5. In the kitchen on closing day, Hallorann shows Wendy the meat in the freezer and the dry food in the pantry, but not those things that fall in between (butter, milk, eggs, and so forth), just as the various weather reports emphasize extremes (for instance, the TV newscast that Wendy watches in the kitchen and the one in Hallorann's Miami bedroom, which mentions both a record heat wave in Florida and a record snowfall in Colorado). So Wendy and Danny watch *Summer of '42* (Robert Mulligan, 1971) on television in the midst of a winter snowstorm, and Jack relives an Overlook ball from the summer of 1921 during a winter in present time.

6. In that Miami bedroom, two paintings showing a black nude woman on opposite walls (mirroring) are seen just before Hallorann experiences a "shining" that occurs between Danny's and Jack's separate visits to Room 237.

7. Two versions of the same nude woman inhabit the green bathroom of Room 237. One is an old hag/corpse who apparently rises out of the bathtub to strangle Danny, and the other is an erotically

inviting siren who "seduces" Jack before transforming herself back into the decomposed and laughing crone.

8. While Danny's "shinings" link him to Jack's unconscious, they also provide a horrific vision into the Overlook Hotel, one that opposes his father's more nostalgic and dreamy "memories." Similarly, Danny's association with cartoon characters and stuffed animals anticipates Jack's grotesque metamorphosis into the Big Bad Wolf coming after the "little piggies" with an ax.

9. Jack "shines" on two occasions, once with each of his two Overlook doubles (Lloyd the bartender and Delbert Grady, the first decidedly American and the other English).

10. The film contains four bathrooms, two associated with both the Torrance family and images of murder (in the Boulder apartment and their Overlook quarters), and two (the green and red ones) associated with Jack's regression into madness and the hotel's past.

11. Not only does the film contain two mazes (the hedge outside and a model inside), but the Overlook itself is a maze and, significantly, it breaks down into two sections, one old and one remodeled, one past and one present. The hotel's old-fashioned "staff wing," for instance, contains the Torrances' rather shabby and cramped apartment, as well as the hallway (worn blue carpet, faded yellow wallpaper) where the two Grady children were murdered. In contrast, the "public" half of the Overlook is dressed out in a mélange of modern and indigenous decorative styles, including authentic Navajo designs and colors, mazelike patterns in the carpeting, and the refurbished (according to Ullman) gold and pink gaudiness of the Gold Room.

12. Finally, mirrors figure prominently in the following settings and scenes: inside the four bathrooms; in the Torrance bedroom at the Overlook (in one scene, a mirror completes a double image of Jack sitting in bed and later converts REDRUM into MURDER); in the hallway entrance inside the Torrance apartment (where Jack's reflection is prominent just *after* he returns from his visit to Room 237); in Hallorann's Miami bedroom; on the wall of the corridor leading to the Gold Room (before both his "shinings" in that room, Jack's reflection in a corridor mirror is shown); behind the bar of the Gold Room; and just inside the doorway of Room 237.

With the possible exception of *2001*, no previous Kubrick film contains as many important details or stimulates as many associative responses. *The Shining* requires several viewings before its secrets are released, and even though like a maze-puzzle it can be assembled into

one or more interpretive designs, mysteries remain which intimate
that there is still more. Like Bowman within his memory room, we
sense a familiar terrain, a kind of private and cinematic *déjà vu*, but
one dislocated from conventional time and space (both real and
filmic) in just enough ways to encourage new perceptions and fresh
understandings, if for no other reason than a desire to escape its powerful hold on our imagination. In that sense, Kubrick's films are always about "shining," about the difficulties of seeing, of choosing, of
creating, *of knowing*. And what is it that makes up good art, or even
good criticism, if not a magical conjunction of informed knowledge
and inspired "shining"? Let us now remove the qualifying marks and
shine on.

The narrative structure of *The Shining* involves a journey from an organized and forward-moving world of time into the disorders of self
and regressions of memory. In some respects, it recalls the first three
parts of *2001* in reverse ("Dawn of Man," Floyd's journey to the Moon,
"Jupiter Mission: 18 Months Later"), in that Jack Torrance, unlike
Bowman as Star-Child, does not escape from his memory room (the
Overlook Hotel) into space, but instead retreats into its dehumanizing order. Through the use of titles on a black screen, Kubrick emphasizes time more than he does space, as the following breakdown
of the film's organization reveals:

Prologue	Credits (Rocky Mountain flight)
Part One	"The Interview" and "Closing Day"
Part Two	"A Month Later"/ "Tuesday"/
	"Thursday"/ "Saturday"/ "Monday"/
	"Wednesday"
Part Three	"8 am" and "4 pm"
Epilogue	Two Frozen Images of Jack (in the
	hedge maze and in the 1921 photograph)

Notice how the progression of events goes from months to days to
hours, a process of reduction and intensification that moves toward a
single moment in time when insanity breaks loose from the restraints
of rational order. As he did so often in other films, Kubrick undermines an audience's faith in the narrative machinery of exposition—
and its cause/effect logic—by, first, establishing its credibility through
a realistic, matter-of-fact style (in part one), only to confuse that un-

derstanding by transforming it into a memory as faint or illusory as Jack's mad quest for the immortality of death. By parts two and three, the periodic screen-titles conform to an associative or symbolic logic, to the film's complex patterns of doubling and reversal (i.e., the every-other-day quality of "Tuesday"/"Thursday," etc., or the movement from "8 am" to "4 pm"), which inevitably mock our desire for temporal sense and rational sequence. Early in the film, for instance, Kubrick creates subtle time confusions that become even more pronounced later on. Wendy tells the doctor that "Tony" first appeared about the same time that Jack, in a drunken rage, separated Danny's shoulder, which, we learn later, happened three years before. Not only does Wendy fail to make the psychological connection between "Tony" and Jack's violence, but she pretends to be reassured by the fact that Jack has been on the wagon for five months, which means that any remorse he felt about his son was either very belated or nonexistent. During Jack's first conversation with the bartender, he acts as if his life in present time were a bad dream from the future (i.e., post-1921), and that *his* imaginary friend Lloyd has as much continuity and corporeality as the members of his own family (his first words, spoken directly into the camera, are "Hi, Lloyd"). Ever so quietly, the film implies from the beginning that psychological time and real time do not operate according to the same causal schedule, that the objective world and its temporal assertiveness may not explain character, but it does provide clues to those who shine.

In the credits, the camera from above moves over water and through mountains with the ease of a bird in flight and the rapidity of a machine in space. Below, on a winding mountain road, Jack's diminutive yellow Volkswagen journeys through a tree-lined maze (the film's second shot), resembling one of Danny's toy cars or the yellow tennis ball seen later from another overhead shot on the maze-patterned carpet (orange and brown colors, with a red center) in the corridor outside Room 237. Above, one experiences the freedom and uncertainty of contingent space, an anticipation of either Star-Gates (*2001*) or Doomsday flights (*Strangelove*), while the theme music (by Wendy Carlos and Rachel Elkind) sounds like a Gregorian chant for the dead (*Dies Irae*) and prepares us for the world below, for paths and endgames within a horizontal labyrinth, where one forgets how to look up and out into the wonders of space. Part one maps out this terrain in a deceptively clear and orderly manner. The interview between Ullman and Jack takes the form of questions and answers, explanations and reassurances—that is, the give and take of rational, linear discourse. Ullman "explains" the caretaker's job, how it is not "physically demanding" but potentially involves problems of adjustment ("cabin fever") for certain kinds of people. Like those disembodied narrators throughout the soundscape of Kubrick's films, his voice and manner serve the requirements of narrative exposition while they fail to explain or acknowledge the mysteries of inner and outer space. Jack smiles and affects a relaxed informality, although his attention becomes more concentrated, even trancelike, when Ullman, himself all smiles, relates as a footnote to the interview a story about the former caretaker who "seemed perfectly normal" but nevertheless cut up his family with an ax and "stacked their bodies neatly in one of the rooms in the west wing." Naturally, he has worked out a reassuring and logical explanation for such an appalling departure from sane behavior (a "claustrophobic reaction"), although Jack's obvious interest (as if it recalls one of his own nightmares) and his insincere congeniality (early signs of a personality malfunction) lead us to believe that the film's definition of his madness will be far more complex.

By the end of the film, the Grady story takes on a larger meaning in the way it not only anticipates Jack's fate but completes a doubling pattern identical to the one between Jack and that smiling figure in the 1921 photograph (that is, as Jack pairs off with a 1921 persona, so Charles Grady in 1970 confronted his Shadow in the figure of Delbert Grady). But all that seems part of another universe in the context of the interview structure of the film's opening, a context and structure that eventually recalls a style of *cinéma vérité* psychodrama familiar in the works of Truffaut (for instance, *The 400 Blows*) and Bergman (*Scenes from a Marriage*, 1973; *Face to Face*, 1976). Is it imitation or parody? Not only in the beginning, but in the other "interviews" of part one (Wendy and the doctor, Jack and Wendy in the car, Hallorann and Danny in the kitchen), Kubrick disturbs the still waters of cinematic normality with something more important than just Danny's bloody shinings. Through his characters' bland, offhand reportage of gruesome acts of horror from the past, he suggests that Ullman's world might have less substance than a madman's phantasms. Charles Grady's butchery and suicide, Jack's earlier violence against his son, the cannibalism of the Donner party, and the threat of Room 237, as well as other "bad" things alluded to by Hallorann in the Overlook's history, become inseparable from all the small talk about "making good time" (Jack's trip from Boulder to the hotel) and making new friends (Wendy's reassurances to Danny), about a "new writing project" and a fresh start (for Jack and his family). Eventually, Jack denies existential time in search of private time, Danny's new friends are two dead girls who want him to play and live with them "forever and ever and ever," and Jack's creative ambitions degenerate into a stack of papers that repeat a single obsessive thought. In the end, *The Shining* concerns old projects and unfinished journeys, secret longings and frustrated desires, movements in reverse rather than movements forward, "interviews" with the Self's dark but hardly imaginary friends.

And what is "Closing Day" all about, if not an attempt to define and place the spatial geography of the film? Like the interview, the closing-day tour puts things in order, establishes relationships, and completes the film's temporal and spatial exposition of the Overlook Hotel. But again there are unexplained confusions and tensions more significant than just Danny's game-room shining (of the two Grady daughters) or the audience's natural tendency to look for the first indications of horror yet to come. Spatially, the tour shows us rooms, places, and objects of importance to later events, while it fails to provide an overview of the whole. Where, for instance, is the Colorado Lounge in relation to the kitchen? or the Gold Room? or Room 237? or the Torrances' apartment?* Like Wendy in her reaction to the kitchen, the audience feels both at home and lost within the hotel's vast public areas and its more intimate corridors and rooms. Like a maze-puzzle, and like the film itself, it has design and purpose, but

---

*Needless to say, some familiarity with Kubrick's maze—namely, his Overlook Hotel set in *The Shining*—helps in placing action and understanding parallels, associations, and repetitions. With that in mind, consider these few items of interest:

1. The reception area, the kitchen (which is behind the reception area), the gold corridor, and the Gold Room occupy the first floor of the Overlook; the model maze sits on a table by a window opposite Ullman's office in the reception area and appears in the background of several scenes (e.g., when Jack first arrives at the hotel, when he calls Wendy to tell her that he has the job, when Wendy pushes a breakfast cart in "A Month Later," and when Hallorann, taking a similar course [from kitchen, through gold corridor, to reception area], is murdered).

2. The Colorado Lounge is located in the center of the second floor of the hotel, and Room 237 appears to be in a wing behind the table where Jack types his manuscript; Danny rides his Big Wheel in a circle ("A Month Later") around the Colorado Lounge, from a service corridor behind the wall with the fireplace and Navajo sand painting, to an alcove by the elevators behind Jack's typing table, past a sign in red advertising "Camera Walk" (Kubrick's joking reference to the Steadicam?) and through the lounge itself, into an alcove on the other side, and back to the original starting point—from there it is not far to the mazelike carpeting (screen right from the elevators) that leads to Room 237.

one that initially requires its inhabitants/players—the characters in the hotel and audience in the theater—to look for signs of that unseen intelligence that created it and that understands its logic. During the interview, for instance, Ullman tells Jack that the Charles Grady killings took place in the "west wing," while he defines the section of the hotel that houses the Torrance apartment as the "staff wing." Is this not one example of an Ullman euphemism (as well as a Kubrick irony), in that the hallway directly opposite the entrance to the apartment leads to the corridor (a dead end) with the faded yellow wallpaper with blue flowers where later Danny shines and sees the butchered Grady daughters? Jack and Wendy stand together in the white bathroom of the apartment, where in part three she will be cornered by his madness, and both express disapproval—Jack through sardonic humor ("homey," he calls it), and Wendy with a look of wifely disappointment—yet neither realizes that, more than likely, they now inhabit an enclosed space that gave birth to a previous caretaker's madness. Besides those extremes implied by the kitchen's two food compartments, Ullman's office and the clash between the spacious Navajo beauty of the Colorado Lounge and the vast but garish modernity of the Gold Room suggest a visual schizophrenia that works to defeat the orderly tendencies of "interviews" and closing-day tours. When the camera follows Jack into his meeting with Ullman, it quickly records a split personality in the decor of the manager's office. Outside the doorway, one sees on the left an abstract painting (red and blue colors, with indications of a human face) that surrealistically mimics the more traditional Navajo art seen elsewhere, and on the right, neatly arranged colored photographs of mountain scenes showing the four seasons. Inside the peach-colored office, this left/right opposition continues; on the left, a multicolored jigsaw county map, a piece of abstract sculpture (of twisted figures), and ancient photographs of the Overlook (a pictorial history in the brownish hues of early-twentieth-century still photography) complement the abstract

---

3. Apparently, the Torrance apartment is located on the third floor in the rear of the hotel in the so-called "staff," or "west," wing, and it is not far from the corridor (yellow wallpaper, blue flowers) where Danny sees the Grady daughters dead.

4. The hedge maze, of course, is behind the hotel. All the exterior location shots of the hotel entrance are the work of a second-unit photography team and show the Timberline Lodge at Mt. Hood National Forest in Oregon, while the "backyard" area with the hedge maze is a full-size replica of the Timberline's exterior, which was built on a backlot at Elstree Studios in England.

painting by the doorway and clash with the orderly arrangement of pictures and awards on the right wall that reflect Ullman's character and his past (e.g., a Boy Scouts Exploring certificate). But there is visual humor as well as counterpoint: next to a small American flag on Ullman's desk sits a metal cup containing pencils and pens—*and* a miniature replica of an ax.

In part one, even though Wendy and Jack appear to be a "normal" heterosexual couple (they call each other "honey" and show other signs of affection), the film visually develops several juxtapositions that objectify latent disorders at work in both their marriage and the family. Shelley Duvall is not a sexually attractive woman; she therefore plays the film's role as Danny's protective mother better than she could the novel's as Jack's lover, which helps clarify the complex symbolism of Jack's meeting with the mysterious nude woman in Room 237. Wendy not only is identified as a "ghost story and horror film addict" (in King, she reads Gothic novels and listens to the music of Bartók), but when first seen she is reading Salinger's *The Catcher in the Rye* and smoking Virginia Slims, while Jack reads *Playgirl* in the hotel's reception area and later smokes Marlboros. On the surface, such details give their respective characters a sexual eclecticism and cultural accessibility, when in truth they anticipate the film's sexist allegory. Jack appears to be a model of liberal politics and education—a writer and teacher, informally dressed in tweed jackets and sweaters, a man who apparently reads *The New York Review of Books*—and Wendy a candidate for modern, liberated womanhood. But he, of course, is a closet sexist, and she is not much more than a dutiful housewife, concerned mother, and nervous mouse who is vulnerable to both Jack's cajolements and his masculine insecurities. Especially in the early scenes, Wendy is visually defined by her role as mother and all that it entails: her world has one central location—the kitchen, not the bedroom—and contains foodstuffs (milk cartons, boxes of cereal) and products (dish detergent, Q-Tips) necessary to her family's welfare and the management of a normal American home. Jack, on the other hand, quietly expresses not only an irritation with the banalities and routines of family life, but something far more dangerous than even he realizes. During a car trip to the Overlook, he barely suppresses an urge to ridicule Wendy's mistaken belief that the Donner incident occurred in Colorado, while he expresses himself more truly in a sarcastic response to Danny's comment that he knows about cannibalism from TV ("See! It's okay, he saw it on the television!"). Jack Nicholson uses both his face (especially his mouth and his villainous eyebrows) and speech to hint at an important dysfunction in the character: after Danny complains to his father that he is hungry, Jack barks out a reply in a primitive, illiterate slur—"you shoulda eaten your breakfast"— which belies his role as "enlightened" teacher/writer. Except for his ability to shine, Danny's character is a picture of normality: he eats peanut butter and jelly sandwiches, drinks milk, watches Roadrunner cartoons on TV, and lives in a child's world inhabited and decorated by characters from Disneyland and "Peanuts," animal books, baseball bats, toy cars, astronauts, his Big Wheel, and stuffed animals. This normal child's world, in the surreal landscape of a resurrected Overlook, undergoes a grotesquely satiric metamorphosis:

1. When Jack moves through the reception area in part two on his way to a shining over the model maze, he throws a yellow tennis ball past a stuffed bear and Danny's Big Wheel, which rests on the very spot (a Navajo circle design) where Hallorann will be murdered (ironically, in front of the cashier's cages).

2. Jack's tennis ball mysteriously rolls into Danny's circle of toy cars just before the boy walks through the open door of Room 237.

3. Wendy uses Danny's baseball bat as a weapon to repel Jack's first murderous advances.

4. Wendy locks Jack in the pantry, where he later eats a "survival" meal closer to a child's than an adult's—peanut butter, roasted peanuts (associated with his drinking), Oreo cookies, and crackers.

5. As Jack breaks through the apartment door with an ax (and the Grady corridor looms in the background), he mocks his role as family man with perhaps his funniest line—"Wendy, I'm *home*"—which prepares for his humorous rendition of both the Big Bad Wolf and the famous introductory pitch from Johnny Carson's *Tonight Show:* "Heeeeere's Johnny!" Behind Jack's grotesquely illuminated face hangs a picture of an idealized, snow-covered cottage.

6. Now the cartoon violence and lyrics of the Roadrunner show take a grimly ironic turn in Jack's Wile E. Coyote ("The coyote's after you") chasing Danny ("If he catches you you're through") into the snow-covered hedge maze, where he is outwitted by the boy's speed and ingenuity ("the coyote is really a crazy clown"). Symbolically, the Overlook Hotel becomes Jack's other Home and other Family, a nightmare world of dismemberment and alienation (where "sliced peaches" and "Heinz Ketchup" recall family massacres, not family meals), in which the mother and child are victims of the father's de-

sire to cannibalize one family to ensure the "survival" of another, to violate one home to resuscitate the corpse of another. Paradoxically, the Monster of *The Shining* wears the face of both masculine brutality and house Fool, one who finds his home amid the polite society of the Overlook's past, and who performs for what Ullman chauvinistically describes as "all the best people."

Jack's madness does not fully emerge until the final day of part two ("Wednesday"), when his unconscious, in unison with the hotel, "awakens" and assumes a life of its own in three remarkable scenes: one in the Gold Room (Jack and Lloyd), one in Room 237 (Jack and the nude woman), and one in the red bathroom of the Gold Room (Jack and Grady). Before these important and symbolic encounters, Kubrick develops a series of visual and aural clues to their meaning. Like the film's musical progression, which, following the credits, moves from the atonalities of Bartók (the ripplings associated with Jack's maze shining and the scrapbook in "A Month Later" and "Tuesday") and Ligeti's "Lontano" (Jack's trancelike states on "Thursday" and "Saturday") to the full dissonance of Penderecki ("The Awakening of Jacob" is especially prominent in the Room 237 episode on "Wednesday"), the visual rhetoric of part two not only objectifies Jack's internal regression but places it in a recognizable mythopoeic context.* Stylistically, the "interview" realism of part one blends into the surrealism of parts two and three, just as a yellow Volkswagen assumes the shape of a tennis ball (which "travels" on the maze carpet into Danny's circle of toy cars) and links Jack's character to the symbolism of a Navajo sand painting. In one striking shot, for instance, the camera tilts up from the typewriter, with a blank piece of paper in its carriage, to reveal the source of a loud pounding noise: in the background, Jack angrily throws a yellow tennis ball against a sand painting, which, uncharacteristically, delineates a totally masculine world.

---

*One of the more interesting aspects of Kubrick's musical selections for *The Shining* is the way they recall the Star-Gate and eighteenth-century memory room sequences in *2001*. Not only does the film use music by György Ligeti ("Lontano"), which sounds like his monolith "Atmospheres" from the earlier film, but many of the selections from Polish modernist Krzysztof Penderecki bear a striking resemblance to the dissonant "journey" and "memory" themes of *2001*. In addition, the film's "theme" music (credits) and the "Rocky Mountains" (the Torrance car trip to the Overlook) by Wendy Carlos and Rachel Elkind recall Penderecki's apocalyptic *Dies Irae Oratorium Ob Memoriam*, what he calls his "music of terror." And finally, Kubrick uses the "Midnight with the Stars and You" tune for the 1920s party and the Epilogue, while an old song called "Home" is heard during the red bathroom scene between Jack and Grady (performed by the Gleneagles Hotel Band).

Within its enclosed design, to include the traditional opening to the East, four male figures (the squarish heads denote masculinity) stand erect and "safe" within the painting's "circle." In the symbolism of most Navajo sand paintings, yellow is a male color, and blue normally identifies the female. (In the mythology of several Indian tribes, yellow denotes death, and blue is associated with sky/happiness/love.) In Kubrick's film, Jack's "colors" begin in the warm part of the spectrum (brown, green, yellow) but inevitably move toward red (e.g., he wears a maroon-colored jacket in the last part of the film, he talks with Grady in the red bathroom, and Danny's blood elevator/REDRUM shinings are associated with his father's unconscious). Conversely, both Wendy and Danny start off in blues and reds, while she, in particular, ends up in greens and browns.

As the film moves closer to Jack's madness and the Overlook's resurrection, the color yellow becomes even more symbolically assertive, although Kubrick usually provides a source light that realistically "explains" it. The Grady murder corridor is decorated in yellow wallpaper; a lamp next to Jack's typewriter gives the paper a yellow texture; his face and eyes turn yellow like the bourbon in his glass during his talk with Lloyd; the hallway into the Torrance apartment is decorated with yellow-flowered wallpaper; as Jack stands outside the bathroom with the ax, his face and the walls take on a yellowish glow from another lamp (while Wendy wears the blue bathrobe inside the blindingly white bathroom); and when he moves on his murderous course to intercept Hallorann, the hotel's interior lighting transforms the walls from daytime white into evening yellow. In addition, the gold corridor and Gold Room convert the warmth and beauty of yellow (as in the aspens behind the credits) into something akin to the unnatural and discordant colors of the Korova Milkbar in *A Clockwork Orange*, especially when mixed with pink upholstered furniture and a bright red bathroom. Symbolically, both Jack's madness and the Overlook's past express a decidedly masculine ethos, one that threatens not only the structures of normality (man/woman, family) but the integrity of psycho/sexual duality. Reminiscent of HAL in *2001*, Jack seeks to command a dead but self-contained world, one that denies existential time as well as contingent space. Significantly, both Jack and HAL are associated with enclosed worlds (spaceship *Discovery* and the Overlook Hotel), with obsessive attitudes toward their "jobs" (the Jupiter Mission and Jack's contract with the Overlook), with a primitive regression disguised by civilized formality (HAL's language and Jack's association with Delbert Grady and the 1920s party), and with the colors yellow and red. HAL's ubiquitous eye (red iris, yellow pupil) not only recalls the leopard's surveillance of a Pleistocene darkness but achieves a humanized incarnation in the sexist coloration of Jack Torrance's insanity.

By the middle section of *The Shining,* the latent schizophrenic tendencies of part one have escaped from the closet and turned both psychological and cinematic "normality" inside out. During Jack's breakfast in bed ("A Month Later"), Kubrick photographs the first half of the scene inside the reflection in the bedroom mirror and the second half outside, a form of visual doubling that goes from a reversed to a "normal" perspective, from a simulacrum to "reality" itself. Yet within the "abnormal," reversed imagery of the mirror (the lettering on Jack's shirt and the illusion that he eats with his left hand), the Torrance couple engage in a banal conversation about staying up late and the difficulties of writing ("lots of ideas, no good ones"), while in the "normal" space outside the mirror Jack talks about *déjà vu* and how he "fell in love" with the Overlook "right away." Soon afterward ("Monday"), Danny visits his now wakeful and unshaven father—sitting on the edge of the same bed and wearing a blue bathrobe—and stands between Jack's mirror reflection on screen-left and his "real" image on screen-right. Even within this touching exchange between father and son, however, Kubrick hints at the macabre awakening of both Jack's dark self and the hotel's past, of a sinister force struggling to escape from the flat surfaces of memory into that three-dimensional world on the other side of the mirror. As the Bartók from his maze-shining plays on the soundtrack, Jack's attention wavers between Danny on his lap ("I love you, Danny, more than anything in the *whole* world") and the seductive intrusion of other visions and other voices: He tells Danny that he can't sleep because of his "work" (the scrapbook), which indicates that his nightmares are learning to walk and to talk; and echoing the Grady daughters' sinister invitation, he tells his son that he would like to stay in the Overlook "forever and ever and ever." In two key scenes, Jack's menacing, godlike isolation *inside* the hotel opposes Wendy and Danny's spirit of *outside* play and exploration. In the first, he shines over the model maze as they playfully race into the hedge maze (and the loser "keeps America clean") and experience its confusion (indicated to the audience by the dizzying motions of the Steadicam). In the second scene ("Thursday"), Wendy and Danny play in the snow below Jack, who, with the sand

Danny translates his father's subconscious into a
mirror image of madness

painting prominent in the background, grins and stares out in a hypnotic, slack-jawed trance from a second-floor window in the Colorado Lounge. As the snowdrifts increase *outside,* the Torrance family becomes more isolated *inside* as normal communication breaks down: Jack sits in the empty but symmetrical "center" of the Overlook, where he reads the scrapbook and translates its collective unconscious into the idiom of his private unconscious; Danny rides his Big Wheel through narrow corridors and sees bloody visions showing the monsters being reborn inside his father's mind; and Wendy tries, with little success, to fight off her loneliness through contacts with the outside world (she watches TV and uses her radio transmitter to say "hello" to a fire-station ranger). But in the surrealistic inversions of part two, that ordinary world now seems as alien to us as did the Jack Torrance who forced himself to smile in the reassuring temporal and spatial masks of part one. The past now speaks through the present, the primitive seems indistinguishable from the civilized, and inner worlds express themselves in strangely familiar dialects and assume familiar shapes. The demons in the mirror have escaped—and not only are they *real,* but they grin in mockery at our bewilderment.

In the climax to part two, Kubrick translates the film's repeated motifs of shining and *déjà vu,* of dreams and recollections, into such an undeniable cinematic and psychological reality that normality itself seems but a distant memory as the Monster both learns to speak our language and discovers its Home. The film starts off with Ullman's recollection of the Charles Grady tragedy, while Danny describes his shinings as dreams faintly remembered, and Jack senses that he's lived in the Overlook Hotel before. Yet before he can remember, Jack must forget. He must forget his past failures and inadequacies as a father, husband, and man of enlightenment. He must forget those responsibilities that bind him to Wendy and Danny. He must forget himself as Jack Torrance in present time, the writer/teacher of part one, and remember that other self who forever waits in a memory room for the lights to be turned on. In *The Shining*, that memory room becomes the Overlook Hotel itself, not as it was, but as Jack would like it to have been. Danny sees the truth—the "horror"—of his father's yearning for the center of the maze, of his macabre quest for the perfection of death, while Jack casts it in the nostalgic afterglow of a formal 1920s mise-en-scène. Sitting at the bar in the Gold Room, Jack looks into the camera and enjoins us—not just Lloyd—to shine with him, not only to drink and be merry, but to share his memory and his disease: a

memory of license, of masculine freedom and violence, one in which
Jack no longer represses either the sexist urge to demean Wendy ("the
old sperm-bank upstairs") or his selfish resentment toward the moral
demands of fatherhood ("I wouldn't hurt a single hair on his god-
damn head! I *love* the little sonofabitch!"). In a remarkable screen
performance, Jack Nicholson captures not only the madman's self-
delusion and self-pity but, what is even more impressive, a psycho-
machia that pits the primitive nuances of "man to man" talk—"You
set 'em up, Lloyd, and I'll knock 'em down"—against the convolu-
tions of rationalization. He takes his first drink (Jack Daniels, naturally), rolls his eyes upward in monstrous bliss, and reenacts before
the sepulchral bartender an act of violence against his son:

> The little *fucker* had thrown all my papers on the floor. All I tried to do
> was *pull* him up [*he violently imitates a jerking motion*]. A momentary loss
> of muscular coordination, a few extra foot pounds of energy per sec-
> ond, per second [*he narrows two fingers into an imaginary measuring de-
> vice, then brings his hands together in a quick 'bone-snapping' motion*].

He tells his ghostly but formal reflection (Lloyd also wears a maroon-
colored jacket) that Wendy won't let him "forget" his brutality against
their son three years before (and in present time, she has just accused
him of strangling Danny), which anticipates the fact that soon he will
forget himself and remember only a once-latent urge to dominate
and to rule.

When Jack shines in the green bathroom of Room 237, he experiences a memory of illicit eroticism, while Danny relives (he shines in
his bed) the grotesque rebirth of the decomposed hag rising out of
the bathwater. Symbolically, both versions of the nude woman (hag/
siren) represent an assault on the integrity of Wendy's role as mother/
wife. Danny is enticed into the room by the mysterious appearance of
the yellow tennis ball that rolls into his circle, an event that coincides
with Jack's nightmare in the Colorado Lounge about killing his family
with an ax. As Danny approaches the open door and the dangling red
key, he calls for Wendy ("Mom, are you in there?") at the very moment that she, from the basement (where she does Jack's "work"),
responds to Jack's cries of terror. But Jack will deny the truth of that
nightmare when he both embraces the young nude woman (Lia Beldam) and retreats in disgust from the laughing crone (Billie Gibson)
—from yet another Kubrickian bathroom that links masturbatory fantasy and death (e.g., Humbert in the bathtub, dreaming of Lolita just

after Charlotte's death).* Sitting on his bed with a tearful Wendy, he tells her that the room was empty, and that Danny must have strangled himself. In other words, Jack *forgets* the green and purple horror of Room 237—that hideous mockery of life itself—and *remembers* only its erotic invitation (the woman and the sexual patterns in the green and purple carpeting). He *forgets* his "contract" with Wendy and *remembers* only that secret agreement he makes with his Shadow in the center of the hotel's maze. As Danny "sees" the blood elevator and REDRUM visions from his bed, Jack's anger mounts to a feverish pitch after Wendy suggests they leave the Overlook. He then severs his responsibilities to one family ("I've let you fuck up my life so far, but I'm not going to let you fuck this up") and reaffirms those to another ("I'm really into *my work*"). As he storms out the apartment door, we notice that his path will take him through the Grady corridor (faded yellow wallpaper) on his way back into the Gold Room and its ghoulish denial of time.

The sounds of a romantic tune lure him back into his Gold Room of memory to celebrate liberation on Independence Day (July 4, 1921) from the restraints of civilization. He tells Lloyd, "It's good to be back, I've been away, but now I'm back," just as a male voice begins

---

*Just before Jack and the Steadicam travel through Room 237 on their way to the green bathroom, Hallorann experiences a long-distance shining from his bedroom in Miami, which reveals a private male world not as complex as Jack's and far more sane. Consider these contrasts between Hallorann's shining and Jack's visit to Room 237:

1. Before Hallorann's shining, Kubrick employs two reverse zooms that recall the kind of visual doubling found in the breakfast scene discussed in the text. In this case, each reverse zoom reveals a picture of a nude black woman; the two pictures are on opposite walls, each a kind of mirror reflection of the other, although they are pictures of *two* different women. Hallorann, seen lying in bed between the two pictures, watches TV in an orange-colored room, which is ordered and symmetrical (there are lamps on each side of the TV and on each side of his bed), but *not* schizophrenic (unlike Ullman's office). However, he does wear blue pajamas that express a kind of visual split personality—the lower half is solid blue (and earlier his color was blue), while the upper half resembles an abstract, mazelike design; overall, Hallorann's decidedly male world expresses balance rather than dissonance.

2. In contrast, the decor of Room 237 is a ghastly combination of different shades of green and purple, colors that in Kubrick's iconography work against each other—green suggests one value (rebirth, in the eighteenth-century room of *2001*), and purple another (Korova decadence); the carpeting in the room is decidedly sexual and mazelike (resembling phallic keyholes inside circles), the wallpaper duplicates the vertical lines of a cage, and just outside the bathroom door hangs a picture of a fox; and, of course, there are two versions of one woman in the green bathroom (with Gold Room trim arching over the tub)—but unlike the pictures on Hallorann's wall, they hardly suggest the workings of a healthy libido. Hallorann has his sexual fantasies well in hand, while Jack's express the extremes of male lasciviousness and disgust.

to sing the lyrics of a song about love, surrender, and remembrance ("Your eyes held a message tender, / Saying 'I surrender all my love to you,' / Midnight brought us sweet romance, / I know, all my whole life through, / I'll be remembering you"). For Jack, shining entails recollection more than extrasensory perception, a nostalgic dream of immortality and pleasure rather than intimations of hidden evil. His brass and vulgar regressions (the ugly American), however, clash with the overdressed European formality of this huge gathering (300 people), just as his ornate recollections oppose the horrific truth of Danny's shinings. Appropriately, Delbert Grady now enters and crashes into Jack, spilling Advocaat (a yellow liqueur) all over his jacket. Inside the red bathroom, reverse camera positions emphasize a mirroring effect (that is, one figure turns his back to the camera and the other faces it), which now doubles Jack with an even more "civilized" but sinister version of Lloyd the bartender. Again, the subject of "recollection" comes up as Jack mistakenly confuses this Grady with Charles Grady ("You *were* the caretaker") and accuses him of murdering his family. (An old song called "Home" is faintly heard throughout this scene.) At first Grady pleads ignorance—"That's odd, I have no recollection of that at all"—but then he remembers and confronts Jack with a new truth: "I beg to differ with you, sir, but *you* are the caretaker, you have *always* been the caretaker." In the film's psychological allegory, this implies that the Jack Torrance/Charles Grady figures of present time "care for" the Overlook by resurrecting its past through a recollection of that other self which sleeps but never dies. And once that memory is found inside the center of the maze (self/hotel), how one got there is quickly forgotten or sublimated within a formal and enclosed artifice. In his first Gold Room shining, Jack remembers how to express his sexist prerogatives ("white man's burden") through the primitive male banalities ("words of wisdom") of that conversation with Lloyd (who says, "Women! Can't live with them, can't live without them!"), only to learn from Grady in the red bathroom how to couch them in the chilling disguise of polite euphemism, in a kind of Overlook Doomsday jargon. Grady describes how, at first, his two daughters did not like the hotel (and one even tried to burn it down), but that he "corrected" them ("and when my wife tried to prevent me from doing my duty, I *corrected* her"). Later, from inside the pantry where Wendy locks him after hitting him with the baseball bat, Jack no longer talks about "bashing her brains out," but instead promises to "deal with the situation" once he is released, in what "Mr.

Grady," from the other side of the door, describes as "the harshest possible way." And Grady knows how to push all the right buttons, especially when he prods Jack's masculine insecurities by commenting on Wendy's unexpected "resourcefulness" and wondering aloud if his American friend has the "belly" for this kind of work.

By part three, Jack's "interviews" with his recollected friends and his tour of the Overlook's psychic history have been completed. His unconscious mind has awakened from a long sleep and now, like the Minotaur, seeks to purify its maze/home of those alien intruders that threaten its rule. In many respects, part three doubles back on part one like a grotesque reflection in a funhouse mirror. Hallorann, for instance, moves through an outside world that looks as if it were shrouded in Jack's madness. He calls Durkin's Garage (Larry Durkin is played by Tony Burton) in Sidewinder, where it's almost completely dark even at mid-morning because of a heavy snowstorm. He passes a traffic accident in which a red Volkswagen is crushed under the weight of a flatbed truck (in the novel, Jack drives a red Volkswagen). He moves in a snowcat ("4 pm") through a dark, eerie corridor of trees that resembles an enlarged version of the Overlook's hedge maze. Inside the hotel, Wendy and Danny sit at breakfast, and Danny watches the Roadrunner show on TV, just as they did in the Boulder apartment of part one. But now Wendy talks to "Tony" exclusively ("Danny isn't here, Mrs. Torrance") as her son's world becomes engulfed by Jack's red madness. Wendy then picks up a baseball bat (toy/weapon) and walks downstairs to the Colorado Lounge, now the Monster's inner sanctum, where she gazes on a manuscript that reveals the nature of Jack's "work" inside the center of the maze. As she frantically leafs through the manuscript, with its seemingly infinite mirror repetitions of "All work and no play makes Jack a dull boy," Kubrick shows us a visual sequence, or history, that objectifies the progress of Jack's insanity (form and spelling become ever more erratic) and clarifies the film's particular use of the maze concept. Not only does the visual sequence resemble a horizontal labyrinth, and therefore suggest fate and psychological entrapment, but it also associates Jack's madness with an image of reduction and repetition. On one page, for instance, his mad litany is typed in the shape of an upside-down pyramid that squeezes his character and his world into a single word ("boy")—as if it were *The Shining*'s Rosebud, except in his film Kubrick portrays a character who obsessively denies complexity (both inner and outer) by searching for the center of existence in

only one memory room (i.e., his unconscious). By part three, Jack no longer explores other ideas—whether good or bad—but moves in straight lines (the gold corridor) or repeated patterns in the center of his horizontal maze. Wendy, on the other hand, has learned how to back up and negotiate the maze without looking (as she retreats from Jack and swings the bat), which reverses her forward turns and movements into the kitchen in part one (where a reverse dolly shot and Hallorann escort her through the maze). Jack has been seduced by the center's illusion of order and timelessness, while its madness and deadly stasis are revealed to us through such typographical disorders as "work" altered to "worm," "boy" to "bog," and "a dull" to "adult."

Only after Jack leaves the hotel to chase Danny into the snow-covered hedge maze does Wendy shine for the first time, and does the Overlook take on the traditional characteristics of a haunted house. In perhaps the film's least convincing sequence, Wendy and the audience see not only the truth of Danny's earlier shinings but the hideous reality of Jack's recollections, which are no longer distorted by nostalgic subterfuge (he has left the inside maze for an outside one). Danny's world as a child and Wendy's harmless interest in ghost stories are transmogrified into a surreal fairy tale about fellatio between a figure in a teddy bear/boar suit (with a piggish snout and fangs) and a gentleman in white tie and tails, skeletons enjoying cocktails and making calls from telephone booths, a man with his head cleaved open ("Great party, isn't it?"), and cascades of blood pouring from an elevator as if from the ruptured artery of a monster. Not only does Wendy's journey through and out of the Overlook's inner maze parallel Danny's movements into and out of the hedge maze, but it provides the film with a series of visual and emotional "effects" that at first seem to satisfy certain expectations but that probably do not resolve an audience's perplexity over the ambiguities of Jack's shinings in Room 237 and the Gold Room or the meaning of that 1921 photograph seen in the last shot of the film. The ending is reminiscent of the ending of *2001:* Kubrick deliberately (some say perversely) gives and takes away at the same time (the Star-Gate ride was not an unexpected event, but what does the eighteenth-century room mean?). But, aesthetically, the maze concept requires that an audience be tested and challenged, even to the point of confusion if it fails to shine and *remember* not only how it got into the film (i.e., the guided tours of narrative exposition) but how it got lost. In retracing those steps, the viewer might discover that it wasn't Kubrick's *The Shining* that betrayed him, but rather all those false expectations that tyrannize audiences into believing that filmic understandings should follow straight paths into a center of meaning.

So what does *The Shining*'s ending "mean"? On its most essential psychological level, it means that Jack Torrance freezes and dies inside the hedge maze because he forgot how to deal with the basic paradoxes of his own nature. Rather than exploring and discovering, making choices and risking both failure and success, he prefers to sit inertly in the center of an enclosed world and shine from above in godlike contemplation of the beauty of his creation. Like Barry Lyndon moving through a formal eighteenth-century maze, Jack forgets to look closely at either his own past or that of the Overlook, at the disorders and complexities that exist inside the structures of personality and civilization. Instead he transforms each into a grotesque vision of duration. He attempts to destroy his family/home in present time because it requires a "contract" that involves not only responsibilities to others and even to another sex (the human world outside the masculine self), but a form of moral/emotional "work" where there are no certainties and very few givens. Jack's "love" for the hotel—rather than for Wendy and Danny—is another Kubrickian version of that mad craving for immortality that animates Strangelove's excitement over the perfection of the Doomsday Machine and HAL's desire to protect an illusion of machine infallibility from the intrusions of humanity. Jack explores and even learns how to control the memory world resurrected from inside the Overlook's maze, while he fails to perceive that, psychologically, it is a denial of *outside* worlds that offer not only the threat of uncertainty but the possibility of hope. Like Johnny Clay's movements into a world outside the temporal and spatial gameboard of his robbery plan, Jack's final journey into the outside maze throws him into a setting that is unresponsive to his obsession for control or recollection. While Bowman wandered through his memory room, only to escape as an enhanced being into the expanses of space, Jack tragically moves from one enclosed maze into another. In the end, he becomes a lonely, anguished figure who cries out in almost inaudible pain from the loss of both his actual and imagined homes. As he did so often within the hotel's maze, he sits down and faces screen right, only now he gazes into a bleak and frozen landscape, into a vision of nothingness that waits in the center of the labyrinth. Like so many others in Kubrick's films, Jack Torrance forgets that in a contingent universe, an obsession with timelessness becomes tantamount to a love affair with death.

In the Epilogue, Kubrick takes us back inside the Overlook Hotel for a final visual tour that paradoxically asserts the continuity of film time and confuses its traditional explanatory function. Reminiscent of a Wellesian journey into Xanadu's fire and the meaning of Rosebud, his camera reaffirms its omniscience and its freedom by traveling through space with an assurance and purpose first glimpsed in the credits. But in this case, it asks the viewers in the theater to shine and recollect, to remember not just one piece in the maze-puzzle (i.e., a Rosebud) but others as well. The camera moves across the reception area of the hotel—from the place where Jack Torrance first was seen and Hallorann was eventually murdered—to a picture that hangs on the wall of the gold corridor in the center of another maze. It reveals a smiling likeness of the grinning monster in the hedge maze, looking up in greeting amid a society of civilized revelers from the past, trapped in the middle of a pictorial manuscript (21 pictures) arranged in three horizontal lines.* This shot not only completes the film's story of Jack Torrance, but it reverses an earlier psychological evolution. In the mazes of parts one and two, Kubrick doubled Jack

*See "Notes & Trivia" for my comments on the role of numbers in the film's maze/puzzle.

the writer/teacher with Jack the Monster, normality with its shadow, present time with a hideous memory lost but not forgotten. Now, past time reflects the image of normality (the 1921 photograph), and present time shows the visage of madness (the frozen, grotesque mask of death in the hedge maze). And as the nostalgic music from the Gold Room party plays again, *The Shining* recalls the ending of another film, Kubrick's own *Barry Lyndon,* as it tries to stimulate our memory—not of a collective unconscious, but of a collective humanity (in the picture) tragically lost and frozen in the maze of our scrapbooks and our history. More than anything else, perhaps, it is Kubrick's dream of civilized life—a remembrance of things forgotten.

9 THE KUBRICKIAN THING
Full Metal Jacket

After the release of *The Shining* in the early summer of 1980, Stanley Kubrick would make only two films in the last nineteen years of his life. It would be seven years almost to the day before he would release his Vietnam war film *Full Metal Jacket* in the summer of 1987, and another twelve years before his thirteenth and final feature, *Eyes Wide Shut,* would be released in July of 1999, four months after his death. Beginning with the completion and release of *Barry Lyndon* in late 1975, Kubrick adopted working habits that increasingly would stretch out the periods between his film projects. To complicate matters, he and his family moved during the shooting of *The Shining* from their home (Abbots Mead) near the Borhamwood studios, where they had lived since 1964, into a manor estate (Childwick Bury) near St.

Albans in rural Hertfordshire. As a result, some of Kubrick's time in the early 1980s was spent converting Childwick Bury into a self-contained creative workplace and home for himself, his wife Christiane, and their daughters. And from all accounts it seems that Kubrick continued to impose even higher standards on his own work than he had in earlier years. He often mentioned how he spent much of his time between films reading on a variety of subjects while searching for the right novel that would "surprise" him and make a connection to his own, very demanding film imagination. But finding such a book was no easy matter for Kubrick, as he confessed to Michel Ciment in a revealing 1976 interview:

> Since I am currently going through the process of trying to decide what film to make next, I realize just how uncontrollable is the business of finding a story, and how very much it depends on chance and spontaneous reaction. You can say a lot of "architectural" things about what a film story should have: a strong plot, interesting characters, possibilities for cinematic development, good opportunities for the actors to display emotion, and the presentation of thematic ideas truthfully and intelligently. But, of course, that still doesn't really explain why you finally choose something, nor does it lead you to the story.

To further complicate his task, Kubrick—particularly since the time of *Dr. Strangelove*—had been going out of his way to bend or subvert the conventions of Hollywood filmmaking, what he once explained to *Newsweek*'s Jack Kroll as a desire to "explode the narrative structure of movies." He obviously had no interest in repeating himself by working with story materials that earlier films already had explored and, undoubtedly in his mind, exhausted. Instead, he wanted "to do something earthshaking." As months turned into years following *The Shining*, I suspect he was thinking along the same lines as the rest of us —that he too wanted the next "Stanley Kubrick Production" to be something special, even by the remarkable standards of his earlier work. It is no wonder that it took so long for him to make his next film, and then his last one.

No doubt another factor contributing to the ever-expanding gaps between his last three films was Kubrick's own perfectionism, his exercise of artistic control and mastery over every aspect of a film's creation. By 1980, with his status as a master filmmaker so firmly established, he could stay off the merry-go-round increasingly being ridden by so many younger American directors who felt compelled by a then

burgeoning Culture of Celebrity and Excess to climb aboard and grab
—over and over again—for the brass ring of success. During this time,
Kubrick continued to repeat how he particularly enjoyed both the
initial development and the editing phases of the creating process. In
the front-end phase, he could work at leisure by letting his mind range
freely over the material involved in the development of a script, and
by exploring every crevice of his imagination's response. In the back-
end phase, now done in his own editing rooms at Childwick Bury, he
would assemble from mountains of footage—collected from numerous takes and retakes of scenes generated by exhausting months of
shooting—his final vision of a project that had had its origins years
before in a single, "spontaneous reaction." Particularly during the
final two decades of his life, it appears that Kubrick envisioned each
film project as being like an evolving life process in miniature, one in
which he could focus on a variety of personal concerns within the
locus of a story's materials. But we must not forget that there was another "life process" going on as well, one we all eventually must face,
and to which one day even Stanley Kubrick would succumb. During
the filming of *Full Metal Jacket,* the fifty-seven-year-old Kubrick must
have experienced, perhaps for the first time in his career, the physical
effects not only of his increasing age but of his quest for perfection in
the film's arduous thirty-nine-week shooting schedule.

As early as the spring of 1980, when he first met Michael Herr,
Kubrick was thinking about doing a war movie. Herr had been a correspondent for *Esquire* during the Vietnam War and had published
his personal accounts in *Dispatches* (1977), a work much admired by
Kubrick, and arguably the single best book ever written on the subject. Herr later would comment that Kubrick "had a strong feeling
about a particular kind of war movie that he wanted to make, but he
didn't have the story." Late in 1982, Kubrick read a novel on the Vietnam War that "surprised" him—Gustav Hasford's surreal and harrowing *The Short-Timers* (1979)—and that would provide him with the
story he needed. According to Herr, Kubrick had found in Hasford's
novel a "book of such agreeable elements and proportions that he
could break it down and build it back up again as a film." By the
middle of 1983, after months of exhaustive research and countless
hours of communication by telephone with both Herr and Hasford,
Kubrick completed a detailed film treatment of the novel and hired
Michael Herr to work with him on the script. Sometime during the
months that followed, he found the inspiration for the movie's title in

a gun catalogue (he thought it "beautiful and tough, and kind of poetic"). Finally, after more than eighteen months of revising the script and supervising the thousands of details involved in pre-production, Kubrick began shooting *Full Metal Jacket,* his twelfth feature film, in August of 1985.

When he first read *The Short-Timers,* Kubrick must have been struck by its uncanny resemblance in theme, style, and tone to several of his own films, particularly *Paths of Glory, Dr. Strangelove,* and *A Clockwork Orange.* Thus it is hardly surprising that, according to Michael Herr, "he knew immediately that he wanted to film it." Hasford's novel, for example, mixes a satiric, understated style of objective reportage with nightmarishly surreal descriptions of the psychological devastation created when a dehumanizing Marine Corps indoctrination program achieves a grotesque apotheosis in the charnel house of Vietnam. Part one ("The Spirit of the Bayonet"), compressed into a chillingly hilarious thirty-three pages, takes place at the Marine Corps Recruit Depot on Parris Island and focuses on the account by Private Joker—the book's first-person narrator—of Private Leonard Pratt's ("Gomer Pyle") cruel initiation into drill instructor Sergeant Gerheim's "beloved Corps" and his evolution from "oat-fed" innocent to hallucinating madman/killer. Part two ("Body Count")—which abruptly jumps into the first of two Vietnam sections in the narrator's matter-of-fact declaration of a change in time and place ("Tet. The Year of the Monkey")—deals with Joker, now a combat correspondent as Hasford was, and his photographer Rafterman joining the Lusthog squad during the 1968 Tet offensive and the battle for Hue City. Part three ("Grunts") climaxes the novel with the main character's promotion from poge to grunt, as he ironically devolves, seemingly like Pyle earlier, from joker to killer during the fighting around the American compound at Khe Sanh in the winter months of 1968. Yet Hasford's Sergeant Joker is no Private Pyle; instead, he's Born Again Hard as a reincarnated version of Master Gunnery Sergeant Gerheim (Hartman in the film). Within this very economic temporal space, Hasford creates an always satiric, mostly fantastical, and sometimes sinister account of a group of post-adolescent American males undergoing a rite of passage that travels through the diabolical landscapes of an antiquated Marine Corps mythology and the brutal devastation of America's most absurd war.

Like *Paths of Glory*, Hasford's novel at times deals with the ironic gaps that exist between the disparate worlds inhabited by the men who fight wars and those who manage them. Only in Hasford, the "managers" are not generals living in remote chateaus—they are sadistic drill instructors living in the men's faces; they are public relations "poges" from the Information Services Office, "who stare at the grunts as though [they] were Hell's Angels at the ballet"; and they are the news manipulators from *Stars and Stripes* who sloganize that Winning the War also requires Winning the Hearts and Minds of the very people whose country they are helping to destroy.* Like most of the fictionalized Vietnam accounts from the 1970s and 1980s, Hasford's novel stays with the men who are doing the fighting and dying. Only rarely does it reflect, as Herr sometimes does in his nonfictional *Dispatches*, on the larger political and social forces responsible for "the horror." But by the late 1970s, when both Hasford and Herr published their books, there was no longer any compelling reason to address such issues. It had become a political given, for all except the most

---

*Naturally, both Hasford and Herr make liberal use of the Gruntspeak commonly heard in the war: "poge," for example, was a derisive term applied to desk-bound soldiers or CIA spooks who couldn't "hack it" and elected to stay "in the rear with the gear"—like *Full Metal Jacket*'s characterization of Lieutenant Lockhart, Joker's Marine news editor, or the poge colonel who reams out Joker about his peace button.

congenital reactionaries, that any policy based on the Domino Theory was doomed to failure. What Hasford does incorporate into Joker's narrative—and which undoubtedly was of great interest to the director of *Dr. Strangelove* and *A Clockwork Orange*—is the suggestion that certain popularized myths of an invidious mass culture had as much to do with the psychological and spiritual damage inflicted by this war as any outmoded Cold War policy.

The most noticeable pop culture paradigm satirized in Hasford's novel, and one that Kubrick incorporates into both the text and the subtext of his film, involves the role of Hollywood as global "dream factory." John Wayne imitations and references to his movies, Westerns and the patterns of male heroism they traditionally embody, Mickey Mouse (as in "what is this mickeymouse shit?"), and the Celebrity Culture that Hollywood epitomizes are all grist for Hasford's commentary. The Parris Island section, for example, starts off with Cowboy, the Stetson-wearing recruit from Texas, introducing himself by asking, "Is that you, John Wayne? Is this me?" Joker, always the mimic, replies in his best rendition of the Duke, "I think I'm going to hate this movie." Just before Cowboy's death in the novel's last section, he gets into a good-natured pissing contest with Animal Mother, the Lusthog squad's natural-born killer, who calls him "Lone Ranger" and says that Cowboy "wears that stetson so the gooks will see that they are dealing with a real Texas lawman." In one of the best scenes in part two, Joker describes the time he and Rafterman went to a movie theater in Da Nang and saw "the funniest movie we have seen in a long time," John Wayne's atrocious right-wing war valentine, *The Green Berets* (1968). He characterizes this first-ever movie about Vietnam as a "Hollywood soap opera about the love of guns." Yet later, as he is overwhelmed by both the dark horrors of war and a darkness emerging from inside him, Joker abandons mimicry and satiric observation as he takes command of the Lusthogs. He tries to stop Animal Mother's futile attempt to save Cowboy from a laughing enemy sniper, which results in a deadly serious threat by Animal Mother: "This ain't no Hollywood movie, Joker. Stand down or I will cut you in half." But before Animal Mother can waste him, Joker raises his grease gun toward Cowboy's face and kills him, with the joking banter of the Texan's final words ringing in his ears: "I NEVER LIKED YOU, JOKER. I NEVER THOUGHT YOU WERE FUNNY." With the killing of Cowboy, "Vietnam, the Movie" ends for Joker the poge—as it no doubt did for his double in real life, Gustav Hasford—and what follows is a real-world sequel in which Sergeant James T. Davis (Joker's actual name), like Gerheim before him, faces the hate of "his men" and becomes "invisible" in their eyes as a human being.

Herr's *Dispatches* played a prominent role not only in Kubrick's thinking and his script preparations for *Full Metal Jacket,* but in Hasford's novel as well, particularly in the way that Herr characterizes the war as a cultural rather than political event. And lest we forget, Hasford acknowledged his indebtedness to Herr's work in an epigraph taken from *Dispatches: "I think that Vietnam was what we had instead of happy childhoods."* Early in his book, Herr talks about how a mythology grew in Nam around the different ways that people who came there rationalized their presence in such a place. There were the grunts who had to be there; the spooks and civilians "whose corporate faith led them there"; and the correspondents like himself, who were there out of "curiosity and ambition." But in the end, according to Herr, "all the mythic tracks intersected, from the lowest John Wayne wet-dream to the most aggravated soldier-poet fantasy," and made "every one of us there a true volunteer." Even though he was not there to "kill gooks," as the grunts were, he participated in something just as dehumanizing—"I was there to watch." Echoing Herr's account, Hasford shows how Joker, prior to his transformation as the grunt sergeant of part three, holds on to the belief that as long as he remains a corporal working for *Stars and Stripes,* an ironic observer of war, he can avoid becoming its victim. While in this role of satiric commentator, Joker briefly equates what he does as a correspondent with what American business does when it wants to sell a product:

> War is good business—invest your son. Viet Nam means never having to say you're sorry. . . . I write that Nam is an Asian Eldorado populated by a cute, primitive but determined people. War is a noisy breakfast cereal. War is fun to eat. War can give you better checkups. War cures cancer—permanently. I don't kill. I write. Grunts kill; I only watch. I'm only young Dr. Goebbels. I'm *not* a sergeant.

Thus Hasford, like Herr, satirizes America's "corporate faith" in a war that could be won if it was handled as if it were just another ad campaign, and in the way such a "myth" supported a desire to remain untainted by the moral and psychological consequences of the war— all of which reflected another intersection, of a more serendipitous kind, between the works by these two writers and several of Kubrick's previous films. But more of that later. For now, consider how the above selections from Herr's *Dispatches* and Hasford's *The Short-Timers* mesh with a comment made by Kubrick in an interview with Penelope Gilliatt at the time *Full Metal Jacket* was released:

> Vietnam was probably the first war that was run—certainly during the Kennedy era—as an advertising agency might run it. . . . It was managed with cost-effective estimates and phony statistics and kill ratios and self-deceiving predictions about how victory was the light at the end of the tunnel.

In his film, during the two editorial meetings involving Lieutenant Lockhart (John Terry) and his staff of Marine reporters, Kubrick draws our attention to a back wall in the Quonset hut, where on prominent display is the cynical motto of the combat correspondent found in Hasford's novel: FIRST TO GO, LAST TO KNOW, WE WILL DEFEND TO THE DEATH OUR RIGHT TO BE MISINFORMED. Like Hasford's narrator, Kubrick no doubt believed that "in war, truth is the first casualty."

Two other prominent Vietnam films, *Apocalypse Now* (Francis Ford Coppola, 1979) and *Platoon* (Oliver Stone, 1986), already had covered some of the territory staked out by Herr and Hasford, but differently than in *Full Metal Jacket*. Michael Herr, in fact, was an advisor on the Coppola film and wrote the voiceover narration for its main character, Captain Willard (Martin Sheen). Stone's film, which was in production during the same time as *Full Metal Jacket,* differs from Coppola's operatic, sometimes over-the-top venture into a pre-MTV surrealist Camp in the way it avoids satiric exaggeration and hallucinatory, rock and roll visions of "the horror." Instead, *Platoon* goes directly for the heart before it informs the head. Stone wants his audience to feel his message, not revel in the messenger's intellectual profundity or his virtuoso use of the medium. Rather than moments of stylistic bravura or verbal sententiousness, he provides a powerful, visceral experience that leads the audience through "the horror" of Vietnam toward a promised land of healing and renewal. Even though both films take as a given the tragically absurd nature of the cultural "myths" described by both Herr and Hasford, they also provide a comfort zone for their audiences—in ways the two books and Kubrick's film never do—by shaping their narratives into familiar moral fables. At first glance, *Apocalypse Now* imitates the revisionist, cynical turn that mainstream Hollywood increasingly took between 1965 and 1975 in such landmark films as *Bonnie and Clyde* (1967), *The*

Graduate (1967), Peckinpah's *The Wild Bunch* (1969)—which still remains one of the first and best of the so-called "anti-Vietnam" films—Altman's *McCabe & Mrs. Miller* (1971), Polanski/Towne's *Chinatown* (1974), and, of course, the two brilliantly conceived *Godfather* films (1972/1974) by Coppola and Mario Puzo. But by 1979, when *Apocalypse Now* was released, revisionism was in decline and was being replaced by a New Classicism engendered by the enormous popularity and traditional mythic resonance of films such as *Jaws* (Steven Spielberg, 1975) and *Star Wars* (George Lucas, 1977). Thus Coppola's film, despite its many stylistic virtues and its technical achievement, did not find a large audience partly because it appeared as a heavy-handed reworking of a Leftist political myth that earlier revisionist films, including his own, had already exhausted. But more significantly, his sometimes silly and always ponderous reworking of the Conradian material (*A Heart of Darkness*) unmasked the fact that he was reinventing the war through another system of fictional analogy, as Stone would do in his own way in *Platoon,* and in later films that explored America's recent political history. In Coppola's version, of course, the "heart of darkness" exists inside American imperialism rather than European colonialism, while in Stone's the civil war raging inside the platoon becomes a metaphor for a "civil war" in America between the Left (Willem Dafoe's Sergeant Elias) and the Right (Tom Berenger's Sergeant Barnes). But *Platoon*'s narrative, unlike the one in *Apocalypse Now,* neatly conforms to the New Classicism of the 1980s, and to a growing desire on the part of the audience to see replicated on their movie screens the emblematic success story known as America *and* Hollywood. Stone's film succeeds partly because it is commercially smarter than Coppola's, particularly in the way it uses the main character, Chris Taylor (Charlie Sheen), to bridge the gap between the story's political polarities to suggest a redemptive future for America. Significantly, Oliver Stone's fictional account of his Vietnam experience owes as much to *Casablanca, On the Waterfront,* and countless other movie parables from Hollywood's classic period as it does to the demythologizing impulses of either Seventies revisionism or novels such as Gustav Hasford's *The Short-Timers.*

But *Apocalypse Now* and *Platoon* both clearly resemble the accounts found in Herr and Hasford in their exploration of what Herr, in his "Foreword" to the screenplay of *Full Metal Jacket* (1987), calls "shadow activity." In their "eternal, recurring telephone call," Herr and Kubrick constantly discussed the Jungian concept of the Shadow, what

Jung called "the most accessible of archetypes, and the easiest to experience." But here again, these two important Vietnam films take a slightly different course from the one found in Hasford's novel. In both Conrad and Coppola, for example, Colonel Kurtz functions as an embodiment of the darkness inside each story's narrator as cultural icon, while in *Platoon,* Sergeant Barnes, associated throughout with death ("I am reality"), represents the shadow "father" fighting for possession of Chris Taylor/America's soul. In both, the main characters go through a ritualized climax in which each journeys through a dark madness objectified in his shadow character, and eventually each, in his own way, exorcises the demon and emerges "reborn" into the possibilities of a new world. Significantly, in whatever ways Hasford's novel can be construed to parallel these two films, Kubrick's *Full Metal Jacket* will all but ignore them. Kubrick omits from his film the evocative, hallucinatory qualities of Joker's waking dreams in Hasford, beginning with the time when he is becoming a "newly minted Marine" on Parris Island, and in the real nightmare of Vietnam, where, as Herr remarks, he confronts war as "the ultimate field of Shadow-activity." In part one, for instance, Joker describes how he "hides in a dark dream" whenever he feels "cold and alone," an internal space where he turns to his rifle (named "Vanessa") for comfort:

> Words come out of the wood and metal and flow into my hands. She tells me what to do. My rifle is a solid instrument of death. My rifle is black steel. Our human bodies are bags of blood, easy to puncture and quick to drain, but our hard tools of death cannot be broken. . . . Blood pours out of the barrel of my rifle and flows up on my hands.

In part three, Joker experiences the waking nightmare of a sniper in Khe Sanh whose "dark laughter draws the blood" from his veins and produces a vision of "Sorry Charlie's" grinning black skull perched on a branch. And, of course, there's the evolution of Joker's character discussed earlier, in which he becomes his own shadow as a Marine instrument of death with the "hard heart that kills." Thus Hasford does not split Joker into two characters and have him do battle with the shadow half, as *Apocalypse Now* does; nor does he follow *Platoon*'s course by positioning Joker between two other characters to represent a struggle between the Angels of Light and Dark. Instead, Joker is Persona *and* Shadow, Eros *and* Thanatos, and in that duality Kubrick found a paradoxical space where, as I have argued throughout this study, his imagination always liked to roam.

Elsewhere in *The Short-Timers,* Hasford explores a very Kubrickian fascination with machines and how they bring both beauty and death into the world. Naturally, Hasford does not neglect to characterize the Marine Corps training regimen as a mechanistic, dehumanizing process: As Pyle moves ever closer to madness, for example, Joker describes him as a "defective instrument for the power that is flowing through him." But Hasford's most evocative descriptions are reserved for the coldly sensual and enduring qualities of the machine itself, and not—as described above—for the soft, vulnerable "bag of blood" known as the human body. Consider the following description by Joker just after he sees a "beautiful" tank, its long barrel inscribed with "BLACK FLAG—*We Exterminate Household Pests,*" and how it captures Hasford's chilling portrait of a dark, utopian Marine Corps dream that links a machine "hardness" used for protection with a human yearning for immortal perfection:

> Military vehicles are beautiful because they are built from functional designs which make them real, solid, without artifice. The tank possesses the beauty of its hard lines; it is fifty tons of rolling armor on tracks like steel watchbands. The tank is our protection, rolling on and on forever, clanking out the dark mechanical poetry of iron and guns.

In consecutive films between 1964 and 1971—*Dr. Strangelove, 2001, A Clockwork Orange*—Kubrick likewise took up the subject of humanity's tragic love affair with its own technological "systems" and creations. But in *Full Metal Jacket,* he chose not to explore that subject as fully as elsewhere, except for the ways in which part one of his film characterizes the "conditioning" program on Parris Island as a Ludovico Technique in reverse and develops Pyle's growing sexual obsession with his rifle. His Private Pyle (Vincent D'Onofrio) confronts the "science" of a systematic Marine Corps training program whose purpose requires that it strip him of his benign, oafish humanity as Leonard Lawrence. And not because this Ludovico Technique in green wants to "cure" him of ultraviolence against the State by turning him into a well-behaved robot, but because it wants to transform him into a Jolly Green Giant who will serve the State as sanctioned killer. In the process, Pyle becomes a Section Eight—a "defective instrument"—whose madness evolves into a "strange love" for his M-14 rifle "Charlene" and *her* "perfect" action and clean, pure "beauty." In a backhanded reference to Major Kong's last ride in *Strangelove* and to a legion of Kubrickian bathrooms, part one of *Full Metal Jacket* eventually climaxes in a latrine with a detonation of violence that brings together man and machine in the grim poetry of Private Pyle *as* Full Metal Jacket.

In its visual and narrative design, *Full Metal Jacket* resembles the military machines described by Joker in Hasford's novel. Its linear, sometimes disjointed structure, its minimalist approach to character, and its functional mise-en-scène create a disorienting effect for the first-time viewer and leave the impression that the film itself is "full metal jacketed." What seems to be missing—with an emphasis on *seems*—are those expected artifices of story as parable, character as archetype, and selected images as iconic reference found in Hollywood "war" films such as *Apocalypse Now, Platoon,* and countless others. The two-part structure of *Full Metal Jacket* seemingly violates the three-act paradigm found in most mainstream films, particularly in the way it abruptly goes from the end of the Parris Island section to the beginning of the Vietnam segment in part two. Before it moves between these two structural units, the film does not provide a plot beat to define its dramatic premise or to focus the remaining action, leaving the impression that part one is disconnected from part two. As a result, the Parris Island scenes resemble a self-contained narrative in three acts, climaxing with Private Pyle's killing of Master Gunnery Sergeant Hartman (Lee Ermey), his own subsequent suicide, and the traditional FADE OUT. Part two then fades in on the incongruity of a Vietnamese street whore (Papillon Soo Soo) in Da Nang strutting her stuff to the sounds of Nancy Sinatra's "These Boots Are Made for Walking," a song associated with another time period and cultural ambience. Thus Kubrick initiates what in many ways seems like an entirely different story, with its own cast of characters, located in a new setting, and one with its own distinct tones and dramatic textures. He provides none of his usual segues or setups to announce or anticipate changes in the film's structural development. Missing from *Full Metal Jacket* are moments like the match cut in *2001* between a hominid's bone and an orbiting space satellite. Or the transition in *Clockwork* from juvenile reverie and arrest to Alex's voiceover lament that we are now entering "the real weepy and tragic part of the story." Or the kinds of deliberate, expository anticipations found in *Barry Lyndon* and *The Shining* that set up later events in two stories about two very different kinds of journeys.

Except for the physical presence and occasional voiceover of Joker (Matthew Modine), along with the reintroduction of Cowboy

(Arliss Howard), part two of *Full Metal Jacket* contains only a handful of the traditional markers that lend unity and continuity to a film narrative. Outwardly, even Joker's appearance has changed, including his now grown-out hair, and in the way he carries himself differently from the recruit/maggot of part one. Nowhere do we get any direct confirmation from him or Cowboy that the events of Parris Island haunt them or have in any way shaped their behavior in the Vietnam section of the story. Specifically, they never mention their betrayal of Pyle in the "blanket party" scene (the soap/towel beating); nor do they mention his madness. However, while Parris Island for Joker and Cowboy may resemble an unpleasant dream long since forgotten, for Kubrick's audience it functions as a forty-five-minute surrealist nightmare and preamble to the narrative proper—the Vietnam "war movie" of part two—that the filmmaker is not about to let us forget.

Kubrick visually characterizes Parris Island as an environment of hard, clean, symmetrical surfaces that demands conformity from its human inhabitants. During the credits, seventeen young men have their heads shaved in preparation for their entry into Gunnery Sergeant Hartman's immaculate world. During his first indoctrination inside the barracks, the drill instructor represents the only animated object as he walks down two lines of twenty men each, rigid at attention and blankly facing each other from across the squad bay like perfectly aligned pawns on two sides of a chessboard. Only Joker's wisecrack and Pyle's grin suggest the presence of an unruly humanity in this setting of rigid conformity. In another scene, Kubrick's wide-angle lens creates a symmetrical mirroring effect when he shows the men in their skivvies lying down in their double bunks holding their rifles at attention and reciting the Rifleman's Creed. We first see the recruits in the top half of the bunks, then those on the bottom, and in each case they alternate from facing right to facing left as the image recedes into a perfectly aligned depth of field. Subsequently, Sergeant Hartman marches the men in two lines down the middle of the squad bay—while Kubrick's camera executes a perfect reverse dolly—and leads them in singing, "This is my rifle! This is my gun! This is for fighting! This is for fun!" Yet even here the young recruits, holding their rifles in one hand and their crotches in the other, stay in cadence and in character. Unlike the audience watching, they repress any indication that they either are amused by this drill or find it absurd. Rigid symmetry and order comically extend even into the latrine, where we see Joker and Cowboy mopping an already spotlessly clean floor between two lines of toilets facing each other at attention. Outside, the men are put through a series of carefully prepared training course obstacles ("Confidence Course") and lectures, but even in this potentially contingent space, removed from the enclosed designs of the barracks, Kubrick does not visually "open up" his film. Instead, we watch the young recruits march or run in lines to the drill instructor's cadences, stand for his inspection, and move over the various obstacles in response to his commands.

Rather than duplicate the often subjective, hallucinatory qualities of Joker's Parris Island account in Hasford's novel, Kubrick chooses to use a visual expression that objectifies—in fact, literalizes—the absurd nature of those events. Because of the narrative context in which they are used, these visual designs ironically remain unobtrusive and invisible for most viewers, probably because Kubrick hoped that his audience would accept them as authentic and functional representations of events on Parris Island. It is reminiscent of what happened during the time when Kubrick was preparing the initial script of *Dr. Strangelove.* He originally intended to do a "serious" treatment of the possibility of a nuclear accident—only to be repeatedly struck by the patent absurdity of then existing military and political policies. Thus, with the help of some highly expressive techniques, he created a film that asked his audience to see how certain comic truths were hidden inside the serious exteriors of the Cold War. In *Full Metal Jacket,* Kubrick takes a more challenging approach by reversing the *Strangelove* model. He puts his audience through its own training course, one separate from Sergeant Hartman's control, and asks us to see the absurd and brutal quality of certain "truths" or givens that all too often we and filmmakers treat with pious respect.

As part one's conventional three-act development unfolds in an efficient, sometimes machine-like linear progression, Kubrick creates as counterpoint several unsettling narrative and stylistic juxtapositions. As the Parris Island scenes move forward in time through a matter-of-fact, "training film" style of presentation, the film pushes characterization into very selective forms of satiric or surreal exaggeration. As he did in the B-52 scenes of *Strangelove,* the middle-class suburbia of *Lolita,* and the eighteenth-century social mazes of *Barry Lyndon,* Kubrick achieves a surreal or heightened effect through a contrast between a realistic, authentic mise-en-scène and satirically heightened performances—between Normality and its Shadow. Lee

Ermey's Gunnery Sergeant Hartman recalls Slim Pickens as Major Kong in the way his performance stands in sharp relief to the more naturalistic styles of the young actors playing the recruits. His rigid Marine carriage and movements, his bulging eyes, and a staccato voice that delivers with AK-47 precision a cascade of vituperation rarely heard in life or in a movie theater—all combine to make Ermey's Hartman a memorable film "character." He spews forth such well-rehearsed satiric gems as "You are nothing but unorganized grabasstic pieces of amphibian shit!" as if they were the natural product of his mother tongue. He is both the drill instructor from hell and a sadistic father surrogate bent on shaping his offspring into his own "hard" and mechanical likeness. Traditional family relationships between fathers and sons meld with a Marine Corps mythology that contends that it must destroy the individual before it can save him (i.e., Inside Every American Boy Is a Marine Trying to Get Out). Hartman represents another version of the Kubrickian Institutional Man—in this case, one who disassembles his male children like an M-14 rifle and then puts them back together as "ministers of death." He takes from these young "ladies" and "faggots" their hair and their manhood; he strips them of their names and their identities, then rebuilds them into killers who not only will bring death into the world, but in death will "live forever" through the Corps. In contrast, we know little or nothing about the young recruits, and except for Joker and Pyle, none stand out. Reminiscent of like situations in *Paths of Glory* and *Barry Lyndon,* the young men of *Full Metal Jacket* become little more than figures in a military geometry of orderly lines for inspection, and of well-drilled units in green marching in unison to their sergeant/ father's cadences.

But Joker's and Pyle's characters are the exceptions. Matthew Modine's laconic, understated performance helps Kubrick establish a tone for both Joker's character and the film itself. As the film develops, for instance, Joker's character and his occasional voiceovers increasingly are used to explain or clarify both *what* we see and hear and *how* Kubrick wants us to see and hear. His two brief voiceovers in part one, expressed in the matter-of-fact language of Joker as "journalist" and recorder, are mostly expository rather than personal, yet indirectly they give us access to more complex subtexts running through the film. Kubrick develops Joker's character, in his twin roles as ironist and wild card, as if he were a mole—an authorial spy—planted inside both the Marine Corps and the film's core. He's Kubrick's One-Eyed Jack—at once a spokesman for the Corps and its severest onscreen critic. He initially characterizes Parris Island as an "eight-week college for the phony-tough and the crazy-brave," while later, in his second voiceover on graduation day, he tells us how the drill instructors are "proud" of the killers they have spawned, and that the "Marine Corps wants to build indestructible men, men without fear." Yet Joker's irony, like Hartman's bulging-eyed ravings, contaminates the very information he reports, and assists Kubrick in his attempt to "train" his recruits—the audience—to see the presence of the surreal beneath the masks of the "real" or naturalistic. In his mimicry of John Wayne and in the "war faces" he creates for Sergeant Hartman in part one, Joker represents one of the "phony-tough," who in part two evolves into a *Stars and Stripes* poge who can "talk the talk" but not "walk the walk." Conversely, Private Pyle in his grotesque madness becomes a precursor of characters such as Animal Mother (Adam Baldwin) and Crazy Earl (Keiron Jecchinis), who in the stark landscapes and rubble of part two have been transformed into the "crazy-brave."

The psychological drama of part one turns on the Joker/Pyle relationship as much as it does on any of the cruelties inflicted by Sergeant Hartman. There are three important story beats in part one, and all involve Joker and Pyle. In the "Virgin Mary" scene, Joker stands up to Hartman's verbal intimidation and is rewarded by being promoted to squad leader and Pyle's caretaker. During the second act of part one, Joker uses gentle persuasion to teach "Leonard" (to his credit, he never addresses him as "Pyle") how to properly disassemble his rifle, lace his boots, make his bed, and perform the Manual of Arms. But Pyle's evolution as a soldier and Joker's as a human being come tumbling down because of one jelly doughnut. Pyle's need and instinct for food, not only for love or acceptance, become another Kubrickian example of the "human factor" that ironically rears its ugly head on a journey toward mechanical perfection. Thus Joker the humanist does not succeed any better than Hartman the martinet in turning Pyle into a better Marine or a better killer. In Joker's betrayal of Pyle in the blanket party scene (the second plot beat of part one), Kubrick, as he did with Colonel Dax's character in *Paths of Glory*, reveals how Joker's attempts at humanity are an absurd incongruity within the barbaric institutions of war.

Immediately after this chilling scene—enhanced by cold blue lighting and an eerie electronic score composed by Abigail Mead (aka Vivian Kubrick)—Pyle rapidly declines into the glassy-eyed stare of madness. But rather than turn on Joker or the members of Platoon 3092 who betrayed the ideal of camaraderie, the soft, effeminate Pyle looks inward and makes contact with the male, stone-cold shadow/killer that lives inside him. Earlier, Hartman literally choked the benignly oafish grin off Pyle's face, and now, with Joker's help, he has turned on the lights inside Pyle's unconscious, where, like Jack Torrance before him, he makes contact with his own paradoxical duality. For Hartman, such a development eventually becomes a cause for celebration: from his ironically prophetic view, Private Pyle has been "born again hard," and like his historical brothers in arms Charles Whitman and Lee Harvey Oswald, he will show "what one motivated marine and his rifle can do!" In the final story beat of part one, Joker confronts Pyle slumped on a toilet in the latrine and loading his rifle's magazine with sleek, shiny live rounds—"seven-six-two millimeter, full metal jacket." He and the audience look on a face caught between a now familiar Kubrickian grin of madness and the pitiful confusions of a lost innocence. Earlier, Joker put his hands to his ears to shut out Pyle's cries of betrayal, but here there is no way he can escape his failed responsibility. This is one mess he cannot shut out, flush down a toilet, or mop into a restored state of antiseptic cleanliness. Like Pyle, he too lives "in a world of shit," and its boundaries are wide and deep. In the events of part two, the film will imply that Joker repressed the violent memory of Pyle's final madness, but without his conscious knowledge it paradoxically bivouacs in the same dark space where Pyle discovered his killer instinct. In a final reversal that produces the climax to *Full Metal Jacket,* Kubrick will ask us to recall Pyle's acts of madness and to understand their part in a paradoxical journey into Joker's humanity.

Jungian theories of human identity appear to influence the subtexts of part one, while in part two Kubrick will give them a full and unique expression in the explosive, disordered surfaces of a violently contingent world called Vietnam. In the psychological regimentation of Parris Island, Joker uses ironic impersonation as a way of salvaging some vestige of his humanity in the face of Hartman's repeated assaults on the individual self. In that sense, Joker resembles Jung's negative archetype of the Trickster, who, if nothing else, has the ability to turn that which is absurd or meaningless into something meaningful, if only for a moment. Jung's Trickster, like Joker in part one, is not an integrated psychological archetype primarily because he lacks a sense of relatedness. He is all Reason (Logos) and no Feeling (Eros). Hence Joker's interruption of Hartman's opening monologue—"Is that you, John Wayne? Is this me?"—represents the rational man's feeble attempt to defend himself against, as well as detach himself from, attacks by the Irrational and the Absurd. Like a black recruit (Peter Edmund as Snowball), a Texan (Cowboy), and Leonard Lawrence (Pyle), however, Private James T. Davis (Joker) is assigned a new name, physically brutalized, and put through a moral/sexual reprogramming by Sergeant Hartman. But Matthew Modine's Joker is not the only impersonator in part one. Lee Ermey plays Hartman as the consummate performer with a loose screw, one so prepared and rehearsed in a role that has enjoyed such a long run that he no longer can distinguish the part from the man. As a caricature of the Shadow Father incarnate, he is both hilarious and frightening, primarily because he has forgotten how to impersonate a real human being. Even when he confronts Pyle and his rifle in the latrine, Hartman stays in character. He engages in a final act of intimidation by trying to stare down Pyle's rebellious madness and, to quote the script of *Full Metal Jacket,* by speaking "in his best John-Wayne-on-Suribachi voice"— *"Now you listen to me, Private Pyle, and you listen good."* In contrast to others, Private Pyle lacks the skills of impersonation, and therefore he is all too human. It is not so much his innocence, physical ineptitude, or lack of gung ho zeal that makes Pyle vulnerable to the rigors of Parris Island, but his lack of sophistication. He can't adopt Joker's pose of ironic detachment, because that requires an intellectual savvy that his innocence does not permit. He can't repress a smile, as the others do, while listening to Hartman's opening harangue, because instinctively and naively he finds its sheer outrageousness funny. He doesn't understand how the game is played, and therefore he doesn't know how to get in character for his role as one of Hartman's squirming maggots. Instead, he is all anima (soft, feminine) and no animus (hard, masculine), the good ol' boy who makes no pretense of being either phony-tough or crazy-brave. Eventually, Private Pyle undergoes a perverse psychological reversal in response to cruelties inflicted by both Hartman and the other recruits. He becomes His Father's Son—a dehumanized caricature of the hard-hearted Marine with the thousand-yard stare.

In an attempt to win the Hearts (Eros) and Minds (Logos) of the young recruits, Hartman's beloved Corps indoctrinates them into the rituals of an ersatz religious order that absurdly flip-flops between a sexualized theology and a theological sexuality. Through this mock-religious paradigm, Kubrick asks us to view these head-shaved young men as monks clothed in cassocks of green and inhabiting an antiseptic, sexless world where they are required to express their fetishistic devotion to a sacred relic through recitations of the Rifleman's Creed. Kubrick reminds us, as he did in *Paths of Glory, Dr. Strangelove,* and *Barry Lyndon,* of the tragicomic history of war and its sometimes lethal mixture of patriotism, religion, sex, and art. As he attempts to cast out from each man's mind the impure memory of "Mary Jane Rotten-crotch in her purty pink panties," Hartman plays the role of the High Camp Priest who marries his young celibates to their M-14s and then requires that they sleep with this "weapon of iron and wood." Consequently, not only does Hartman's dehumanized regimen take aim at the men's moral identity by converting them into killers, but it also wants to eradicate their sexual duality. All things female are expelled, repressed, or—in Pyle's case—grotesquely transformed by the perverted ideals of this all-male dystopia disguised as a Marine Corps boot camp. Even Joker, primarily through Matthew Modine's projection of a non-threatening, even sweet asexuality into his characterization, seemingly blends into Hartman's vision of a homoerotic paradise.

As he did through both *Strangelove*'s sexual allegories and *Clock-work*'s behaviorist dreams turned nightmare, Kubrick once again shows how quests for moral or social "perfection"—whether engineered by the Left or the Right—represent denials of the contingent realities of life itself. In one scene, Joker and Cowboy mop the latrine into a spotless cleanliness that eliminates any sign of the body functions and male fantasizing that take place there—of the fact that the young men of Parris Island also live "in a world of shit" and "erect nipple wetdreams." Being natural impersonators, however, Joker and Cowboy only mimic the drill instructor's catechisms while remaining faithful to their naturally overactive libidos. Yet while Joker playfully remarks that he wants to slip his "tubesteak" into Cowboy's sister, Pyle talks to his rifle "Charlene" and compliments her on her smooth, clean "action." And in the climax we get to see Pyle and Charlene in action, joined together in the cold blue light of the latrine and, to the electronic sounds of full metal madness, erupting in an orgasm of blood and brain all over the white, antiseptic surfaces of Hartman's utopian dream.

The paradoxical dualities and reversals of *Full Metal Jacket* become even more apparent in part two and provide ways of viewing the film as a continuous and unified whole. The cleanly polished and regimented world of Parris Island is replaced by the dirty, smoke-filled, chaotic world of Vietnam. The blue skies of Parris Island become either a blinding white ceiling, like those that pressed down on the trenches of *Paths of Glory,* or a smoke-filled reminder of the Inferno. While everything and everyone had their proper place within Hartman's straight-lined geometry, in Nam everything and everybody occupy the same cluttered space. The clean-cut, well-starched, obedient recruit maggots of part one adopt the protective coloration of their new environment in part two and evolve into scruffy, slouching, profane survivors. Instead of boys playing at war with pugil sticks and dummy rounds, the jolly green grunts of part two wear the raiment of death all over their bodies and kill everything in sight. Hartman's vision of erotic displacement and male purity gives way to the profane hustles of "suckee-suckee" and "boom-boom long time." Even the vacuous country and western pop songs that introduce each section, in the way they combine into a male/female duet, reflect a pattern of ironic, reverse dualism. As recruits are being shorn of their hair, Johnny Wright's "Hello Vietnam" introduces us to Parris Island with the man's lament of "wars that never end" and the pangs of separation from his "sweetheart" that they produce. At the start of part two, the woman answers back—while we follow a Da Nang hooker looking for business—in the brash rhythms of Nancy Sinatra's complaint to her lover that he has "been a-messing where you shouldna been a-messing." Joker's playful mimicry of John Wayne, his war faces, and other simulacra of Hollywood male heroism and death have all but disappeared—and in their place arises an existential world of actual death and poignantly absurd acts of real heroism. Joker's increasingly ironic reticence in the presence of Hartman's brutal assaults has changed into a satiric verbosity that often flaunts itself before now powerless superiors. Pyle's smile of innocence and his grin of death are transposed onto Joker's face as he increasingly confronts death's naked reality and undergoes a reverse progression in which he makes contact with a repressed humanity that lurks beneath his mask of "the joker."

Significantly, the Jungian subtexts closeted inside part one's artificial shell of Hartman's male utopia and Kubrick's visual naturalism erupt onto the surfaces of part two and prowl with Joker, Rafterman (Kevyn Major Howard), and the Lusthogs through the rubble of a shadow world that is now palpable to the senses. Standing next to a lime pit filled with the bodies of the dead, Joker is confronted by a colonel (Bruce Boa)—or rather the caricature of a colonel—who demands an explanation for the "sick joke" of his wearing BORN TO KILL on his helmet and a peace symbol on his jacket. Joker explains that he was trying to suggest something about "the duality of man, the Jungian thing." In this context, "the Jungian thing" is consistent with Joker's glibly explicit assumption of superiority in the face of a ubiquitous military stupidity. However, in less visible ways it also suggests the presence of a "Kubrickian thing" working itself out through the often schizophrenic and always complex dualities and paradoxes of *Full Metal Jacket*.

Kubrick develops part two through a progression of five plot beats that climax with the killing of a young Vietnamese female sniper. But it is through a system of associations and subtexts both within and between these segments, as well as their implied importance to the Parris Island events, that he structures the final story of *Full Metal Jacket*. The idea of "Vietnam, the Movie," for instance, doesn't just start with a comment made by Cowboy in Hue City, but with a hooker in the first scene posing for Rafterman's camera and a young Da Nang street warrior impersonating Bruce Lee as he makes his getaway with the Nikon. Joker, still the mimic, Bruce Lees him back, and later, inside the Marine Corps compound, expresses his admiration for the "little sucker's moves" while reassuring a disconsolate Rafterman that "it's just business." What we soon realize is that Joker and Rafterman, in their respective roles as correspondent and photographer for *Stars and Stripes,* are in the "business"—as in show business—of turning the war into entertainment. Lieutenant Lockhart instructs Rafterman on how he wants pictures of Ann-Margret ("fur and early morning dew"), reminds Joker how they run two basic kinds of stories (Winning Hearts and Minds; Winning the War), and in general defines how their job is to "rewrite" their war story and "give it a happy ending." Thus "search and destroy" is changed to an antiseptic euphemism—"sweep and clear"—that would earn both John Wayne's and Parris Island's Good Housekeeping Seal of Approval.

Yet the world we are seeing is anything but the sanitized, surgical operation found in either *The Green Berets* or the televised briefings of Desert Storm. Inside the newspaper's Quonset hut, the table around which the men sit and the walls that surround them are cluttered with a collection of papers, pictures, and objects that reflect an untidy world inhabited not by robots or imitation movie stars, but by characters who look like real human beings. Pictures of Snoopy the dog and Mickey Mouse figurines occupy the same space as newspaper clippings, the American flag, photographs, girlie pictures, and the combat correspondent's motto that ironically defends the "right to be misinformed." But as it often does, an untidy, contingent world—the one that eventually we organize into "history"—intrudes into this fenced-in outpost "in the rear with the gear" and forces it to change. Following the first plot beat of part two (the Tet offensive coming to "Dogpatch"), the *Stars and Stripes* office takes on the first signs of the real war that they have reported as if it were a segment for *Entertainment Tonight.* Combat helmets, cartridge belts, hand grenades, and guns are scattered over the table, and the "staff" members now are dressed for combat rather than for a visit by Ann-Margret. Wearing a field jacket with grenades hanging from it, even Joker looks like a real soldier. But appearances can be deceiving. Now there is "that damn button" on his jacket and Lockhart's whining complaint—"How's it gonna look if you get killed wearing a peace symbol?"—to keep alive Joker's function as onscreen entertainer.

During the early scenes of part two, Joker's character develops only to the extent that the satiric persona he was forced to repress on Parris Island can be more fully expressed in the less regulated but equally absurd world of the U.S. Marine Corps compound in Da Nang. In fact, there is a displacement in the film between, on the one hand, Joker the stand-up comic and stand-in for Kubrick and, on the other, Joker the evolving character within the serious drama of Kubrick's *Full Metal Jacket*. In itself, Joker's satiric outspokenness should not be seen as a significant moment in the film's arcing of his character. Kubrick merely indicates that Vietnam provides his character with a protective coloration under which he can hide from the psychological and moral truth of what happened to Pyle and what is happening all around him. He not only mimics Bruce Lee and cynically accepts what he does as "business," but now functions as an onscreen commentator for Kubrick's satiric development of "Vietnam, the Movie."

Yet in two Da Nang scenes Kubrick does anticipate later developments in which Joker will evolve from mouthpiece to character. In a hooch scene, ironically counterpointed on our soundtrack with another vapid, totally inappropriate love song (the "gonna get married" refrain of the Dixie Cups' "Chapel of Love"), Joker complains from his bunk that he is bored and wants to get "back in the shit." Payback (Kirk Taylor), with a tits-and-ass girlie magazine on his lap, counters with his rendition of a popular Marine mystique that sounds as if it originated in Hollywood before it found a home in that real-world place called Vietnam. He says you can tell that Joker has never been in the bush, because he doesn't have the "thousand-yard stare" that tells every one "you've really seen beyond." Rather than lying in rigid attention in their bunks, reciting the Rifleman's Creed, the Marines in Da Nang lazily play-act the Corps' myths in a series of post-adolescent pissing contests. Joker predictably employs his John Wayne impersonation ("Listen up, pilgrim") as a way of making fun of Payback's "bullshit" and of warning "new guy" Rafterman away from a delusional view that spiritualizes killing by elevating it into the realm of "The Beyond." Lockhart subsequently orders a very reluctant Joker to take Rafterman with him to Phu Bai ("in the bush") with an admonition— "You're responsible for him"—that Kubrick hopes will remind us of Joker the character's earlier failure of responsibility in his betrayal of Private Leonard Lawrence (Pyle).

Joker now begins a journey that will take him into the heart of his humanity, one that paradoxically reverses and merges with Pyle's earlier descent into "a heart of darkness." Thus Kubrick alerts us early on that his tale will not follow the Conradian model—at least not in the case of Joker's character. But we also should notice that it is a journey for Rafterman as well, one that eventually takes his character in a direction that reverses the film's development of Joker's character. As the two poge journalists travel into the field by helicopter, they confront one of Hartman's "crazy-brave" graduates in a door-gunner (Tim Colceri) who laughs and yells, "Get some! Get some!" as he fires on Vietnamese farmers who happen to be in the path of his M-60 machine gun. Rafterman, who earlier expressed his desire to get some "trigger time" in the field, throws up throughout the entire ride, while Joker noticeably does not laugh as the gunner explains "how" he can kill women and children—"Easy, you just don't lead 'em as much. Ain't war hell?" (Now, that's funny—and a Vietnam anecdote right out of Herr's *Dispatches*.) Eventually, Rafterman completes his initiation into the crucible of Vietnam in a manner that would make both his father and Hartman proud. This blond, scrubbed-face all-American boy eventually develops the "stare" and becomes a stone-cold "heart-breaker" and "life-taker" when he later stands in celebration over the body of a bullet-riddled fifteen-year-old female sniper. In contrast, Joker's contrary development begins in an earlier scene, as he stands looking down into a pit. Kubrick starts by showing us his face in close-up, staring down and backlit by an oppressively empty white sky, then follows with a reverse zoom that reveals a blank, lime-covered death staring back up at Joker and the onlookers who line each side of an excavated pit. As he looks down at the remains of twenty Vietnamese civilians killed by the NVA (North Vietnamese Army), Joker's face shows the first signs of a humanity breaking through the hard shell of the Trickster's mask. It is a pure Kubrickian moment—recalling earlier paths of death, not of glory—that both reminds us of where we have been (Pyle's white madness in a latrine) and prepares us for where we are going.

As Joker's character begins to take on a more complex duality, the serious Kubrick film that lurks beneath the Kubrick satire called "Vietnam, the Movie" likewise begins to emerge and show its face. Particularly in the events prior to the Lusthogs' final movement into the concrete inferno of Hue City, Kubrick ratchets up the film's disjointed narrative surfaces, as well as its thematic interest in Jungian dualities, by squeezing his film into a still unsettling but now purposeful schizophrenic unity. Increasingly he reverses his earlier strategy of suggesting, for instance, that beneath the naturalistic and satirically rendered surfaces of Parris Island there existed as counterpoint a more seriously considered subtext. In part two of *Full Metal Jacket*, both text and subtext—the satiric and the serious—mingle and cohabit in a now single schizophrenic film space. In the lime pit scene, for example, Kubrick juxtaposes Joker's facial acknowledgment of death's naked presence with a young lieutenant (Ian Tyler) who poses for Rafterman's camera and the poge colonel's mindless conviction that "inside every gook there is an American trying to get out." All the while, a silent image of death in white looms in the background. Elsewhere, he dramatically alternates between scenes depicting the sobering truth of death and satiric renderings that turn death into another form of entertainment.

Joker and Rafterman hook up with Cowboy and the Lusthog squad inside the courtyard of a Vietnamese pagoda (the second plot beat of part two), and with the nonsense lyrics of "Wooly Bully" as accompaniment, they once again engage in the post-adolescent rites of manhood. Talking in the ironic banter that defined their association on Parris Island, Joker and Cowboy reaffirm their friendship through the age-old traditions of male bonding. As Sam the Sham's "Watch it, watch it" continues to play on the soundtrack, Joker confronts in Animal Mother an imposing, "crazy-brave" presence—a helmet inscribed with I AM BECOME DEATH, cartridge belts crisscrossing his chest, and an oversized gun—that resembles a heavy metal rock star's impersonation of death. He passes through Animal Mother's test of manhood ("You seen much combat?") by once again flipping his face back over and using a parlor trick invented by the Duke ("Well, pilgrim"). But the tone of the scene suddenly changes when Crazy Earl unveils for Rafterman's camera an image of actual death in the lifeless, whitened face of a young NVA soldier. For the first time, Kubrick's camera becomes Rafterman's camera—and like Joker staring down into the lime pit, we are directly confronted by the white face of death. Crazy Earl, kneeling beside a dead boy masquerading as an enemy grunt, looks into *our* camera and tells *us* how much the Lusthogs love being "jolly green giants, walking the earth with guns," and how when "we rotate back to the world, we're gonna miss not having anyone around that's worth shooting." Kubrick now challenges his audience to engage more directly his medium of sight and sound—to *see* and *hear* in ways that go deeper than the hard, polished surfaces of Parris Island. To not only see and hear the "crazy-brave" in the detached landscapes of satire—of "Vietnam, the Movie"—but to see and hear the frightening presence of our own very human fear of death gazing back at us from the heart of *Full Metal Jacket*.

As "Full Metal Jacket, the War Movie" begins in earnest with the Marine advance on Hue City, it still must compete with "Vietnam, the Movie." Shot in an abandoned gasworks in the East London neighborhood of Beckwith, the Hue City scenes increasingly show the presence of real fear—not some Hollywood simulacrum—on the faces of Joker, Rafterman, Cowboy, and even Animal Mother. The Lusthogs move into a gray, almost blank landscape of concrete, twisted iron, and rubble, where the only noticeable color comes from billowing clouds of blackened smoke, orange volcanoes of fire, and Vietnamese advertising billboards staring down in pop culture mockery. It is a concrete nightmare in broad daylight, a firebombed Dresden on the day after, that oddly resembles the blank, vacant New York urban corridors from the last part of *Killer's Kiss*. Kubrick now uses a ground-hugging Steadicam and returns to Abigail Mead's electronic drums and twangs to give an emotional, visceral charge to events that momentarily exist outside the artifices of satire and impersonation. During this initial advance, a familiar grinning Vietnamese face looms down on the men from a billboard. It is identical to one seen in the backgrounds of downtown Da Nang advertising beer and toothpaste, only here, rather than being a piece of functional background decor, it is a surreal reminder of other, more sinister faces of madness and death. Without warning, just after Crazy Earl guns down a handful of the remaining VC (Viet Cong) in the city, the fighting stops, and the moronic sounds of "Surfin' Bird" become part of a schizophrenic segue that takes us into four consecutive scenes that flip-flop between satire and drama. It is as if the theater has now entered the theater of war.

In the first of these scenes, for example, Kubrick introduces a three-man Marine camera crew conducting interviews of the Lusthog squad. While tanks continue to reshape the jagged, concrete skyline of Hue City, the crew sweeps by the weary soldiers, who, rather than providing the usual newsreel fodder, bombard the camera with responses destined for the cutting room floor. Cowboy gets the ball rolling with a title for their film—"Start the cameras, this is Vietnam—the Movie!"—while the other squad members pick the genre and cast themselves for star turns in a Hollywood oater with cowboys and Indians. Appropriately, Joker is assigned the part of John Wayne by Eightball (Dorian Harewood), while the "gooks" will play the Indians. We then cut from "Vietnam, the Movie" to Kubrick's serious movie—the "shadow" inside the parody—through an overhead shot looking down on the dead, bloodied remains of Lieutenant Touchdown (Ed O'Ross) and Hand Job (Marcus D'Amico). Like Joker earlier, the Lusthogs and the audience look down on the stark face of death. Standing in a circle around the bodies, the men say their goodbyes in a series of low-angle shots that frame each character's face against either an empty white sky or the gray ruins of Hue City. Rafterman, who as New Guy still lacks the "stare" that Sees Beyond, offers the official party line—"At least they died for a good cause . . . Freedom" —while Animal Mother coldly looks down and corrects him with, "This is a slaughter. If I'm gonna get my balls blown off for a word . . . my word is *poontang*." The next scene, again abruptly, takes us back to the camera crew and fourteen separate "interview" inserts of the Lusthogs talking into the camera and expressing several of the film's conflicting tonal and thematic dichotomies. Cowboy's observation that the urban warfare of Hue City reminds him of a real war—i.e., World War II and all the movies, from *Battleground* (1949) to *Saving Private Ryan* (1998), that depict it as the "good war"—is counterpointed by Doc Jay's (John Stafford) marvelous parody of LBJ's folksy political evasions of the Vietnam issue in the 1964 presidential campaign. And Rafterman's photogenic gingoism ("I mean *we're* the best. . . . Mother Green and her killing machine!") stands in sharp relief to Joker's "Have a Nice Day" happy face put-on in the final insert: "I wanted to see exotic Vietnam, the jewel of Southeast Asia . . . I wanted to be the first kid on my block to get a confirmed kill."

Before the Lusthogs go into war's concrete inferno for the last time, where Kubrick will complete the serious intentions of *Full Metal Jacket,* the film says its final goodbye to "Vietnam, the Movie." The wreckage of a Hue City movie theater, first seen behind Doc Jay and Joker during the "interviews," provides an iconic backdrop for the film's last satiric assault on Hollywood as global mythmaker. A painted billboard (MAO-GIANG) on the front of the theater portrays the chiseled physique of a romanticized Hollywood male warrior against a Western movie landscape. The young Lusthogs, standing and sitting outside this setting in rows of broken movie seats, greet the arrival of an ARVN (Army, Vietnam) pimp/soldier and his teenage hooker on a motor scooter with a chorus of libidinous hoots and hollers. Not much more than a boy himself, the pimp starts the bidding, while the Vietnamese girl, dressed like an American teenage queen in dark shades (Cowboy calls her "little schoolgirl"), stands with her hands on her hips, ready for inspection. Racial and sexual myths intermingle in ironic, humorous ways as the girl confirms that the black grunt Eight-ball doesn't "pack too much meat" by seeing for herself his "magnificent specimen of pure Alabama blacksnake." As we watch this performance in the foreground, the background setting reminds us of another source for the myths of racial/sexual stereotyping. Signs advertise the movie playing at this ruined theater—*The Lone Ranger*—and display the likeness of a Hollywood Indian on the warpath. In Kubrick's "Vietnam, the Movie," however, Animal Mother is cast as "Kemosabe," and the "little yellow sister" as his faithful companion "Tonto."

As Animal Mother pushes the young hooker into the theater for some "boom-boom," the serious drama of *Full Metal Jacket* hopes that its audience will recall both the scene with the Da Nang hooker where "Vietnam, the Movie" began and the sexually dehumanized regimen of Sergeant Hartman in part one. Reminiscent of Alex's "rebirth" in *A Clockwork Orange,* male sexuality has been resuscitated by the chaotic disorders of Vietnam. It has escaped from the mock-religious strait-jacket of Hartman's reverse Ludovico Technique. Sex no longer remains closeted inside the mind or inside the white latrines of Parris Island. It now roams in broad daylight with the Lusthogs and their weapons of war in hormonal unity. In the paradoxical, inside-out world of *Full Metal Jacket,* war sexually liberates these young grunts from the social mechanisms of repression, because ultimately its disorders are beyond human management. In a typically Kubrickian paradoxical reversion, the Lusthogs represent not only "ministers of death" but a raunchy, raucous life-force—albeit a post-adolescent, sexist one—that affirms the presence on a devastated landscape of both the human and the inhumane. It is Kubrick's sexual parable of a journey *out of* the "heart of darkness"—re-titled here as "Vietnam, the Pornographic Movie"—that eventually casts out the "shadow" of sexual dehumanization.

The third plot beat of part two sends the Lusthogs back to the battleground of Hue City, and the film's paradoxical moral parable toward its climax. In a violation of a narrative film convention, Kubrick does not "show" us the plot beat that forces the Lusthogs back into action, but merely has Joker, in voiceover, "tell" us. Joker reports that Intelligence believes that the NVA pulled out of the area during the night, and that the squad is being sent on patrol to check it out. In contrast, Kubrick will challenge the audience to *see, hear,* and *understand* his cinematic voice during these compelling, climactic events through the way they complete patterns and subtexts developed throughout the film. More important, Kubrick once again will demonstrate his remarkable genius for extracting a complex range of emotions and ideas from the jaws of that time-bound, linear machine called film narrative. In this final twenty-five minutes of the film, which pivots on the death of Cowboy and climaxes with Joker standing over a dying VC sniper, a moral drama unfolds that eventually completes the film's complex dualities and reversals.

Following Crazy Earl's death by booby trap, and with Cowboy now in charge, the Lusthogs become lost in the increasingly burning, defoliated rubble of Hue City. Tragically, they "change direction" right into the path of death itself. Sent ahead as scout, Eightball, the "nigger behind the trigger," walks under the sights of the sniper's rifle, and for the first time Kubrick's camera looks down on this devastated landscape through the "enemy's" stone-cold stare. Now it is a Marine who is a tiny, faceless figure in the background, not the NVA or VC soldiers gunned down in earlier scenes. As the sniper lures the other squad members into its killing field, sections of Eightball's body explode before our eyes like one of those "bags of blood" so chillingly described in Hasford's novel. At first, Cowboy wants to "sit tight" and wait for the tanks, but with no tanks forthcoming, he orders the Lusthogs to pull out. But Doc Jay and then Animal Mother show that a human spirit, not just an *esprit de corps,* lives inside them. They don't go after Eightball because they believe in freedom or poontang, nor because they mindlessly follow a Marine Corps dictum that you don't leave your buddies behind. They defy Cowboy's orders and charge off—headlong and "crazy-brave"—in response to an instinct that sets aside a concern for individual survival in the interest of saving another human life. Following Doc Jay and Animal Mother's acts of crazy-brave courage, the other moral and instinctual dominoes start to fall. Since he is now the squad leader, Cowboy reluctantly assumes the moral, rather than tactical, responsibility for what follows. Reason tells him that both Eightball and Doc Jay are "wasted"—and Kubrick makes sure that we share that conviction as he shows them being torn to pieces by the sniper's fire—while his emotional bond with these young men urges him to follow Animal Mother's mad dash into death. Moreover, Kubrick no longer allows his audience to detach itself from these events through satiric impersonation or exaggeration. His on-screen ironic mouthpiece for "Vietnam, the Movie" is developing into a fully realized character. Significantly, Joker and Rafterman volunteer to go with Cowboy—Joker out of friendship, and Rafterman out of a desire to "see beyond"—as Kubrick continues to foil their respective characters. Now that two-headed caricature of the "phony-tough" and "crazy-brave" has a thoroughly human face that, within the stark landscapes of Hue City, becomes both absurd and tragically poignant.

Following Cowboy's death (the fourth plot beat of part two), Kubrick turns the focus of his moral drama onto Joker, and completes not only a reverse doubling between Joker and Rafterman, but a more important one between Joker and Pyle. With a burning concrete monolith in the background—a Kubrickian sign for an important evolutionary moment—Joker holds a dying Cowboy and tries to reassure him ("You're gonna be all right") and keep him alive through the joking, latrine banter ("I wouldn't shit you man. You're my favorite turd") that has defined their friendship since Parris Island. But Cowboy can't "hack it," despite his dying appeal to that familiar Marine incantation, while Joker's face now shows the presence of a cold anger that erases once and for all the Trickster's mask of bemused contempt. Animal Mother, whose face moves back and forth between brief expressions of fear and a more dominant steely hardness, coldly recites the grunt's predictable response: "Let's go get some payback." As the climax makes clear, however, Kubrick chooses not to take Joker's character along the path followed by Pyle and Animal Mother.

The surviving members of the Lusthogs now travel through a dark and smoky world of orange burning fires, pockmarked buildings, and mountains of rubble to a showdown with a fifteen-year-old Eurasian angel (Ngoc Le) transformed into a slant-eyed VC grunt. The surreal, mechanical sounds of Abigail Mead's electronic score link this climatic scene to both the betrayal of Pyle in the towel-beating scene and the grotesque face of his madness in the latrine's cold blue light. In what appears to be the ruins of a Vietnamese temple, Joker and Kubrick's audience confront a female version of Private Pyle's madness, and, echoing his response in part one, Joker stands helpless before its explosion of AK-47 full metal madness. Only now he can't shut out its sounds or its face by covering his ears or closing his eyes. He looks, along with Kubrick's audience, at a young girl's once-beautiful face disfigured by male fury—a Vietnamese diminutive of both Pyle the madman and Animal Mother the killer grunt. Suddenly, her body explodes before our eyes from offscreen bursts of fire from an M-16 rifle. Rafterman, as Lone Ranger and Supergrunt, has come to Joker's rescue. Rafterman's development is now complete, as he stands over the shattered remains of this child, coldly laughing in celebration and speaking in a vulgar, pop-culture argot that chillingly trivializes the profound ("Am I bad? Am I a life-taker? Am I a heart-breaker?"). Kubrick again shows Joker standing with others in a circle looking into the face of death. Only here, the young girl is still alive, at first praying, then begging for someone to kill her, in a moment that expresses her lost innocence. Joker now confronts his betrayal of Pyle and his part in the sacrifice of another innocent on the altar of Sergeant Hartman's beloved Corps. Significantly, Joker's face transfigures from the grunt's thousand-yard stare that gazes into a void to the contortions of human compassion. He challenges Animal Mother's authority as the new squad leader by insisting that they can't leave the young girl to suffer. In what becomes the last beat in a Kubrickian moral parable, Joker has to choose between proving to Animal Mother that he can "walk the walk" or proving to himself that he can act as a morally responsible human being. Kubrick's camera holds on Joker's face for more than a minute as it twists itself into a paradoxical act of moral courage—what Kubrick wryly described in an interview as "humanity rearing its ugly head." After firing his gun into the young girl, Joker continues to look down as a predictable offscreen chorus violates the sanctity of this moment. Rafterman's "Joker, we're gonna have to put you up for the Congressional Medal of . . . *Ugly!*" and Donlon's (Gary Landon Mills) "Hard, core man" are no longer amusing or appropriate expressions of Gruntspeak. They now have the hollow ring of hollow men.

Kubrick ends *Full Metal Jacket* with a coda that draws together and unifies the events of parts one and two of the film. In the final shots, lines of moving soldiers fade into silhouettes as they journey across a black and orange landscape, singing not the "Halls of Montezuma" but the Mickey Mouse Club song ("Forever let us hold our banner high"). Kubrick uses Joker's final voiceovers to rejoin his schizophrenic twins, "Vietnam, the Movie" and "Full Metal Jacket, the Movie." Once again we hear the satiric journalist of Da Nang ("We have nailed our names in the pages of history enough for today") and the irreverent impersonator of Parris Island ("My thoughts drift back to erect nipple wetdreams about Mary Jane Rottencrotch"). But we also hear the voice of Joker the character, who is no longer confined by his function as Kubrick's satiric mouthpiece—the one who looked down into the terrible faces of death and eventually confronted his own failed responsibility toward Leonard Lawrence/Pyle. Like Pyle,

Joker believes that he lives in "a world of shit," but he also has a modest hope for the future: "I am so happy that I am alive, in one piece and short. I'm in a world of shit, yes. But I am alive and I am not afraid." Rather than following Hasford's lead and turning his main character into one of Sergeant Hartman's killers ("indestructible men, men without fear"), Kubrick has Joker confront and acknowledge his fear of death, and thereby save himself from the greater fear of losing his humanity.

In the final analysis, such understated nuances of character and theme do not conform to the kind of redemptive ending that an audience expects, and that it got in several of the Vietnam films before *Full Metal Jacket.* Unlike those films, Kubrick's journey into darkness moves through a conceptual and emotional space that lacks those moral or ideological rest areas that provide an audience the opportunity to reconnoiter and to fit the film into a familiar parabolic design. Rather than ingratiating himself, Kubrick repeatedly challenges the audience by undermining popular mythologies and, from one film to the next, by working out his own unique responses to the complex nature of human experience. That may be why some see in *Full Metal Jacket* only the fragments and not the whole of its characterization, structure, theme, or tone. Understandably, they then might conclude that his work lacks the kind of "center" found in other films, without realizing that inside Kubrick's mazes, the center is everywhere and nowhere. Perhaps Kubrick's various film odysseys always have taken too many sharp and unexpected turns. In the various ways it evolved, expanded, and repeatedly twisted itself into new shapes throughout his film career, Kubrick's vision might have always been too personal and idiosyncratic for most viewers. But if for no other reason, the fragmented yet brilliantly whole film experience of a Kubrick film such as *Full Metal Jacket* keeps drawing audiences back into his theater because of a very human fascination with the sheer plasticity of genius.

10 HOUSE CALLS
Eyes Wide Shut

In the years between the 1987 release of *Full Metal Jacket* and the early months of 1996, when *Eyes Wide Shut* was in pre-production, Kubrick worked on three separate projects dealing with subjects that had dominated his imagination throughout his career. Between *The Killing* and *Paths of Glory*, he co-authored a screenplay for MGM with Calder Willingham based on a story by Viennese writer Stefan Zweig called *The Burning Secret*. By all accounts, Kubrick was extremely enthusiastic about Zweig's sardonic Freudian account of sexual infidelity. Eventually the script was shelved, but not before it had stimulated his interest in doing a film about what he would later describe as "the sexual ambivalence of a happy marriage." Although the exact date remains unknown, he also discovered Arthur Schnitzler, another Viennese writer whose work is profoundly psychological, as well as satiric, and deals primarily with the repressed sexual fears and desires of the bourgeoisie. During the 1960s and 1970s, Kubrick repeatedly mentioned to acquaintances his desire to make a film based on Schnitzler's 1926 novella *Traumnovelle* ("Dream Story"). In 1971, as *A Clockwork Orange* was being prepared for release, Warner Brothers announced that he would adapt the Schnitzler story for his next film. But in an interview with Michel Ciment some months later, Kubrick admitted that he had not begun work on the project, and eventually he went on to make *Barry Lyndon.* As early as 1958, Kubrick expressed his view on a human response to the psychological and moral stresses of middle-class life that closely resembles the approach to character found in the works of Zweig and Schnitzler: "many people have learned to accept a kind of grey nothingness, to strike an unreal series of poses in order to be considered normal." And in 1960, in an article written for *The Observer,* he mentioned his desire to make a contemporary story

> that really gave a feeling of the times, psychologically, sexually, politically, personally. I would like to make that more than anything else. And it's probably going to be the hardest film to make.

As it turned out, that film was not *Lolita,* which he had begun shooting in England when the above comment was published; nor would it be his near-futuristic "psychological myth" of some ten years later, *A Clockwork Orange.* Almost forty years after first reading Stefan Zweig's *The Burning Secret,* and quite possibly the stories and plays of Arthur Schnitzler, Stanley Kubrick began work with Frederic Raphael on a script inspired by *Traumnovelle* that eventually would become *Eyes Wide Shut* (1999).

Kubrick not only worked on two other scripts during the period after *Full Metal Jacket,* but even completed some of the pre-production for both projects before putting them aside in 1996 and focusing all his energies on *Eyes Wide Shut.* One was a futuristic epic about global warming and a robot boy's quest to be human, titled *A.I.* (Artificial Intelligence), based on a short story by science-fiction writer Brian Aldiss called "Super Toys Last All Summer Long." The other was a historical piece titled *The Aryan Papers,* about Jewish survival during the Holocaust as seen through the eyes of a small boy in Nazi-occupied Poland, based on Louis Begley's 1991 novel *Wartime Lies.* Each story focuses on a boy's experience with the interrelationship between the

psychological and cultural processes of dehumanization/humaniza-
tion, a paradoxical subject that increasingly dominated Kubrick's
work from *Dr. Strangelove* to *Full Metal Jacket.* He worked on *A.I.* with
Aldiss and at least three other writers between 1990 and 1995, which
means that in the period between late 1994 and Christmas of 1995,
when Frederic Raphael was collaborating with him on the script for
Eyes Wide Shut, Kubrick was simultaneously working with another
writer, Sara Maitland, on *A.I.* By early 1993, Kubrick had completed
the script for *The Aryan Papers,* and Warner Brothers announced it as
his next film. Locations were scouted in Denmark, and filming was
scheduled to start in the late fall of that year.

For reasons that seem to have been connected to Steven Spielberg, he canceled his plans for *The Aryan Papers* and resumed working
on what he called his "Pinocchio" story, *A.I.* By the spring of 1993,
Spielberg was filming *Schindler's List* in Poland, and later that same
year his *Jurassic Park* became a summer hit. By all reports, Kubrick was
so impressed by the computer-generated effects of *Jurassic Park* that it
gave him renewed confidence that his futuristic vision for *A.I.* could
be realized on the screen. Not only did he hire Maitland to help him
solve the nagging problem of creating a workable myth and script
from Aldiss's short story, but he began collaborating with technical
artists on the visual design of the film's futuristic world. There is little
doubt that he was excited about this project, but as Sara Maitland
finally concluded, "You just can't load two and a half thousand millen-
niums onto the poor little Pinocchio story." In the end, the decision
probably came down to the fact that the script for *Eyes Wide Shut*
reached fruition first, and that Kubrick, after an almost ten-year hia-
tus, was eager to once again be behind the camera on a movie set.
After almost forty years, he would attempt to realize his goal of creating a contemporary film story about sex and marriage out of the *fin-
de-siècle* Viennese world of Schnitzler's *Traumnovelle.*

In his chronicle of their collaboration, Frederic Raphael records
in several places Kubrick's insistence that their script follow Schnitzler's plot beats. What this means, I think, is that Kubrick had complete confidence in the structural integrity of *Traumnovelle,* even
though, as with Raphael's first reaction to reading the novella, he
probably agreed that it was a "bit dusty" (dated). No doubt Kubrick
sought out Raphael not only for his considerable skills as a storyteller,
but for his stylish and often witty treatment of contemporary sexual
mores and for his ability to adapt difficult literary material to the

screen.* Thus it became Raphael's job to help remove the "dust," and to translate Schnitzler's story into a contemporary, end-of-the-twentieth-century New York City cultural ambience. In the film, the two principal characters, Dr. William Harford (Tom Cruise) and his wife, Alice (Nicole Kidman), are upscale New York City yuppies living in a beautifully appointed apartment on Central Park West. Bill's patients include the *crème de la crème* of the New York City social register, extravagantly wealthy and powerful men such as Victor Ziegler (Sydney Pollack), who reward the young doctor for making "house calls"— as well as for being discreet about their medical and sexual histories —by inviting the Harfords to their lavish Christmas parties. Instead of the novel's Viennese red light district, the film locates Bill's nocturnal wanderings in Greenwich Village, where it emphasizes such things as rowdy college boys loudly throwing verbal brickbats that ridicule both Bill's manhood and his sexuality; college girls who study sociology and hook their way through school (Domino and Sally); jazz clubs such as the Sonata Café, where Bill's college chum Nick Nightingale (Todd Field) plays piano; and a coffee house (Sharkey's) that serves up a Mozart requiem with its lattes and cappuccinos.

While retaining Schnitzler's dialogue in a handful of key scenes— in Alice's confession about the naval officer and in her description of a dream, in the masked ball/orgy scene, and in the final reconciliation between Bill and Alice—the language of the film overall conforms to its contemporary mise-en-scène. Particularly in scenes created by Kubrick and Raphael, the film not only removes the "dust" from the Schnitzler story, but develops a number of subtexts that become crucial to the film's conceptual aspirations. The early Christmas party sequence, for instance, introduces Gayle (Louise Taylor) and Nuala (Stewart Thorndike), two fashion models whose sexual double entendres are matched only by the slithering gyrations of their bodies as they practically snake their way into Dr. Harford's pants. In contrast, there are the absurdly dated sexual come-ons in the oily, Old World charm of the Hungarian Lothario, Sandor Szavost (Sky

---

*Frederic Raphael's screenplay credits include *Darling* (1965), for which he earned an Oscar; *Two for the Road* (1967); and the adaptation of Thomas Hardy's *Far from the Madding Crowd* (1967), Iris Murdoch's *A Severed Head* (1971), and Henry James's *Daisy Miller* (1974). For Raphael's account of his collaboration with Kubrick, see *Eyes Wide Open: A Memoir of Stanley Kubrick* (1999), which includes a summary of the Schnitzler story (pp. 17–23); for more on the Raphael book, consult the "Notes & Trivia" section of this volume.

Dumont), who quotes Ovid's *Art of Love* as he tries to lure Alice upstairs to look at Victor's sculpture gallery and to engage in an act of
sexual infidelity. Here and elsewhere, the dialogue indirectly implies
that satiric commentary is being directed not only against a smarmy
lounge lizard such as Szavost, but against Bill and Alice as well.

In the Harfords' younger world of hip, liberated sexual parlance,
Szavost's old-fashioned, sexist-tainted utterances about the art of
"making love" have been replaced by the honest vulgarity of "fuck"
and "fucking," which ironically implies that they may be less adept
than the aging roué at understanding or expressing the deeply private and intimate language of unfulfilled sexual yearning. Certain
phrases used by Bill and Alice betray an unfortunate shallowness that
encourages the audience to dismiss them as yuppie social climbers in
need of less acculturation and more actual self-examination. Expressions such as "I'm just trying to find out where you're coming from"
(Alice to Bill) and "You're putting me on" (Bill to Nick) illustrate a
form of cultural mimicry that belies the overall impression that this
beautiful couple are intelligent, sensitive members of a privileged
class. In the end, we will discover, along with Bill and Alice, that there
is a great deal more to their characters than the imprimaturs of
an upwardly mobile cultural order that they unconsciously imitate
through the various masks they assume in their daily lives.

The script of *Eyes Wide Shut* retains the following plot beats (referred to by Kubrick as "Arthur's beats") from the novella: Albertina/
Alice's confession to Fridolin/Bill of an unfulfilled sexual desire for
another man; Marianne/Marion's confession of love to Fridolin/Bill
in the presence of her dead father; Fridolin/Bill's encounters on separate nights with two different prostitutes; Fridolin/Bill's chance encounter with Nightingale in which he learns the password for a
masked party; the masked party/orgy scene and a mysterious woman's
intervention that "saves" Fridolin/Bill; Albertina/Alice's account of a
dream in which she mocks her husband; the death of the mysterious
woman from the orgy and Fridolin/Bill's visit to the morgue to view
her body; and Fridolin/Bill's confession ("I will tell you everything")
to Albertina/Alice when confronted by the mask on the pillow. Significantly, the Victor Ziegler character and the related story of Mandy
(Julienne Davis) have very little authority in *Traumnovelle,* except in
Schnitzler's fondness for generalizing about aristocratic decadence,
and in his introduction of the voluptuous naked woman at the
masked party who first warns and then "redeems" Fridolin, and who is

later identified as a "Baroness" who mysteriously dies from poison in a fashionable hotel.

The Victor/Mandy story is central to the Christmas party sequence, the masked ball/orgy sequence, Bill's discovery of Mandy's death and his visit to the morgue, and a final important scene between Victor and Bill around a pool table at the wealthy sybarite's mansion. In addition, the film often alters the effect of Schnitzler's plot beats through changes in character motivation that not only "update" the story but develop some decidedly Kubrickian themes. Bill's character, for instance, is less internalized than Schnitzler's Fridolin, as is evidenced by the script's focus on a psychological journey that gradually forces Dr. William Harford to abandon the impersonal, artificially erected masks of his public status and to confront his considerable shortcomings as a doctor, husband, father, and man. Reminiscent of character developments found in *Barry Lyndon* (Redmond Barry) and *Full Metal Jacket* (Joker), *Eyes Wide Shut* once again shows a Kubrickian male character discovering his own paradoxical duality— and ultimately a more fully realized humanity—in an evolution that brings Bill Harford into contact with the intertwined psychological realms of Persona and Shadow.

Another way in which the script contemporizes the Schnitzler story is through the sexual and sometimes sexist fireworks that define Bill and Alice's marriage. Although in both versions the women are more emotionally and psychologically explored than their mates, the film turns Alice into a much more complex, layered character than Schnitzler's Albertina, particularly in the way she is differentiated from her husband, Bill. Both female characters are more honest than the men about their unfulfilled sexual desires, and each expresses, in a slightly differing way, a declaration of heartfelt love for her husband in a manner that exists outside his emotional vocabulary. From the beginning, however, the film gives Alice's character not only more psychological autonomy than Schnitzler allows Albertina, but also a restless sexual volatility that foreshadows and eventually parallels the later misadventures experienced by Bill. While Albertina's anger toward Fridolin remains safely tucked away in her unconscious, and therefore finds expression only in a dream in which she celebrates Fridolin's crucifixion at the hands of vengeful women, Alice's resentment toward Bill—as well as other men—exists closer to the surface of her consciousness.

In the early scenes, emboldened by too much champagne in one instance and pot in another, she becomes "aggressive" (Bill's diagnosis) and makes fun of both the absurdly stilted sexual manner of Sandor Szavost and the smug "professionalism" of Dr. Bill. While dancing with the Hungarian, she mockingly teases him by exclaiming, *"Fascinating!"* in response to his story about women from a Victorian past who got married only so they could lose their virginity and then be with the men they really desired. The following evening, in an argument with Bill about the differing sexual attitudes of men and women, she becomes impatient with Bill's patronizing evasions and screams, "Why can't you ever give me a straight fucking answer!" In two other instances, she gazes at her mirror reflection in gestures of muted psychological exploration, whether in the act of love with Bill when they are doing the "bad, bad thing" mentioned in the Chris Isaak song or while retrieving a hidden stash of pot from a medicine cabinet. Alice's description of her dream in the middle of the film is less vengeful than Albertina's account in Schnitzler, but it does express both her desire for sexual freedom and her resentment toward the impersonal mask of sexual propriety worn by her husband. In the dream, she laughs at Bill while he watches her "fucking" other men, which recalls Alice's earlier real-time "fucking laughing fit" (to quote Bill in a fit of exasperation) after his sexist response—"Women basically don't think like that"—to her question about whether his female patients have sexual fantasies about him. In such ways *Eyes Wide Shut* explores more fully than does the novella the often unresolved psychological and sexual undercurrents that, to one degree or another, are universal to the institution of marriage—whether they exist in a "repressed" period such as Schnitzler's Vienna or in a contentious and "liberated" era such as the late twentieth century. Kubrick's avowed interest in the "sexual ambivalence" of marriage becomes central to the film's ending, in which Alice, like Albertina in *Traumnovelle*, becomes the focal point of a reconciliation that provides closure for the serious-minded "Dream Story" of *Eyes Wide Shut*. Unlike her counterpart in Schnitzler, however, while standing with her family in a toy store, surrounded by stuffed animals, Barbies, and a Muzak rendition of "Jingle Bells," Alice utters a single word—"Fuck"—that functions as a coda for the film's shadow story, the "Sex Comedy" of *Eyes Wide Shut*. But more on that later.

Not since *Killer's Kiss* and *Lolita*—and, coincidentally, in the same period when he probably first read *Traumnovelle*—had Kubrick worked with psychological material as sexually provocative as Schnitzler's novella. Like Davy Gordon and James Mason's Humbert Humbert, Schnitzler's protagonist is drawn toward a series of women, some little more than overly pubescent children, who arouse unconscious desires that turn both his waking and his sleeping life into a phantasmagoria. Reminiscent of Davy and Humbert's gradual absorption into the shadow world of a Saturnalian alter ego (Rapallo/Quilty), Fridolin is overtaken by what he describes as the "unreal and phantomlike" qualities of a pornographic luxuriousness, which in his case include suggestions of misogyny, pedophilia, and necrophilia. Like Jack Torrance in *The Shining*, he expresses a latent male urge to blame his wife for all his inadequacies as a husband and father, and "to loosen all the bonds of human relationships." At one point, as he contemplates the possibilities of a restored male freedom, he abstracts all women into a menacing, collective "they" who engage in dark conspiracies of mockery against his manhood. But unlike Jack Torrance, he comes to his senses before making that fateful decision to "correct" his wife by going to the woodshed for an ax.

Throughout his nightmarish experiences, the good doctor repeatedly tries to reassure himself through personal diagnosis that he is suffering from nothing more than a "delirium." In a passage that probably inspired Kubrick's choice of title for *Eyes Wide Shut,* Schnitzler sardonically describes a moment when his protagonist prematurely declares himself cured:

> Fridolin opened his eyes as wide as possible, passed his hand over his forehead and cheeks and felt his pulse. It scarcely beat faster. Everything was right. He was completely awake.

Even after the ending reconciliation, when a "victorious ray of light" announces the arrival of a new day, Schnitzler suggests that Fridolin's eyes, in the expression of the film, are still in many ways *wide shut.* Thus Fridolin, as Davy Gordon, Humbert Humbert, and Jack Torrance likewise do, suffers at the expense of the author's satiric humor. But again like Kubrick, Schnitzler also invests his character with oddly poignant and touching qualities, particularly in the way Fridolin struggles to put the pieces of his domestic and psychological life back together:

> Everything he put his hands to turned out a failure. Everything seemed unreal: his home, his wife, his child, his profession, and even he himself, mechanically walking along through the nocturnal streets with his thoughts roaming through space.

In the end, Fridolin never truly reconciles the divided quality of his newly discovered desires, partly because of the limitations of his imagination, but primarily because—like Davy Gordon, Barry Lyndon, and Dr. William Harford of *Eyes Wide Shut*—he is pathologically middle-class and normal.

The narrative design of *Eyes Wide Shut* integrates a series of contrasts, reversals, and paradoxical doublings that recall the schizophrenic structure of *Full Metal Jacket*. As he did for most of his career, Kubrick combines in his final film a number of contrasting story developments, tones, and themes that seem to pull in opposite directions and to cancel each other out rather than meld into a narrative unity. In *Eyes Wide Shut,* however, he reverses the equation between the "serious" and "satiric" found in *Lolita, Dr. Strangelove, A Clockwork Orange, Barry Lyndon,* and *Full Metal Jacket,* in which satirically rendered surfaces were countered by, then surrealistically absorbed into, serious narrative subtexts. Instead, *Eyes Wide Shut* resembles the more deceptive narrative strategy found in *2001* and *The Shining,* in which predominantly solemn and naturalistic surface orders are at war with an internal satiric disarray caused by unacknowledged irrational forces that exist within the structures of both personality and civilization. In *2001,* the evolutionary progressions of an odyssey into space were countered by the devolutions of an Earth-inspired comedy, while in *The Shining* the horrific present-time story of a decline into madness by Jack the Responsible Family Man ("all work and no play") was opposed by a grotesquely satiric past-time account of a retreat by Jack the Crazy Clown into a primitive, nostalgic pursuit of pleasure ("all play and no work").

Kubrick, however, incorporates the disparate narrative elements of *Eyes Wide Shut*—the "Dream Story" and the "Sex Comedy"—into a classic three-act unity that metaphorically imitates the instrumental musical form of the sonata. Not only does one of the film's plot beats occur in a Greenwich Village jazz club called the Sonata Café, but, as we shall see, its overall structure recalls the sonata's organization of contrasting forms and keys into the three primary movements of Exposition, Development, and Recapitulation:

Part 1: Exposition
> First Night: Home with the Harfords/Victor's Christmas Party
> A Day in the Life of the Harfords

Notice the strong presence of alternating and contrasting "keys" and "movements" in the three-part structure of *Eyes Wide Shut,* beginning with the contrast in the "Exposition" of part 1 between the Harfords' attractive upper-middle-class domesticity and Victor's vulgar American-rich opulence. What follows are contrasts: Between the repetitious, mundane routines of the Harfords' daily life in part 1 and the nightmarish experience of their nocturnal peregrinations in part 2, whether—in Alice's summation during the coda—"they were real or only a dream." Between the overly familiar and often silly disputes of male/female conjugality in part 1 and the responses in parts 1 and 2 to the aphrodisiac of flirtations, confessions, dreams, and missed sex-

ual opportunity. Between Alice's haunting confession of an irresistible sexual attraction for a stranger (the naval officer) in part 1 and
Marion's (Marie Richardson) desperate confession of love for Dr. Bill
in part 2. Between the mysteries of voluptuous sexuality offered to Bill
in part 2 in a chance encounter with Domino (Vinessa Shaw) during
his first nocturnal journey and the banality of Bill's college-boy sexual
come-ons to Domino's roommate Sally (Fay Masterson) in his second
night out. Between two scenes in part 2 with Milich (Rade Sherbed-
gia) and his pubescent child-daughter (Leelee Sobieski) at Rainbow
Fashions, one during a night filled with dreamlike sexual encounters
and the other in the crass, businesslike light of day. Between the
masked party's ritualistic Christian solemnity and its pagan Saturnalian orgy. Between Bill's voyeuristic migration through the masked,
naked obscenities of Somerton and Alice's description of her sexual
release in a dream in which she revels in her own nakedness and
laughs at her voyeuristic husband. Between Mandy's naked presence
as an overdosed hooker in an upstairs bathroom at Victor's party in
part 1 and as an undressed corpse on a morgue's slab in part 2. Between Victor Ziegler as Bill's charming patient/host in the "Exposition" of part 1's Christmas party and Victor Ziegler as the good doctor's cynical teacher in the "Recapitulation" of part 3. And finally,
between Alice's frank, often tearful confessions of both her sexual
desires and her most profound fears in parts 1 and 2, and Bill's tearful
confession ("I will tell you everything") of his previously unacknowledged desires and fears in the "Climax" of part 3.

The sonata-like narrative of *Eyes Wide Shut* also integrates a pattern of twos and repetitions that alternate in tone and concept between the film's contrasting "keys" and "movements" of the serious
("Dream Story") and the satiric ("Sex Comedy"). Not only does the
film use a married couple for its psychological and emotional focus,
but in part 1 it establishes a potentially lethal instability in the Harfords' happy marriage through Alice's haunting confession of extramarital sexual desire, and then provides in the climax/reconciliation
of part 3 a symmetrical match for Alice's earlier declaration in Bill's
emotional confession. In part 1, we see the two faces of Victor Ziegler:
the charming mask that he wears as downstairs host, in the company
of his guests and wife, Ilona (Leslie Lowe), and that of the partially
undressed debauchee standing over the nude Mandy in his upstairs
bathroom. During that important scene, we see two nude women in
almost identical poses: the drug-overdosed Mandy, sprawled out in a

semi-conscious state on a red chair, and a nude portrait of a woman in a state of uninhibited sexual invitation on the wall. During the Christmas party in part 1, Bill flirts with two models (Gayle and Nuala), who promise to take him "where the rainbow ends," and then in part 2 he takes two nocturnal journeys that develop events which both mirror and reverse each other. Not only does Bill make two calls on Marion, one to express condolences as the doctor of her dead father and the other (a phone call) to set up a sexual liaison, but he also makes two separate trips to Domino's apartment, the Sonata Café, Rainbow Fashions, and Somerton. In a Greenwich Village apartment, he has two sexual encounters with two different young women, the first (Domino) interrupted by a phone call from Alice, and the second (Sally) interrupted by the revelation that Domino has tested positive for HIV. He encounters two Japanese gentlemen (Togo Igawa, Eiji Kusuhara) in each of his two trips to Rainbow Fashions, where he is propositioned twice, once by Milich's daughter whispering into his ear, and once by a previously outraged Milich now pimping for his daughter. Two naked women, their identities obscured by colorful Venetian carnival masks, confront Bill during the orgy at Somerton; one seductively invites him to go with her to someplace more private, and the other mysteriously warns him of danger and begs him to leave.

Primarily through a system of narrative and sexual teases, not only does Kubrick separate the "Sex Comedy" from the serious "Dream Story" of *Eyes Wide Shut,* but these devices help him integrate as well both the Bill/Alice marriage story and the mysterious Somerton story. Toward that end, the film's narrative develops a series of carefully placed *interruptions* that often make fun of Bill Harford's emotional and psychological shortcomings, but that also satirize those members of the movie audience who, not unlike Bill, seek vicarious forms of erotic titillation. The film's first image—seen only briefly in the blink of a camera's eye—shows Alice shedding an elegant black dress and revealing her stunning nude body, only to be cut short by the "interruption" of the film's title card. During the Christmas party, Bill is interrupted twice, once during a conversation with Nick when Victor's secretary (Michael Doven) comes for the piano player ("Nick, I need you for a minute"), and the other by Ziegler's personal assistant (Randall Paul) in the middle of Bill's flirtation with the two models. The first interruption connects Nick to Victor and prepares for the piano player's involvement in the events at Somerton, while the second concerns the Bill/Alice marriage story and each character's coquettish behavior at the party during separate sexual encounters. Bill is ushered into an upstairs bathroom, where sex between Victor and Mandy has been interrupted by her overdose, a scene that provides the audience with its second startling image of nude female sexuality. Stimulated by the party's genteel yet sexually charged atmosphere, Bill and Alice make love while standing in front of their bedroom mirror, but for the audience, at least, it recalls the film's opening image in the way Kubrick "interrupts" what we're seeing through a sudden, unexpected fade-out. The Harfords no doubt go on and do the "bad, bad thing," but Kubrick quite literally turns his "Sex Comedy" into a "mind fuck" for the audience by shutting down his camera and not allowing his viewers to watch with their eyes wide open. Bill and Alice's pot-induced lovemaking the next night leads to *coitus interruptus,* as a result of their argument about the differing sexual attitudes of men and women. Structurally, this important plot beat in part 1 creates a rift in the couple's "happy" marriage that will not achieve closure until the film's coda in part 3. Marion's declaration of love is interrupted by the sudden arrival of her fiancé, Carl (Thomas Gibson), which not only saves Bill from an embarrassing moment but ironically puts the lie to his confident belief, expressed in his argument with Alice, that "women basically don't think like that."

During Bill's two nocturnal journeys in part 2, Kubrick continues to use interruptions to develop the "Sex Comedy" of *Eyes Wide Shut.* In Greenwich Village, Bill and the audience are titillated by Domino's sudden, voluptuous appearance, as well as by an implied promise of uninhibited sexual adventure on the other side of her apartment building's red doors. But two forces conspire to frustrate this anticipated climax to the film's foreplay. Because of Bill's reticence and his fear of letting himself go, Domino has to do all the preliminary sexual work ("Shall we?") prior to the phone call from Alice that interrupts them at the very moment when it was to be Bill's next move ("Was that Mrs. Dr. Bill?" Domino asks). Interestingly, this "interruption" not only allows Bill to technically remain "faithful" to his marriage vows, but it saves a doctor who should know better from having "unsafe" sex with a woman who unknowingly carries the AIDS virus. At Rainbow Fashions, Bill interrupts Milich's sleep, and they both interrupt the young daughter's involvement in a *ménage à trois.* In this case, the audience arrives too late for the sexually appointed moment and in the wrong company. As Milich rants and raves about "decency," he unknowingly conspires with the filmmaker in comically frustrating an-

other voyeuristic opportunity for the audience. At Somerton, although the discovery of Bill's identity "interrupts" the sexual proceedings, it does not happen until after both his and the audience's "eyes"
have been made "wide open" by the masked party's absurdly grotesque display of opulent female pulchritude. Yet once again, the joke
is on both Bill and the audience. In his movements from room to
room, in which every imaginable sexual act is being performed, Bill
has what he calls a "good look around," but that's about all he does.
He, like the audience, remains frustrated and locked into his voyeurism through the untimely intervention of another interruption. Just
as he is about to retire into a room with a naked young woman ("Do
you want to go somewhere a little more private?"), the mysterious
woman in the feathered mask takes him away and warns him. Afterward, Bill is saved from the embarrassment of being forced to strip off
his clothes and expose his nakedness to the masked assembly by an
interruption caused by the mysterious woman's declaration that she
will "redeem" him. In the next scene, Bill interrupts Alice's Somerton-
like dream orgy of her "fucking other men" by waking her up. And
during his second nocturnal journey, Bill's sexual advances against
Sally are interrupted by her revelation about Domino's blood test. Bill
Harford may be unlucky in love, but in the parlance of a sensational-
ized *New York Post* headline seen later, he is also LUCKY TO BE ALIVE.
In the final scene, the film brings closure to the emotional and sexual
chasm that has separated Bill and Alice since an argument interrupted their lovemaking two nights before in part 1. Alice utters a
single, magic word—"Fuck"—that not only anticipates the completion, following the film's last fade-out, of some unfinished sexual business in the Harfords' marriage, but completes as well the film's "mind
fuck" of those members of the audience whose prurient interest in
watching two movie celebrities—Tom Cruise and his wife Nicole Kidman—do a simulation of the "bad, bad thing" has kept them in their
seats for what must have been an excruciating 158 minutes.

Through separate, contrasting images of Alice and Bill Harford, Kubrick begins *Eyes Wide Shut* with a sly authorial maneuver that not only
anticipates divisions that will form in the couple's marriage some forty
minutes later, but also sets up a number of psychological and conceptual concerns for development in part 2. That brief, well-lit peek at
Alice undressing and exposing her striking nude body is countered
by the film's first shot of Bill, standing in the exact same spot in the

couple's now darkened dressing room, completing the finishing touches of dressing for Victor's party. Thus Kubrick establishes the film's contrary motifs of undressing/confession and emotional exposure, versus the defensive mechanisms of covering up/denial and psychological masking. Initially, all seems right in the Harfords' world as we follow this trophy couple moving through their gorgeous Central Park West apartment, which they have beautifully decorated in a way that complements our first impression that theirs is a perfect marriage within a perfect family. Paintings of vegetables and vegetable gardens, of plants and domestic pets, done in brightly rich greens, yellows, and oranges—the work of Kubrick's wife Christiane and stepdaughter Katharina Hobbs—adorn the walls and help create the impression that this late-twentieth-century American Adam and Eve inhabit a New World garden. They have the requisite child—an adorable seven-year-old daughter who wears angel wings over her pajamas and watches a performance of "The Nutcracker" on TV—consistent with a yuppie family "lifestyle" that looks as if it belongs on the pages of *Cosmopolitan* or *Vanity Fair*. (The only thing missing is a puppy, and Helena later mentions that to her father as a desired Christmas present.)

While Bill's eyes are always "wide open" to a number of social and sexual opportunities, in the beginning they are "wide shut" when it comes to seeing himself or his marriage. He looks, but he does not see. As the couple go through hurried preparations to leave, accompanied on the soundtrack by the gliding, graceful harmony of Shostakovich's "Waltz 2 from Jazz Suite," Alice asks Bill two simple questions that require that he look at her and give her honest answers. But in each case, he continues to focus on his own appearance in the bathroom mirror as he answers her with the stock responses that she looks "perfect" and that her hair looks "great," even though at the time she's sitting behind and below him on the toilet. (And, yes, even in that posture, she looks fantastic.) Irritated by his second answer, Alice remonstrates, "You're not even looking at it." But Bill saves the day by turning and "looking" at his wife, with his mask of adoring husband now in place, and saying with obviously studied sincerity and pride, "It's beautiful. . . . You always look beautiful." As Bill and Alice are leaving, we are also asked to notice—to keep our eyes and ears wide open to—the signs of other disorders that exist behind the attractive façades of this perfect couple's life. We notice, for instance, that Bill does not seem especially attentive to domestic family matters, particularly in the way he plays the "absent-minded" husband who depends on Alice to help him with such trivia as locating his wallet and remembering the name of the babysitter, Roz (Jackie Sawiris). In contrast, he also has a very smooth and practiced manner in the way he can play the gracious, considerate "Dr. Harford" in the company of the hired help ("I'll hold our cab tonight to take you home," he tells Roz).

In contrast to this attractive New World domesticity, the long Christmas party sequence (17 minutes) ushers both the Harfords and the audience into Victor Ziegler's American-rich version of a decadent Old World vulgarity. Bill and Alice are only invited guests—two innocents abroad, rather than official members—of this high society of the rich and powerful, because, as the young doctor says to his wife, "this is what you get for making house calls." Except for Nick Nightingale's presence on the bandstand and the window dressing provided by young models such as Gayle and Nuala, Victor's guests are noticeably older and more distinguished looking than the Harfords. From all appearances, the Zieglers have invited "all the best people" (to cite a phrase used to describe the overdressed ghouls at the Overlook Hotel's 1921 party), while undoubtedly they are the same people who will preside over the flip side of Victor's Christmas party, the masked orgy at Somerton in part 2. Only here, rather than carnival masks, they hide behind the masks of social normality while keeping their hookers and sexual liaisons discreetly out of sight, either in an ornate upstairs bathroom or in a sculpture gallery. Reminiscent of the contrast in *The Shining* between the Torrance family as caretakers of the Overlook during a winter in present time and as resuscitators of a male-dominated, Jazz Age Pleasureland in the summer of past time, *Eyes Wide Shut* sets up the now familiar Kubrickian concern for the disparities not only between the psychological realms of Persona and Shadow, but also between the enlightened and primitive faces of human civilization.

Particularly in this sequence, Kubrick establishes a series of contrasts and parallels between the dualities of Old World/New World, male dishonesty/female honesty, old/young, and clothed/naked that will dominate the psychological, sexual, and cultural concerns of *Eyes Wide Shut*. Initially, the Christmas party masks are in place as we follow Bill and Alice through a gauntlet of greetings, mixing, dancing, and, when the opportunity arises, flirtations with the opposite sex. Victor plays the perfect host as he greets the Harfords with hardy enthusiasm by complimenting Alice on her appearance ("Alice, look at you!

You're absolutely stunning"), and by thanking Bill for past medical advice that improved his tennis game. But very quickly Bill and Alice respond to the aphrodisiac of the party and cease being the "perfect couple" on display for others' admiration. They split up and engage in separate but parallel wanderings, as if unconsciously seeking both a release from their stifling perfection and the kind of sexual adventure that will come to dominate their waking and sleeping lives in part 2. Instead of a Shostakovich waltz as a complement to the harmonious appearances of their marriage, Kubrick selects music from three popular American love songs—"I'm in the Mood for Love," "It Had to Be You," and "When I Fall in Love"—as ironic counterpoint to the Harfords' separate flirtations. While Alice drinks champagne and dances with the overly insistent Hungarian Szavost, Bill talks about old times with college chum Nick Nightingale and flirts with two sexually aggressive models. In the process, the film lays the groundwork for a contemporary male/female sexual parable, one that eventually will be central to the seriocomic development of both the "Dream Story" and the "Sex Comedy" of *Eyes Wide Shut*.

Bill and Nick, for instance, appear to be contrasting male types, when, in fact, the film will reverse their roles in part 2 and show the many ways they are psychologically alike. But at the Christmas party, what we notice most are the ritualized, frat-boy power handshakes, pats, and joking banter that typify two guys momentarily reliving a freer time that existed prior to the responsibilities of career and family. Bill makes light of the fact that, unlike Nick, he stuck it out in medical school and became a success ("Once a doctor, always a doctor"), while the itinerant piano player freely admits that "it was a nice feeling" to walk away from a medical career, and that he continues the same practice in other areas of his life ("I do it a lot"). At the Sonata Café in part 2, we find out that Nick abandoned his wife and four sons in Seattle with a typical male excuse ("You gotta go where the work is") that occurs at the very moment when Bill is eagerly searching for any sexual opportunity to get revenge against Alice for laughing at him and for her frank confession of extramarital desire. The Bill/Nick doubling suggests the first signs of Bill's unconscious desire to "walk away" from his obligations to his wife and his daughter Helena (Madison Eginton), and to rediscover a male freedom that he gave up in the interest of molding himself into the successful professional and the perfect family man.

Conversely, Alice's teasing flirtation with Szavost during the Christmas party sequence shows how her restlessness is likewise connected to a desire for sexual freedom. The suave Hungarian asks Alice a question about the Roman erotic poet Ovid, who, he contends, had "a *very* good time." But in a witty retort to Szavost's antiquated sexual technique, Alice makes it clear that she is not one of Victor's models or hookers: "Didn't he wind up all by himself? Crying his eyes out in some place with a very bad climate?"* But more important, through both her politely mocking banter and her increasingly angry defense of marriage in the face of Szavost's ungentlemanly persistence, Alice openly expresses a deeper resentment toward the dishonesty and arrogance of men. Not only does she seem to resent Bill's adoring view of her as a prized social trophy for the public admiration of others, but she also objects to Szavost's assumption of an equally primitive male prerogative in viewing her as nothing more than a potential sexual conquest. As Kubrick's treatment of the masked party/orgy in part 2 will reveal, Szavost does more for the film's story than stimulate Alice's sexual imagination, which leads to her doing the "bad, bad thing" with Bill in front of a bedroom mirror. Both Szavost and Victor Ziegler eventually come to represent an aging male order that ruthlessly defends the ugly, primitive myth of its own social and sexual authority in a world where that power is being challenged by a younger generation of successful men with chiseled physiques (Bill/ Tom Cruise as a 1990s "Yuppie Hunk") and of liberated women with buffed self-confidence (Alice/Nicole Kidman as a 1990s "New Woman").

Kubrick also uses the events at Victor's Christmas party to create an ambivalent portrait of Bill Harford as professional man and doctor. Especially in the scenes downstairs that parallel Bill and the two models with Alice and Szavost, as well as the one upstairs of Bill with Victor and Mandy, he suggests the presence of unexplored shadows hiding behind the various masks of Bill's social persona. Gayle reminds Dr. Harford that she once was his patient, and that he was "such a gentleman" when he removed "half of Fifth Avenue" from her eye. Bill's self-deprecating reply—"Well, that is the kind of hero I can be

---

*Ovid evidently practiced what he wrote, in that his life was dominated by the pursuit of pleasure until he was exiled by the emperor Augustus to an uncivilized outpost of the Roman Empire on the Black Sea; during the last ten years of his life, he waited for a message of recall from Rome that never came. For a libertine such as Ovid, it undoubtedly was a place with a very bad climate.

. . . sometimes"—shows how easily he moves between a polished bedside manner and a charming social insouciance. In addition, Tom
Cruise's performance hints at another kind of reversal—this one involving Bill's ambivalent sexuality—that the film will more fully develop during the character's sexual adventures in Greenwich Village.
As he flirts with Gayle and Nuala, Bill takes on a traditional female
coyness in the way he pretends ignorance ("Where exactly are we going . . . exactly?") before their blatant assault on his mask of respectability. Gayle uses outrageous sexual double entendres in her reference to how doctors are "so knowledgeable" (about women's bodies),
and how she and Nuala are prepared to take him "to where the rainbow ends"—where, it is implied, he will be in the middle of an undu-
lating sex sandwich. But perhaps it is not only a heterosexual rainbow
that Dr. Harford unconsciously seeks; in Greenwich Village, rowdy
college boys will berate Bill's manhood by calling him a "switch-hitter," and a gay hotel desk clerk will sidle up next to him in a gesture
of sexual familiarity. In such ways will Kubrick gradually encourage us
to view Bill's character through the paradoxical perspectives of satiric irony ("Sex Comedy") and sympathetic understanding ("Dream
Story").

Parallels and contrasts are further developed during the Christmas party when Dr. Harford makes an unscheduled "house call" in
response to his host's predicament over Mandy's overdose. Just as he
began *Eyes Wide Shut* with contrasting images of Alice undressing and
Bill dressing, Kubrick will conclude the Christmas party sequence by
juxtaposing the mannered, overdressed formality of events downstairs
with a sudden, startling image of a partially undressed Victor standing
over Mandy's sprawling, defenseless nudity in an upstairs bathroom.
While downstairs Victor puts his opulently appointed wealth and
power on display, clothed in a gracious but patronizing civility, upstairs he hurriedly covers up his ugly, naked vulnerability just as the
young doctor arrives. Significantly, during his initial panic, Victor
shows no respect for Mandy's unfortunate condition by covering up
her exposed nakedness, and only after she regains consciousness,
when she no longer represents a public or legal embarrassment for
him, does he put on any show of regard for her. Even though Bill's
concern seems as shallow as Victor's, particularly in the way he assumes a patronizing bedside manner to gently lecture Mandy about
the necessity of rehab ("You are a very, very lucky girl"), he does reject
Victor's callous desire to "get some clothes on her and get her out of

here." To his credit, Bill insists that Victor keep her in the house longer, and that someone take her home. Unlike Alice, however, who makes fun of Szavost's aging male authority, Bill mostly stays in character as the socially ambitious young professional. He does not, for instance, use Victor's sudden vulnerability as an opportunity to exercise power over him, either by laughing at the pantaloon's absurd sexual appetites or by lecturing him on the dangers of promiscuous sexual activity. Instead, he automatically takes on the role of male confidant—like one of those ubiquitous polite young men who work for Victor—and unknowingly becomes just another hired hand who protects a prominent member of the Old Boys Club from exposure. Because he is a wealthy patient who helps support the Harfords' lavish middle-class existence, Victor—rather than Mandy—receives almost all of the doctor's professional and emotional attention. Through a series of bizarre and often nightmarish "house calls" in parts 2 and 3, in which his emotional and moral failures as a doctor will be exposed, Dr. William Harford's social and professional masks will be stripped away as the film completes its own examination and diagnosis of his character.

Part 1 of *Eyes Wide Shut* concludes by focusing on the Bill/Alice marriage story, and by developing the plot beat that will provide the impetus for Bill's psychological journey in parts 2 and 3. In an extremely abrupt transition, Kubrick goes from Alice flashing her wedding ring and rejecting Szavost's overtures ("because I'm married") to her standing naked before her bedroom mirror in a state of sexual readiness. As he did in the film's opening shot and in Victor's upstairs bathroom, Kubrick once again cuts to an unexpected image of a naked female body, only in this case it asserts a dynamic erotic presence that moves to its own sexual rhythms. In the film's first image, he framed Alice's nakedness and our voyeurism within a painterly composition of white pillars and red curtains, bathed in a golden light that made her resemble one of those Renaissance bronzes later mentioned by Szavost. While here, in the sexually explicit context of Bill and Alice's response to the Christmas party, she is the onscreen voyeur who looks at herself making love with Bill inside the mirror's frame. Although we at first assume that their separate flirtations at Victor's party provided the stimulus for their doing the "bad, bad, thing," their argument the next night will make us wonder if there were other, less visible and more unconscious forces at work. In Alice's case, it may be that she was more aroused by her suspicion (or hope)

Looking into the mirror of desire

that Bill came down from his pedestal and "fucked" the two models than by the aphrodisiac of Szavost's irritating attentions; while in Bill's case, it may be that he was more aroused by his view of Mandy's unconscious, voluptuous passivity than by Gayle and Nuala's aggressive sexual explicitness. Throughout this dreamlike episode, Kubrick keeps the focus on Alice, who seems to be looking with her "eyes wide open" for something more than just sexual gratification beneath the reflected surfaces of her marriage.

During the argument/confession scene (Schnitzler's first plot beat), Kubrick brings the contrasting seriocomic tonalities of *Eyes Wide Shut* into narrative conjunction for the first time as he concludes the "Exposition" of part 1. While the Harfords' argument continues to develop the "Sex Comedy" established in the Christmas party sequence, Alice's confession sets up the haunting "Dream Story" and prepares for the film's later integration of the marriage story into the mysterious Somerton masked party/orgy story. In her earlier defense of marriage during Szavost's cynical Old World assault on the revered American institution, Alice countered his humorous denigration— "Is it as bad as that?"—with her New World faith in the limitless possibilities of conjugal bliss ("No, as good as that"). Yet her optimism takes on a hollow ring as we watch the well-mannered surfaces of the Harfords' "perfect" marriage come apart during their argument, primarily due to the unruly presence of Alice's resentment toward Bill and her own unfulfilled desires. As this scene makes clear, Bill wants to remain in ignorant bliss and preserve the illusion of their perfect life, while Alice—like Eve in the Garden—grows restless in paradise and wants to explore the dangerous knowledge of unconscious desire. Yet neither character seems prepared to face what the film shows us—that rather than being privileged members in a Brave New World of liberated, psychosexual chic, they are in most respects poignantly unexceptional and normal. Like Nick, Bill has a typical male yearning to "walk away" from the constraints of fidelity, while Alice, like Marion in part 2, has an ordinary female desire for a passionate, illicit sexual experience outside the restrictions of duty and commitment. What we have, therefore, is a story that could easily evolve into an updated "Sex Comedy" remake of a classic melodrama such as *Casablanca* (1942)—except in this case, Tom Cruise's Bill would play the part of the sententious, asexual bore Victor Laszlo (Paul Henreid) rather than the role of the sexually mysterious Rick Blaine (Humphrey Bogart). It is no wonder that Alice, like Ingrid Bergman's Ilsa Lund, has become so restless and sexually vulnerable to the memory of a naval officer's dreamlike appearance and disappearance during a summer vacation with her family.

Stripped down to their underwear and smoking pot, away from the masks of social civility and sexual predation, the Harfords become ensnared in a private psychosexual dispute that exposes the fraudulent nature of their "perfect" marriage. During the heat of their argument, Bill holds to the antiquated double standard that women just don't think the same way about extramarital sex with other men as do men about having sex with other women (i.e., what is good for the gander is *not* good for the goose). He staunchly defends his "professionalism" in the face of Alice's satiric disbelief by declaring that he has never had sexual thoughts about any female patient while he was "feeling tits," nor have his female patients ever had "fantasies about what handsome Doctor Bill's dickie might be like." He goes on to claim that he is the "exception" to the rule that makes it "understandable" why Szavost wanted to "fuck my wife"—because, as he tells Alice, "we both know what men are like." Given his behavior with the two models at Victor's party, however, and the fact that Gayle was once his patient, these comments represent blatantly silly denials on Bill's part. Thus the film raises a question about Bill's motives for not giving Alice a "straight fucking answer" and admitting that, as other men might do, he did think about having sex with the two models. Conversely, Alice's motives for starting the argument are much clearer. She is angered by Bill's smug assumption of male superiority, by the impersonal mask he wears as the "knowledgeable" doctor, and by his basic emotional dishonesty. No matter how stimulated or irritated she might have been by Szavost's arrogant attentions, at least he, unlike her husband, was reasonably direct and honest about what they were. When the Hungarian proposed that they go upstairs and look at Victor's "sculpture gallery," Alice did not turn coy by pretending ignorance, while, in contrast, Bill asked Gayle for clarification of what she meant by her reference to "where the rainbow ends." Consequently, Alice seems willing to admit that her flirtation with Szavost created in her the "desire" for illicit sex, which may partially explain her glances into the mirror while making love with Bill the night before. On the other hand, Bill's stubborn denials and his smug certainty about his wife's desires ("I'm sure of *you*," he tells her) prompt Alice's paroxysm of laughter and her confession of sexual desire for the naval officer.

Primarily through Alice's confession, however, Kubrick makes it clear that *Eyes Wide Shut* will not become just another send-up of a classic movie story. As he has done so often before, in films as disparate in tone and genre as *Killer's Kiss, Lolita, 2001, Barry Lyndon,* and *The Shining,* Kubrick slows down the scene and directs his performers toward a fuller emotional exposition of their characters. Both Tom Cruise and Nicole Kidman reveal the presence of turbulent shadow worlds that exist behind the attractively placid façades of the Harfords' marriage. Because Alice is ready to confront her emotional and sexual ambivalence, Kidman's performance during this scene is the more noteworthy, primarily because Cruise's "Dr. Bill" has not as yet started his psychological journey. What we gradually do see on Bill's face, however, are the early shadows of confused anger and jealousy that later will do battle with the masks of his social persona. The scene's deliberate pace allows Kidman to take her character through a slow emotional bloodletting, in which Alice gradually releases all the resentment and frustration that has built up in the course of her marriage. She explodes into the satiric ridicule of what Bill angrily calls her "fucking laughing fit," in which she makes fun of her husband in ways that complement what the film, almost invisibly, has been doing with his character since the beginning. Then just as suddenly, reinforced only by Jocelyn Pook's haunting musical piece ("Naval Officer"), Kidman takes Alice's character from doubled-over mockery into the dreamlike reverie of memory, unconscious desire, and confession.

In a tone more wistful and uncomprehending than it is scornful, Alice confesses to Bill that, in response to an overwhelming sexual desire, she was once willing "to give up everything. You, Helena, my whole fucking future," while at the same time she admits that this dreamlike experience produced in her an equally powerful love for him "that was both tender and sad." Kidman also reveals Alice's willingness to face the presence of unconscious fears that occupy the same emotional space as her sexual desires. On the day after she first saw the naval officer, Alice says that she awoke in "panic" and "didn't know if I was afraid he had left or that he might still be there." But when she discovered that the naval officer had indeed left, she confesses to Bill that she was "relieved." Thus Alice's confident persona as the New Woman eager to "explore" her sexuality is replaced by a shadowy figure who undresses herself emotionally in front of her husband and exposes her fear that a firestorm raging inside her unconscious might turn both her marriage and her waking life into a nightmare. In an analogous fashion, Kubrick uses this important plot beat to fully reveal the "Dream Story" that occupies the same narrative space as the "Sex Comedy" within the complex structure of *Eyes Wide Shut*. While Alice will continue to dream and to explore her unconscious, a jealous and resentful Bill will journey into the waking nightmares of part 2. And only after he accumulates the memories of these dreamlike "adventures," in which he confronts his unconscious desires and his fears, will Bill break down into tearful confession before Alice and complete the psychological unmasking of his character.

Reminiscent of other Kubrickian one-eyed jacks, Bill Harford is forced to confront the confusions of a paradoxical duality that live on the other side of a carefully erected social identity. Particularly through a series of ironically developed "house calls" in parts 2 and 3, *Eyes Wide Shut* psychologically undresses Dr. William Harford's character and exposes the fraudulent nature of his professional persona. Part 2, for example, begins and ends with scenes of Bill confronting the face of death. In the first, he maintains his unctuous bedside manner before Marion Nathanson's grief and death's stark presence, as he performs a perfunctory service ("to go over there and show my face," he tells Alice) over the corpse of a wealthy patient. By contrast, in a highly emotional moment during the final plot beat of part 2, Bill looks down into the whitened face of another dead patient (Mandy) and, as Joker did over the shattered remains of a young female sniper in *Full Metal Jacket*, confronts both his failed responsibilities and his own humanity. Elsewhere, Bill's facial masks vary according to either the social requirements of a given situation or the emotional shifts in his character that announce the presence of his own fears and desires. During his house call on Marion and her dead father (Kevin Connealy), Bill manages to repress the jealous anger created by Alice's confession and to maintain his professional composure in the presence of death through the practiced, mechanical nature of his bedside manner. He places his hand on the dead father's head and then bows his own in a studied gesture of respect, before showering the grieving daughter with the narcotic of facial condolence and of familiar, whispered reassurances ("I'm sure your father died peacefully in his sleep"). But Marion's desperate confession explodes in his face, forcing a startled Dr. Bill and his innocuous bedside manner to retreat in hurried disarray. For the second time in a single night, Bill confronts a woman's confession of illicit sexual desire—for which she is willing to sacrifice her "whole fucking future"—and once again he struggles unsuccessfully to hold together the structured surfaces of a relationship (husband/wife; doctor/patient) in the presence of a woman's emotional honesty.

Bill trades on his charm and professional status when he first pays a visit to Domino's apartment in response to her proposition on the street ("How'd you like to have a little fun?") and when he calls on Milich at Rainbow Fashions to rent a costume. Before he gets down to business, Bill's coyness in the company of attractive women returns as he compliments Domino on her pathetic Christmas tree ("nice tree") and her cramped, messy apartment ("cozy"). Once again a woman asks Bill a direct question about his desires ("What *do* you wanna do?"), and once again he does not give her a "straight fucking answer." Instead, he deflects her question by asking one of his own ("What do you recommend?"). Rather than cast aspersions on his manhood, as Schnitzler's prostitute does with Fridolin, Domino finds

Bill's sexual reticence charming and makes an awkward situation easier for him by "getting in character" and by answering him in kind ("I'd rather not put it into words"). Unexpectedly, in a scene that easily could have degenerated into an erotically trashy, guilty pleasure for a voyeuristic audience, Kubrick creates an extraordinarily poignant and ironic unmasking of Bill's basic decency through Domino's female sensitivity. Their roles are reversed as Bill becomes Domino's patient ("How about you just leave it up to me?") and agrees to follow the "doctor's" orders ("I'm in your hands"). Driven by jealous anger and feelings of humiliation following Alice's dream story, Bill makes a second house call on Domino's apartment in the guise of a gentleman caller bearing gifts (pastries), only to transform into a smirking, libidinous college boy/"john" in the company of her roommate Sally. But it is all to no avail. When Sally interrupts his ardor with the truth about Domino's blood test, Bill's puffed and strutting manhood shrinks like a deflated condom before the sudden declarations of female honesty and the fearful reminder that death also makes "house calls." In a moment that recalls the scene with Marion and her dead father, and that anticipates the sight of Mandy's once voluptuous body on a morgue's cold slab (an image of Domino's possible fate), Dr. Harford beats a hasty retreat from the unseen face of death rather than the visible proof of female desire.

In his first "house call" on Rainbow Fashions, Bill travels from Domino's dreamy world of feminine sensuality into Milich's male world of mercenary business transactions. While Domino reluctantly accepts Bill's money for services not rendered, Milich, who negotiates like Shakespeare's infamous merchant of Venice, is more impressed by the good doctor's extra $200 ("for the inconvenience," says Bill) than by either his charm or his medical credentials. In this bizarre, mostly satiric encounter between Old World horse trader and New World medicine man, Kubrick foreshadows the long sequence at Somerton, in which the seriocomic tonalities of *Eyes Wide Shut* will come together in surreal unison. Reminiscent of a scenario from the *commedia dell'arte*—only here the masks are worn by Milich's mannequins rather than Kubrick's characters—the film once again directs its satire against a patriarchal order confronting the power of female desire. Milich plays the outraged father/Pantalone who bellows about "decency" and his daughter's "depravity" while he meritoriously tends to business ("Couldn't you see that I try to serve my customer?"). As the young daughter's straight man, Bill unwittingly assumes the role of the witless Dottóre, who finds himself on the receiving end of her sexually inviting glances and shocking whispers, all in total disregard of her father's moral harangue. In his second visit to Rainbow Fashions, in the harsh glare of broad daylight and cinematic naturalism, Bill confronts Milich's transformation into Old World whoremaster as he accommodates his daughter's desire to the interest of business. Significantly, Bill's exploitation of his own professional status, which he glibly trades on in the pursuit of nocturnal desire, is now countered for the first time by his own moral outrage at the sight of Milich as father/pimp.

Following his first visit to Rainbow Fashions, Bill continues his round of "house calls" by putting on a carnival mask and crashing the party at Somerton, a setting not unlike those opulent homes inhabited by his wealthy patients. During this important plot beat, roles are reversed as the "good doctor" (Milich's expression) ironically becomes the patient who is commanded by a male authority figure ("Red Cloak") to take off his mask—to "show" his face—and to remove his clothes. Unsettled by Somerton's nightmarish and humiliating exposure, Dr. Bill finally makes a "house call" on his own family, in which he treats his wife as if she were just another neurotic female patient like Marion. Using the guise of concerned doctor and loving husband, he coaxes Alice into recounting the frightening details of her dream. As her earlier confession had, Alice's dream acts here as a catalyst that sends her husband into a second round of nightmarish "house calls," and that will further expose the presence of Bill's now conscious fears and desires.

In the course of Bill Harford's two nocturnal journeys, Kubrick also develops and climaxes a male/female sexual parable established in part 1. In the journeys of part 2, however, the film shows a greater interest in Bill's sexual duality than in either his denial or his repression of sexual desire. Unlike Schnitzler's Fridolin, Bill Harford's sexual psychology does not involve the aberrations of misogyny, pedophilia, and necrophilia, but rather an ambivalent response to issues of his own manhood within a cultural mise-en-scène dominated by an older male order and the demands of a young female independence. Thus the film does not seem particularly interested in developing the "bisexual" possibilities (Bill as "switch-hitter") of Bill's character, except in those selected contexts where they help raise in the character's mind questions about his manhood. *Eyes Wide Shut,* therefore, continues Kubrick's exploration of the Jungian struggle between animus (male) and anima (female) found in *Barry Lyndon, The Shining,* and *Full Metal Jacket,* except that in this film he defines the Harfords as typical ("normal") representatives of a contemporary cultural mise-en-scène in which sexual roles exist in a state of flux. Through Bill's recurring, progressive fantasy of sex between Alice and the naval officer (Gary Goba), Kubrick transfers the dreamy nature of Alice's female desire into the graphic male landscape of Bill's sexual imagination. Not only do these separate black and white episodes fuel Bill's jealousy, and therefore motivate his sexual desire for a number of women during his two journeys, but they also turn him into a voyeur who "watches" his wife having passionate sex with another man. Alice's touching memory of female sexual desire becomes in the theater of Bill's male imagination a "blue movie" that foreshadows his voyeuristic participation in the grotesque pornography of Somerton, in which women are not much more than masked, unclothed mannequins who are obedient to the will of male fantasy. By the end of part 2, however, after Bill acquires haunting memories of his own fears and desires, he experiences an emotional catharsis over Mandy's nude corpse, and during the confrontation/"recapitulation" scene with his aging male alter ego (Victor) in part 3 that clarifies the film's ambivalent treatment of his sexuality. In his tearful confession during the film's climax, Bill Harford will finally show the kind of "tender" and "sad" regard for Alice that she expressed for him in her confession of desire for the naval officer.

In part 2, Kubrick continues to structure the visual progression of *Eyes Wide Shut* into a series of contrasting, alternating "keys" that not only help clarify the film's psychological, sexual dualities (persona/shadow; male/female), but also develop its tonal (serious/comic) and cultural dualities (Old World/New World; old/young). Victor Ziegler's Old World ostentation, for instance, is replicated in the cold and formal artifice of the French Regency decor seen in the Nathanson bedroom, which both complements the pallid death mask worn by the patriarch and conspires to repress the emotional disorders of Marion's female desire. The Nathansons' luxurious apartment stands in sharp relief to the warm, earthy sensuality of Domino's Greenwich Village flat decorated with colorful African masks, a stuffed tiger, an "I ♥ NY" sticker, and her sexual presence. At Rainbow Fashions, presided over by an older transplanted European who makes fun of the young American doctor's choice of a black costume ("a cloak with a hood and a mask"), Bill moves through a colorful backroom display of masked mannequins and period costumes that, according to Milich, "look like live." This romantic, Old World wax museum suddenly becomes a comically surreal bordello in red for Milich's "little whore" and two male pedophiles dressed only in female wigs and makeup, a *ménage à trois* who undoubtedly believe that they have found "where the rainbow ends." All of which anticipates the overwrought, pretentious Old World Italian artifice of the masked party/ orgy at Somerton, an event that joins together the film's schizophrenic twins—"Dream Story" and "Sex Comedy"—through its suggestion of the December Christian/pagan celebrations of Christmas Mass and Saturnalian pleasure.

Kubrick develops the long Somerton sequence (17 minutes) and the scene that follows, in which Alice describes to Bill her harrowing dream, into a contrasting and parallel unity that forms the narrative centerpiece of *Eyes Wide Shut*. In the masked party's surreal carnival of Venetian *màschere* and mock Roman Catholic ritual, Kubrick creates the flip side of Victor's Christmas party in part 1. Old World art and ritual in this setting, however, provide cover for the social personas of the American rich and powerful, while they paradoxically expose an ugly cultural shadow world over which they preside.* Fresh from the humiliations of Rainbow Fashions, Bill wanders into this Italian *commedia dell'arte* amalgam of Catholic solemnity, pagan virgin sacrifice, and Saturnalian pornography wearing the colorful, ornamental mask of a feminized male hero rather than that of the foolish Dottóre. It is no wonder that the members of the masked assembly so easily notice his presence. Even when unofficially "masked" as the up-

---

*Not only did Kubrick have Venetian carnival masks created for this important sequence, some of which were inspired by the Italian *commedia dell'arte,* but he reminds us of the popular Saturnalian celebration in Italy that traditionally begins on December 17th and has enjoyed a long historical association with the Christmas season. In addition, the mock religious overtones of the masked party are decidedly Catholic, and, of course, the seat of Roman Catholicism resides in Italy. The Hungarian Szavost mentions the Roman poet Ovid and alludes to Victor's collection of "Renaissance bronzes" (Italian), while the interior of Somerton imitates the ornate Adriatic/Moorish style of Venetian baroque architecture prevalent during the Renaissance. In the scene in which Alice's phone call interrupts Bill and Domino, she is sitting in her kitchen watching *Blume in Love* (Paul Mazursky, 1973) on TV, a movie that also deals with the problems of "contemporary" marital infidelity, and that takes place in both the Italian and California cities of Venice. The "password" for admittance into Somerton is "Fidelio" (Italian for "He who is faithful"), which, as Nick Nightingale tells Bill at the Sonata Café, refers to an 1805 German opera written by Beethoven known for its high moral seriousness. And when Bill is shadowed through the dark streets of Greenwich Village by a mysterious man, he walks by the "Verona Restaurant."

and-coming young doctor, Bill indulges in cultural mimicry through his New World, yuppified projection of confident manhood. But more to the point, he is the only male in attendance who is not wearing the kind of misshapen or dehumanized mask that projects either the ruthless power and mockery of an aging male order or the unbridled pleasures of Saturnalian lust. If Bill had only chosen a stern, forbidding mask like the one worn by the party's presiding figure ("Red Cloak"), or one that resembled a Saturnalian figure such as Pan, he might have gone undetected (until, of course, they found the receipt from Rainbow Fashions in his overcoat).

Through this sequence's disparate mise-en-scène and its clashing musical tonalities, Kubrick slyly (perversely, his critics might say) throws the audience into a confusion that, in many respects, replicates Bill's disordered state of mind. As Bill wanders through this seriocomic nightmare, in which Somerton is transformed into an absurdly ornate cathouse, Jocelyn Pook's haunting scores ("Masked Party" and "Migrations") clash with the humorous intrusion of "Strangers in the Night," heard when a blindfolded Nick is shown being escorted through a ballroom of naked couples dancing, and the pounding notes of Dominic Harlan's unnerving piano rendition of Ligeti's "Musica Ricercata II." In such ways does Kubrick force his audience to experience both the confusions of Bill's sexual desire and his fearful intimations of death. When he is escorted into Somerton's great hall to stand as the accused before the masked assembly and "Red Cloak" (Leon Vitali), Bill's eyes remain "wide shut" to the objective truth of what is happening to him. Because he responds to the events of Somerton through the confusions of his increasingly conscious desires and fears, he does not notice that "Red Cloak," now sitting on a throne, plays the dual roles of Grand Inquisitor and King of Carnival. He does not notice that the mysterious woman in the feathered mask (Abigail Good), who seriocomically appears and announces that she will "redeem" him, noticeably overacts her part. He does not understand what the Venetian masks imply; nor does he notice how most of them gaze at him not only in stern, patriarchal disapproval, but also in grotesque attitudes of laughter and mockery. Dr. William Harford unknowingly becomes a key player in a cruel "charade" in which an older male order not only exercises its sexual power over young women, but also administers a comeuppance to a young doctor who threatens its rule.

In contrast, Alice's account of what she calls her "horrible" dream in the following bedroom scene is not staged, even though it contains descriptions of female nakedness, a mocking male presence (the naval officer "laughs" at her), indiscriminate "fucking," and voyeurism that strikingly parallel Bill's journey through Somerton's masked party/orgy. Bill awakens his sleeping wife in the midst of her second "laughing fit" and confronts in his own marriage the surreal presence of his own repressed fears and desires. These two events, in addition to Alice's confession in part 1, are nothing more than separate articulations of a psychological realm that the characters and their culture unknowingly inhabit called the collective unconscious. Here, however, the mise-en-scène shifts from Somerton's Old World masked fakery to the honest emotional landscape of Alice's Brave New World of female sexual expression. In her dream, she revels in her nakedness ("I felt wonderful . . . lying in a beautiful garden, stretched out naked"), a moment made possible only after Bill leaves her in search of their clothes and takes with him the presence of his male gaze. But her reverie ends when the naval officer suddenly appears and "laughs" at her. As she clings to Bill on their bed, Alice tearfully reveals how her dream of liberation turned into a nightmare of her "fucking" different men and of Bill watching her, in which she eventually experienced an overwhelming urge to laugh in her voyeuristic husband's face. While we watch Bill's face once again become clouded with resentment and anger, Alice unmasks a paradoxical shadow that lurks behind her dream of female sexual freedom. It is the shadow of her fear that an unbridled expression of desire not only will destroy her marriage but, like the roles assumed by Milich's daughter and the women of Somerton, will further subject her to the sexual tyranny of men.

Kubrick concludes the visual and psychological journeys of part 2 by taking an emotionally distraught Bill Harford into the cold, stainless-steel world of a hospital's morgue, with its drab beige walls decorated only by skeletal X-ray "portraits" of the human chest. Rather than masked mannequins in colorful costumes or voluptuous naked women in carnival masks, the morgue's inhabitants are the unclothed and unmasked remains of the dead. During his earlier "house call" on a naked, semi-conscious Mandy in Victor's upstairs bathroom, Bill repeatedly asked her to "look" at him ("Mandy, look at me"), while in the morgue his former "patient" exposes the good doctor's own failures of sight by "looking" up at him with her lifeless eyes wide open. Rather than gaze on Mandy's naked body in voyeuristic satisfaction,

or react in smug male mockery to ("laugh at") a young woman's comeuppance, Bill's eyes are now wide open as they confront the fearful
shadows that live behind his New World dream. As Dr. Harford bends
down over Mandy's face and looks with feeling into her death mask,
accompanied on the soundtrack by a haunting rendition of Liszt's
"Grey Clouds," Kubrick creates an important moment in his character's development. He not only connects the body to the mysterious
woman at Somerton who "saved" him, but he recognizes the face of a
young patient whom he failed to save. No longer looking through the
eyes of the male voyeur, Bill now gazes on a naked female body and
sees both the truth of his own desires and the fear that lurks behind
those desires. Bill now shows the kind of tender regard for Mandy
that was missing in his earlier examination in Victor's upstairs bathroom. As he once again looks into her eyes, however, he flinches in
the face of the corpse's accusatory stare by closing his own eyes. And
rather than assume his mask of "impersonal" professionalism, as he
did in his "house call" on Marion's dead father, Bill now expresses his
human frailty by closing his "eyes wide shut" before the terrifying
truth of his own mortality and of his failures as a doctor and as a human being.

In Bill Harford's two final house calls in part 3, Kubrick "recapitulates" and climaxes the psychological, sexual, and cultural journeys of
Eyes Wide Shut. In doing so, he gives the audience a final opportunity
to understand—with their "eyes wide open"—how those journeys began, how they developed, and what, as they reach their final destination, they mean. As he is ushered through Victor's lavish home for a
second time, Bill continues to wear the congenial mask of the polite
young doctor who makes "house calls" on the rich, only now his face
shows the strain of disturbing memories from his two nocturnal journeys. Victor continues to play the gracious host as he greets Bill with
hearty appreciation inside the oversized male space of a library/game
room. Its wood-paneled walls, its art and artifacts (e.g., a collection of
portraits from another time, a large model of a schooner), and its red
pool table project a masculine respectability that recalls how, in parts
1 and 2, the American-rich opulence of Victor's mansion anticipated
Somerton's Old World decadence. Now Victor's room recalls those
separate rooms seen during Bill's "migration," in which Somerton's
great manor home was transmuted into a surreal Animal House for
the world's most outrageous stag party. In contrast to the Christmas
party, however, the male rites of glad-handing and backslapping—of

dominance and deference—are exchanged in unnatural and awkward ways. Even though during the past two nights both men have encountered potentially harrowing experiences in the company of women, they remain uncomfortable in a situation that requires the language of emotional exposure. Kubrick now wants us to clearly see the fakery in a charming male insouciance that was not as visible in the "Exposition" of part 1. Facing Bill across the pool table, Victor begins his "confession" about the events of Somerton ("I have to be completely frank"). Not only does he, like Alice before him, unmask the young doctor's pretense of innocence ("What the hell are you talking about?"), but, more significantly, Victor unknowingly reveals an emotional void that exists behind his mask of patriarchal affability.

Rather than being an emotionally haunting account, as Alice's confession was, Victor's "recapitulation" treats Mandy's unfortunate death as if it were nothing more than an impersonal statistic in the life of a "hooker" with "great tits" who overdosed because it was "always just gonna be a matter of time with her." As Victor throws Bill's earlier words back in his face ("Remember, you told her so yourself?"), the film reminds us of the young doctor's mechanical bedside manner in the "house calls" of part 2. During Victor's account, Bill's face instinctively searches for cover. He bends his head down, walks away and turns his back to Victor, and eventually sits down and shields his face from Victor's increasingly frank and graphic revelations. To his credit, Bill ignores Victor's crude attempt to ease an uncomfortable emotional moment by refusing to take part in the wealthy man's Old Boys' Club banter about "that prick" Nick being safely home and "banging Mrs. Nick." Instead, Bill responds to a basic decency in his character that has been present from the beginning. He not only defends Nick and takes the blame, but he also forces the issue about Mandy and finds out that she was the mysterious woman at Somerton, and that the Grand Inquisition was only a "charade" designed to "scare the living shit" out of him.* Now the masks and the gloves come off as this "civilized" discussion between two men turns into tribal combat. Even though he once again suffers exposure and humiliation before an older male's inquisition, Bill now "shows" a face different from the one that hid behind the carnival mask at Somerton. In-

---

*See "Notes & Trivia" for my comments on the potential confusion caused by Kubrick's casting of two different actresses in the twin roles of Mandy/Mysterious Woman.

stead of reacting in social embarrassment and fear, he finally turns his face toward Victor's callous indifference and expresses an angry, moral indignation. When Bill confronts Victor with an accusation ("Do you mind telling me what kind of fucking charade ends with somebody turning up dead?"), his male adversary defends his threatened power by cutting "the bullshit" and indirectly scoffing at Bill for believing in the "play-acted, 'take me' phony sacrifice" by the mysterious woman at Somerton.

Thus Kubrick uses this long scene (12 minutes) not only to clarify on an objective level Victor and Mandy's involvement in the masked party/orgy story, but as an important plot beat that both "recapitulates" and objectifies Bill's psychological/moral development. Particularly in the scene's final moments, he reminds us of Dr. Bill's earlier failure to acknowledge the unseen link between sexual promiscuity and death in a post-AIDS cultural environment. Following Victor's harsh reclamation of power, Bill again turns his back on the older man, but this time not from the embarrassment caused by social exposure. His anguished face reveals, as it did over Mandy's body, his confrontation with the harsh truths of death and of his own moral failures. Only now, the change in Bill's emotional character is objectified through the way his face, in two-shot, stands in sharp relief to the mask of Victor's restored power. Anger no longer clouds Victor's face, as he automatically resumes the now ugly and cloying role of gracious host. He comes up from behind and lays his hands on the shoulders of the disconsolate young doctor, in a condescending magnanimity that older men have when they reclaim power over a defeated adversary. But what Kubrick wants us to see is the moral and psychological role reversal that has taken place between the two men.

In the Christmas party sequence of part 1, Victor was exposed as the unclothed debauchee/pantaloon frightened by the prospect of a "hooker" dying in his own bathroom, while Bill seemed to be the "knowledgeable" doctor who ruled over the processes of life and death. Now, however, in the "Recapitulation" of part 3, Victor pompously assumes the role of the wise patriarch who dispenses his bromides about the transitory nature of human life as if he has found an elixir for the ages:

> Listen, Bill. Nobody killed anybody. Someone died. It happens all the time. Life goes on. It always does until it doesn't. But you know that, don't you?

Victor unwittingly becomes the fatuous "Dr. Bill"/Dottóre of parts 1 and 2, a figure "laughed at" by Alice, Milich, and Somerton's masked assembly, while Bill's face now shows the profound emotional effect of his encounters not only with conscious desire but with his unconscious fear of death. Dr. Harford may have been "knowledgeable" about the biological functions and frailties of the human body, but he was abysmally ignorant of his own psychological and moral frailty. He may have been privy to the medical secrets of his wealthy patients, but he cast a blind eye to their moral and sexual corruption. The film now asks us to remember ("recapitulate") Bill's earlier argument with Alice, in which he defended his position that "sex is the last thing" on a female patient's mind because of her fear of what he "might find." Like any doctor, Bill commands a certain power over his patients through his authority to "examine" them and to "expose" their naked vulnerability before his fearful knowledge of death. It is no wonder, therefore, that an aging male order perceives him as a threat to its power and secretly relishes an opportunity to humble the young doctor. Yet the film has shown that Bill rarely exercises that power, partly because of his own essential decency, but also because, like his patients, his eyes are "wide shut" to his own fear of death and its often unseen presence in everyday life. Mandy's "unlucky" death, therefore, forces Bill to confront the snake that mocks his transience from the shadows of his and Alice's New World Eden.

In the film's climactic scene, in which the marriage story moves toward closure, Bill makes his final house call and once again confronts his emotional betrayal of a woman. Simultaneously, Kubrick climaxes the film's contrasting tonal and visual disparities by moving from a scene dominated by verbal recapitulation and well-lit cinematic naturalism to a scene dominated by emotional disclosure in a bedroom's shadowy atmosphere of dreams, nightmares, and confessions. The contrasting tonalities between the "Dream Story" and the "Sex Comedy" of *Eyes Wide Shut* once again form a seriocomic unity as the film not only comes full circle, but also closes the circle. Only now it is Alice's turn to play doctor and to expose her husband's denials by sleeping with the "hero's" mask from Somerton, which, in its ornamental emptiness, "recapitulates" her life with the masks of Bill's social persona. In the film's initial plot beat (the confession), Bill engaged in denial because he preferred to live in ignorant bliss, and because, unlike his wife, he had not confronted his own unconscious desires and fears. In doing so, he repressed his own male/female duality by clinging to an antiquated concept of "manhood" that helped perpetuate the kind of grotesque pornography found at Somerton. As he looks down on his own mask, and gazes into its sightless eyes, Bill relives the shattering experience over Mandy's death mask. But rather than flinch and close his eyes at the sight of his now conscious fears and failures, he finally succumbs to his own human decency by "crying his eyes out" for Mandy and by telling Alice "everything" through the cathartic of confession.

In the coda to *Eyes Wide Shut,* Kubrick completes his contemporary fable about "the sexual ambiguities of a happy marriage." And even though the dialogue in the Kubrick/Raphael script adheres faithfully to Schnitzler's final plot beat, its emotional and psychological implications have been altered in order to complete the film's contrasting "keys" and "movements." Kubrick partly accomplishes his purposes by transferring the reconciliation scene in *Traumnovelle* from the couple's bedroom to the bright colors of a contemporary toy store decorated for Christmas.* In doing so, Kubrick creates a counterpoint between the visualized setting and the couple's use of "words" as they struggle to redefine their marriage and to reconcile themselves to the disturbing memories of confessions, dreams, and nocturnal adventure. Reunited with their daughter Helena, Bill and Alice walk through the toy store's rainbow of colors and attempt to piece their marriage back together and to understand how they have changed. Bill now asks the questions ("Alice, what do you think we should do?") in the hope that the "knowledgeable" Alice will have the answers. Like Schnitzler's Albertina, Alice remains committed to an ambivalent

---

*The color progression of *Eyes Wide Shut* not only travels through the six colors of the rainbow, but it adds blacks and whites for contrasting effect; the color red stands out in the way it is used throughout to develop the contrasting associations of sexual desire (the Harfords' bedroom; Milich's backroom bordello; Somerton's carpeting; Victor's pool table) and of Christmas (seasonal decorations; the toy store). In part 2, the film continues to use red as a dominant color (the Sonata Café; Domino's apartment; Somerton), but it also introduces darker shades of black and purple, as well as the cooler hues of blue and white, to suggest the cold presence of fear and emotional exposure (the Nathanson bedroom; the streets of Greenwich Village; the morgue). Particularly in the three important scenes that take place in the Harfords' bedroom—inside the realm of dreams and confessions—the lighting and color become more muted, especially during the dream account of part 2 and the mask on the pillow scene of part 3; in both instances, the reds inside the bedroom are transmuted into a deathlike shade of Korova purple. Thus, even though the film's final scene creates the visual impression that the Harfords have regained paradise and once again live "under the rainbow," internally it asserts the presence of a psychological shadow that the couple will carry with them into an uncertain future.

course, even though she once again applies the balm of being "re-lieved" (in this case, "grateful") that she and Bill have survived their adventures, "whether they were real or only a dream." Kubrick also keeps intact the novella's implication that the protagonist's nocturnal adventures were nothing more than shadows of his character's un-conscious, but, as the scene with Victor makes clear, he also confers on those events a cultural objectivity not found in Schnitzler. Thus Bill—as Fridolin does—now admits to Alice that "no dream is just a dream," meaning that he recognizes both the psychological truth con-tained in her earlier account and her greater emotional courage in confronting her fears and desires. Like Schnitzler's married couple, Bill and Alice express their hope for the future through the wife's declaration that they are "awake now and hopefully for a long time." When Bill, however, tries to reconstitute his crumbling New World dream by saying "forever" in response to Alice's modest hope, she frowns and tells him that she is frightened by "that word."

Thus Kubrick climaxes the marriage story of *Eyes Wide Shut* by turning Alice into the most psychologically complete character found in any of his films, one whom he allows to speak in his voice. In a way unique in Kubrick's work, Alice acknowledges that her optimism oc-cupies the same emotional space in her character as the knowledge of her own transience and of the fragile nature of her "happy" marriage. In contrast, Kubrickian characters as different as Johnny Clay in *The Killing*, Humbert Humbert in *Lolita*, and Jack Torrance in *The Shining* were thrown into either the resignations of despair or the delusions of madness when confronted by such knowledge. Lest we forget, how-ever, "forever" in Kubrick's contingent film universe resides in the exclusive domain of deluded male desire. It exists in Strangelove's vision of civilization's glorious rebirth in the mine shafts of a post-apocalyptic future, in Barry Lyndon's attraction to the illusory perma-nence of aristocratic style and title, and in Jack Torrance's quest to live "forever and ever" in a nostalgic dream of male freedom and plea-sure. Consequently, Alice Harford becomes the strongest female pres-ence created by Kubrick in any of his films, a presence that also illu-minates his male protagonist's nocturnal encounters with Marion, Domino, and Sally in part 2. In some respects, therefore, Bill success-fully completes his psychological and moral journey, because, in ways he does not always perceive, he benefits from the company of honest women who show him, through personal example, how to confront his unconscious fears and desires. Like other Kubrickian males (Hum-

bert, *Barry Lyndon*, Joker), Bill eventually realizes a fuller humanity
by responding to a latent female sensitivity in his character.*

Kubrick leaves Schnitzler's *Traumnovelle* in the dust by ending *Eyes
Wide Shut* with a final image of Bill and Alice standing together in
a toy store decorated in the delights and colors of childhood innocence, temporarily outside the stark light or frightening shadows of
death. Alice again plays the "knowledgeable" wife to Bill's "absent-
minded" husband, as she reminds him of the unfinished business of
their marriage ("There is something very important we need to do as
soon as possible"). Significantly, Alice takes on the important job
of keeping Bill's male desires within the existential context of the
Here and Now. She counters his "forever" with a word that does not
frighten her—"Fuck"—and once again puts the lie to Bill's earlier
belief that "women basically don't think like that." But she also shows
her desire to unmask the unconscious—the world of the "Dream
Story"—and to expose it to the full light of day. Not only, therefore,
does her single word create the promise of closure for the *coitus interruptus* of part 1, but it also becomes a coda for the film's affirmative
New World response to Somerton's grotesque Old World transmuta-
tion of Christian ritual into Saturnalian pornography. Likewise, Kubrick uses this final moment to provide a coda for the "Sex Comedy"
of *Eyes Wide Shut,* in the way its voice, through the character of Alice
Harford, transmutes the scoffing laughter of satiric ridicule into the
compassionate forgiveness of romantic comedy.

---

*See "Notes & Trivia" for my comments on a reported cameo appearance by Kubrick
in the Sonata Café scene, and on how *Eyes Wide Shut* is undoubtedly his most "personal"
film.

POSTSCRIPT

Death made a house call on Stanley Kubrick before he could complete the unfinished business of his creative life. Within a matter of days after completion, *Eyes Wide Shut* unexpectedly was transmuted into a brilliant climax for a distinguished film career that had officially begun fifty-eight years earlier, during a thirteenth-birthday celebration. Had he lived into the twenty-first century, Stanley Kubrick undoubtedly would have continued to confuse and to dazzle the world with his wit, his unflinching honesty, his humane understanding, and his film genius.

FILMOGRAPHY

Day of the Fight (1951)
Director/Photography/Editor/Sound: Stanley Kubrick
Commentary: Douglas Edwards
Documentary short on Walter Cartier, middleweight prizefighter
Running Time: 16 minutes
Distributor: RKO Radio

Flying Padre (1951)
Director/Photography/Editor/Sound: Stanley Kubrick
Documentary short on the Reverend Fred Stadtmueller, Roman Catholic missionary of a New Mexico parish that covers 400 square miles
Running Time: 9 minutes
Distributor: RKO Radio

The Seafarers (1953)
Director/Photography/Editor: Stanley Kubrick
Script: Will Chasan
Producer: Lester Cooper
Narrator: Don Hollenbeck
Documentary short in color about the Seafarers International Union
Running Time: 30 minutes

Fear and Desire (1953)
Production Company: Stanley Kubrick Productions
Producer: Stanley Kubrick
Associate Producer: Martin Perveler
Director/Photography/Editor: Stanley Kubrick
Script: Howard O. Sackler
Dialogue Director: Toba Kubrick
Music: Gerald Fried
Cast: Frank Silvera (Mac), Kenneth Harp (Corby), Virginia Leith (The Girl), Paul Mazursky (Sidney), Steve Coit (Fletcher), David Allen (Narrator)
Running Time: 68 minutes
Distributor: Joseph Burstyn

Killer's Kiss (1955)
Production Company: Minotaur
Producers: Stanley Kubrick, Morris Bousel
Director/Photography/Editor: Stanley Kubrick
Script: Stanley Kubrick, Howard O. Sackler
Music: Gerald Fried
Choreography: David Vaughan
Cast: Frank Silvera (Vincent Rapallo), Jamie Smith (Davy Gordon), Irene Kane (Gloria Price), Jerry Jarret (Albert), Ruth Sobotka (Iris), Mike Dana, Felice Orlandi, Ralph Roberts, Phil Stevenson (Hoodlums), Julius Adelman

(Mannequin Factory Owner), David Vaughan, Alec Rubin (Convention-eers)
Running Time: 64 minutes
Distributor: United Artists

The Killing (1956)
Production Company: Harris-Kubrick Productions
Producer: James B. Harris
Director: Stanley Kubrick
Screenplay: Stanley Kubrick, based on the novel *Clean Break,* by Lionel White
Additional Dialogue: Jim Thompson
Photography: Lucien Ballard
Editor: Betty Steinberg
Art Director: Ruth Sobotka Kubrick
Music: Gerald Fried
Sound: Earl Snyder
Cast: Sterling Hayden (Johnny Clay), Jay C. Flippen (Marvin Unger), Marie Windsor (Sherry Peatty), Elisha Cook, Jr. (George Peatty), Coleen Gray (Fay), Vince Edwards (Val Cannon), Ted de Corsia (Randy Kennan), Joe Sawyer (Mike O'Reilly), Timothy Carey (Nikki), Kola Kwariani (Maurice), James Edwards (Parking Lot Attendant), Jay Adler (Leo), Joseph Turkel (Tiny)
Running Time: 83 minutes
Distributor: United Artists

Paths of Glory (1957)
Production Company: Harris-Kubrick Productions
Producer: James B. Harris
Director: Stanley Kubrick
Screenplay: Stanley Kubrick, Calder Willingham, Jim Thompson, based on the novel by Humphrey Cobb
Photography: George Krause
Art Director: Ruth Sobotka Kubrick
Editor: Eva Kroll
Music: Gerald Fried
Sound: Martin Muller
Cast: Kirk Douglas (Colonel Dax), Ralph Meeker (Corporal Paris), Adolphe Menjou (General Broulard), George Macready (General Mireau), Wayne Morris (Lieutenant Roget), Richard Anderson (Major Saint-Auban), Joseph Turkel (Private Arnaud), Timothy Carey (Private Ferol), Peter Capell (Colonel Judge), Suzanne Christian (German Girl), Bert Freed (Sergeant Boulanger), Emile Meyer (Priest), John Stein (Captain Rousseau), Ken Dibbs (Private Lejeune), Jerry Hausner (Tavern Owner), Harold Benedict (Captain Nichols)
Running Time: 86 minutes
Distributor: United Artists (presented by Bryna Productions)

Spartacus (1960)
Production Company: Bryna Productions
Executive Producer: Kirk Douglas
Producer: Edward Lewis
Director: Stanley Kubrick

Screenplay: Dalton Trumbo, based on the novel by Howard Fast
Photography: Russell Metty
Additional Photography: Clifford Stine
Art Director: Eric Orbom
Set Decoration: Russell A. Gausman, Julia Heron
Screen Process: Super Technirama-70
Color: Technicolor
Titles: Saul Bass
Editors: Robert Lawrence, Robert Schultz, Fred Chulack
Production Designer: Alexander Golitzen, Saul Bass
Technical Adviser: Vittorio Nino Novarese
Costumes: Peruzzi, Valles, Bill Thomas
Music: Alex North
Music Director: Joseph Gershenson
Sound: Waldo O. Watson, Joe Lapis, Murray Spivack, Ronald Pierce
Assistant Director: Marshall Green
Cast: Kirk Douglas (Spartacus), Laurence Olivier (Marcus Crassus), Jean
    Simmons (Varinia), Charles Laughton (Gracchus), Peter Ustinov
    (Batiatus), John Gavin (Julius Caesar), Tony Curtis (Antoninus), Nina Foch
    (Helena), Herbert Lom (Tigranes), John Ireland (Crixus), John Dall
    (Glabrus), Charles McGraw (Marcellus), Joanna Barnes (Claudia), Harold
    J. Stone (David), Woody Strode (Draba), Peter Brocco (Ramon), Paul Lam-
    bert (Gannicus), Robert J. Wilke (Captain of Guard), Nicholas Dennis
    (Dionysius), John Hoyt (Roman Officer), Fred Worlock (Laelius), Dayton
    Lummis (Symmachus)
Running Time: 196 minutes
Distributor: Universal Pictures

Lolita (1962)

Production Company: Seven Arts/Anya/Transworld
Producer: James B. Harris
Director: Stanley Kubrick
Screenplay: Vladimir Nabokov, based on his novel
Photography: Oswald Morris
Editor: Anthony Harvey
Art Director: William Andrews
Set Design: Andrew Low
Music: Nelson Riddle, "Lolita's Theme" by Bob Harris
Sound: H. L. Bird, Len Shilton
Assistant Directors: Roy Millichip, John Danischewsky
Cast: James Mason (Humbert Humbert), Sue Lyon (Lolita Haze), Shelley Win-
    ters (Charlotte Haze), Peter Sellers (Clare Quilty), Diana Decker (Jean
    Farlow), Jerry Stovin (John Farlow), Suzanne Gibbs (Mona Farlow), Gary
    Cockrell (Dick Schiller), Marianne Stone (Vivian Darkbloom), Cec Linder
    (Physician), Lois Maxwell (Nurse Mary Lord), William Greene (Mr. Swine),
    C. Denier Warren (Mr. Potts), Isobel Lucas (Louise), Maxine Holden (Hos-
    pital Receptionist), James Dyrenforth (Mr. Beale), Roberta Shore (Lorna),
    Eric Lane (Roy), Shirley Douglas (Mrs. Starch), Roland Brand (Bill), Colin
    Maitland (Charlie Holmes), Irvin Allen (Hospital Attendant), Marion
    Mathie (Miss Lebone), Craig Sams (Rex), John Harrison (Tom)
Running Time: 153 minutes
Distributor: Metro-Goldwyn-Mayer

Dr. Strangelove; or How I Learned to Stop Worrying and Love the Bomb (1964)

Production Company: Hawk Films
Producer/Director: Stanley Kubrick
Associate Producer: Victor Lyndon
Screenplay: Stanley Kubrick, Terry Southern, Peter George, based on the novel
    Red Alert, by Peter George (Bryant)
Photography: Gilbert Taylor
Editor: Anthony Harvey
Production Design: Ken Adam
Art Direction: Peter Murton
Special Effects: Wally Veevers
Music: Laurie Johnson
Aviation Adviser: Captain John Crewdson
Sound: John Cox
Cast: Peter Sellers (Group Captain Lionel Mandrake, President Muffley, Dr.
    Strangelove), George C. Scott (Buck Turgidson), Sterling Hayden (General Jack D. Ripper), Keenan Wynn (Colonel Bat Guano), Slim Pickens
    (Major T. J. "King" Kong), Peter Bull (Ambassador de Sadesky), Tracy Reed
    (Miss Scott), James Earl Jones (Lieutenant H. R. Dietrich, D.S.O.), Glenn
    Beck (Lieutenant W. D. Kivel, Navigator), Shane Rimmer (Captain G. A.
    "Ace" Owens, Co-pilot), Paul Tamarin (Lieutenant B. Goldberg, Radio
    Operator), Gordon Tanner (General Faceman), Robert O'Neil (Admiral
    Randolph), Roy Stephens (Frank), Laurence Herder, John McCarthy, Hal
    Galili (Members of Burpleson Base Defense Corps)
Running Time: 94 minutes
Distributor: Columbia Pictures

2001: A Space Odyssey (1968)

Production Company: Metro-Goldwyn-Mayer
Producer/Director: Stanley Kubrick
Screenplay: Stanley Kubrick, Arthur C. Clarke, based on Clarke's short story
    "The Sentinel"
Photography: Geoffrey Unsworth
Screen Process: Super Panavision, presented in Cinerama
Color: Metrocolor
Additional Photography: John Alcott
Special Photographic Effects Designer and Director: Stanley Kubrick
Editor: Ray Lovejoy
Production Design: Tony Masters, Harry Lange, Ernie Archer
Art Direction: John Hoesli
Special Photographic Effects Supervisors: Wally Veevers, Douglas Trumbull,
    Con Pederson, Tom Howard
Music: Richard Strauss, Johann Strauss, Aram Khachaturian, György Ligeti
Costumes: Hardy Amies
Sound: Winston Ryder
Cast: Keir Dullea (David Bowman), Gary Lockwood (Frank Poole), William
    Sylvester (Dr. Heywood Floyd), Daniel Richter (Moon-Watcher), Douglas
    Rain (HAL's Voice), Leonard Rossiter (Smyslov), Margaret Tyzack (Elena),
    Robert Beatty (Halvorsen), Sean Sullivan (Michaels), Frank Miller (Mission Control), Penny Edwina Carroll, Mike Lovell, Peter Delman, Dany
    Grover, Brian Hawley

Running Time: 141 minutes
Distributor: Metro-Goldwyn-Mayer

A Clockwork Orange (1971)

Production Company: Warner Brothers/Hawk Films
Producer/Director: Stanley Kubrick
Executive Producers: Max L. Raab, Si Litvinoff
Associate Producer: Bernard Williams
Screenplay: Stanley Kubrick, based on the novel by Anthony Burgess
Photography: John Alcott
Color: Warnercolor
Editor: Bill Butler
Production Design: John Barry
Art Direction: Russell Hagg, Peter Shields
Music: Ludwig van Beethoven, Edward Elgar, Gioacchino Rossini, Terry Tucker, Henry Purcell, James Yorkston, Arthur Freed, Nacio Herb Brown, Nikolai Rimsky-Korsakov, Erika Eigen
Original Electronic Music: Walter Carlos
Songs: Gene Kelly, Erika Eigen
Costumes: Milena Canonero
Special Paintings and Sculpture: Herman Makkink, Cornelius Makkink, Liz Moore, Christiane Kubrick
Production Assistant: Andros Epaminondas
Sound: Brian Blarney
Assistant to Producer: Jan Harlan
Cast: Malcolm McDowell (Alex), Patrick Magee (Mr. Alexander), Michael Bates (Chief Guard), Warren Clarke (Dim), John Clive (Stage Actor), Adrienne Corri (Mrs. Alexander), Carl Duering (Dr. Brodsky), Paul Farrell (Tramp), Clive Francis (Joe the Lodger), Michael Gover (Prison Governor), Miriam Karlin (Miss Weber, the Cat Lady), James Marcus (Georgie), Aubrey Morris (Mr. Deltoid), Godfrey Quigley (Prison Chaplain), Sheila Raynor (Em), Madge Ryan (Dr. Branom), John Savident (Conspirator), Anthony Sharp (Minister of the Interior), Philip Stone (Pee), Pauline Taylor (Dr. Taylor/Psychiatrist), Margaret Tyzack (Conspirator), Steven Berkoff (Constable), Lindsay Campbell (Inspector), Michael Tarn (Pete), David Prowse (Julian), Jan Adair, Vivienne Chandler, Prudence Drage (Handmaidens), John J. Carney (CID Man), Richard Connaught (Billyboy), Carol Drinkwater (Nurse Feeley), Cheryl Grunwald (Rape Girl), Gillian Hills (Sonietta), Barbara Scott (Marty), Virginia Wetherell (Stage Actress), Katya Wyeth (Girl), Barrie Cookson, Gaye Brown, Peter Burton, Lee Fox, Craig Hunter, Shirley Jaffe, Neil Wilson
Running Time: 137 minutes
Distributor: Warner Brothers

Barry Lyndon (1975)

Production Companies: Warner Brothers/Hawk Films/Peregrine Productions
Producer/Director: Stanley Kubrick
Associate Producer: Jan Harlan
Screenplay: Stanley Kubrick, based on the novel by William Makepeace Thackeray
Photography: John Alcott

Editor: Tony Lawson
Production Design: Ken Adam
Art Direction: Roy Walker
Music: Johann Sebastian Bach, Frederick the Great, George Frideric Handel, Wolfgang Amadeus Mozart, Giovanni Paisiello, Franz Schubert, Antonio Vivaldi
Music Adaptation: Leonard Rosenman
Costumes: Ulla-Britt Søderlund, Milena Cannonero
Screen Process: Panavision
Color: Metrocolor
Sound: Rodney Holland
Assistant Director: Brian Cook
Cast: Ryan O'Neal (Barry Lyndon), Marisa Berenson (Lady Lyndon), Patrick Magee (The Chevalier), Hardy Kruger (Captain Potzdorf), Marie Kean (Mrs. Barry), Gay Hamilton (Nora Brady), Murray Melvin (Reverend Runt), Godfrey Quigley (Captain Grogan), Leonard Rossiter (Captain Quin), Leon Vitali (Lord Bullingdon), Diana Koerner (Lischen), Frank Middlemass (Sir Charles Lyndon), André Morell (Lord Wendover), Arthur O'Sullivan (Captain Freny), Philip Stone (Graham), Steven Berkoff (Lord Ludd), Anthony Sharp (Lord Hallum), Michael Hordern (the narrator)
Running Time: 185 minutes
Distributor: Warner Brothers

The Shining (1980)
Production Companies: Warner Brothers/Hawk Films/Peregrine Productions
Produced in association with The Producer Circle Company: Robert Fryer, Martin Richards, Mary Lea Johnson
Producer/Director: Stanley Kubrick
Executive Producer: Jan Harlan
Screenplay: Stanley Kubrick, Diane Johnson, based on the novel by Stephen King
Photography: John Alcott
Editor: Ray Lovejoy
Production Design: Roy Walker
Music: Béla Bartók, Wendy Carlos, Rachel Elkind, György Ligeti, Krzysztof Penderecki
Music for strings, percussion, and celesta/Conductor Herbert Van Karajan, Recorded by Deutsche Grammophon
Costumes: Milena Canonero
2nd Unit Photography: Douglas Milsome, Gregg Macgillivray
Steadicam Operator: Garrett Brown
Art Direction: Les Tomkins
Assistant Director: Brian Cook
Assistant to Producer: Andros Epaminondas
Personal Assistant to Director: Leon Vitali
Cast: Jack Nicholson (Jack Torrance), Shelley Duvall (Wendy Torrance), Danny Lloyd (Danny Torrance), Scatman Crothers (Hallorann), Barry Nelson (Stuart Ullman), Philip Stone (Delbert Grady), Joe Turkel (Lloyd), Anne Jackson (Doctor), Tony Burton (Larry Durkin), Lia Beldam (Young Woman in Bath), Billie Gibson (Old Woman in Bath), Barry Dennen (Watson), David Baxt (Forest Ranger 1), Manning Redwood (Forest Ranger 2), Lisa Burns, Louise Burns (The Grady Girls), Alison Coleridge (Ullman's

Secretary), Jana Sheldon (Stewardess), Kate Phelps (Overlook Reception-
ist), Norman Gay (Injured Guest with Head-Wound)
Running Time: 146 Minutes*
Distributor: Warner Brothers

Full Metal Jacket (1987)

Production Companies: Warner Brothers/Hawk Films/Harrier Productions
Director/Producer: Stanley Kubrick
Screenplay: Stanley Kubrick, Michael Herr, Gustav Hasford, based on Hasford's
novel *The Short-Timers*
Executive Producer: Jan Harlan
Lighting Cameraman: Douglas Milsome
Steadicam Operators: John Ward, Jean-Marc Bringuier
Production Designer: Anton Furst
Original Music: Abigail Mead
Additional Music: "Hello Vietnam" (Johnny Wright), "The Marines Hymn,"
"These Boots Are Made for Walking" (Nancy Sinatra), "Chapel of Love"
(The Dixie Cups), "Wooly Bully" (Sam the Sham), "Paint It Black" (Rolling
Stones)
Sound Editors: Nigel Galt, Edward Tise
Editor: Martin Hunter
Art Directors: Rod Stratford, Les Tomkins, Keith Pain
Special Effects: Supervisor John Evans
Technical Adviser: Lee Ermey
Casting: Leon Vitali
Cast: Matthew Modine (Joker), Adam Baldwin (Animal Mother), Vincent
D'Onofrio (Pyle/Leonard Lawrence), Lee Ermey (Gunnery Sergeant Hart-
man), Dorian Harewood (Eightball), Kevyn Major Howard (Rafterman),
Arliss Howard (Cowboy), Ed O'Ross (Lieutenant Touchdown), John Terry
(Lieutenant Lockhart), Keiron Jecchinis (Crazy Earl), Kirk Taylor (Pay-
back), Tim Colceri (Doorgunner), John Stafford (Doc Jay), Bruce Boa
(Poge Colonel), Ian Tyler (Lieutenant Cleves), Sal Lopez (T.H.E. Rock),
Gary Landon Mills (Donlon), Papillon Soo Soo (Da Nang Hooker), Peter
Edmund (Snowball), Ngoc Le (V.C. Sniper), Leanne Hong (Motorbike
Hooker), Tan Hung Francione (ARVN Pimp), Marcus D'Amico (Hand
Job), Costas Dino Chimona (Chili), Gil Kopel (Stork), Keith Hodiak
(Daddy Da), Peter Merrill (TV Journalist), Herbert Norville (Daytona
Dave), Nguyen Hue Phong (Camera Thief), Duc Hu Ta (Dead N.V.A.)
Running Time: 116 minutes
Distributor: Warner Brothers

Eyes Wide Shut (1999)

Production Companies: Warner Brothers/Pole Star/Hobby Productions
Director/Producer: Stanley Kubrick
Screenplay: Stanley Kubrick, Frederic Raphael, inspired by *Traumnovelle*, by Ar-
thur Schnitzler
Executive Producer: Jan Harlan

---

*Before releasing *The Shining*, Kubrick previewed it for a London audience, after
which he deleted an ending showing Wendy recuperating and talking with Ullman in a
hospital.

Lighting Cameraman: Larry Smith
Second Unit Photography: Patrick Turley, Malik Sayeed, Arthur Jaffa
Steadicam Operators: Elizabeth Ziegler, Peter Cavaciuti, Jim C. McConkey
Editor: Nigel Galt
Assistant Directors: Brian Cook, Adrian Toynton, Becky Hunt, Rhun Francis
Production Designers: Les Tomkins, Roy Walker
Original Music: Jocelyn Pook
Additional Music: Dmitri Shostakovich's "Jazz Suite 2" (Royal Concert Gebouw
    Orchestra), "Chanson d'amour" (Victor Silvester Orchestra), "Old Fash-
    ioned Way" (Victor Silvester Orchestra), "I'm in the Mood for Love" (Vic-
    tor Silvester Orchestra), "When I Fall in Love" (Victor Silvester Orchestra),
    "It Had to Be You" (Tommy Sanderson and The Sandman), "I Only Have
    Eyes for You" (Victor Silvester Orchestra), "I Got It Bad (And That Ain't
    Good)" (The Oscar Peterson Trio), "Baby Did a Bad, Bad Thing" (Chris
    Isaak), "If I Had You" (Roy Gerson), "Blame It on My Youth" (Brad Mehl-
    dau), "Strangers in the Night" (Peter Hughes Orchestra), "Musica ricercata
    II" by György Ligeti (piano by Dominic Harlan), "I Want a Boy for Christ-
    mas" (The Del-Vets), "Nuages gris" by Franz Liszt (piano by Dominic Har-
    lan), "Wien, du Stadt meiner Traume" by Rudolf Sieczynski, "Requiem
    K626, Rex tremendae" by Wolfgang Amadeus Mozart (Berlin Radio Sym-
    phony Orchestra)
Art Director: John Fenner
Venetian Masks Research: Barbara Del Greco
Original Paintings: Christiane Kubrick, Katharina Hobbs
Costume Designer: Marit Allen
Casting: Denise Chamian, Leon Vitali
Cast: Tom Cruise (Dr. William Harford), Nicole Kidman (Alice Harford), Syd-
    ney Pollack (Victor Ziegler), Marie Richardson (Marion Nathanson), Rade
    Sherbedgia (Milich), Todd Field (Nick Nightingale), Vinessa Shaw
    (Domino), Alan Cumming (Hotel Desk Clerk), Sky Dumont (Sandor
    Szavost), Fay Masterson (Sally), Leelee Sobieski (Milich's Daughter), Thom-
    as Gibson (Carl), Madison Eginton (Helena Harford), Jackie Sawiris (Roz),
    Leslie Lowe (Illona), Peter Benson (Bandleader), Michael Doven (Zieg-
    ler's Secretary), Louise Taylor (Gayle), Stewart Thorndike (Nuala Wind-
    sor), Randall Paul (Harris), Julienne Davis (Mandy), Lisa Leone (Lisa, Re-
    ceptionist), Kevin Connealy (Lou Nathanson), Mariana Hewett (Rosa),
    Dan Rollman, Gavin Perry, Chris Pare, Adam Lias, Christian Clarke, Kyle
    Whitcombe (Rowdy College Boys), Gary Goba (Naval Officer), Forian
    Widorfer (Café Sonata Maitre d'), Togo Igawa (Japanese Man 1), Eiji Kusu-
    hara (Japanese Man 2), Sam Douglas (Cab Driver), Abigail Good (Mysteri-
    ous Woman), Leon Vitali (Red Cloak), Brian W. Cook (Tall Butler), Car-
    mela Marner (Waitress at Gillespie's), Phil Davis (Stalker), Cindy Dolenc
    (Girl at Sharkey's), Treva Eteinne (Morgue Orderly)
Running Time: 158 minutes
Distributor: Warner Brothers

SELECTED BIBLIOGRAPHY
Additional sources can be found in "Notes & Trivia."

Comprehensive Studies, Biographies, Essays, and Interviews
Andrew, Dudley. *André Bazin.* New York: Oxford University Press, 1978.
Andrew, J. Dudley. *The Major Film Theories: An Introduction.* New York: Oxford University Press, 1976.
Baxter, John. *Stanley Kubrick: A Biography.* New York: Carroll and Graf, 1997.
Bernstein, Jeremy. "Profiles: How about a Little Game?" *The New Yorker,* 12 November 1966, pp. 70–110.
Bordwell, David. *Making Meaning: Inference and Rhetoric in the Interpretation of Cinema.* Cambridge, Mass.: Harvard University Press, 1989.
Bordwell, David, and Kristin Thompson. *Film Art: An Introduction.* 5th ed. New York: McGraw-Hill, 1997.
Braudy, Leo. *The World in a Frame.* Garden City, N.Y.: Anchor Books, 1977.
Cavell, Stanley. *The World Viewed: Reflections on the Ontology of Film.* Enlarged ed. Cambridge, Mass.: Harvard University Press, 1979.
Ciment, Michel. *Kubrick: The Definitive Edition.* Translated from the French by Gilbert Adair; additional material translated by Robert Bononno. New York: Faber and Faber, 2001.
Coyle, Wallace. *Stanley Kubrick: A Guide to References and Resources.* Boston: G. K. Hall, 1980.
Falsetto, Mario. *Stanley Kubrick: A Narrative and Stylistic Analysis.* Westport, Conn.: Praeger, 1994.
Falsetto, Mario, ed. *Perspectives on Stanley Kubrick.* New York: G. K. Hall, 1996.
Feldmann, Hans. "Kubrick and His Discontents." *Film Quarterly,* Fall 1976, pp. 12–19.
Gelmis, Joseph. *The Film Director as Superstar.* Garden City, N.Y.: Doubleday, 1970, pp. 293–315.
Gorchakov, Nikolai M. *Stanislavsky Directs.* Translated by Miriam Goldina. New York: Funk and Wagnalls, 1954.
Henderson, Brian. *A Critique of Film Theory.* New York: E. P. Dutton, 1980.
Herr, Michael. *Kubrick.* New York: Grove Press, 2000.
Houston, Penelope. "Kubrick Country." *Saturday Review,* 25 December 1971, pp. 42–44.
Kagan, Norman. *The Cinema of Stanley Kubrick.* Expanded ed. New York: Holt, Rinehart, and Winston, 1990.
Kawin, Bruce F. *Mindscreen.* Princeton: Princeton University Press, 1978.
Kohler, Charles. "Stanley Kubrick Raps." *Eye,* August 1968, pp. 84–86.
Kolker, Robert Phillip. *A Cinema of Loneliness.* Third Edition. New York: Oxford University Press, 2000, pp. 97–174.
Kubrick, Stanley. "Director's Notes: Stanley Kubrick Movie-Maker." *The Observer* (London), 4 December 1960.
Kubrick, Stanley. "Kubrick Dissects the Movies." *Newsweek,* 2 December 1957, pp. 96–97.
Kubrick, Stanley. "Words and Movies." *Sight and Sound,* Winter 1960/61, p. 14.
LoBrutto, Vincent. *Stanley Kubrick: A Biography.* New York: Donald I. Fine Books, 1997.
Nelson, Thomas Allen. "Film Styles and Film Meanings." *Film Criticism,* Spring 1979, pp. 2–17.

Nelson, Thomas Allen. "Through a Shifting Lens: Realist Film Aesthetics." *Film Criticism*, Fall 1977, pp. 15–23.

Norden, Eric. "Interview with Stanley Kubrick." *Playboy*, September 1968, p. 85.

Phillips, Gene D. "Interview with Stanley Kubrick." *Film Comment*, Winter 1971/72, pp. 30–35.

Phillips, Gene D. *Stanley Kubrick: A Film Odyssey*. New York: Popular Library, 1975.

Pudovkin, V. I. *Film Technique*. Enlarged ed. Translated by Ivor Montagu. London: George Newness, 1933.

Rapf, Maurice. "A Talk with Stanley Kubrick." *Action*, January/February 1969, pp. 15–18.

Stang, Jonathan. "Film Fan to Film-Maker." *New York Times Magazine*, 12 October 1958.

Stanislavsky, Konstantin. *Stanislavsky, on the Art of the Stage*. Translated with introductory essay by David Magarshack. New York: Hill and Wang, 1961.

Strick, Philip, and Penelope Houston. "Interview with Stanley Kubrick." *Sight and Sound*, Winter 1971/72, pp. 62–66.

Taylor, John Russell. *Directors and Directions: Cinema for the Seventies*. New York: Hill and Wang, 1975, pp. 101–35.

Walker, Alexander, with Sybil Taylor and Ulrich Ruchti. *Stanley Kubrick, Director: A Visual Analysis*. New York: W.W. Norton, 1999.

Walter, Renaud. "Entretien avec Stanley Kubrick." *Positif*, Winter 1968/69, pp. 19–39.

The Early Films

Alpert, Hollis. "The Day of the Gladiators." *Saturday Review*, 12 October 1960.

Cobb, Humphrey. *Paths of Glory*. New York: Viking Press, 1935.

Crowther, Bosley. "Shameful Incident of War." *New York Times,* 27 December 1957.

Gurnseley, Otis L. "Review of *Fear and Desire*." *New York Herald-Tribune*, 1 April 1953.

Lambert, Gavin. "Killer's Kiss." *Sight and Sound*, Spring 1956, p. 198.

Lambert, Gavin. "The Killing." *Sight and Sound*, Autumn 1956, pp. 95–96.

Lambert, Gavin. "Paths of Glory." *Sight and Sound*, Winter 1957/58, pp. 144–45.

"Review of *Fear and Desire*." *Time*, 3 April 1953.

"Review of *The Killing*." *Time*, 4 June 1956, p. 106.

White, Lionel. *Clean Break*. New York: E. P. Dutton, 1955.

Lolita

Appel, Alfred. *The Annotated Lolita*. New York: McGraw-Hill, 1970.

Appel, Alfred, Jr. *Nabokov's Dark Cinema*. New York: Oxford University Press, 1974.

Corliss, Richard. "Cherishing Lolita." *Film Comment*, September/October 1998, pp. 34–39.

French, Brandon. "The Celluloid *Lolita*: A Not-So-Crazy Quilt." In *The Modern American Novel and the Movies*, ed. Gerald Peary and Roger Shatzkin. New York: Frederick Ungar, 1978, pp. 224–35.

Nabokov, Vladimir. *Lolita: A Screenplay*. New York: McGraw-Hill, 1974.

Nabokov, Vladimir. *Strong Opinions*. New York: McGraw-Hill, 1973.

Toffler, Alvin. "Interview with Vladimir Nabokov." *Playboy*, January 1964, pp. 35–45.

Dr. Strangelove

Bryant, Peter. *Red Alert*. New York: Ace Books, 1958.

George, Peter. *Dr. Strangelove*. New York: Bantam, 1963.

Linden, George W. "*Dr. Strangelove*." In *Nuclear War Films*, ed. Jack G. Shaheen. Carbondale: Southern Illinois University Press, 1978, pp. 59–67.

Macklin, Anthony. "Sex and *Dr. Strangelove*." *Film Comment*, Summer 1965, pp. 55–57.

Maland, Charles. "*Dr. Strangelove:* Nightmare Comedy and the Ideology of Liberal Consensus." *American Quarterly*, Winter 1979, pp. 697–717.

Milne, Tom. "How I Learned to Stop Worrying and Love Stanley Kubrick." *Sight and Sound*, Spring 1964, pp. 68–72.

2001: A Space Odyssey

Agel, Jerome, ed. *The Making of "2001."* New York: New American Library, 1970.

Bizony, Piers. *"2001": Filming the Future*. London: Aurum, 1994.

Clarke, Arthur C. *The Lost Worlds of 2001*. New York: New American Library, 1972.

Clarke, Arthur C. *2001: A Space Odyssey*. New York: New American Library, 1968.

Daniels, Don. "A Skeleton Key to *2001*." *Sight and Sound*, Winter 1970/71, pp. 28–33.

Daniels, Don. "*2001:* A New Myth." *Film Heritage*, Summer 1968.

Dumont, J. P., and J. Monod. "Beyond the Infinite: A Structural Analysis of *2001: A Space Odyssey*." *Quarterly Review of Film Studies*, Summer 1978, pp. 297–316.

Geduld, Carolyn. *Filmguide to "2001: A Space Odyssey."* Bloomington: Indiana University Press, 1973.

Hoch, David G. "Mythic Patterns in *2001: A Space Odyssey*." *Journal of Popular Culture*, Summer 1970, pp. 961–65.

Lightman, Herb. "Kubrick's *2001*." *American Cinematographer*, June 1968.

Macklin, F. A. "The Comic Sense of *2001*." *Film Comment*, Winter 1969, pp. 10–15.

McKee, M. "*2001:* Out of the Silent Planet." *Sight and Sound*, Autumn 1969, pp. 204–207.

Michelson, Annette. "Bodies in Space: Film as 'Carnal Knowledge.'" *Art-forum*, February 1969, pp. 54–63.

Robinson, W. R., and Mary McDermott. "*2001* and the Literary Sensibility." *Georgia Review*, Spring 1972, pp. 21–37.

Trumbull, Douglas. "Creating Special Effects for *2001*." *American Cinematographer*, June 1968.

A Clockwork Orange

Alpert, Hollis. "Milk-Plus and Ultra-Violence." *Saturday Review*, 25 December 1971, p. 40.

Bailey, Andrew. "A Clockwork Utopia." *Rolling Stone*, 20 January 1972, pp. 20–22.

Boyers, P. "Kubrick's *A Clockwork Orange:* Some Observations." *Film Heritage*, Summer 1972, pp. 1–6.

Burgess, Anthony. "Author Has His Say on 'Clockwork' Film." *Los Angeles Times*, *Calendar* section, 13 February 1972.

Burgess, Anthony. *A Clockwork Orange*. London: Heinemann, 1962.

Burgess, Anthony. *A Clockwork Orange*. New York: Norton, 1963.

Burgess, Anthony. "Juice from *A Clockwork Orange*." *Rolling Stone*, 8 June 1972, pp. 52–53.

Burgess, Anthony. *1985*. Boston: Little, Brown and Co., 1978.

Ciment, Michel. "Interview with Kubrick." In Ciment, *Kubrick,* pp. 148–65.

Gilbert, Basil. "Kubrick's Marmalade: The Art of Violence." *Meanjin Quarterly,* Winter 1974, pp. 157–62.

Gumenik, A. "*A Clockwork Orange:* Novel into Film." *Film Heritage,* Summer 1972, pp. 7–18.

"Interview with Anthony Burgess." *Playboy,* September 1974, pp. 68–86.

Jackson, Kevin. "Real Horrorshow: A Short Lexicon of Nadsat." *Sight and Sound,* September 1999, pp. 24–27.

Kubrick, Stanley. *A Clockwork Orange: A Screenplay.* New York: Ballantine Books, 1972.

LoBrutto, Vincent. "The Old Ultra-Violence." *American Cinematographer,* October 1999, pp. 52–61.

McCracken, Samuel. "Novel into Film; Novelist into Critic: *A Clockwork Orange* . . . Again." *Antioch Review* 32, no. 3 (1978): 427–36.

Barry Lyndon

Alcott, John. "Photographing Stanley Kubrick's *Barry Lyndon.*" *American Cinematographer,* March 1976, p. 268.

Ciment, Michel. "Interview with Kubrick." In Ciment, *Kubrick,* pp. 166–79.

Dempsey, Michael. "Barry Lyndon." *Film Quarterly,* Fall 1976, pp. 49–54.

DiGiulio, Ed. "Two Special Lenses for *Barry Lyndon.*" *American Cinematographer,* March 1976, pp. 276–77.

Houston, Penelope. "*Barry Lyndon.*" *Sight and Sound,* Spring 1976, pp. 77–80.

Kael, Pauline. "Kubrick's Gilded Age." *The New Yorker,* 29 December 1975, pp. 49–52.

Nelson, Thomas Allen. "*Barry Lyndon:* Kubrick's Cinema of Disparity." *Rocky Mountain Review,* Winter 1978/79, pp. 39–51.

Sarris, Andrew. "What Makes Barry Run?" *Village Voice,* 29 December 1975, pp. 111–12.

Schickel, Richard. "Kubrick's Grandest Gamble." *Time,* 15 December 1975, pp. 72–78.

Spiegel, Alan. "Kubrick's *Barry Lyndon.*" *Salmagundi,* Fall 1977, pp. 194–208.

Thackeray, William Makepeace. *The Luck of Barry Lyndon.* Edited by Martin F. Anisman. New York: New York University Press, 1970.

Westerbeck, Colin L. "*Barry Lyndon.*" *Commonweal,* March and April 1976, p. 208.

The Shining

Alberton, Jim, and Peter S. Perakos. "*The Shining.*" *Cinefantastique,* Fall 1978, p. 74.

Brown, Garrett. "The Steadicam and *The Shining.*" *American Cinematographer,* August 1980, p. 786.

Ciment, Michel. "Interview with Kubrick." In Ciment, *Kubrick,* pp. 180–97.

Hofsess, Jim. "The Shining Example of Kubrick." *Los Angeles Times, Calendar* section, 1 June 1980, p. 1.

Huss, Roy, and T. J. Ross, eds. *Focus on the Horror Film.* Englewood Cliffs, N.J.: Prentice-Hall, 1972.

Jameson, Richard T. "Kubrick's Shining." *Film Comment,* July–August 1980, pp. 28–32.

Kael, Pauline. "Devolution." *The New Yorker,* 1 June 1980, pp. 130–47.

Kennedy, Harlan. "Kubrick Goes Gothic." *American Film,* June 1980, pp. 49–52.

King, Stephen. *The Shining.* New York: Doubleday, 1977.

Kroll, Jack. "Stanley Kubrick's Horror Show." *Newsweek,* 26 May 1980, pp. 96–99.

Kubrick, Vivian. *The Making of the Shining*. BBC.

Leibowitz, Flo, and Lynn Jeffress. "The Shining." *Film Quarterly,* Spring 1981, pp. 45–51.

Lightman, Herb. "Photographing Stanley Kubrick's *The Shining:* An Interview with John Alcott." *American Cinematographer,* August 1980, p. 760.

Mayersberg, Paul. "The Overlook Hotel." *Sight and Sound,* Winter 1980/81, pp. 54–57.

Perakos, Peter S. "Interview with Stephen King." *Cinefantastique,* Winter 1978, pp. 12–15.

Romney, Jonathan. "Resident Phantoms." *Sight and Sound,* September/October 1999, pp. 8–11.

Titterington, P. L. "Kubrick and *The Shining*." *Sight and Sound,* Spring 1981, pp. 117–21.

Wood, Robin. "Return of the Repressed." *Film Comment,* July–August 1978, pp. 25–32.

Full Metal Jacket

Castle, Robert, and Stephen Donatelli. "Kubrick Ulterior War." *Film Comment,* September/October 1998, pp. 24–28.

Clines, Francis X. "Stanley Kubrick's Vietnam." *New York Times,* 21 June 1987.

Corliss, Richard. "Welcome to Vietnam, the Movie: II." *Time,* 29 June 1987, p. 66.

Gilliatt, Penelope. "Heavy Metal." *American Film,* September 1987, pp. 20–23, 50–52.

Hasford, Gustav. *The Short-Timers*. New York: Bantam Books, 1979.

Herr, Michael. *Dispatches*. New York: Alfred A. Knopf, 1977.

Herr, Michael. "Foreword" to Stanley Kubrick, Michael Herr, and Gustav Hasford, *Full Metal Jacket: The Screenplay*. New York: Alfred A. Knopf, 1987, v–vii.

Kroll, Jack. "1968: Kubrick's Vietnam Odyssey." *Newsweek,* 29 June 1987, pp. 64–65.

Magrid, Ron. "Full Metal Jacket: Cynic's Choice." Including an interview with Douglas Milsome. *American Cinematographer,* September 1987.

Maslin, Janet. "Inside the 'Jacket': All Kubrick." *New York Times,* 5 July 1987.

Moore, Janet C. "For Fighting and for Fun: Kubrick's Complicitous Critique." *Velvet Light Trap* 31 (1993): 39–47.

Pursell, Michael. "*Full Metal Jacket:* The Unraveling of Patriarchy." *Literature/Film Quarterly* 16 (1988): 218–25.

Rose, Lloyd. "Stanley Kubrick, at a Distance." *Washington Post,* 28 June 1987, p. FO1.

Willoquet-Maricondi, Paula. "Full Metal-Jacketing, or Masculinity in the Making." *Cinema Journal* 33 (1994): 5–21.

Eyes Wide Shut

Booth, Cathy. "Three of a Kind." *Time,* 5 July 1999, pp. 72–74.

Gross, Larry. "Too Late the Hero." *Sight and Sound,* September 1999, pp. 20–23.

Jameson, Richard T. "Sonata Ghost." *Film Comment,* September/October 1999, pp. 27–28.

Kroll, Jack. "Dreaming with 'Eyes Wide Shut.'" *Newsweek,* 19 July 1999, pp. 62–63.

Kubrick, Stanley, and Frederic Raphael. *Eyes Wide Shut* (which also includes Schnitzler's *Dream Story*). New York: Warner Books, 1999.

Maslin, Janet. "Review of *Eyes Wide Shut*." *New York Times*, 16 July 1999.

Raphael, Frederic. *Eyes Wide Open: A Memoir of Stanley Kubrick*. New York: Ballantine Books, 1999.

Schickel, Richard. "All Eyes on Them." *Time*, 5 July 1999, pp. 65–70.

Schnitzler, Arthur. *Rhapsody: A Dream Novel*. Translated from the German by Otto P. Schinnerer. New York: Simon and Schuster, 1927.

Smith, Adam. "The Eyes Have It." *Empire*, October 1999, pp. 90–97.

Smith, Larry. "A Sword in the Bed." *American Cinematographer*, October 1999, pp. 28–38.

Taubin, Amy. "Imperfect Love." *Film Comment*, September/October 1999, pp. 24–26, 30–33.

Turan, Kenneth. "Eyes That See Too Much." *Los Angeles Times*, 16 July 1999.

Whitehouse, Charles. "Eyes without a Face." *Sight and Sound*, September 1999, pp. 38–39.

Wilmington, Michael. "Review of *Eyes Wide Shut*." *Chicago Tribune*, 16 July 1999.

Postscript

Bogdanovich, Peter. "What They Say about Stanley Kubrick." *New York Times Magazine*, 4 July 1999, pp. 1–22.

Goldstein, Patrick. "The Kubrick Mystique." *Los Angeles Times*, 10 March 1999.

Herr, Michael. "Kubrick." *Vanity Fair*, August 1999, pp. 136–50, 184–89.

Hunter, Stephen. "Appreciation: Stanley Kubrick's Odyssey." *Washington Post*, 15 March 1999.

James, Nick. "At Home with the Kubricks." *Sight and Sound*, September 1999, pp. 12–18.

Kroll, Jack. "Kubrick's View." *Newsweek*, 22 March 1999, pp. 66–67.

Magid, Ron. "Quest for Perfection." *American Cinematographer*, October 1999, pp. 40–51.

Maslin, Janet. "Farewell to a Fearless Imagination." *New York Times*, 14 March 1999.

Schickel, Richard. "Art Was His Fragile Fortress." *Time*, 22 March 1999.

Turan, Kenneth. "An Appreciation: Passionate Director Seems Forever Young." *Los Angeles Times*, 8 March 1999.

NOTES & TRIVIA

1. The Shaping of a Film Imagination

2–4: For a fuller discussion of the biographical material from the early period, see John Baxter, *Stanley Kubrick: A Biography* (New York: Carroll and Graf, 1997), pp. 9–44; Vincent LoBrutto, *Stanley Kubrick: A Biography* (New York: Donald I. Fine Books, 1997), pp. 5–42; Jeremy Bernstein, "Profiles: How about a Little Game?" *The New Yorker*, 12 November 1966, pp. 70–110; Alexander Walker, *Stanley Kubrick, Director: A Visual Analysis* (New York: W. W. Norton, 1999), pp. 7–37; Gene D. Phillips, *Stanley Kubrick: A Film Odyssey* (New York: Popular Library, 1975); and Joseph Gelmis, "Interview with Stanley Kubrick," in Gelmis, *The Film Director as Superstar* (Garden City, N.Y.: Doubleday, 1970), pp. 293–315. I am indebted to John Morgan's Internet site, "The Unknown Kubrick," for descriptions and illustrations of Kubrick's photographic assignments for *Look* magazine.

5: V. I. Pudovkin, *Film Technique*, enlarged ed., trans. Ivor Montagu (London: George Newness, 1933). On p. 7 of *Film Technique*, Pudovkin says that "the film is yet young, and the wealth of its methods is not yet extensive." As a result, he felt, a limitation had to be imposed on the "scale of theme," and, in fact, he faulted Griffith's *Intolerance* for its thematic overreaching, characterizing the film as "ponderous," with a theme too deep for the film's "superficiality of form."

7: "Director's Notes: Stanley Kubrick, Movie-Maker," *The Observer* (London), 4 December 1960.

9–10: "Kubrick Dissects the Movies," *Newsweek*, 2 December 1957, pp. 96–97; Walker, *Stanley Kubrick, Director*, p. 38.

10–15: For a discussion of film theory, see J. Dudley Andrew, *The Major Film Theories: An Introduction* (New York: Oxford University Press, 1976); see also André Bazin, "The Evolution of the Language of Cinema," in *What Is Cinema?*, vol. 1, trans. Hugh Gray (Berkeley and Los Angeles: University of California Press, 1967), pp. 23–40; Thomas Allen Nelson, "Through a Shifting Lens: Realist Film Aesthetics," *Film Criticism*, Fall 1977, pp. 15–23; Thomas Allen Nelson, "Film Styles and Film Meanings," *Film Criticism*, Spring 1979, pp. 2–17; and Brian Henderson, "Two Types of Film Theory," *Film Quarterly*, Spring 1971, pp. 33–42. The Henderson essay contains an interesting comparison of Bazinian ("relation to real") and Eisensteinian ("part-whole") theories; Henderson believes that developments in film since the late 1950s have gone far beyond the explanatory capacities of the classical film theories. For an excellent collection of essays in film theory, see Bill Nichols, ed., *Movies and Methods: An Anthology* (Berkeley: University of California Press, 1985).

13–14: Dudley Andrew, *André Bazin* (New York: Oxford University Press, 1978), p. 121.

14: Penelope Houston, "Kubrick Country," *Saturday Review*, 25 December 1971, pp. 42–44; Seymour Krim, *Shake It for the World, Smartass* (New York: Dial Press, 1970), p. 349.

15: See Andrew, *The Major Film Theories*, pp. 185–211.

16–17: For more on these subjects, see Max Planck, *The New Science*, trans. James Murphy and W. H. Johnston (New York: Meridian Books, 1959); Martin

Gardner, *The Ambidextrous Universe* (New York: Basic Books, 1959); Hans Pagel, *The Cosmic Code: Quantum Physics as the Language of Nature* (New York: Simon and Schuster, 1982); Richard Poirier, *The Performing Self* (New York: Oxford University Press, 1971), pp. 86–111; Erving Goffman, *The Presentation of Self in Everyday Life* (New York: Doubleday, 1959); R. D. Laing, *The Politics of Experience* (New York: Pantheon Books, 1967); Maz'ud Zavarzudeh, *The Mythopoeic Reality* (Urbana: University of Illinois Press, 1976), pp. 3–67; Arthur Herman, *The Idea of Decline in Western History* (New York: Free Press, 1997); and Isaac Asimov, *Today and Tomorrow and . . .* (Garden City, N.Y.: Doubleday, 1973) and *The Collapsing Universe* (New York: Walker, 1977).

2. From *Fear and Desire* to *Paths of Glory*

20: For production notes and biographical material associated with Kubrick's first four features, see the accounts in LoBrutto, *Stanley Kubrick,* pp. 71–157, and Baxter, *Stanley Kubrick,* pp. 45–102. A critic who responded very early to Kubrick's promise as a filmmaker was *Sight and Sound*'s Gavin Lambert. See his separate reviews of *Killer's Kiss* (Spring 1956, p. 198), *The Killing* (Autumn 1956, pp. 95–96), and *Paths of Glory* (Winter 1957/58, pp. 144–45).

25: James Naremore's analyses of *Touch of Evil* and *Psycho* warrant reading; see *The Magic World of Orson Welles* (New York: Oxford University Press, 1978) and *A Filmguide to "Psycho"* (Bloomington: Indiana University Press, 1973).

43: In Cobb, the chateau is first mentioned on p. 135, but is not described until pp. 203–204, just before the court-martial. Assolant's (Mireau's) headquarters is located in the *mairie* of a nearby town.

45–46: Cobb's pre-attack account begins at "zero minus thirty minutes" and takes up nine pages (121–29), while the description of the attack, which lasts thirty-five minutes, takes up less than two pages (130–31).

49: Cobb's novel provides very little description of the ambience of the court-martial, which is presented in the form of a question-and-answer transcript (pp. 207–22).

53: Walker, *Stanley Kubrick, Director,* p. 66.

53–55: None of these scenes between Dax and Broulard has a source in Cobb; nor does the last scene of the film. The novel ends with the execution and a description of Sergeant Boulanger shooting each of the already dead soldiers in the head.

3. *Lolita*

56: For an informative description of Hollywood in the 1950s, one that discusses the impact of television, the rise of independent production companies, and the blacklist years, see Arthur Knight, *The Liveliest Art,* rev. ed. (New York: Macmillan, 1978), pp. 241–54. For a discussion of this period in Kubrick's career, see LoBrutto, *Stanley Kubrick,* pp. 166–226, and Baxter, *Stanley Kubrick,* pp. 103–64.

58: Kubrick discusses the *Spartacus* experience in the following sources: Gelmis, *The Film Director as Superstar* ("I was disappointed in the film. It had everything but a good story," p. 314); Renaud Walter, "Entretien avec Stanley Kubrick," *Positif,* Winter 1968/69, pp. 19–39; and Phillips, *Stanley Kubrick,* in which Kubrick remarked, "It is the only film over which I did not have absolute control. I have since involved myself in the administrative side of film production because it is in this area that many artistic battles are won and lost" (pp. 65–66).

59: In later years, Kubrick discussed his interest in historical battles in the context of his postponed *Napoleon* project: "I think that it's extremely important to communicate the essence of these battles to the viewer, because they all have an aesthetic brilliance that doesn't require a military mind to appreciate. There's an aesthetic involved; it's almost like a great piece of music, or the purity of a mathematical formula. It's this quality I want to bring across as well as the sordid reality of battle. . . . There's a weird disparity between the sheer visual and organizational beauty of the historical battles sufficiently far in the past, and their human consequences" (Gelmis, *The Film Director as Superstar,* pp. 296–97).

60: Kubrick, to his credit, avoided Humphrey Cobb's Christ symbolism in the execution scene in *Paths of Glory.* Cobb has Langlois say, "Those posts make it look like the Crucifixion, don't they? And if we keep in this order, it will be Ferol who will play the role of Christ. That's the proper touch of irony, all right."

See also Michael Herr's excellent essay "Kubrick," *Vanity Fair,* August 1999, in which he maintains that Olivier's Crassus in *Spartacus* "is the most complex character ever to appear in an epic-genre film, almost Shakespearean, and I'm sure Stanley wrote and otherwise informed a lot of those scenes" (p. 186).

61: Alvin Toffler, "Interview with Vladimir Nabokov," *Playboy,* January 1964, pp. 35–45.

61–63: Vladimir Nabokov, *Lolita: A Screenplay* (New York: McGraw-Hill, 1974). See also Vladimir Nabokov, *Strong Opinions* (New York: McGraw-Hill, 1973), a collection of his "occasional English prose" (interviews, essays, etc.), with some comments on Kubrick's film. Alfred Appel, Jr., *Nabokov's Dark Cinema* (New York: Oxford University Press, 1974); see especially the section "Making of *Lolita,*" pp. 228–45. Appel, I think, overrates Nabokov's screenplay and underrates Kubrick's film; he is disappointed that Kubrick did not imitate or adapt the style of the American *noir* road films. See also Brandon French, "The Celluloid *Lolita:* A Not-So-Crazy Quilt," in *The Modern American Novel and the Movies,* ed. Gerald Peary and Roger Shatzkin (New York: Frederick Ungar, 1978), pp. 224–35. French, like Appel, regrets the lack of a visual style the equal of Nabokov's prose style: "There are a number of directors whose obtrusive, highly visible styles might have provided such an equivalent: Orson Welles, Bernardo Bertolucci, Luchino Visconti, Roman Polanski . . . but the best directorial equivalent . . . is Josef von Sternberg" (p. 233). In 1970, Kubrick again clarified why *Lolita* was filmed in England and in the studio for MGM: "I would have done it at the time if the money had been available in America. But as it turned out the only funds I could raise for the film had to be spent in England. There's been such a revolution in Hollywood's treatment of sex over just the last few years that it's easy to forget that when I became interested in *Lolita* a lot of people felt that such a film couldn't be made—or at least couldn't be shown. . . . And filming in England we obviously had no choice but to rely mainly on studio shooting" (Gelmis, *The Film Director as Superstar,* p. 299). Kubrick's discussion of how he preferred the studio to actual locations for a psychological film can be found in "Stanley Kubrick, Movie-Maker," *The Observer* (London), 4 December 1960.

63–64: Pudovkin, in *Film Technique,* pp. 105–20, discusses his concept of the role of the actor. Like Griffith, he relied on editing and the close-up for emotional effect, something that is only an occasional technique in Kubrick's work. Konstantin Stanislavsky, *Stanislavsky, on the Art of the Stage,* trans. with introductory essay by David Magarshack (New York: Hill and Wang, 1961); Stanislavsky's description of the three types of actor (the creative, the imitative, and the stagehack) has interesting applications to film acting. Translate "creative" as method actor, "imitative" as conventional studio actor, and "stagehack" as character actor. See Nikolai M. Gorchakov, *Stanislavsky Directs,* trans. Miriam Goldina (New

York: Funk and Wagnalls, 1954). This book came out between *Fear and Desire* and *Killer's Kiss,* but as has been mentioned in the text, Kubrick did not have the money at that time to hire actors trained well enough to put his reading into practice. For a helpful and informative summary of film acting and the history of acting styles, see James F. Scott, *Film: The Media and the Maker* (New York: Holt, Rinehart, and Winston, 1975), pp. 209–59. Obviously, I keep seeing parallels between Kubrick's films and Buñuel's which, as far as I know, had not been widely discussed when I first wrote this chapter. Buñuel himself said the following about Kubrick: "I'm a Kubrick fan, ever since *Paths of Glory.* Fabulous movie; that's what it's all about: codes of conduct, the way people behave when the codes break down. *A Clockwork Orange* is my favorite. I was very predisposed against the film. After seeing it, I realized it's the only movie about what the modern world really means." See Carlos Fuentes, "The Discreet Charm of Luis Buñuel," in *The World of Luis Buñuel: Essays in Criticism,* ed. Joan Mellen (New York: Oxford University Press, 1978), p. 65. Mellen provides a description of Buñuel's style that, in some ways, could apply as well to Kubrick's *Lolita:* "Not content to play about the surfaces of reality, Buñuel would bring the unconscious into view by so integrating it with everyday life that the film itself renders it empirically real" (p. 5).

64: The comment by Kubrick can be found in Jonathan Stang, "Film Fan to Film-Maker," *New York Times Magazine,* 12 October 1958.

66: For Kubrick's comments about changes made to satisfy the Production Code and the Legion of Decency, and why he began the film with the murder of Quilty, see Gelmis, *The Film Director as Superstar,* pp. 300–301.

4. *Dr. Strangelove*

82–83: Helpful biographical and production information on the making of *Dr. Strangelove* can be found in LoBrutto, *Stanley Kubrick,* pp. 227–51; Baxter, *Stanley Kubrick,* pp. 165–98; Phillips, *Stanley Kubrick,* pp. 107–109; and Gelmis, *The Film Director as Superstar,* pp. 301–302, 309–11. The quotation from Kubrick can be found in Walker, *Stanley Kubrick, Director,* p. 114.

84–85: Peter Bryant, *Red Alert* (New York: Ace Books, 1958). In his "Foreword," George tries to impress the reader with the topicality of his novel: "It is a story that could happen. It may even be happening as you read these words. And then it really will be two hours to doom." Each chapter is titled by a reference to one of the three settings and three different times (Greenwich, Moscow, Washington). The novel ends this way: "The President sank into the seat he had used during the action. He was very weary, but he felt that his biggest effort was still to come. Yet he looked forward to it. He felt, like Zorubin [the Russian Ambassador], that no-one who had lived through that time could ever again take any action which might lead to war" (p. 191). See also Peter George's novelization of the screenplay, *Dr. Strangelove* (New York: Bantam, 1963).

85: Quoted comment by Kubrick in Gelmis, *The Film Director as Superstar,* p. 309.

87: At the time, Terry Southern's claim to fame was a comic novel about Southern California mores called *Flash and Filigree* (1958).

87: For a good discussion of the "mythopoeic" in fiction, see Zavarzudeh, *The Mythopoeic Reality,* and John W. Tilton, *Cosmic Satire in the Contemporary Novel* (Lewisburg, Pa.: Bucknell University Press, 1977). The latter, incidentally, briefly compares Burgess's *A Clockwork Orange* with Kubrick's 1971 film.

88: Alexander Walker, in particular, has some interesting things to say about the actors and acting styles of *Dr. Strangelove* in *Stanley Kubrick, Director,* pp. 114–

58. Originally, Peter Sellers was to have played the Kong part, but because he had trouble with the Texas accent and was injured just before the filming of the B-52 scenes, Kubrick turned to Pickens. George C. Scott once described his portrayal of Buck Turgidson as his best film role. Another notable performance of his—as Patton—involved another general officer and a certain degree of caricature.

89: Quoted in Norman Kagan, *The Cinema of Stanley Kubrick*, expanded ed. (New York: Holt, Rinehart, and Winston, 1990), p. 111.

93–95: Quoted in Gelmis, *The Film Director as Superstar*, p. 309; quoted in Walker, *Stanley Kubrick, Director*, p. 127; see F. Anthony Macklin, "Sex and *Dr. Strangelove*," *Film Comment*, Summer 1965, pp. 55–57; George W. Linden, "*Dr. Strangelove*," in *Nuclear War Films*, ed. Jack G. Shaheen (Carbondale: Southern Illinois University Press, 1978), pp. 59–67. See Kagan, *The Cinema of Stanley Kubrick*, pp. 136–37, for another listing of sexual allusions.

5. The Ultimate Cinematic Universe

103: For biographical and production information, see LoBrutto, *Stanley Kubrick*, pp. 255–320, and Baxter, *Stanley Kubrick*, pp. 199–330. See also Jerome Agel, ed., *The Making of "2001"* (New York: New American Library, 1970), which includes reprints of interviews, reviews, production notes, special effects information, stills, and a wide assortment of commentary and trivia; it also anthologizes Clarke's "The Sentinel," pp. 15–23. Needless to say, Agel's book is invaluable. Some of the more interesting technical features of *2001* are that (1) it was the first film to use large-scale front projection—for "The Dawn of Man," a front projection screen covered with highly reflective materials measured 40' × 90'; (2) for the moon excavation set, Kubrick had a pit constructed, 60' × 120', containing sand washed to resemble the color of the Moon's surface; (3) *Discovery*'s fictional size was 770' long, whereas in actuality it was a 54' model, and the exterior detail was done by hand so that in close-up it would look authentic; (4) *Discovery*'s centrifuge cost $300,000, was 38' across with an 8' interior, and rotated at speeds up to 3 mph; and (5) Douglas Trumbull's slit-scan special effects for the Star-Gate were a major innovation at the time. See *American Cinematographer*, June 1968, for essays on the technical effects of *2001*, especially those by Douglas Trumbull and Herb A. Lightman. Material here has been incorporated and summarized in several chapters and articles on the film, such as Agel's collection and Carolyn Geduld's *Filmguide to 2001: A Space Odyssey* (Bloomington: Indiana University Press, 1973), and the biographies by LoBrutto and Baxter.

104: Kubrick's statement quoted from Phillips, *Stanley Kubrick*, p. 148. In the *Playboy* interview, still one of the best background sources for *2001*, Kubrick discusses the scientific reading and philosophic speculation that went into the making of the film.

105: Arthur C. Clarke, *The Lost Worlds of 2001* (New York: New American Library, 1972), contains script material and ideas not used in the final film; it is something of a grab-bag, and not as helpful as one might hope. Kubrick, it appears, kept his own counsel during much of the time he collaborated with Clarke. Clarke breaks down the "authorship" of *2001* this way: 90 percent Kubrick, 5 percent special effects crew, 5 percent Clarke.

106: Arthur C. Clarke, *2001: A Space Odyssey* (New York: New American Library, 1968), based on a screenplay by Stanley Kubrick and Arthur C. Clarke. According to Clarke, Kubrick declined to share co-authorship of the novel.

107: Because his special effects crew could not come up with a credible Saturn model (the rings were the problem), Kubrick decided on Jupiter. In the novel, Floyd is identified as the chairman of the National Council of Astronautics and a widower. In the novel, he does not sleep in either *Orion* or *Aries,* and when he talks over the Picturephone in the novel, he talks with his housekeeper.

110: Kubrick, in the Gelmis interview, defines some of his intentions regarding character: "One of the things we were trying to convey in this part of the film is the reality of a world populated—as ours soon will be—by machine entities who have as much, or more, intelligence as human beings, and who have the same emotional potentialities in their personalities as human beings" (p. 307).

111: These psychological and symbolic patterns resemble the folklore and literature of the Sleeper Awakened (i.e., *The Arabian Nights,* Shakespeare's *A Midsummer Night's Dream,* the Rip Van Winkle story). The scene of Moon-Watcher with the bone is the only episode in *2001* that was filmed outside the studio. It was shot on a lot at the Borehamwood studio. Clarke says that as Kubrick walked back to the studio after finishing the scene, he kept tossing bones into the air and shooting them with a handheld camera.

111: In Clarke, HAL's name is explained as an abbreviation for *H*euristically programmed *AL*gorithmic computer; he is the "brain and nervous system of the ship" (p. 95). The fact that the name is one letter displaced in the alphabet for IBM was, according to Kubrick, nothing more than a happy coincidence.

113: After a preview before an audience in New York City, Kubrick trimmed *2001* from a running time of 161 to 141 minutes. Before that, he had deleted the prologue material (mostly prepared statements by leading scientists), which is printed in Agel.

115: In Clarke, Floyd does not appear suddenly on a screen in HAL's "brain." There, after disconnecting the computer, Bowman talks with Mission Control and Floyd, who then explains the purpose of the mission (the reader has been told by the narrator earlier). Three months then pass before he arrives at Saturn and goes through the Star-Gate. Kubrick alters and compresses these events and develops associative effects not found in the novel.

117: On the subject of language, Kubrick once said, "Perhaps it has something to do with the *magic of words.* If you can talk brilliantly about a problem, it can create the consoling illusion that it has been mastered" (in Walker, *Stanley Kubrick, Director,* p. 184). Here is an example of what Clarke refers to as Mission Control "Technish," which occasionally is duplicated in the film: "Mission Control, this is X-ray-Delta-One. At two-zero-four-five, on-board fault prediction center in our niner-triple-zero computer showed Alpha Echo three-five unit as probable failure within seventy-two hours. Request check your telemetry monitoring and suggest you review unit in your ship systems simulator" (p. 121).

118: While shooting, Kubrick tried to create a working "mood" or atmosphere by playing classical music, even though at the time he had hired veteran Hollywood composer Alex North (who composed the music for *Spartacus*) to score the film; sometime later, he decided on the now famous classical selections for *2001.* He once remarked that the von Karajan version of "The Blue Danube" is ideal for "depicting grace and beauty in turning. It also gets about as far away as you can get from the cliché of space music" (in Agel, *The Making of "2001,"* p. 88).

119: For a discussion of how motifs from "The Dawn of Man" (waterhole, bone, etc.) inform later sequences, see Don Daniels, "A Skeleton Key to *2001,*" *Sight and Sound,* Winter 1970/71, pp. 28–33. Other essays on the film are listed in the Selected Bibliography.

122: Two interesting visual parallels come to mind during the Moon monolith scene: The shape of the excavation resembles the horseshoe table in the conference room (where a man also photographs Floyd); and when the five figures line up for the photograph, with Floyd centered, it recalls the five judges of *Paths* who face the prisoners from across a marble floor on another Kubrickian gameboard.

125: On the subject of machines as man's children, consider this comment by Kubrick: "All man's technology grew out of his discovery of the tool-weapon. There's no doubt that there is a deep emotional relationship between man and his machine-weapons, which are his children. The machine is beginning to assert itself in a very profound way, even attracting affection and obsession. Man has always worshiped beauty, and I think there's a new kind of beauty in the world" (in Phillips, *Stanley Kubrick*, p. 126). According to Clarke, he and Kubrick decided that the shape of *Discovery* should be a matter of "aesthetics rather than technology" (*The Lost Worlds of 2001*, p. 124).

In his novel, Clarke describes the spaceship as shaped like an "arrow," which may explain the symbolism of Bowman's name. Kubrick evidently decided on the film's version (the fossilized appearance of an extinct mammal or reptile) sometime after Clarke had finished his work.

127: In Clarke, HAL detects the "fault" in the AE-35 unit just after Poole's birthday celebration; in the film he detects it during a conversation with Bowman about his drawings and the secret preparations for the mission (a scene not found in the novel).

129: Carolyn Geduld's *Filmguide* study of *2001* contains an extensive analysis of the "uterine" imagery in the film. In places her discussion is quite good, but elsewhere she exhibits an unexplained hostility toward the film.

130: The subject of "normality" appears once again in a Kubrick film, this time just before HAL is disconnected. HAL assures Bowman that he is all right: "I know I have made some poor decisions lately, but everything is now back to normal." The most touching moment of the film comes when Bowman is disconnecting HAL. HAL's refrain "I can feel it, I can feel it" provides a haunting, emotional prelude to Bowman's eventual death and rebirth.

131: In Clarke's novel, Bowman's last transmission to Earth as he is being sucked into the Star-Gate reads: "The thing's hollow—it goes on forever—and— oh my God!—*it's full of stars!*" (p. 191).

132: Kubrick explained his problems with the ending thus: "The ending was altered shortly before shooting it. In the original, there was no transformation of Bowman. He just wandered around the room and finally saw the artifact. But this didn't seem like it was satisfying enough, and we constantly searched for ideas until we finally came up with the ending as you see it" (Agel, *The Making of "2001*," p. 157). The title of the Walter Tevis novel refers to the fall of Icarus, a mythological analogy the reverse of the Homeric pattern of Kubrick's *2001,* for the superior alien in the novel descends to Earth and failure, never to return home. The film *The Man Who Fell to Earth,* directed by Nicolas Roeg, was released in 1976.

133: Quoted from Gelmis, *The Film Director as Superstar,* p. 304.

134: It may or may not be significant that Bowman is wearing a green helmet when he disconnects HAL.

135: In Clarke, the Star-Child looks on Earth as a toy and brings death before giving life: "A thousand miles below, he became aware that a slumbering cargo of death had awoken, and was stirring sluggishly in orbit. The feeble energies it contained were no possible menace to him; but he preferred a cleaner sky. He put forth his will, and the circling megatons flowered in a silent detonation that brought a brief, false dawn to half the sleeping globe. Then he waited, marshaling his thoughts and brooding over his still untested powers. For though he was master of the world, he was not quite sure what to do next. But he would think of something" (p. 221).

6. *A Clockwork Orange*

136: For biographical material and information about the production of *A Clockwork Orange,* its economics (a budget of less than $2 million), and its technology, see the following sources: LoBrutto, *Stanley Kubrick,* pp. 321–76, and Baxter, *Stanley Kubrick,* pp. 231–67; Phillips, *Stanley Kubrick,* pp. 157–70; Philip Strick and Penelope Houston, "Interview with Stanley Kubrick," *Sight and Sound,* Winter 1971/72, pp. 62–66; Michel Ciment's interview, reprinted in Ciment, *Kubrick,* trans. from the French by Gilbert Adair (New York: Holt, Rinehart, and Winston, 1980), pp. 148–65; Penelope Houston, "Kubrick Country," *Saturday Review,* 25 December 1971, pp. 42–44; Andrew Bailey, "A Clockwork Utopia," *Rolling Stone,* 20 January 1972, pp. 20–22; and Vincent LoBrutto, "The Old Ultra-Violence," *American Cinematographer,* October 1999, pp. 52–61.

137: Quoted material from Houston, "Kubrick Country," p. 42, and Bailey, "A Clockwork Utopia," p. 22. In the novel, Dr. Branom provides a definition of Alex's Nadsat: "Odd bits of old rhyming slang. . . . A bit of gypsy talk, too. But most of the roots are Slav. Propaganda. Subliminal penetration" (p. 114, American ed.); see also Kevin Jackson, "Real Horrorshow: A Short Lexicon of Nadsat," *Sight and Sound,* September 1999, pp. 24–27.

138: From "Interview with Anthony Burgess," *Playboy,* September 1974, pp. 69–86. In this interview and in Anthony Burgess, "Juice from *A Clockwork Orange,*" *Rolling Stone,* 8 June 1972, pp. 52–53, Burgess comments on his intentions in *A Clockwork Orange.* Although brief, the *Rolling Stone* article is excellent.

139: Kubrick explained why he felt it unnecessary to seek Burgess's collaboration on the screenplay of *Clockwork:* "I wasn't particularly concerned about this because in a book as brilliantly written as *A Clockwork Orange* one would have to be lazy not to be able to find the answers to any questions that might arise within the text of the novel itself. I think it is reasonable to say that, whatever Burgess had to say about the story was said in the book" (Strick and Houston, "Interview with Stanley Kubrick," p. 63). Burgess, on the other hand, had this to say about Kubrick's film: "very much a Kubrick movie, technically brilliant, thoughtful, relevant, poetic, mind-opening. It was possible for me to see the work as a radical remaking of my own novel, not as a mere interpretation and this—the feeling that it was no impertinence to blazon it as 'Stanley Kubrick's *A Clockwork Orange*'—is the best tribute I can pay to the Kubrickian mastery" (Anthony Burgess, "Author Has His Say on 'Clockwork' Film," *Los Angeles Times,* Calendar section, 13 February 1972, p. 1). In the British edition of Burgess's novel (London: Heinemann, 1962), Alex—in a chapter not included at the end of the American version—comes to the conclusion that Youth itself is nothing more than a clockwork toy: "But Youth is only being in a way like it might be an animal. No, it is not just like being an animal so much as being like one of those malenky toys you viddy being sold in the streets, like little chellovecks made out of tin and with a spring inside and then a winding handle on the outside. . . . Being young is like being like one of these malenky machines" (p. 195).

139: A good source for Burgess's theological and philosophical ideas is his essays collected in *1985* (Boston: Little, Brown and Co., 1978). In an essay titled "Cacotopia," he discusses the polarity of "Pelagian" and "Augustinian" thinking.

Concerning the violence in *A Clockwork Orange*, its negative impact (i.e., aversive) on an audience, and art's responsibilities, Burgess and Kubrick, respectively, said the following: "Art never imitates. It merely takes over what is already present in the real world, such as violence, and makes an aesthetic pattern out of it, or tries to explain it, or tries to relate it to some other aspect of life" (*Playboy* interview with Burgess, p. 72); "Art consists of reshaping life but it does not create life or cause life" (Strick and Houston, "Interview with Stanley Kubrick," p. 63). In the novel, Alex reads aloud from F. Alexander's book (the "other" *Clockwork Orange*) the overly ripe passage cited in my text. He calls it a "very high type preaching goloss," and Dim rewards his recitation with a Bronx cheer (pp. 21–22, American ed.). Later, Alex describes how he understands the meaning of Alexander's book: "The name was about a clockwork orange. Listening to the J. S. Bach, I began to pony better what that meant now, and I thought, slooshying away to the brown gorgeousness of the starry German master, that I would like to have tolchocked them both harder and ripped them to ribbons on their own floor" (p. 34).

139: See B. F. Skinner, *Beyond Freedom and Dignity* (New York: Alfred A. Knopf, 1971), especially pp. 150ff. A comment particularly appropriate to a study of Alex's mindscreen is Skinner's belief that "it is the environment that acts upon the perceiving person, not the perceiving person who acts upon the environment" (p. 188). Kubrick's quoted comment can be found in Bailey, "A Clockwork Utopia," p. 22. For more on the same subject, see the interview with Michel Ciment.

140: Quoted in Houston, "Kubrick Country," p. 42.

141: In the novel, Alex talks about how the "Bad" comes from the self and how the self is created by God, which prompts this analysis of the State: "But the not-self cannot have the Bad, meaning they of the government and the judges and the schools cannot allow the Bad because they cannot allow the self" (p. 40, American ed.).

143: Cited in Kagan, *The Cinema of Stanley Kubrick*, p. 167.

144: Throughout chapter 6 I have made use of Bruce F. Kawin's extremely useful terminology on the crucial subject of first-person film aesthetics found in *Mindscreen* (Princeton: Princeton University Press, 1978), particularly pp. 3–22. Here is how he summarizes the three ways of signifying subjectivity within a first-person narrative film, all of which involve distortion: (1) through what a character *says* (voiceover); (2) through what a character *sees* (subjective focus, imitative angles of vision); and (3) through what a character *thinks* (memory, fantasy, emotion, etc.). By "mindscreen," he means the last category. Significant to this study, of course, is that *A Clockwork Orange* exhibits all three, while it requires an audience to perceive the "mindscreen" of its creator, the filmmaker himself. Within this authorial subjectivity, "the image does not simply *appear,* but gives the audience the impression of having been *chosen.*" An invaluable source of study for Kubrick's *Clockwork* is the published screenplay (New York: Ballantine Books, 1972), which was assembled by Kubrick and staff members after a frame-by-frame analysis; it contains more than 700 stills from the film.

146: Here is what Kubrick once said about Walter Carlos's electronic music: "I think Walter Carlos is the only electronic composer and realizer who has managed to create a sound which is not an attempt at copying the instruments of the orchestra and yet which, at the same time, achieves a beauty of its own employing electronic tonalities. I think that his version of the fourth movement of Beethoven's Ninth Symphony rivals hearing a full orchestra playing it, and that is saying an awful lot" (Strick and Houston, "Interview with Stanley Kubrick," p. 64).

152: The huge heads of the laughing dummies on the derelict casino stage recall the "mannequin" imagery common to earlier films, i.e., the factory scene in *Killer's Kiss* and Johnny Clay's mask in the robbery scene of *The Killing*. In *Clockwork*, of course, the performing styles of Aubrey Morris (Deltoid) and Patrick Magee, in particular, suggest that of animated but decidedly mechanical toys. In several ways, Magee's performance recalls Sellers as Strangelove. In contrast, the dehumanized "maskies" worn by Alex and his droogs during the first HOME sequence resemble the activity of "zannies" from the *commedia dell'arte* or figures out of a George Méliès magic-show film such as "The Magic Lantern." Interestingly, Kubrick's final film, *Eyes Wide Shut*, also makes extensive use of Venetian carnival masks, mannequins, and satiric characterization reminiscent of the *commedia dell'arte*.

155: First a musical play (1973), and later a midnight horror-camp phenomenon of the first order, *The Rocky Horror Picture Show* (directed by Jim Sharman) parodies horror films in general, and especially those from the Hammer Studio. One scene is a take-off on the very scene from *The Curse of Frankenstein* (1957) that appears on a drive-in movie screen in Kubrick's *Lolita* (it shows the monster unwrapping himself). *The Rocky Horror Picture Show* also pays homage to *Dr. Strangelove*—a character named Dr. Scott, with a German accent, appears in a wheelchair. Two recent essays that discuss the film and the subject of midnight audiences are Kenneth von Gunden, "The RH Factor," *Film Comment*, September–October, 1979, pp. 54–56, and Jonathan Rosenbaum, "The Rocky Horror Picture Cult," *Sight and Sound*, Spring 1980, pp. 78–79. Writer/director Quenten Tarantino's *Pulp Fiction* (1994) upgrades this tradition, but his film also includes several allusions to Kubrick's work.

156: When Alex is expelled from his own home by the presence of Joe the lodger, Pee and Em's new "son," the mournful sounds of the slow movement from the "William Tell Overture" return as an accompaniment to both his piteous solicitations and his thoughts of suicide on the Thames Embankment.

158: In response to a question about his interest in Napoleon as a film subject (Strick and Houston, "Interview with Stanley Kubrick"), Kubrick made the following backhanded reference to *Spartacus:* "First of all, I start from the premise that there has never been a great historical film, and I say that with all apologies and respect to those who have made historical films, including myself" (p. 66).

158: Alex's comment about the first Ludovico film—that "it was a very good like professional piece of sinny"—comes directly from the novel (p. 102, American ed.), while the added phrase "like it was done in Hollywood" is Kubrick's interpolation. In the novel, the sinny-cinema pun can be appreciated more easily than in the film.

165: Someone pointed out to me an interesting parallel between Alex's last vision and the Ascot musical number in the film version of the Lerner-Loewe musical play *My Fair Lady* (1964, George Cukor), both of which are adaptations of Shaw's *Pygmalion*. When one thinks about it, *A Clockwork Orange* is a kind of upside-down version of the Pygmalion legend, as are countless other fairytales, a version that involves in its popular form the "awakening" of Eliza's full human potential by the misogynist Dr. Henry Higgins. Also, it concerns the pros and cons of "conditioning," develops a linguistic theme (i.e., phonetics), and comments on the shallowness of social distinctions (the primitive and her civilized detractors). As an element in Kubrick's cinematic self-references, it would have to be considered in the same company as "Singing in the Rain," which, incidentally, returns as musical accompaniment to the end titles, only this time in its original form with Gene Kelly singing the lyrics.

7. Barry Lyndon

166: Biographical material from the period between *A Clockwork Orange* and *Barry Lyndon* can be found in LoBrutto, *Stanley Kubrick,* pp. 377–408, and Baxter, *Stanley Kubrick,* pp. 268–94. Recommended readings on the production, economics, technology, and aesthetics of *Barry Lyndon* include John Alcott (Director of Photography), "Photographing Stanley Kubrick's *Barry Lyndon,*" *American Cinematographer,* March 1976, p. 268; Ed DiGiulio, "Two Special Lenses for *Barry Lyndon,*" *American Cinematographer,* March 1976, pp. 276–77; Richard Schickel, "Kubrick's Grandest Gamble," *Time,* 15 December 1975, pp. 72–78; Colin L. Westerbeck, Jr., "*Barry Lyndon,*" *Commonweal,* March and April 1976, p. 208; and a very revealing interview with Kubrick in Michel Ciment, *Kubrick,* pp. 166–77. For a sampling of initial review opinions, see Penelope Houston, "*Barry Lyndon,*" *Sight and Sound,* Spring 1976, pp. 77–80; Michael Dempsey, "*Barry Lyndon,*" *Film Quarterly,* Fall 1976, pp. 49–54; Pauline Kael, "Kubrick's Gilded Age," *The New Yorker,* 29 December 1975, pp. 49–52; and Andrew Sarris, "What Makes Barry Run?," *Village Voice,* 29 December 1975, pp. 111–12. Highly recommended as a summary of negative opinion is *Mad Magazine*'s spoof "*Borey Lyndon,*" September 1976, pp. 4–10, listed under the "Kubrick-A-Brac Dept." For more extensive coverage, see Hans Feldmann, "Kubrick and His Discontents," *Film Quarterly,* Fall 1976, pp. 12–19; Alan Spiegel, "Kubrick's *Barry Lyndon,*" *Salmagundi,* Fall 1977, pp. 194–208; Thomas Allen Nelson, "*Barry Lyndon:* Kubrick's Cinema of Disparity," *Rocky Mountain Review,* Winter 1978/79, pp. 39–51; and Robert Phillip Kolker, *A Cinema of Loneliness* (New York: Oxford University Press, 1980), pp. 123–38.

167: All references to Thackeray's *The Luck of Barry Lyndon* come from the critical edition prepared and edited by Martin F. Anisman (New York: New York University Press, 1970). In addition, I am indebted to the discussion by Robert A. Colby in *Thackeray's Canvass of Humanity: An Author and His Public* (Columbus: Ohio State University Press, 1979).

168: Thackeray, *The Luck of Barry Lyndon,* p. 351.

168: Thackeray, *The Luck of Barry Lyndon,* pp. 47, 49.

168–69: Thackeray, *The Luck of Barry Lyndon,* p. 315.

169: Thackeray, *The Luck of Barry Lyndon,* p. 167. The film's *Epilogue* reads as follows: "It Was in the Reign of George III That the Aforesaid Personages Lived and Quarrelled. Good or Bad, Handsome or Ugly, Rich or Poor, They Are All Equal Now."

171: Quoted comment from Richard Schickel, "Kubrick's Grandest Gamble," p. 76.

172: In several places, Kubrick's camera and the narrator's commentary *are* in perfect harmony, especially when slow zooms move in for close-ups of Barry's face as the narrator explains or interprets what he is thinking or feeling (e.g., while Barry stands by a campfire and ponders his disappointment with military life, or as he decides to desert the British army by stealing a gay officer's horse and identity). This method of psychological penetration, however, tends to be less prominent in part II, as the narrator's authority diminishes.

173: In a particularly revealing passage, Thackeray's Redmond Barry describes his father's death: "At length, after his great day of triumph before his sacred majesty at Newmarket, Harry's fortune was just on the point of being made, for the gracious monarch promised to provide for him. But alas he was taken in charge by another monarch, whose will will have no delay or denial,— by Death, namely, who seized upon my father at Chester races, leaving me a helpless orphan. Peace be to his ashes! He was not faultless, and dissipated all our princely family property; but he was as brave a fellow as ever tossed a bumper or called a main, and he drove his coach-and-six like a man of fashion" (p. 51).

180: Kubrick's casting for *Lyndon* deserves some comment, especially in light of the critical snickers occasioned by the selection of Ryan O'Neal and Marisa Berenson. Besides looking the part (a man/boy), O'Neal had a strongly emotional acting character and face (e.g., *Love Story*), as well as a talent for light comedy (e.g., *Paper Moon* and *What's Up Doc?*); Marisa Berenson was not only a professional model who wore clothes well (a not unimportant aspect of Lady Lyndon's characterization), but her face possessed a naturally sad expressiveness. Elsewhere, Kubrick used first-rate performers (mostly English character actors), some of whom, like Philip Stone, Patrick Magee, Leonard Rossiter, and Anthony Sharp, appear in more than one Kubrick film.

183: Quoted comments can be found in Strick and Houston, "Interview with Stanley Kubrick," p. 65.

184: Here is how John Alcott (in "Photographing Stanley Kubrick's *Barry Lyndon*") explained the film's visual style from his position as Director of Photography: "Each composition is like a painting by one of the Old Masters, and they link one onto the other like the tiles of a wondrous mosaic" (p. 270); "As I saw it, the story of Barry Lyndon took place during a romantic type of period —although it didn't necessarily have to be a romantic film. I say 'a romantic period' because of the quality of the clothes, the dressing of the sets, and the architecture of that period. These all had a kind of soft feeling" (p. 274). Ed DiGiulio, who helped devise the still-camera lens used for the candlelight scenes, said that Kubrick wanted "to preserve the natural patina and feeling of those old castles at night as they actually were," and that they were not intended as a "gimmick" ("Two Special Lenses for *Barry Lyndon*," p. 318).

194: Except for the 1789 reference, which has a clear importance to the film's thematic/structural intentions, the other dates do not seem historically significant. The marriage date (June 15, 1773) differs from that in Thackeray's novel (May 15, 1773), which could mean that Kubrick shot the early scenes of part II during the summer, or that he wanted to suggest a form of seasonal progression. If so, part II goes from the mythological height of Barry's fortune (Summer) to the discontents and death of Winter (December 1789). Or, heaven forbid, it may mean nothing at all.

8. *The Shining*

195–96: Stephen King, *The Shining* (New York: Doubleday and Co., 1977). For biographical background that covers the 1975–1980 period, see LoBrutto, *Stanley Kubrick*, pp. 409–54, and Baxter, *Stanley Kubrick*, pp. 295–325. Kubrick's comment is quoted in Jack Kroll, "Stanley Kubrick's Horror Show," *Newsweek*, 26 May 1980, p. 99. For a sampling of other reviews and reactions, see Richard Schickel, "Red Herrings and Refusals," *Time*, 2 June 1980, p. 69; Richard T. Jameson, "Kubrick's Shining," *Film Comment*, July–August 1980, pp. 28–32; Pauline Kael, "Devolution," *The New Yorker*, 1 June 1980, pp. 130–47; John Hofsess, "The Shining Example of Kubrick," *Los Angeles Times*, *Calendar* section, 1 June

1980, pp. 1, 25; and Paul Mayersberg, "The Overlook Hotel," *Sight and Sound,* Winter 1980/81, pp. 54–57; see also Jonathan Romney, "Resident Phantoms," *Sight and Sound,* September 1999, pp. 8–11, which echoes several of the ideas expressed in my chapter, first published in the 1982 first edition; and Michel Ciment's interview in *Kubrick,* pp. 180–97.

196: Robin Wood, "Return of the Repressed," *Film Comment,* July–August 1978, pp. 25–32.

197: Diane Johnson, who in the late 1970s was a college literature professor at a California university, had written five novels and a biography of George Meredith's first wife, Mary Ellen Peacock (*Lesser Lives*). Her work examines character with Gothic wit and humane understanding, and it could be that Kubrick sought her assistance not only with plot/character ideas (since the film changes so much from King's novel) but with the problem of giving the film a contemporary American sound (dialogue) and ambience. After all, he had been away for a long time.

199: Production details on the making of *The Shining* ($18 million budget) and comments by Stephen King can be found in Jim Alberton and Peter S. Perakos, "*The Shining,*" *Cinefantastique,* Fall 1978, p. 74; Peter S. Perakos, "Interview with Stephen King," *Cinefantastique,* Winter 1978, pp. 12–15; David Chute, "King of the Night: An Interview with Stephen King," *Take One,* January 1979, pp. 33–38; and Harlan Kennedy, "Kubrick Goes Gothic," *American Film,* June 1980, pp. 49–52. Of particular significance are the comments about the film's remarkable lighting and extensive use of the Steadicam by John Alcott (Director of Photography) and Garrett Brown (Steadicam Operator) in *American Cinematographer,* August 1980: see Herb Lightman's interview with Alcott ("Photographing Stanley Kubrick's *The Shining*"), p. 780, and Garrett Brown, "The Steadicam and *The Shining,*" p. 786.

204: For a helpful summary of mazes and labyrinths, see W. H. Matthews, *Mazes and Labyrinths: Their History and Development* (London: Longmans, Green, and Co., 1922). It may be only a coincidence, but in some ancient maze legends the emblem of a double ax plays an important role. See especially the stories in Jorge Luis Borges, *Ficciones,* trans. Anthony Kerrigan (New York: Grove Press, 1962).

212: For a discussion of Navajo sand paintings, their mythology and symbolism, see Leland C. Wyman, *The Windways of the Navaho* (Colorado Springs: The Taylor Museum, 1962). Jack's passion for the enclosed order of the maze resembles the Navajo circle that protects one from malevolent outside forces, except that Kubrick's films usually reverse that mythology and characterize such worlds as entrapping, while outside space offers both uncertain exploration and hope. Like the maze, however, the Indian circle has an opening (toward the east) for both entrance and escape. Throughout the film, Danny is associated with circles. These, although they recall the Navajo circle of protection from outside evil, ironically enclose rather than banish the evil that exists inside his home (the circle/maze of Jack's madness).

226: Here are a few observations (partly facetious) on the role of numbers in *The Shining:* Danny wears a jersey numbered 42, and he briefly watches with Wendy the Robert Mulligan film *Summer of '42.* Forty-two is 21 doubled (1921, 21 pictures on the gold corridor wall). Twelve is a mirror image for 21, the radio call number for the Overlook is KDK 12, and the two screen titles for part three ("8 am" and "4 pm") add up to 12, which means that the film both duplicates and reverses the numbering of *2001* if you omit the zeroes. In *2001,* we learn that HAL's birthday (the day he became operational in Urbana, Illinois) is 12

January 1992, which not only reverses the numerical title of the film (12), but if added together, the year's numbers (1+9+9+2) equal 21. Kubrick changed Room 217 in the novel to 237 (one published report explains it as a "legal" necessity). The numbers 237 added together equal 12. Numerically speaking, *The Shining* is a *2001* in reverse gear. Double, double, toil and trouble.

9. *Full Metal Jacket*

228: For a biographical account of the period between 1980 and 1987, see LoBrutto, *Stanley Kubrick,* pp. 455–91, and Baxter, *Stanley Kubrick,* pp. 326–53. For background on the making of *Full Metal Jacket* and the critical reaction to the film, see *American Cinematographer,* September 1987; Walker, *Stanley Kubrick, Director,* pp. 314–43; Francis X. Clines, "Stanley Kubrick's Vietnam," *New York Times,* 21 June 1987; Richard Corliss, "Welcome to Vietnam, the Movie: II," *Time,* 29 June 1987, p. 66; Janet Maslin, "Inside the 'Jacket': All Kubrick," *New York Times,* 5 July 1987; Jack Kroll, "1968: Kubrick's Vietnam Odyssey," *Newsweek,* 29 June 1987, pp. 64–65; Penelope Gilliatt, "Heavy Metal," *American Film,* September 1987, pp. 20–23, 50–51; Lloyd Rose, "Stanley Kubrick, at a Distance," *Washington Post,* 28 June 1987, p. FO1; Robert Castle and Stephen Donatelli, "Kubrick's Ulterior War," *Film Comment,* September/October 1998, pp. 24–28.

229: Ciment, *Kubrick,* p. 167; Kroll, "1968," p. 65.

230: Michael Herr, *Dispatches* (New York: Alfred A. Knopf, 1977); Gustav Hasford, *The Short-Timers* (New York: Bantam Books, 1979). The quoted comments can be found in Michael Herr, "Foreword," in Stanley Kubrick, Michael Herr, and Gustav Hasford, *Full Metal Jacket: The Screenplay* (New York: Alfred A. Knopf, 1987), pp. v–vi.

232: See Grover Lewis's interview with Hasford in "The Several Battles of Gustav Hasford," *Los Angeles Times Magazine,* 28 June 1987, pp. 18–23, 35.

233: *The Short-Timers,* pp. 177–78.

234: *Dispatches,* p. 20.

234–35: *The Short-Timers,* p. 60; Gilliatt, "Heavy Metal," p. 22.

236: For more on distinctions between classic and revisionist Hollywood narrative, see Robert B. Ray, *A Certain Tendency of the Hollywood Cinema, 1930–1980* (Princeton: Princeton University Press, 1985), and Thomas Schatz, *Hollywood Genres* (New York: Random House, 1981).

236: Herr, "Foreword," pp. v–vii.

237: *The Short-Timers,* p. 32.

238: *The Short-Timers,* p. 78.

239: On the subject of "plot beats," John Baxter reports that Kubrick, while working with Brian Aldiss on the script for *A.I.,* would repeatedly emphasize the necessity of creating a minimum of "six really good non-submersible units" within a given story's structure (*Stanley Kubrick,* p. 356). By "non-submersible units," Kubrick meant plot beats, which reveals that although *Full Metal Jacket* does not seem to conform to a conventional three-act film structure, it is still held together by a series of plot beats that occur about every twelve to fifteen minutes in both part 1 and part 2.

239: The resemblance between Lee Ermey's performance and the performance by Michael Bates as "Chief Guard" in *A Clockwork Orange* is striking. Visually, the prison sequence in *Clockwork* and the Parris Island scenes of *Jacket* are also very similar.

245: For reference, see *The Basic Writings of C. G. Jung,* edited with an Introduction by Violet Staub De Laszlo (New York: Modern Library, 1959); Robert H. Hopcke, *A Guided Tour of the Collected Works of C. G. Jung* (Boston: Shambala,

1989); for a definition of the "Trickster" as Jungian archetype, see Andrew Samuels et al., *A Critical Dictionary of Jungian Analysis* (London: Routledge and Kegan Paul, 1986), pp. 152–53.

258: Quoted comment by Kubrick can be found in Gilliatt, "Heavy Metal," p. 22.

10. *Eyes Wide Shut*

260: For biographical information covering the 1987–1998 period, see LoBrutto, *Stanley Kubrick*, 495–501, and Baxter, *Stanley Kubrick*, 354–64. Production notes on the making of *Eyes Wide Shut* can be found in Manuel Harlan, "The Eyes Have It," *Empire*, October 1999, pp. 12–13, 90–97; Cathy Booth, "Three of a Kind," *Time*, 5 July 1999, pp. 72–74; Larry Smith, "A Sword in the Bed," *American Cinematographer*, October 1999, pp. 28–38. For a sample of initial critical reactions, see Richard Schickel, "All Eyes on Them," *Time*, 5 July 1999, pp. 65–70; Jack Kroll, "Dreaming with 'Eyes Wide Shut,'" *Newsweek*, 19 July 1999, pp. 62–63; Michael Wilmington, "Review of *Eyes Wide Shut*," *Chicago Tribune*, 16 July 1999; Janet Maslin, "Review of *Eyes Wide Shut*," *New York Times*, 16 July 1999; Kenneth Turan, "'Eyes' That See Too Much," *Los Angeles Times*, 16 July 1999; Alexander Walker, "It's a Sex Odyssey," *London Standard*, 24 June 1999; Larry Gross, "Too Late the Hero," *Sight and Sound*, September 1999, pp. 20–23; Charles Whitehouse, "Eyes without a Face," *Sight and Sound*, September 1999, pp. 38–39; Amy Taubin, "Imperfect Love," *Film Comment*, September/October 1999, pp. 24–26, 30–33; and Richard T. Jameson, "Sonata Ghost," *Film Comment*, September/October 1999, pp. 27–28. Tim Kreider, "Eyes Wide Shut," *Film Quarterly* Spring 2000, pp. 41–48.

261: Quoted comment from "Director's Notes: Stanley Kubrick, Movie-Maker," *The Observer* (London), 4 December 1960. For material that covers Kubrick's early interest in the work of Stefan Zweig and Arthur Schnitzler, see LoBrutto, *Stanley Kubrick*, p. 131, Baxter, *Stanley Kubrick*, pp. 86–88, and Kubrick's own comments in Ciment, *Kubrick*, pp. 154–55.

262: Quoted comment by Sara Maitland can be found in "My Year with Stanley," *The Independent*, 12 March 1999. See also her review of Frederic Raphael's *Eyes Wide Open: A Memoir of Stanley Kubrick* and Alexander Walker's *Stanley Kubrick, Director*, in the *New York Observer*, 19 July 1999, p. 33.

262: Frederic Raphael, *Eyes Wide Open: A Memoir of Stanley Kubrick* (New York: Ballantine Books, 1999), pp. 23–24. See also the published screenplay, which includes a reprint of Schnitzler's novella, in Stanley Kubrick and Frederic Raphael, *Eyes Wide Shut* and *Dream Story*, by Arthur Schnitzler (New York: Warner Books, 1999). All references to the novella are from Arthur Schnitzler, *Rhapsody: A Dream Novel*, translated from the German by Otto P. Schinnerer (New York: Simon and Schuster, 1927).

267: *Dream Story*, p. 97.

267: *Dream Story*, p. 138.

285: Recommended sources on the *commedia dell'arte* are two books by Allardyce Nicoll: *Masks, Mimes, and Miracles: Studies in Popular Theatre* (New York: Cooper Square Publishers, 1963), and *The World of the Harlequin: A Critical Study of the Commedia dell'Arte* (Cambridge, England: Cambridge University Press, 1963).

293: Kubrick used two different actresses to play the dual roles of Mandy and the Mysterious Woman at Somerton, even though it is clear from a voice-over used during the morgue scene and in Victor's "recapitulation" that, at least on an objective level, Bill and the audience believe they are one and the same. It could have been a decision prompted by the long shooting schedule (fifteen months), meaning that Julienne Davis (Mandy) might not have been available during the period that the masked party sequence was shot; or it could be a matter of "body type," in that Abigail Good (Mysterious Woman) stands out among all the other nude actresses not only because of her distinctive feathered mask, but also because of her imposing sexual presence.

297: *Empire* (October 1999), a British film magazine, incorrectly reported that Kubrick made his first-ever cameo appearance in the Sonata Café scene. Ill-founded rumors aside, however, *Eyes Wide Shut* remains his most "personal" film: Kubrick's father was a New York City doctor; Kubrick and his family—like the Harfords—once lived in an apartment on Central Park West prior to their final move to England in 1962; as a young photographer and aspiring filmmaker, Kubrick lived in Greenwich Village, where he was a frequent habitué of Village jazz clubs such as the Sonata Café; his wife Christiane and stepdaughter Katharina's paintings are prominently displayed inside the Harford apartment; and it becomes increasingly evident in the film that Kubrick developed a real fondness for his two main characters, which may indicate a personal attachment he formed during the long shoot with Tom Cruise and Nicole Kidman. In addition, the film could be read as Kubrick's personal acknowledgment that he, like Bill Harford, had also benefited from the company of women (i.e., his wife and three daughters). Thus, *Eyes Wide Shut* may represent an "unmasking" of Kubrick's emotional response to his own conscious fears and desires—a personal journey, I think, that becomes noticeable in the intimations of mortality that increasingly dominate the emotional textures of his last four films. In that respect, *Barry Lyndon* may represent a major turning point in Kubrick's personal life and in his creative life.

Postscript

298: For tributes and reminiscences by people who knew Kubrick, see the references listed in the "Selected Bibliography." I highly recommend the comments found in the *New York Times Magazine,* the *Vanity Fair* essay by Michael Herr, Nick James's interview with Kubrick's wife Christiane, stepdaughter Katharina, and daughter Anya ("At Home with the Kubricks"), and Michael Herr's personal reflections in *Kubrick.*

INDEX

Thomas Allen Nelson is Professor of
English at San Diego State University and
author of *Shakespeare's Comic Theory*.